"No one is satisfied with America's fiscal prospect. Much of what is proposed does not stand up to serious analysis. Bill Gale and this important book offer a set of well thought out, humane proposals for our fiscal future. His ideas should be very seriously considered by whoever is the president of the U.S. on January 20, 2021."

—Lawrence H. Summers, Charles W. Eliot University Professor and President Emeritus, Harvard University; former Secretary of the Treasury.

"Great nations do not stay strong if their debt gets out of control. *Fiscal Therapy* is the perfect book for a moment when glaring problems are ignored and toxic partisanship has replaced responsible governing. *Fiscal Therapy* explains the issues fairly and with great insight and proposes immensely sensible and achievable solutions. Let's hope our political leaders read this book—and you should too."

—Maya MacGuineas, President, Committee for a Responsible Federal Budget

"America's debt burden is enormous and growing. Finding sensible and balanced ways to reduce it has been an immense and intractable problem. Bill Gale, one of America's finest economists, has given us a roadmap that problem-solving people of every political coloration could and should embrace. Gale both analyzes where the problems are in both revenues and expenditures and provides solutions that preserve the safety net, maintain and even expand programs essential to growth, and provide the best ways of reforming our tax system, improving fairness and reducing inequality. *Fiscal Therapy* should be read by every concerned citizen, but especially by the members of Congress who need to act."

—Norm Ornstein, Resident Scholar, American Enterprise Institute

"Bill lays out a roadmap to achieve our fiscal health, based on economic facts instead of ideological fictions. The economic challenges we face are not easy but they are doable. It is a must read for anyone who cares about the future of this country – it should be required reading for anyone entering political office."

—Diane Swonk, Chief Economist, Grant Thornton LLP

"Deficit reduction is certain to return to the center stage of political debate in Washington at some point. Bill Gale is a veteran of past debates and is well equipped to guide the public and policymakers through a jungle filled with traps involving taxes, health policy, retirement programs, national defense and many others. Those wishing to separate real, long-term solutions from those that promise more than they can deliver will find an objective, nonpartisan map in *Fiscal Therapy*."

—Bruce Bartlett, former economic policy adviser to Presidents Reagan and George H.W. Bush and author of *The Benefit and the Burden: Tax Reform—Why We Need It and What It Will Take*

Fiscal Therapy

CURING AMERICA'S DEBT ADDICTION AND INVESTING IN THE FUTURE

WILLIAM G. GALE

OXFORD
UNIVERSITY PRESS

OXFORD
UNIVERSITY PRESS

Oxford University Press is a department of the University of Oxford. It furthers
the University's objective of excellence in research, scholarship, and education
by publishing worldwide. Oxford is a registered trade mark of Oxford University
Press in the UK and certain other countries.

Published in the United States of America by Oxford University Press
198 Madison Avenue, New York, NY 10016, United States of America.

© William G. Gale 2019

Library of Congress Cataloging-in-Publication Data
Names: Gale, William G., author.
Title: Fiscal therapy : curing America's debt addiction and investing in the future / William G. Gale.
Description: New York : Oxford University Press, 2019. |
Includes bibliographical references and index.
Identifiers: LCCN 2018031184 (print) | LCCN 2018033225 (ebook) |
ISBN 9780190645427 (UPDF) | ISBN 9780190645434 (EPUB) | ISBN 9780190645410 (hardback)
Subjects: LCSH: Finance, Public—United States. | United States—Economic Policy—
21st century. | United States—Economic conditions—21st century. |
United States—Social policy—21st century. | BISAC: BUSINESS & ECONOMICS / Public Finance. |
POLITICAL SCIENCE / Public Policy / Economic Policy. |
BUSINESS & ECONOMICS / Economic Conditions.
Classification: LCC HJ257.3 (ebook) | LCC HJ257.3 .G35 2019 (print) | DDC 336.73—dc23
LC record available at https://lccn.loc.gov/2018031184

9 8 7 6 5 4 3 2

Printed by Sheridan Books, Inc., United States of America

To Danny and Becca

Contents

13. Taxing Consumption

14. Improving the Environmental Outlook

Epilogue

Acknowledgments

Like the federal government, I have accumulated a lot of debts. Through re-search and policy analysis, I have been working on the topics discussed in this book for many years. I owe gratitude to many co-authors, who have taught me an immense amount and made it fun. Special thanks to Alan Auerbach, with whom I have published alternative "shadow budget" projections for almost 20 years. Peter Orszag and I wrote numerous papers that helped form my under-standing of many topics discussed in the book. Long-time collaborations with Len Burman and Ben Harris have been very productive.

The work was funded by the Arjay and Frances Fearing Miller Chair at Brookings and by grants from donors that are anonymous to me.

I have received extremely helpful comments on earlier drafts from a very large number of Brookings colleagues and other people. I am leery of writing down a list for fear of leaving someone out, but here it goes: Alan Auerbach, Leonard Burman, Gary Burtless, Stan Collender, E.J. Dionne, Jennifer Doleac, Robert Dugger, Jason Fichtner, Matthew Fiedler, Ted Gayer, Howard Gleckman, Jonathan Goldman, Marc Goldwein, Ben Harris, Ron Haskins, Aaron Klein, Michael Klein, Richard Kogan, Donald Marron, Jonathan Meer, Michael O'Hanlon, Alice Rivlin, Isabel Sawhill, Louise Sheiner, Joel Slemrod, Martin Sullivan, Alan Viard, David Wessel, and Darrell West.

I owe a deep debt of gratitude to a long string of stellar assistants who worked on various parts of this project, including Samuel Brown, Alec Camhi, Chelsey Crim, Ilana Fischer, Sarah Holmes, Erin Huffer, Victoria Johnson, Bryan Kim, Leah Koestner, David Logan, Abigail Major, Leah Margulies, Brian McGrail, Emily Parker, Bryant Renaud, Katie Rodihan, Fernando Saltiel, Spencer Smith, Rebeka Sundin, and Elaine Yang.

I owe special thanks to several people. Whitford Schuyler, Vivian Sisskin, and Ali Rodway helped me overcome numerous obstacles.

Hilary Gelfond spent two years at Brookings doing superb work on a wide range of chapters and supervising the submission of the manuscript. Aaron Krupkin was indispensable and did just about everything that needed to be done, from writing first drafts to managing the budget calculations and even coming up with the book's subtitle.

Lawrence Haas was an amazing editor, able to take massive, meandering first drafts and turn them into short, coherent essays. The book literally could not have been written without his wise guidance and strong editing.

Diane Lim—The Economist Mom—not only came up with the title; she was everything I needed and everything she always is: encouraging, supportive, joyful, patient, and loving.

Abbreviations

ACO	Accountable Care Organization
AGI	adjusted gross income
ACA; Obamacare	Affordable Care Act
AFDC	Aid to Families with Dependent Children
AMT	alternative minimum tax
AOTC	American Opportunity Tax Credit
ASCE	American Society of Civil Engineers
ATRA	American Tax Relief Act
AMI	area median income
BEAT	base erosion and anti-abuse tax
BCA	Budget Control Act
BEA	Budget Enforcement Act
CO_2	carbon dioxide
CMS	Centers for Medicare and Medicaid Services
CHIP	Children's Health Insurance Program
CTC	child tax credit
CBO	Congressional Budget Office
CPI	consumer price index
VA	Department of Veterans Affairs
DoD	Defense Department/Department of Defense
DI	Disability Insurance
HHS	Department of Health and Human Services
DBCFT	destination-based cash-flow tax
EITC	Earned Income Tax Credit
ECI	employment cost index
Freddie Mac	Federal Home Loan Mortgage Corporation
FNMA [Fannie Mae]	Federal National Mortgage Association
FPL	Federal Poverty Level

FDA	Food and Drug Administration
FDII	foreign-derived intangible income
FDR	Franklin Delano Roosevelt
FAFSA	Free Application for Federal Student Aid
FRA	full retirement age
FYDP	Future Years Defense Program
GILTI	global intangible low-taxed income
GHG	greenhouse gases
GDP	gross domestic product
GNP	gross national product
HSA	health savings account
HD	high-deductible
HFC	hydrofluorocarbon
IRA	individual retirement account
IPCC	Intergovernmental Panel on Climate Change
IRS	Internal Revenue Service
IMF	International Monetary Fund
LLC	Lifetime Learning Credit
LIHEAP	Low-Income Home Energy Assistance Program
MIT	Massachusetts Institute of Technology
MID	mortgage interest deduction
MTO	Moving to Opportunity
NASA	National Aeronautics and Space Administration
NHE	National Health Expenditures
NIH	National Institutes of Health
NSLP	National School Lunch Program
NSF	National Science Foundation
NIIT	net investment income tax
NNP	net national product
OMB	Office of Management and Budget
OASDI; Social Security	Old-Age, Survivors, and Disability Insurance
OASI	Old-Age and Survivors Insurance
OECD	Organisation for Economic Co-operation and Development
OCO	overseas contingency operation
PAYGO	pay-as-you-go
PIA	primary insurance amount
QBI	qualified business income
QTPs	Qualified Tuition Plans
R&D	research and development
SBP	School Breakfast Program

SCC	social cost of carbon
SSA	Social Security Administration
WIC	Special Supplemental Nutrition Program for Women, Infants, and Children
SMI	Supplemental Medical Insurance
SNAP	Supplemental Nutrition Assistance Program
SPM	supplemental poverty measure
SSI	Supplemental Security Income
TCJA	Tax Cuts and Jobs Act
TANF	Temporary Assistance for Needy Families
TARP	Troubled Asset Relief Program
UI	unemployment insurance
UBI	universal basic income
VAT	value-added tax
VRR	VAT revenue ratio
VHA	Veterans Health Administration

Fiscal Therapy

Introduction

The American economy in 2019 is in great shape in many ways. After nine straight years of economic expansion, the stock market is up, consumer confidence is booming, and unemployment has fallen to historically low levels.

But dig beneath the surface and trouble looms. America faces two distinct but related challenges that policymakers must address in the coming years if they hope to provide a brighter future for the nation and its people.

The first challenge is rising government debt. Federal debt is already higher as a share of the economy than at any time in our history, except for a few years around World War II, when a massive military buildup required immense borrowing. Under current policies, debt will rise steadily to unprecedented levels over the next decade and to unsustainable levels over the next 30 years and beyond. If we don't rein in the debt, it will slowly but surely make it harder to grow our economy, boost our living standards, respond to wars or recessions, address social needs, and maintain our role as a global leader.

The increase in debt will be driven mainly by an aging population and rising healthcare costs that boost federal spending on Social Security, Medicare (for the elderly), and Medicaid (for some of the poor and elderly). In addition, tax revenues are not expected to grow very fast. Rising red ink is often described as just a spending problem, but it isn't intrinsically a spending problem or a tax problem, any more than one side of the scissors does the cutting. It's the *imbalance* between the two that creates rising debt. Addressing the debt challenge will require both slowing the spending trajectory and raising taxes.

The second challenge is changing the *way* we tax and spend. The nation has increasingly split into a fractured society with groups separated by disparities in income, education, and opportunity. This growing divide is not only inequitable, it is outright wasteful, reducing opportunities for tens of millions of Americans. To make Americans more productive and expand opportunity, we need more public investment—in education, health, childcare, nutrition, public infrastructure, and scientific research. But public investments in these areas (other than healthcare) are slated to shrink as a share of the economy to their lowest levels

1

in more than half a century. And we need to improve the tax system and raise revenues to finance public investment, encourage growth, and distribute tax burdens fairly both within and across generations. What matters is not just the debt, but how we raise and spend the money.

How and when we address these twin challenges will help determine the future we build for ourselves, our children, and future generations. How can we address our rising debt rather than bury ourselves in red ink? How can we invest wisely so our economy does not corrode? How can we refashion taxes and spending to best support opportunity and prosperity?

In the pages that follow, I explore these twin challenges and offer a plan to remedy the problems in ways that would help us build a stronger, fairer economy.

The analysis rests on five guideposts. First, facts and evidence should play a key role in policy analysis. Too often, ideology rules people's positions. There is, in fact, a significant body of evidence that can be brought to bear on the issues in this book. As Daniel Patrick Moynihan, former White House official, US ambassador, and senator once said: "Everyone is entitled to their own opinion but not to their own facts."[1]

Second, public policy should reflect our values as a people, including freedom, fairness, opportunity, and individual and social responsibility—toward one another, between rich and poor, and from generation to generation. Our policies should reflect who we are, what we care about, what we aspire to be. But these values often conflict with one another, as we will see repeatedly as we aim to address the nation's problems.

Third, both the private sector and the government can—and must—be part of the solution to our problems. The private sector does many things well, but it can't address all the challenges we face by itself. Although it surely makes mistakes, government is essential to addressing such challenges as defending the nation, providing social insurance, guaranteeing equal opportunity, protecting our environment, and giving private markets incentives to function more efficiently.

Fourth, taxes and spending are inextricably linked, and policymakers should consider them together when crafting solutions to our fiscal and investment challenges. We impose taxes to finance spending—the more we want of the latter, the more we need of the former. Political leaders and the public often focus on these items separately. When President Donald Trump says he is giving us a "giant tax cut for Christmas," he neglects to mention that he is also sending us the bill—in terms of higher future taxes or lower future spending.[2] Thinking about taxes and spending together spurs different, and more responsible, answers than thinking about them separately. Ask people if they want a tax cut, and many say yes. Ask them if they want a tax cut if it means the debt will rise or the tax cut will necessitate cuts to Social Security, healthcare, education, or environmental programs, and a majority will say no.[3]

Fifth, and finally, we should focus on realistic solutions. For every social problem, there is a simple, radical proposal that looks good on paper, but inevitably wilts under closer examination or conflicts with broader policy goals. Tried-and-true strategies, or reforms that make existing programs work better, are usually the right approach even if they don't generate the same excitement as scrapping what we have and starting anew.

With these guideposts providing a framework, my proposals have three core themes:

- *Control entitlement spending:* The proposals would contain spending growth in Social Security, Medicare, and Medicaid while also preserving and enhancing the programs' anti-poverty and social insurance roles.
- *Invest in the future:* By stipulating major new public investment in human and physical capital, the proposals would boost the potential for Americans to lead productive lives.
- *Raise and reform taxes:* The proposals would raise adequate revenue to pay for government spending in a fair and efficient manner.

Taken together, the proposals would put debt on a stable course by reducing the growth of spending and raising taxes. In the absence of reform, the federal government's debt will rise inexorably and unsustainably—to almost 180 percent of GDP by 2050 and by increasing amounts after that. Annual budget deficits would exceed 9 percent of GDP, well above historical averages and fueling a vicious circle of increasing debt and higher interest rates.

Under the proposals, debt would be stabilized at a sustainable level—60 percent of annual gross domestic product (GDP)—lower than today's as a share of the economy (Figure I.1). Annual budget deficits would eventually shrink to zero (Figure I.2). Federal spending would fall significantly from its projected levels. The reduction would come from lower interest payments because the debt would be lower. Non-interest spending would be a higher share of the economy than it is today (Figure I.3), but that is almost inevitable given the aging of the population. Federal revenues would rise to levels substantially higher than we've experienced in the past but still less than what most European countries experience today (Figure I.4). Appendix Table I.1 provides numerical details.

The plan would boost economic growth. By controlling the debt, it would release huge amounts of capital for private investment. Corporate tax changes, as outlined below, would boost business investment. New resources for children, education, and the safety net would increase human capital and make workers

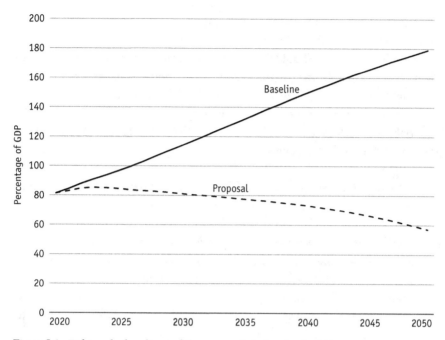

Figure I.1. Debt under baseline and the proposal. Author's calculations.

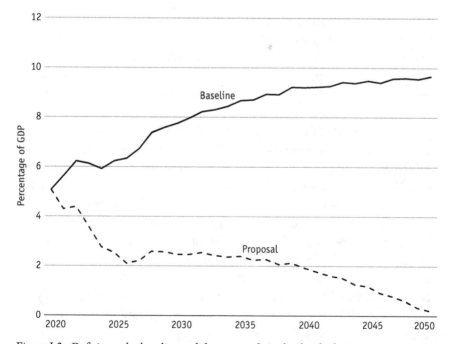

Figure I.2. Deficits under baseline and the proposal. Author's calculations.

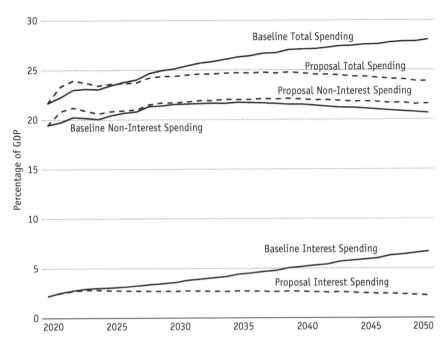

Figure I.3. Spending under baseline and the proposal. Author's calculations.

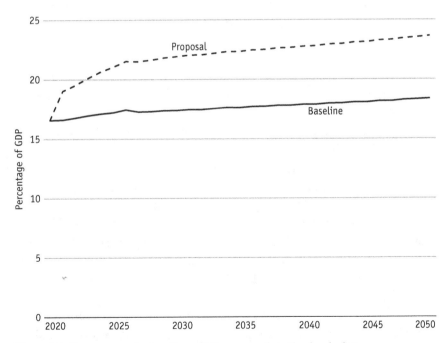

Figure I.4. Revenues under baseline and the proposal. Author's calculations.

more productive. Additional public infrastructure and research and development investment would generate efficiency and innovation.

The plan would reduce inequality by helping the poor and taxing the rich, raise low- and middle-income living standards by helping to equalize and expand economic opportunity, provide better protection to people who came upon hard times, and provide a more economically and environmentally sound world to our children and grandchildren.

The proposals are realistic. They are administratively feasible. They build off existing programs and ideas that have already proven achievable in the United States or around the world. There are no appeals to "magic asterisks" or future but unspecified spending cuts. There is no advocacy of imposing a balanced budget rule (or worse, a constitutional amendment) without specifying how to reach that goal. There is no appeal to faster economic growth as a painless way to solve the fiscal problem (although the plan should boost growth).

I've modeled the changes as if they would be implemented starting in 2021—this provides some time to enact the necessary legislation and gives people and businesses time to react. The changes could be delayed. Indeed, it is doubtful that Congress could pass such a wide-ranging package in one fell swoop. Rather, the notion behind *Fiscal Therapy*, like physical therapy, is that resolving problems will take a concerted and consistent effort to address trouble spots. But we should not wait very long to start addressing these issues. As President Kennedy said, "The time to repair the roof is when the sun is shining."[4] And the longer we wait to implement changes, the larger and potentially more abrupt the changes will have to be.

The proposals won't appeal to everyone, and that's fine. If you don't like the ideas, I encourage you to decide how you'd address the challenges. It's harder than you might think, but there are ample tools available to help. My colleagues at the Brookings Institution's Hutchins Center have an online software package, "The Fiscal Ship," that showcases both the possibilities and problems in designing a plan.[5] The Committee for a Responsible Federal Budget—a non-partisan budget watchdog organization in Washington, DC—has another good calculator.[6] Other sources of ideas are the Bowles-Simpson Commission, convened by President Obama in 2010; the Debt Reduction Task Force, chaired by Pete Domenici and Alice Rivlin in 2010; and a collection of plans commissioned by the Peterson Foundation.[7] Just don't ignore the problem and don't think that there are painless solutions.

This book is divided into two sections. In the first, I explain the problems as well as the factors that should drive a solution. Together, we explore what the federal government does and what we can learn from prior experiences with debt. We compare estimates of where we're headed (in terms of the size of public debt) with where we should be headed (debt at a sustainable level that's consistent with a strong economy). We show how much policy needs to change to reach the appropriate debt level. We explore how government debt affects the economy, what a fair solution would include, and why political considerations can make a solution more elusive.

Against that backdrop, the second section lays out a plan to reach the proposed debt target and make critical investments. Four chapters cover major spending programs—healthcare, Social Security, investments in people, and investments in infrastructure, research, and defense. Four additional chapters cover revenue options—including proposals to reform the personal income tax and the corporate income tax, and to create a new national value-added tax and a carbon tax. Each chapter in this section provides background information to frame the issue and then discusses the proposed reform.

Chapter 1 provides an overview of what the federal government does. In 2018, total federal spending was about 21 percent of the economy and revenue was around 17 percent, creating a *deficit* that year of 4 percent. The public *debt*— the sum of all previous annual deficits, minus all surpluses, since the nation's founding—was 78 percent of the economy.

While the government runs thousands of programs, more than two-thirds of all spending goes to just four: Social Security, healthcare, defense, and interest payments on the debt. This means that reforming these programs (other than interest, which we must pay to avoid defaulting) will be central to addressing our long-term fiscal challenges. But to address those challenges only by reducing spending, we would have to cut those programs so much that we'd essentially destroy them. So, we need to look for more revenue as well. More than 80 percent of revenue comes from individual income and payroll taxes, the rest from taxes on corporate income, very large estates, gasoline, alcohol, and tobacco. While we can raise those taxes, we'll also need to look for new revenue sources.

Compared to other advanced countries, the United States has significantly lower taxes—especially on consumption and energy use—and lower public spending on children, but much higher spending on defense. We have more inequality and less economic mobility. While we don't want to necessarily copy the tax and spending policies of other countries, we can learn something from what they do.

We also can learn from our own history, the topic of Chapter 2. From the nation's founding until about 1980, debt as a share of the economy rose only when we were at war or in recession, and it only rose temporarily. After the war or recession ended, debt fell rapidly. Ronald Reagan's tax cuts and other policies in the 1980s changed that pattern, raising debt significantly. After

Reagan left office, tax increases and defense cuts under Presidents George H. W. Bush and Bill Clinton helped turn persistent deficits into surpluses by the end of the century. But tax cuts and spending increases under Presidents George W. Bush, Barack Obama, and Donald Trump, along with the Great Recession of 2007 to 2009, greatly boosted current and projected levels of future debt.

Our history provides several lessons. The main one is that *this time is different*.[8] Because the source of our rising debt isn't a war or recession but, instead, a built-in and growing imbalance between taxes and spending, the problem won't disappear when a war ends or as the economy grows. That is, we can't solve this problem by cutting defense, which is already a much smaller share of the economy than in the past. Nor can we "grow our way" out of the problem, as we did after World War II. We would need far higher economic growth than we can reasonably expect to generate. Consequently, we'll need to make tough choices about which programs to cut and which taxes to raise.

Chapter 3 outlines the fiscal challenge. Under current tax and spending policies and reasonable assumptions about how the economy will perform, the debt will grow more or less continuously from about 78 percent of GDP in 2018 to almost 180 percent by 2050. That's largely because, as noted, spending for Social Security, Medicare, and Medicaid will grow in the future as the baby boomers retire, swelling the ranks of elderly people who are eligible for those programs. Healthcare costs will likely keep rising faster than overall inflation, further boosting spending for Medicare and Medicaid. Interest payments on the debt will also grow swiftly both because the debt will rise and because interest rates are likely to rise from their very low levels of recent years. All other spending— defense, investment, social programs—will shrink as a share of the economy. Meanwhile, taxes won't grow as fast as spending, leaving an ever-widening gap between the two. The projections are to some extent uncertain, of course, but the basic problem should be clear: we have a fundamental and growing mismatch between what people expect from government and what they've committed to contribute.

We don't need to eliminate the debt or even balance the budget in, or by, any particular year. But we need to reduce the debt to manageable levels and put it on a sustainable path. A 2050 target of debt at 60 percent of GDP, as I propose, would do that. That's relatively high for the United States in historical terms, but even so, it would require significant, and politically painful, tax and spending reforms. For example, if we act by 2021, the net changes needed would be equivalent in size to a 24 percent increase in all federal taxes, a 50 percent increase in the income tax alone, or a 21 percent reduction in all non-interest spending.

As discussed in Chapter 4, debt isn't always bad. We've had good reason to borrow money at times in the past—to fight wars and recessions and to make investments. Nevertheless, virtually all leading experts agree—and empirical evidence confirms—that following our current debt path and spending the borrowed funds as projected would be a significant problem. Rising deficits and debt will cause gradual, significant, and durable long-term problems for the economy and reduce our ability to grow and improve living standards; respond to war, recession, or social needs; and remain a global leader in economic and political matters. Notably, all of this will occur even if rising debt does *not* bring about a financial crisis. The United States remains the world's safest place to invest, so investors will continue to buy our Treasury securities, and we have the resources to pay the interest on our debt for decades to come.

Who should pay higher taxes and receive fewer benefits? What's fair? As explored in Chapter 5, debt, taxes, and spending redistribute resources within and across generations. In recent decades, we have set aside the historical notion that each generation should pay off its debts. At the same time, it is no longer automatic that each generation will be better off than the one before it. Thus, one reason to address the debt problem is to avoid unduly burdening our children and grandchildren.

The United States used to have high income inequality but also significant economic mobility: people who worked hard could ascend the income ladder. In recent years, though, the gap between rich and poor has grown to its highest level since the Roaring Twenties, but rates of mobility haven't improved. Indeed, the increase in inequality limits economic mobility, which then increases inequality, potentially creating a vicious cycle. While we can't and shouldn't use public policy to offset the entire growth in inequality created over the past 40 years, we should narrow inequality in ways that are economically productive and fiscally sound and that distribute opportunities and outcomes more fairly. We should invest more in education, health, nutrition, neighborhoods, and employment programs, and we should judiciously raise taxes on high-income households.

Fiscal responsibility aligns with both conservative and liberal goals. Conservatives don't want the government to spend money it doesn't have. Liberals value a proactive and constructive government, which requires a solid financial foundation. Citizens of all stripes can support the notion of making life better for our children and grandchildren. So, why is it so hard to generate politically acceptable fiscal solutions?

Long-term fiscal reform has all the classic elements of a difficult political problem, as discussed in Chapter 6. The economic benefits would accrue slowly over time, mainly to people who aren't old enough to vote now or aren't even born yet and, thus, aren't a front-of-mind concern of elected officials. In contrast, the costs—benefit cuts and tax increases—are easy to identify and evoke harsh reactions among those who would be affected. As a result, deficit reduction is usually no one's first choice—liberals want more spending, conservatives want lower taxes. Nor does public opinion give policymakers a clear mandate: polls show that Americans deplore rising red ink but also oppose most of the very measures required to reduce deficits and debt to sustainable levels. Meanwhile, the rising political partisanship of recent years has poisoned the environment for compromise across the political parties. But when one party controls all the levers of government, deficits and debt tend to go up, not down. Lastly, the fiscal problem is gradual and growing, but it is not a *crisis* that demands policymakers' immediate attention.

Nevertheless, a long-term solution to our fiscal challenges should be within reach. Absent a crisis that might bring the sides together, we will need strong leadership to rally the country, much like President Roosevelt provided in the 1930s around the New Deal and President Reagan provided in the 1980s around tax reform. A motivated citizenry could galvanize political leaders to act. The fact that no solution is currently feasible politically does not imply there is no solution. It just means that whatever solution eventually emerges will be something that is currently considered infeasible. And it highlights the importance of not using current political feasibility as a criterion to critique reforms.

Given the fiscal state of America, we next turn to solutions. "Something that can't go on forever," the economist Herb Stein used to say, "will stop."[9] That's true, but *how* it stops matters. A plane that runs out of gas can glide into a smooth landing, or it can crash. We need a plan to address the long-term fiscal challenge that gives the economy a smooth landing.

As Chapter 7 documents, healthcare already accounts for more than a quarter of federal spending, and that share will grow significantly as the population ages and medical technology generates higher health expenditures. Almost half of Americans get their health insurance through government programs, of which Medicare and Medicaid are the most prominent. The government also finances or provides healthcare for children in low- to moderate-income families, members of the military, and veterans. Government has an important role to play as it can help correct market failures in health insurance markets. But the United States spends substantially more of its income on healthcare than any other advanced country without always getting good value for the money. Rising healthcare costs threaten to weaken the economy, slow the growth of workers' wages, and increasingly drive our long-term fiscal problems.

Policymakers should aim to expand coverage and reduce expenditures. To expand coverage, the government should reinstate the penalty for individuals who do not purchase health insurance and convince states to expand their Medicaid programs as much as they can under the Affordable Care Act (ACA) and recent rules. Giving more people access to healthcare improves their health, reduces financial hardship, and saves lives. To reduce expenditures, government should reform Medicare to pay medical providers based on the quality of care they provide and the patient outcomes they secure, not the services they perform. Medicare should expand its use of competitive bidding, and it should get the same drug price discounts as other government health programs. Policymakers should reduce tax subsidies that encourage people to use more healthcare than they need and should tax alcoholic beverages at a rate that reflects the social costs of drinking. These and other reforms would cut costs and wasteful procedures and improve the health of Americans by expanding coverage and enhancing the quality of care.

Social Security is among the nation's most popular and successful programs, as discussed in Chapter 8, providing a crucial foundation of income every year for tens of millions of people, including retirees, surviving spouses, dependents, and the disabled. But the program is financially unsustainable. The taxes that today's workers pay go mainly to cover the benefits of today's retirees. As a result, the coming rise in the number of retirees relative to workers will leave the program with too little revenue to pay all the benefits starting in about 2034. Payroll taxes will have to rise, benefits will have to fall, or policymakers will have to find other ways to fund the program.

Policymakers should enact a 2016 plan proposed by a Bipartisan Policy Center commission (of which I was a member). It would bring Social Security into long-run fiscal balance by raising taxes and cutting benefits in a progressive manner, protecting the poor, encouraging people to work longer, and fixing the way Social Security calculates inflation.

The most precious asset the nation has is its people. But we are leaving far too many behind, as discussed in Chapter 9. Economic growth is a prerequisite for raising incomes, but it's no longer sufficient to ensure that Americans at all income levels can climb the ladder of success. Investing more in children should be a high national priority, for both equity and efficiency reasons. Children are not responsible for the obstacles to advancement that they face, and they are the future of the country. There is now significant evidence that programs that provide struggling individuals and families with cash, food, healthcare, childcare, education, jobs, and appropriate incentives not only help the beneficiaries, but they also pay off for the economy as a whole over time.

To capitalize on these opportunities to reduce poverty, expand opportunity, and boost mobility, we should provide an additional 1 percent of the economy per year in funds through 2050 to programs that invest in people. This would be a significant increase relative to projected levels of spending on these programs, but it represents just a fifth of what we currently spend on Social Security and an eighth of income tax revenues. The changes should focus on five goals: investing in children, patching holes in the safety net, raising educational attainment, providing jobs and job training to people who need them, and making work pay better.

The federal government makes other investments that are critical to the nation's well-being in areas in which the private sector would invest too little, as outlined in Chapter 10. Because federal spending in these areas has fallen significantly in recent years and because interest rates are low relative to historical levels, I propose sizable increases for infrastructure as well as for research and development. The increases in infrastructure spending will provide the resources needed to update our aging roads, bridges, and public transit systems, while higher research and development spending will allow the United States to enhance the development of cutting-edge technologies, health innovations, and more.

Not all the investment would come on the domestic side, however. To enable the US military to protect the nation and meet its global obligations, policymakers should provide the funds to enable the Department of Defense (DoD) to carry out its plans through 2030 and to grow modestly after that. That would allow for a continuing presence overseas, but it would not assume that the United States engaged in new wars. If war broke out, policymakers presumably would provide the additional *temporary* funds to ensure that America emerges victorious.

In *Annie Hall*, Woody Allen tells a joke about two people at a Catskills summer resort: one says the food is bad, the other agrees and complains that the portions are too small. That's how it is with our tax system, too. The taxes we have are not very good, and we don't have enough revenues. The solution is to reform the structure of the tax system in a manner that also raises revenues.

The income tax is the centerpiece of the federal tax system, as explored in Chapter 11, raising almost half of all federal revenues in a progressive manner. Despite a constant droning from some quarters that taxes destroy the economy, the evidence suggests that variations in the income tax have very little impact on economic growth. We need reform that is fiscally responsible, raises taxes on wealthy households, and tightens enforcement of the tax. To that end, I propose closing capital gains loopholes, repealing several features of the 2017 tax overhaul, replacing the mortgage interest deduction with a first-time homebuyers credit, and installing new enforcement measures. Meanwhile, the estate tax has shrunk dramatically over the past 40 years, making it a small revenue source for the federal government. By taxing the transfer of wealth, however, it retains an important role in making taxes progressive. The estate tax could be made more effective by transforming it into a tax on inherited assets.

Chapter 12 argues that sensible business taxation is central to any well-functioning economy. Ideally, a business tax would be neutral; firms would make choices about investing, hiring, and so on based on economic criteria rather than the tax implications. On that basis, our current system fails badly. A major tax overhaul in 2017 helped in some ways and hurt in others. Replacing the corporate income tax with a 25 percent cash-flow tax on corporations would improve investment incentives, raise revenues, and simplify the system. Additionally, we should streamline the tax treatment of pass-through businesses by repealing certain provisions in the 2017 tax act and closing various loopholes.

Since we need more revenue than we can generate just by raising existing taxes, we need to think about new taxes, starting with a broad-based national consumption tax, as discussed in Chapter 13. Value-added taxes (VATs) are the world's most common consumption tax, in place in more than 160 countries, including every economically advanced nation except the United States. In fact, while states and localities have sales taxes, we've never had a national consumption tax. A VAT is really a sales tax on consumers, but it's collected in parts at each stage of production rather than all at once at the retail level. A broad-based, 10 percent value-added tax should be a central part of the fiscal solution. Such a tax would raise substantial revenues. It wouldn't distort incentives to save or invest, and it's simpler to administer than other broad-based consumption taxes.

In Chapter 14, I propose that we impose a tax on carbon. The tax would burden emissions of carbon dioxide and other greenhouse gases that arise from the burning of coal, oil, and natural gas. When released in the atmosphere, these gases raise global temperatures and pollute the air, threatening the environment and our livelihoods. Currently, businesses and people don't need to consider how their decisions on what to make and what to buy will increase pollution and generate climate change because they don't bear the full cost of their choices. A properly designed tax would make producers and consumers face those costs by raising energy prices, prompting them to use less energy (or more efficient energy sources), which, in turn, would reduce emissions. For these reasons, the carbon tax is routinely considered one of the best ways to address global warming.

Through our taxing and spending policies, we can expand our economy or let it wither; make our society more equal, or less; expand opportunity or let tens of millions of struggling families continue to fend for themselves. We face a big fiscal challenge, but we also have substantial opportunities to strengthen our nation and build better lives for our children and grandchildren if we're wise enough to seize them. We are not "broke." We do not have to kill popular programs like Social Security, Medicare, and Medicaid or starve government. Indeed, a primary reason to get the fiscal house in order is to maintain and enhance the vital functions that government provides. We need to act responsibly, to pay for the government we want, and to shape that government in ways that better serve us.

I propose a comprehensive plan through which to address our twin challenges of reducing our rising red ink while investing in our future. It would help ensure that we lay the foundation for a better future for those who come after us. It would plant the seeds for fiscal sustainability, stronger economic growth, higher living standards, less inequality, and more opportunity for those in the middle and at the bottom.

Notes

1. Moynihan (2010).
2. Ballhaus (2017).
3. CBS News (2017); Hacker and Pierson (2005).
4. Kennedy (1962).
5. Hutchins Center on Fiscal and Monetary Policy (2018).
6. Committee for a Responsible Federal Budget (2017).
7. Debt Reduction Task Force (2010); National Commission on Fiscal Responsibility and Reform (2010); Peter G. Peterson Foundation (2011, 2015).
8. This expression is taken from the title of a comprehensive historical analysis of financial collapses by Reinhart and Rogoff (2009). They mean their title ironically—in that they document that different financial crises tend to have the same broad patterns and effects, even though participants in each crisis tend to think the situation they face is unique. In contrast, I mean the statement literally. The debt problem today is different in source and magnitude than the ones we've faced in the past and will require different solutions.
9. Stein (1997).

Appendix Table I.1. **Fiscal Aggregates**

	Deficit	Revenue	Non-Interest Spending	Interest	Total Spending	Debt
2018	*4.0*	*16.6*	*19.0*	*1.6*	*20.6*	*78.0*
2050 - Baseline	*9.7*	*18.4*	*21.3*	*6.7*	*28.0*	*179.0*
Healthcare Reform	−1.5	0.6	−0.3	−0.7	−0.9	−18.2
Social Security Reform	−1.8	0.6	−0.4	−0.8	−1.2	−22.5
Investment in People	2.0	0.0	1.0	1.0	2.0	28.5
Investment in Infrastructure & R&D	1.9	0.0	1.0	0.9	1.9	25.4
Investment in Defense	0.7	0.0	0.5	0.2	0.7	6.7
Income Tax Reform	−2.4	1.2	0.0	−1.2	−1.1	−31.7
Business Tax Reform	−1.8	1.0	0.0	−0.8	−0.8	−22.0
Value-Added Tax	−5.1	1.0	−1.5	−2.6	−4.1	−69.8
Carbon Tax	−1.5	0.9	0.0	−0.7	−0.7	−18.4
Net Change	**−9.5**	**5.3**	**0.2**	**−4.4**	**−4.2**	**−121.9**
2050 - Under the Proposal	*0.2*	*23.6*	*21.6*	*2.2*	*23.8*	*57.0*

Note: All figures are reported as a percentage of GDP. Total may not equal sum due to rounding. The key figures are for the deficit and the debt. The decomposition of the policy changes into tax and spending components is subject to definitional and price level issues. For example, the revenue increases include at least 1.1 percent of GDP in net reductions of tax expenditures by 2050 (as detailed in Chapters 7, 11, and 12), which are in many ways more appropriately thought of as reductions in government spending than increases in taxes. Likewise, the decomposition of the effects of the value-added tax between revenue and spending depends on how the price level changes (see Chapter 13). Details of all revenue and spending calculations may be found in an online document entitled "Fiscal Therapy: Calculation of Spending and Revenue Effects of Policy Proposals" at https://www.brookings.edu/FiscalTherapyCalculations.

Source: Author's calculations.

1

Government at a Glance

In a recent poll, the typical respondent thought foreign aid comprised 28 percent of federal spending, and a fifth of respondents thought it accounted for more than 40 percent.[1] In an online quiz, more than a third of people thought the government spent more on foreign aid than on Social Security.[2] In fact, foreign aid accounts for less than 1 percent of federal spending. We spend more on Social Security in about two weeks than on foreign aid all year.[3]

Confusion about foreign aid—a result that appears in poll after poll—reflects a broader problem: Americans routinely mistake the relative size of controversial budget items—from the salaries we pay members of Congress, to the subsidies we allot for public television, to the cost of running the Education Department. Many want to believe that if we can just eliminate the least popular items, we can eliminate prospects of rising red ink without breaking a sweat. But the numbers show how wrong that is. The programs that cost the most money—Social Security, Medicare, Medicaid, and the military—receive strong public support.

We can't reasonably set tax and spending priorities and choose between alternative paths if we don't understand what the government does. After all, as Mark Twain reportedly put it, "What gets us into trouble is not what we don't know. It's what we know for sure that just ain't so."[4] So, we need to start with some basic questions: How much does the government spend and collect? Where does the money come from? Where does it go? The answers to these questions, though, are not just numbers. They represent a living manifestation of who we are, what we care about, and what we aspire to be.

The federal government spent $4.1 trillion in 2018, raised $3.3 trillion in revenues, and borrowed $0.8 trillion.[5] Federal spending was about 21 percent of the nation's gross domestic product (GDP), the value of all goods and services produced in the United States. Revenues were less than 17 percent.

These totals vary over time for many reasons. For example, during recessions, as more people seek government benefits and income falls, spending and deficits tend to be higher than average, while taxes tend to be lower. Over the past 50 years, spending has trended upward slightly as a share of GDP, averaging about 20 percent. Federal taxes averaged more than 17 percent over the same period.

Though people often confuse the deficit and debt, the distinction is simple. The *deficit* is the excess of spending over revenues in a particular year. (If revenues exceed spending, which last occurred in 2001 and won't occur again for a long time, the result is a surplus.) In 2018, for example, the deficit was $0.8 trillion (about 4 percent of GDP), the difference between the spending and revenue figures noted earlier.[6]

In contrast, the *debt* (more formally, net debt held by the public) is the total accumulation of deficits, minus surpluses, since the nation's founding.[7] By the end of 2018, the debt stood at about $16 trillion, or 78 percent of GDP, the highest share of GDP in US history ever except for a few years around World War II.[8] In Chapter 3, we will see that the deficit and the debt are slated to rise inexorably over the next several decades to levels that are both unprecedented and unsustainable.

Federal revenue comes in four basic categories: individual income taxes, payroll taxes, corporate income taxes, and other taxes (Figure 1.1). Together, individual income and payroll taxes accounted for about 84 percent of all federal revenues in 2018.

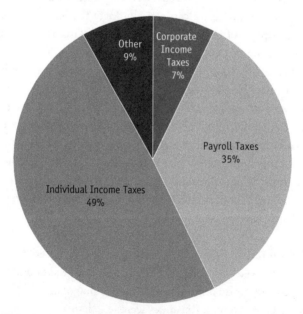

Figure 1.1. Federal revenue by source, 2018. The "other" category includes the following revenue sources: excise taxes (3%); Federal Reserve (2%); customs duties (1%); miscellaneous fees and fines (1%); and estate/gift taxes (1%). Congressional Budget Office (2018a).

The individual income tax raised $1.6 trillion in 2018, about 8 percent of GDP, and almost half of federal revenues. It applies to wages, salaries, some investment earnings, and profits from "pass through" businesses (including sole proprietors, partnerships, and S-corporations). Perhaps nowhere in the fiscal system is the clash of values more apparent than in the income tax.

The tax is progressive, reflecting the widely shared view that the more you make, the greater share of your income you should pay in taxes. People don't pay any taxes on an initial amount of their income; married couples with no children, for instance, didn't owe taxes on the first $24,000 of their 2018 income. Additional income is taxed at rates that rise gradually from 10 percent up to 37 percent. High-income households also face a 3.8 percent surtax on income from interest, dividends, capital gains, and other "passive income."

But, in an effort to limit progressivity or pursue other goals—such as more investment, family support, or work effort—policymakers routinely insert economic incentives and social policies into the income tax code. Tax experts refer to these provisions—which include tax credits, deductions, and lower tax rates for certain types of income—as tax preferences, or "tax expenditures" because many of them are the economic equivalent of spending programs. Tax expenditures cost the government an enormous amount. In 2018, for example, income tax expenditures were about 80 percent as large as actual individual income tax revenues, or about 6.3 percent of GDP.[9] By reducing the amount of income subject to taxation, tax expenditures reduce government revenue or force policymakers to impose higher tax rates on the remaining taxable income to raise a given amount of revenue.

People often call tax expenditures "loopholes"—suggesting that taxpayers are exploiting some unintended or narrowly offered benefit. And while there are some narrowly targeted screamers (for professional sports stadiums, for example), the costliest tax preferences offer benefits to many millions of households. These include subsidies for certain pass-through businesses; employer-provided health insurance; mortgage interest; charitable gifts; state and local taxes; retirement saving; capital gains (that is, on the profit from asset sales); and people who work, raise children, and pursue education.

Everyone should pay his or her fair share in taxes, and the successful efforts of the wealthy to avoid taxes often breed resentment. At the other end of the income spectrum, about 44 percent of households did not pay any federal income taxes in 2018. This also breeds resentment. Both outcomes, however, are the result of policies that receive widespread and bipartisan support. For example, everyone receives a certain tax-exempt amount of income. Policymakers of both parties have long held that poor people shouldn't pay any income tax. Repeated expansions of credits for low-income workers and parents have enjoyed strong bipartisan support over the years. Both credits are "refundable"—not only do they reduce the taxes that eligible working people pay, but they also provide cash refunds to those taxpayers who don't owe any income tax. Almost everyone who doesn't owe any federal income tax is either low income—and still pays federal payroll taxes—or retired.[10]

Social insurance taxes rank second as a federal revenue source, raising about 35 percent of all revenues ($1.2 trillion) in 2018 (Figure 1.1). The biggest of them by far are the payroll taxes that finance Social Security and Medicare, which an employer and employee pay in equal amount. Social Security taxes are 12.4 percent of wages, with the employer and employee each paying 6.2 percent, up to a cap of $128,400 of the employee's earnings in 2018. Self-employed workers pay both parts of the tax. The earnings cap rises each year at the same rate as average national wages. Medicare taxes are 2.9 percent on *all* wages, with 1.45 percent paid by each the employer and employee. Employees in high-income households also pay a 0.9 percent Medicare surtax, so the overall Medicare tax is 3.8 percent on earnings or self-employment income (the same as the surtax on investment income described earlier). The government also collects other taxes to finance social insurance, such as the tax on employers to fund unemployment insurance.

Income and payroll taxes differ in important ways. In the budget, income taxes are part of general revenues and are not earmarked for any particular spending program; payroll taxes, by contrast, go into dedicated trust funds that finance specific programs—most prominently, Social Security and part of Medicare. Income taxes apply to a broad measure of income; most payroll taxes apply only to wages. Income tax rates rise with income; payroll taxes are a fixed rate over a broad range of income, and most fall to zero above that cap. The income tax exempts many low-income households and, in fact, goes further by subsidizing their work efforts through refundable tax credits to low-income working families. Payroll taxes, by contrast, apply from the first dollar of earnings.

Although the legal burden to remit payroll taxes is often shared between the worker and employer, most economists believe that workers really bear close to the entire burden of the payroll tax—even the employer share. That is, if employers weren't paying the tax, they'd pay higher wages to those employees.[11] Counting the employer share, most households pay more in payroll taxes than income taxes. Among households in the bottom 80 percent of the income distribution, payroll taxes exceed income taxes on average (Figure 1.2).[12] Payroll taxes are regressive when considered in isolation, but when the benefits are included, Social Security and Medicare are progressive programs. Lower-income beneficiaries receive greater benefits, relative to their income and tax contributions, than higher-income beneficiaries.

Ranking third as a revenue source is the corporate income tax, which raised about 7 percent of federal revenue ($242 billion) in 2018 (Figure 1.1). Corporations are taxed at a flat 21 percent rate on their domestic earnings. A number of complex provisions aim to limit the extent to which companies can move profits offshore.

Although companies pay the government what they owe in corporate taxes, they don't bear the burden of those payments. Instead, the burden is borne by either customers (via higher prices), workers (via lower wages), input suppliers (via lower demand for inputs), shareholders (via lower profits), or all capital holders (as investments move into the non-corporate sector and reduce returns there). Most studies in the United States suggest that workers bear up to one-third of the burden, while shareholders and capital owners bear the rest.[13]

A grab-bag of other revenue sources accounts for the remaining 8 percent ($278 billion) of revenues in 2018. Federal taxes on gasoline—18.4 cents per gallon of unleaded gas, 24.4 cents per gallon of diesel fuel—help fund federal grants to states to repair and maintain roads. Taxes on alcohol and tobacco products, sometimes called "sin" taxes, are designed to raise revenues and reduce the use of these products.

The federal estate and gift tax does not generate much revenue (0.8 percent of revenue in 2018) but adds significant progressivity to the tax system. Only the very rich pay it—the first $22.4 million of a married couple's estate is exempt from tax as of 2018. With this high exemption and a variety of loopholes, fewer than one out of every 1,000 people who die owe estate taxes.[14] Gift taxes aim to prevent well-to-do people from avoiding the estate tax by passing down their estate in the form of gifts while they're still alive.[15]

Taking account of all federal taxes, the federal tax system is progressive—typically, the share of income that people pay in taxes rises as their income rises. Among households in the top 1 percent, federal tax burdens—including all of the taxes noted above—account for 30 percent of their income (Figure 1.2). In the middle fifth, the average tax rate is just over 12 percent. In the bottom fifth, the average tax rate is less than 4 percent.[16] That's mainly due to the income tax, which, as noted above, is progressive because tax rates rise with income and an initial amount of income is tax exempt (Figure 1.2). Households in the top 1 percent pay 24 percent of their income in federal income taxes. The rest of households in the top 20 percent pay about 10 percent.[17] Households in the bottom 40 percent on average receive net refunds from the income tax system because of income that's exempt from taxes and because of the tax credits they receive.

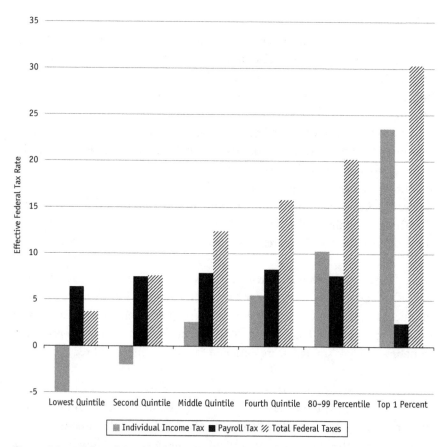

Figure 1.2. Effective federal tax rates by income group, 2018. The 80–99 percentile group is a weighted average by total income from the 80–90, 90–95, and 95–99 percentile groups. Income is measured by "expanded cash income," which equals cash income plus tax-exempt employee and employer contributions to health insurance and other fringe benefits, employer contributions to tax-preferred retirement accounts, income earned within retirement accounts, and food stamps. The income percentile classes used in this table are based on the income distribution for the entire population and contain an equal number of people, not tax units. The breaks are (in 2017 dollars): 20% $25,000; 40% $48,600; 60% $86,100; 80% $149,400; 90% $216,800; 95% $307,900; 99% $732,800; 99.9% $3,439,900. Tax Policy Center (2017b, 2018).

On the spending side, here's a key fact to keep in mind: although the federal government operates thousands of programs each year, four items—Social Security, healthcare, defense, and interest on the debt—account for almost 70 percent of all spending.[18]

Social Security accounted for about 23 percent of spending ($967 billion) in 2018 (Figure 1.3) and includes two programs. President Roosevelt and Congress created the Old-Age and Survivors Insurance (OASI) program in 1935, in the

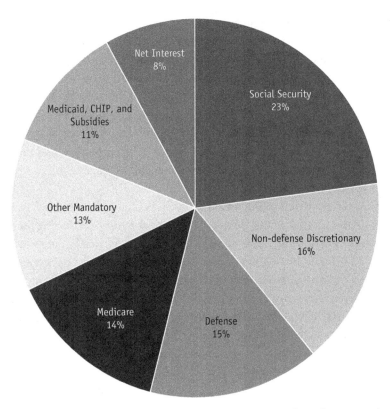

Figure 1.3. Federal outlays by category, 2018. Sum may not equal 100 due to rounding. Congressional Budget Office (2018a).

midst of the Great Depression, at a time of intense focus on the tens of millions of people who were suffering. It provides cash benefits to retirees, their spouses and dependents, and survivors of deceased workers. President Eisenhower and Congress created the Disability Insurance (DI) program in 1956, expanding the breadth of support that Social Security offers to vulnerable Americans. It provides cash benefits to disabled workers and eligible dependents. Each program is funded through payroll taxes. More than 60 million Americans—about a fifth of the population—receive benefits in a given year, mostly through the retirement program. Social Security helped up to 26 million people avoid poverty in 2016, and it provides most of the retirement income for most elderly households.[19]

Medicare accounted for 14 percent of spending ($583 billion) in 2018.[20] President Johnson and Congress enacted the program in 1965 as part of the Great Society, which Johnson built on Franklin Delano Roosevelt's (FDR's) New Deal. Medicare provides the elderly with basic health insurance. President George W. Bush and Congress added prescription drug coverage in 2003. Medicare now covers about 60 million beneficiaries in a given year and is financed by a combination of payroll taxes, insurance premiums, and general revenues.[21]

Medicaid, which Johnson also pushed through Congress in 1965, accounted for 9 percent of spending ($383 billion) in 2018. It provides medical coverage to some low-income families—who account for about a third of its spending—and to disabled people and the elderly. Medicaid covered 74 million beneficiaries in 2018.[22] The federal government and the states jointly fund the program through general revenues, and the states administer it. The government also provides subsidies to help people buy private insurance and offers a Children's Health Insurance Program (CHIP).

Defense accounted for 15 percent of federal spending ($622 billion) in 2018. About 20 percent of the core Defense Department budget (excluding the costs of overseas operations such as the wars in Iraq and Afghanistan) goes to "procurement"—that is, buying weapons and other items. The rest pays mainly for operations and maintenance, personnel, and research and development.

Interest payments on the national debt accounted for about 8 percent of spending ($316 billion) in 2018. The level of interest payments depends on the size of the debt and the interest rate. While the debt continues to rise as the government runs deficits each year, the government has benefited in recent years from unusually low interest rates. In 2018, the government paid an average interest rate of roughly 2.2 percent, which is low by historical standards.

The remaining 29 percent of federal spending includes everything else the government does—safety net programs for the poor, education and science programs, core functions of government like diplomacy and law enforcement, and so on.

Outside of Social Security, Disability Insurance, Medicare, and Medicaid, the major safety net programs include Temporary Assistance for Needy Families (TANF), the Supplemental Nutrition Assistance Program (SNAP, formerly called food stamps), housing assistance, unemployment insurance, Supplemental Security Income (SSI), and the refundable parts of the earned income tax credit and child tax credit. These programs provide benefits to an enormous number of people. In an average month, SNAP provided food assistance for more than 40 million Americans in 2018. In 2016, SSI benefited 8 million people per month on average. Over 26 million families and children received some benefit from the earned income tax credit (EITC) in 2016. Combined, the safety net and similar programs accounted for about 13 percent of spending in 2018. They lifted as many as 18 million people out of poverty in 2016.[23]

About 16 percent of the budget goes to other domestic programs, many of which can be reasonably called investments. This includes education, training, and social services; science, medical, and technological research; and transportation and infrastructure. Education, training, and social services programs include grants to state and local governments, training programs at the Labor Department, social services at the Department of Health and Human Services (HHS), and Pell Grants to help lower-income students attend college. Science, medical, and technological research includes funds for the National Aeronautics and Space Administration (NASA), the National Institutes of Health (NIH), and the National Science Foundation (NSF). Transportation and infrastructure spending includes grants to states for highway maintenance and improvements.

And, of course, the government funds core functions: for example, the Justice Department for law enforcement activities, the Department of Homeland Security to protect America on the domestic front, the Environmental Protection Agency to protect our natural resources, the National Park Service to maintain the parks, and the State Department to conduct our diplomatic efforts and provide international security assistance. The government also provides retirement and health benefits to veterans and federal workers.

All told, about 61 percent of spending comes through "mandatory" programs (and another 8 percent from net interest); the rest are "discretionary." In mandatory programs, the law determines a person's eligibility for benefits based on certain criteria (age, income, or other factors), and anyone who is eligible is entitled to those benefits; that's why the programs are often called "entitlements." Like tax laws, mandatory programs continue on auto-pilot from year to year, under the terms set in the law, unless the president and Congress change them. Social Security, Medicare, and Medicaid are mandatory programs, as are safety net programs such as TANF, SNAP, and unemployment compensation, as well as farm subsidies.

By contrast, policymakers authorize discretionary programs only for a set period—typically, but not always, a year. Discretionary spending tends to fund many of government's traditional functions. About half goes to defense and homeland security. About another quarter goes to investments, including the education and training, science and space, and infrastructure projects discussed above. Other discretionary spending covers housing, environmental protection, food safety, government operations like law enforcement and tax collection, and many other functions.

The distinctions between discretionary and mandatory spending matter because of the way the president and Congress prepare the budget. As noted, mandatory spending programs generally continue as is unless they are changed. Discretionary programs are typically authorized for only a limited period, usually a year, and so expire unless they are actively extended.

In principle, the budget process works like this. In February, the president submits a budget for the next fiscal year to Congress, proposing levels for spending on discretionary programs and changes to the laws regarding taxes and mandatory spending. The president's budget director and other top officials promote the budget at congressional hearings. By April 15, Congress adopts a budget resolution that sets congressional targets for the overall level of taxes, mandatory spending, and each of 12 discretionary spending categories. Each chamber of Congress passes 12 appropriations bills to fund discretionary programs, as well as any bills to change revenue or spending on mandatory programs. The House and Senate reconcile each of these bills, after which each chamber passes the conference report, and the president signs the budget into law—all by September 30, in advance of the October 1 start of the fiscal year.

In practice, the process almost never works that way and is routinely described as "broken." Congress designed this process in 1974. Since then, in only four years has it passed all of the appropriations bills for discretionary spending on time. In most years since 2010, Congress has not even passed a budget resolution.[24] In some years, Congress combines some or all of the discretionary spending proposals into an "omnibus appropriations bill." Alternatively, the president and Congress can enact a short-term "continuing resolution" to fund the discretionary part of the government, typically at the previous year's levels, until they agree on new spending levels. If they don't enact any of these measures on time, the federal government "shuts down." Vital services such as defense, however, continue to operate.

The nation has a legal limit on the debt it can accumulate—often called the "debt ceiling." Until World War I, every issuance of government debt required presidential and congressional approval. During the war, President Wilson and Congress eliminated that rule and created an overall limit to make it easier to finance the mobilization. Since then, Democratic and Republican presidents and Congresses have raised or suspended the debt ceiling more than 100 times, including more than 75 times since 1960 and more than 15 since 2001.[25] Congress usually raises or suspends (i.e., temporarily abolishes) the ceiling before the limit is reached, but the party out of power often dissents.[26]

The debt limit is an odd duck and is greatly misunderstood. First, for historical and legal reasons, it applies to what is called "gross debt," the sum of net debt *plus* intragovernmental loans. Net debt is what the government owes the public—including investors, pension funds, domestic or foreign central banks—and it is a measure that economists consider to be important. Intragovernmental debt is what one part of the government owes the other part. Because it is akin to your right pocket owing your left pocket money, intragovernmental debt *has no economic content*. By extension, then, gross debt is a legal concept that has no economic significance.[27] Sadly, the popular discussion, even among many so-called experts—sometimes focuses on "gross debt." Even Manhattan's "national debt clock" focuses on gross debt.[28] That's a mistake.

A second problem is that voters often assume—and lawmakers often assert—that a vote to raise the debt ceiling is a vote for more red ink. In fact, however, raising the debt limit is about paying for past choices. Debt limit debates are about whether Congress should authorize the government to borrow to pay for spending that *Congress has previously authorized.* The debate about accumulating more debt occurred (or should have occurred) when policymakers voted to raise spending or cut taxes in the first place.

Oddly enough, when Congress authorizes new spending and new taxes, it does not automatically authorize the borrowing needed to make up any difference.[29] Among other advanced countries, only Denmark has a separate debt limit rule like ours—and they don't use it as a political football. Arguing about increasing the debt limit is like having a person charge vacation expenses to his credit card and debating whether he should pay the credit card company when the bill comes due. He should have considered the payment before he took the vacation.

If government debt hits the ceiling, the Treasury Department can typically use any of several accounting gimmicks to postpone the day of reckoning. But these typically last only a few months and then the government would have to default on interest payments or other obligations—for example, military pay, tax refunds, or safety net payments. The economic consequences of a large-scale, intentional default are unknown, but predictions range from the merely bad to the truly catastrophic.[30]

When it comes to fiscal policy, the debt ceiling is not America's only peculiarity. In many ways, our tax and spending systems are unusual among major industrialized powers. To some extent, the differences represent differing values and circumstances. The differences can also offer ideas about how to address our own challenges—as we do in the chapters to come.

Despite what certain policymakers have claimed, the United States has substantially *lower* taxes than other advanced nations. In 2015, the most recent year for which we have comprehensive data, US government at all levels—federal, state, and local—collected 26 percent of GDP in taxes, the lowest share in the G7—which also includes Canada, France, Germany, Italy, Japan, and the United Kingdom—and far below the non-US G7 average of 36 percent. Over the last 40 years, US federal, state, and local governments raised an average of 8 percent of GDP less in revenue than the other G7 countries.

The composition of US taxes also is quite different. The other G7 countries rely less on income taxes and much more on consumption, payroll, and energy taxes.

In 2015, they raised almost three times as much in consumption taxes as America did—a difference of almost 4 percent of GDP (Figure 1.4). All of those countries—and more than 160 countries worldwide—have a national value-added tax, which is a general tax on consumption of goods and services (as discussed further in Chapter 13). In the United States, the federal government imposes taxes on tobacco, alcohol, and gasoline, but not on overall consumption. State and local governments levy sales taxes, but they constitute a small share of all US revenue.

Payroll taxes, which fund social insurance programs, are almost twice as large in the other G7 countries—a difference of almost 6 percent of GDP in 2015 (Figure 1.4).[31]

The United States relies less on corporate taxes. Corporate taxes raise less revenue—2.2 percent of GDP across all levels of government in America in 2015—than in other G7 countries, which averaged 2.6 percent of GDP. Corporate taxes are slated to drop substantially in the United States following the 2017 tax act.

Finally, the United States imposes very low taxes on energy compared to other nations (not shown). The average combined federal and state gasoline tax

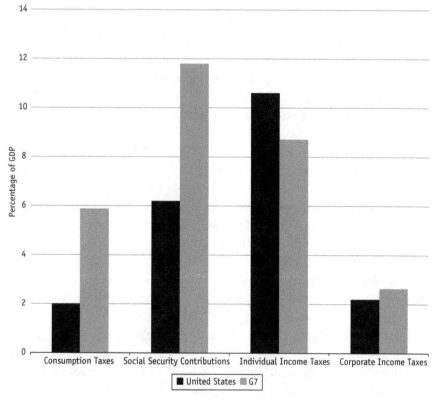

Figure 1.4. Major United States and G7 general government revenue sources, 2015. G7 average is weighted by GDP and does not include the United States. OECD (2017d).

in 2015 was 49 cents per gallon for petroleum and 54 cents for diesel fuel.[32] In other G7 nations, effective tax rates on fuel for road use were *16 times* higher for petroleum, and *nine times* higher for diesel fuel.[33]

The level and composition of spending also differs in the United States compared to other G7 countries.[34] For statistical reasons, the spending data are not directly comparable to the data in the previous section. The United States spent about 38 percent of GDP in combined federal, state, and local spending in 2015, compared to 45 percent for the other G7 countries. Over the past 20 years, US spending has been about 8 percent of GDP lower than in the rest of the G7.[35]

Other countries spend much more on the social safety net and infrastructure, and much less on defense, than the United States (Figure 1.5).[36] Other G7 countries spent 2.1 percent of GDP on benefits for families with children in 2013 (the most recent year with comprehensive data), including cash payments and

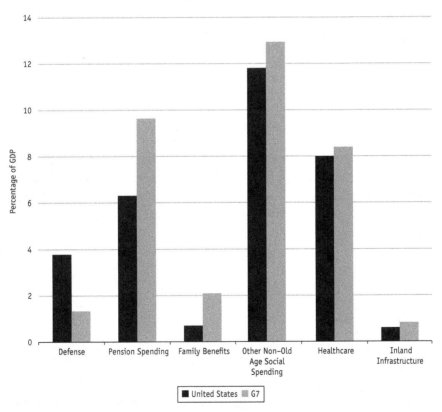

Figure 1.5. Selected general government spending categories as a share of gross domestic product (GDP), 2013. G7 average is weighted by GDP and does not include the United States. OECD (2016, 2017a, 2017b, 2017c).

services, compared to 0.7 percent in the United States, which ranks last in the G7 in this category (Figure 1.5). That's partly because the United States provides more benefits than some G7 countries through tax deductions and credits for low-income households. Even with that included, however, the United States still provides the smallest family benefits, as a share of GDP, of any G7 country.[37]

For elderly households, the social safety net is more extensive in the other G7 countries. The United States spent 6.3 percent of GDP on old-age and pension-related social spending in 2013 (not including healthcare), while the other G7 countries spent 9.6 percent of GDP—or 50 percent more. Other countries have older populations, younger retirement ages, and longer life expectancies, as well as more generous annual benefits under their retirement programs.

Other countries also invest more in infrastructure, with the rest of the G7 spending 0.8 percent of GDP on inland infrastructure investment (including roads, railways, inland waterways, ports, and airports) compared to 0.6 percent in the United States. On the other hand, the United States spends far more on defense than its G7 colleagues—3.8 percent of GDP in 2013, for instance, compared to 1.3 percent in the other countries. Although total (public and private) US healthcare spending far exceeds that of other G7 countries—16.3 percent of GDP compared to 10.4 percent in 2013—the difference lies in private spending; public spending on healthcare is about the same.

That the United States has developed tax and spending patterns different from those of other G7 nations may not be surprising, for our patterns reflect the unique challenges that America has faced at home and abroad since its birth more than two centuries ago. Our fiscal history not only explains how we got to where we are on taxes and spending, it also offers a window into how we will have to address our fiscal problems in the years ahead. And it's our history to which we now turn.

Notes

1. Kaiser Family Foundation (2013).
2. Pew Research Center (2014).
3. Williamson (2018) argues that people's interpretations of what constitutes foreign aid varies, which can partially explain why common estimates of the size of the foreign aid budget are so large. For example, among those who include military spending in their perceptions of foreign aid, estimates of the size of the foreign aid budget are 55 percent higher, potentially reflecting differing interpretations of what is included in budget categories rather than lack of knowledge. Nevertheless, there is still a huge mismatch between reality and perceptions. All defense plus foreign aid accounts for only 16 percent of federal spending.

4. This quote has been attributed to Mark Twain, but versions of the saying may have actually been written by Josh Billings (Quote Investigator 2015).

5. All 2018 numbers refer to fiscal year 2018, which ran from October 1, 2017, to September 30, 2018. Unless otherwise stated, the data are from the Congressional Budget Office (CBO), the Office of Management and Budget (OMB), or the US Treasury. The Center on Budget and Policy Priorities' (2018a) "Policy Basics" series provides very useful and readable summaries of many of the topics covered in this chapter.

6. The unified budget deficit (or surplus) is the difference between all spending and revenues. The primary budget deficit (or surplus) is the difference between non-interest spending and revenues. The cyclically adjusted deficit estimates what the deficit would be if the economy were at full employment. I focus on the unified deficit unless otherwise mentioned.

7. This statement is not literally true—there are some items, called "below the line" financing, that break the exact link between debt and accumulation of prior deficits. But the items are small, and they generally do not affect the analysis in the rest of the book. The budget usually reports costs on a cash-flow basis, with the exception of credit programs, where the budget records the subsidy component rather than the cash flow.

8. About half of current, publicly held debt is owned by US private investors and the Federal Reserve System. The rest is held by foreign investors. The federal government also holds significant financial assets. As recently as 2008, financial assets were small relative to the debt, primarily composed of the Treasury's operating cash balance and direct and guaranteed loans. Since then, federal financial asset holdings have increased due to provisions in the Troubled Asset Relief Program (TARP), the conservatorship of the Federal National Mortgage Association (FNMA [Fannie Mae]), and the Federal Home Loan Mortgage Corporation, known as Freddie Mac, as well as changes to student loan policies. Net financial assets held by the federal government were about 8 percent of GDP in 2018.

9. Joint Committee on Taxation (2018).

10. Tax Policy Center (2017c); Williams (2015).

11. Fullerton and Metcalf (2002); Gruber and Krueger (1990).

12. Tax Policy Center (2018).

13. Congressional Budget Office (2018b); Cronin et al. (2012); Fullerton and Metcalf (2002); Joint Committee on Taxation (2013); Nunns (2012).

14. Tax Policy Center (2017a).

15. Johnston (2001); Tax Policy Center (2016). Gift taxes apply to gifts between two people (e.g., an elderly person who is close to death and one of his children) of over $15,000 per year in 2018. Individual donors receive lifetime gift tax exclusions of $11.2 million, above the $15,000 per year threshold. The tax exempts gifts for education and health expenses that an individual pays directly to an institution.

16. Tax Policy Center (2017b). This calculation defines income as expanded cash income, which includes cash income (wages and salaries, employee contribution to tax-deferred retirement savings plans, business income or loss, farm income or loss, interest income, taxable dividends, realized net capital gains, social security benefits received, unemployment compensation, energy assistance, TANF, worker's compensation, veterans' benefits, supplemental security income, child support, disability benefits, taxable individual retirement account [IRA] distributions, total pension income, alimony received, and other income including foreign-earned income), tax-exempt employee and employer contributions to health insurance and other fringe benefits, employer contributions to tax-preferred retirement accounts, income earned within retirement accounts, and food stamps. Expanded cash income is a broader measure of income than adjusted gross income, which is reported on tax forms.

17. Tax Policy Center (2018).

18. While it is easy to specify how much money the government spends, it is much harder to pin down the precise size—the influence—of the federal government. There is a

natural tendency to equate the size of government with government spending, but the two concepts can be quite different. The government can impose regulations that affect business and individual choices but don't show up as spending. Some programs (for example, Medicare) collect user fees that the government counts as negative outlays and thus that reduce official spending figures. Tax expenditures—which, as noted above, can substitute for spending programs—expand the role and influence of government with no increase in spending and actually a reduction in revenue (Marron and Toder 2013).

19. Fox (2017). In 2016, Social Security provided more than 90 percent of income for more than a third of the elderly and more than half of income for about two-thirds of the elderly (Social Security Administration 2016).

20. This represents gross Medicare outlays of 3.5 percent of GDP, less offsetting receipts of 0.6 percent of GDP.

21. Boards of Trustees (2018); Centers for Medicare and Medicaid Services (2018).

22. Centers for Medicare and Medicaid Services (2018).

23. Center on Budget and Policy Priorities (2018b); Food and Nutrition Service (2018); Sherman (2017); Social Security Administration (2017).

24. Desilver (2018).

25. Austin (2015); US Department of the Treasury (2018).

26. For example, in 2006, then-senator Barack Obama voted against an increase under President Bush.

27. The gross debt measure is such a misleading concept that if, for example, the government runs a surplus in the Social Security trust fund, the gross debt measure goes up. When Social Security runs a surplus—that is, when payroll tax receipts and interest payments from Treasury exceed benefit payouts and other net costs in a given year— the Social Security Trust Fund gives the surplus to the Treasury Department and, in return, receives a bond from Treasury (which counts as gross government debt) that it can redeem for those funds when it needs them to pay benefits. The asset that Social Security obtains is exactly offset by the new intragovernmental debt that Treasury faces. Other major trust funds, which contribute to intragovernmental debt, include those for civil service retirement, military retirement, part of Medicare, disability insurance, and highways.

28. Kadet (2017).

29. At various points since 1980, the House of Representatives did automatically authorize the needed debt payments along with the passage of a non-binding congressional budget. But this so-called Gephardt rule was ultimately repealed in 2011 (Heniff 2015).

30. US Department of the Treasury (2013).

31. This measure groups all Social Security contributions from the employer, employee, and the self-employed. Earmarked income taxes are also included.

32. American Petroleum Institute (2015).

33. For more comparisons of energy taxes, see OECD (2018).

34. For a variety of reasons, the measures of spending used in cross-national studies by the Organisation for Economic Co-operation and Development (OECD) are harder to make comparable than tax data. They are available for fewer years, and they tend to overstate what we would consider to be spending under conventional accounting definitions.

35. Total spending data are not available for Canada. Data for Japan are not available until 2005.

36. Defense data are missing for Canada.

37. OECD (2016).

2

How We Got Here, Why It Matters

The United States was born amid debates over taxes and debt, and we've been arguing about them ever since. Our current budget situation derives from policy choices and economic events over a long period. We can't fully understand where we are, or where we should go, unless we know where we've been and how we got here.

The overarching story of US fiscal history is straightforward, reflecting the circumstances and values that Americans have brought to fiscal policy since the nation's earliest days.[1] From the signing of the Constitution all the way to 1980, debt buildups were sporadic and brief. They occurred only in times of emergency—wars or depressions—and presidents and Congresses rapidly reversed them after each crisis. This pattern has its roots in a deep-seated cultural aversion to debt, which was often viewed as a sign of moral weakness.

In the 1980s, with tax cuts and a defense buildup that he pushed through Congress, Ronald Reagan ushered in the first sustained growth in debt at a time of peace and prosperity. But policymakers' continuing distaste for fiscal profligacy led to a remarkable series of politically difficult but largely bipartisan decisions in the 1980s and 1990s to correct the debt path. These changes, combined with strong economic growth in the 1990s, turned deficits into surpluses by the end of the century.

Those surpluses disappeared rapidly under President George W. Bush, due to two tax cuts, two wars, higher domestic spending, and a weak economy. Then came the financial crisis and Great Recession in 2007–2009, which boosted debt enormously. President Obama's 2009 stimulus package, which cut taxes and raised spending, added to short-term deficits. Obama and a Republican-led Congress had several budget showdowns over the ensuing years that reduced short-term spending, and long-term debt projections fell due to reductions in interest rates and expected healthcare spending. But in 2017 and 2018, President Trump and a Republican-led Congress reversed course and enacted a major tax cut and a major spending increase that will raise future debt considerably.

History may well just be "one damned thing after another," as historian Arnold Toynbee put it, but US fiscal history offers lessons for thinking about our fiscal future.[2] We learn, for instance, that the nation's leaders make major corrective fiscal policy changes only rarely, and often only if they perceive a crisis. But when they do, they tend to make them through a series of incremental steps rather than a single "Grand Bargain." The steps typically include both tax increases and spending cuts. Deficit reduction between 1982 and 1993 reflects that pattern. History suggests that cutting taxes as a way to constrain spending—the "starve the beast" theory—does not work very well.

Even with many policy changes and vociferous debates over the years, the basic building blocks of our fiscal system have existed for a long time. We've had a progressive income tax, a corporate tax, and an estate tax for more than 100 years, though corporate and estate taxes have steadily shrunk over time. Most major tax credits, deductions, and other subsidies date back more than 50 years, some more than 80. On the spending side, Medicare and Medicaid were established more than 50 years ago. A person born when Social Security was created in 1935 is now old enough to have collected benefits for 20 years. Because these programs are well entrenched and popular, policymakers may find it hard to change them radically.

Unfortunately, our fiscal history also shows that policymakers tend, mistakenly, to try to move toward balanced budgets during times of economic weakness. Such policies backfired in the 1930s, and they slowed the recent recovery from the Great Recession. While policymakers should focus more on long-term fiscal issues than they do, they should not confuse the benefits of short-term deficits in a weak economy with the costs of chronic long-term deficits (as discussed in Chapter 4).

Ironically, however, the most important lesson that our history presents— in conjunction with the budget outlook presented in Chapter 3—is that the future debt solution can't be like previous ones. We are in uncharted territory. The fiscal situation we now face differs in nature and magnitude from previous episodes. Some of the current problems reflect inherited debt, due to war costs, the economy, and tax cuts, just like previous debt buildups. This time, however, we also have an enduring problem that's rooted largely in demographics: the aging of the population means that spending on federal retirement and health programs will grow more rapidly than the revenues that finance government.

But before we turn to the future, let's start at the beginning.

The United States borrowed heavily to finance the Revolutionary War. The Continental Congress issued most of the debt, but the states issued a sizable share as well. The Articles of Confederation, however, gave the power to tax exclusively to the states. All 13 states had to approve any national tax, leaving the federal government with no real way to pay its debts.

As a result, the United States in the 1780s endured a lengthy fiscal crisis, defaulting on interest payments and falling behind on principal payments. It was not uncommon for governments created in the fire of revolution to default on the debt they inherited. Consequently, borrowers perceived American debt as risky and demanded high interest rates on the country's bonds. To confront these and other issues, later in the decade, the authors of the Constitution gave the national government the power to "lay and collect taxes" and "borrow money on the credit of the United States." Still, creditors remained unsure whether the fledgling nation would pay its debts.

Enter Alexander Hamilton, the nation's first treasury secretary. In his 1790 "Report on the Public Credit," he argued that the government should not only repay all of its debt but also assume and pay the states' debts. These steps, he believed, would solidify the country's reputation as credit-worthy, ensuring its ability to borrow and establish the trade and credit markets needed for economic development. As Hamilton wrote, "A national debt, if it is not excessive, will be to us a national blessing."[3] Hamilton favored a strong and activist federal government. He lived in New York and echoed the values and priorities of bankers and merchants from that city, who stood to gain from expanded credit markets. He also represented the views of the northern states, which still owed substantial debts.

Thomas Jefferson and James Madison had a different view. As representatives of southern agrarian interests, they did not want to reward New York speculators who had purchased steeply discounted Treasury debt immediately after seeing Hamilton's report—and before news of it had spread across the country. Nor did they see why the southern states, which had already significantly paid down their debts, should have to subsidize the debt of other states. They also feared the political and economic implications of a significant national debt and thought each generation should pay off the debts it incurred. In Madison's words, "a public debt is a public curse."[4]

In a political compromise, Jefferson and Madison agreed that the federal government would repay its full debt and assume the states' debt, while Hamilton agreed to support moving the nation's capital to the South, from Philadelphia to what is now Washington, DC.

Although Hamilton won the battle over the federal assumption of state debt, Jefferson and Madison won the war about how to use federal debt over the next century and beyond. From 1790 until the Second World War, the "fiscal cycle" was straightforward: the government ran big deficits and increased public debt only during wars or depressions. When those episodes ended, the government ran surpluses and rapidly paid off the debt (Figure 2.1). Limited government and fiscal conservatism took precedence over almost everything else, and it came at the expense of other key national priorities such as transportation, utilities, and other infrastructure, which were left to state and local governments.

After the Constitution's ratification, the government's first major act was to establish a revenue system, featuring mainly tariffs on imported goods. The government's main fiscal activity over the next 20 years was to use those revenues to pay down the debt. The one major exception is notable. After Jefferson became president, the government borrowed $11 million (about 2 percent of GDP at that time) to finance the Louisiana Purchase in 1803, an almost perfect example of how Hamilton had envisioned using debt to promote national economic interests. In any case, as creditors gained confidence in the government's ability and willingness to pay its debt, interest rates fell. By 1811, debt had fallen to 6 percent of GDP from around 30 percent in 1790.

The War of 1812 restarted the fiscal cycle. Spending rose and a financing crisis ensued; significant borrowing came only after the nation's leaders made heroic efforts to find people willing to extend credit. The government was continually short of funds and frequently couldn't pay soldiers and contractors on time—that is, it defaulted on numerous occasions.

After the war, the government ran surpluses, paying down the debt rapidly. Andrew Jackson, elected president in 1828, viewed debt as economic bondage

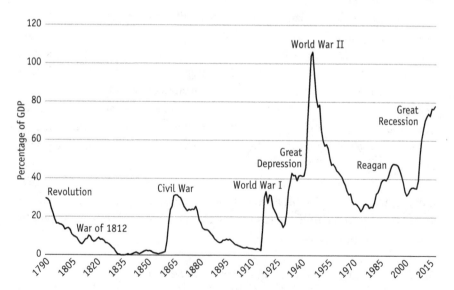

Figure 2.1. Debt as a percentage of gross domestic product (GDP), 1790–2018. For years 1790–1928: Congressional Budget Office (2010); for years 1929–1940: Congressional Budget Office (2010) and Bureau of Economic Analysis (2013); for years 1941–2018: Office of Management and Budget (2018).

and paid off the entire national debt by 1835. A year later, the federal government sent surplus funds to the states, but a financial crisis in 1837 ignited a deep recession, ending such revenue sharing and generating new federal debt. Nevertheless, 50 years after the Constitutional Convention, the nation had made good on its reputation for paying what it owed, and US debt was highly regarded.

The Civil War restarted the fiscal cycle, but on a much larger scale. Spending soared, reaching 12 percent of GDP (compared to 4 percent during the War of 1812), most of which the government funded by borrowing. Federal debt, which was just 2 percent of GDP in 1860, skyrocketed to 31 percent by the end of the war. During the war, President Lincoln and Congress imposed excise taxes on a vast array of consumption goods, accounting for most of the new revenue. Because those taxes were regressive, policymakers added a progressive inheritance tax and, in 1861, the nation's first income tax, with rates that reached 10 percent on incomes over $10,000 by 1866. About 10 percent of Union households had incomes high enough to face the tax. To administer these taxes, policymakers created a new agency—the Office of Internal Revenue—the forerunner of today's Internal Revenue Service (IRS).

After the war, the government again ran surpluses and paid off much of its debt. The debt-to-GDP ratio fell to 7 percent in 1893. As surpluses rolled in, the government eliminated many taxes, including the income tax in 1871. The nation resumed its reliance on tariffs but also retained Civil War–era excise taxes on alcohol and tobacco.

With the end of progressive income and inheritance taxes and with rising wealth and income inequality, populist concerns grew over the tax code's regressivity. The "Panic of 1893," which threw the economy into a depression and ended the series of budget surpluses, exacerbated these concerns. In response, policymakers created America's second income tax in 1894—designed more to increase social justice based on "ability to pay" rather than to generate substantial revenue. Before the tax took effect, however, the Supreme Court ruled it unconstitutional.[5] Public opposition to the decision was strong, though, and the movement for progressive taxation gathered steam. In 1909, Congress created a 1 percent corporate profits tax, the precursor to the modern corporate income tax. President Taft proposed a constitutional amendment to authorize an income tax. Congress overwhelmingly passed the Sixteenth Amendment, and the necessary three-quarters of states ratified it by 1913.

That same year, the president and Congress created the nation's third income tax, and though the third time wasn't exactly a charm, the tax has nonetheless survived to this day. Originally, it was a "class tax"—only the top 2 percent of Americans had to pay it, much less than during the Civil War. Rates ranged from 1 to 7 percent, with a tiny fraction of people paying the top rate. The tax offered deductions for interest payments and for state and local taxes. Life insurance proceeds, gifts, and inheritances were exempt, as were the first $20,000 ($480,000 in today's dollars) of dividends. The tax form was only three pages long, with one page of instructions!

The 1916 Revenue Act raised the top income tax rate to 15 percent, boosted corporate tax rates, and introduced the estate tax. Thus, as of 100 years ago, all major pieces of the modern tax system, except the payroll taxes that fund Social Security and Medicare, were already in place.

The familiar fiscal cycle returned as America entered World War I in 1917. Spending soared to 20 percent of GDP. The government borrowed massively and raised taxes. The debt-to-GDP ratio jumped from 3 percent in 1916 to 33 percent in 1919. Policymakers boosted income tax rates dramatically, raised corporate taxes, and imposed an excess profits tax.

After the war and a brief but deep recession, the economy recovered, the Roaring Twenties arrived, and fiscal policy returned to its normal postwar state. The government ran surpluses, cut spending, and repaid debt. The debt-to-GDP ratio fell by more than half—to 15 percent—by 1929. Under Treasury Secretary Andrew Mellon's guidance, policymakers cut tax rates several times in the 1920s, dropping the top rate from 77 to 25 percent and repealing the excess profits tax. But with the personal and corporate income taxes in place and accounting for most federal revenue, the nation's revenue structure was much more progressive than in the past.

The 1929 stock market crash and the Great Depression launched another fiscal cycle, and the two events demonstrate why short-run federal fiscal policy is important. In response to a collapsing economy, policymakers mistakenly tried to balance the budget. President Hoover and Congress raised tariffs in 1930 and boosted personal and corporate income taxes in 1932. Raising taxes during a downturn hurt the economy; the tariffs ignited a trade war. Unemployment rose to 25 percent by 1933. The debt rose from 15 percent of GDP in 1929 to 43 percent by 1934, mainly because the economy cratered so badly. At the time, this was the largest peacetime increase in the debt-to-GDP ratio in US history.

Over the next few years, the government ran substantial deficits and the economy recovered rapidly. By 1937, unemployment had fallen considerably but was still high at 14 percent. President Roosevelt—who ran on a balanced budget platform in both 1932 and 1936—decided the nation could afford fiscal restraint. He and Congress let a one-time veterans' bonus end and imposed new taxes (for Social Security). Again, tax hikes made a weak economy even weaker.[6]

After 1938, though, the federal government returned to substantial deficits and the economy grew rapidly heading into World War II.

Overall, the 1930s saw a substantial increase in the size of government. Federal spending more than doubled as a share of the economy, from less than 4 percent in 1930 to more than 9 percent in 1940. Roosevelt's New Deal included massive public works, jobs, farm and housing programs, welfare, and Social Security. Federal taxes rose substantially as well. But, after the initial drop in GDP helped boost the debt-to-GDP ratio to 43 percent in 1934, the substantial growth of the economy over the rest of the decade kept the debt-to-GDP ratio in check despite sizable federal deficits in most years. By the end of the decade, the ratio stood at 42 percent.[7]

When the United States entered World War II, the familiar fiscal cycle began again, but on a far larger scale. The government enacted the largest fiscal stimulus in history. Federal spending quadrupled as a share of GDP between 1941 and 1945 and comprised more than 40 percent of GDP by the war's end. Borrowing financed most of the war costs, with annual deficits averaging almost 25 percent of GDP from 1943 to 1945 and the debt-to-GDP ratio rising to an all-time high of 106 percent by 1946.

The war also brought massive tax changes. The Revenue Act of 1942 transformed the income tax from a "class tax" to a "mass tax," dramatically reducing the income level at which people paid taxes and boosting the number of taxpayers tenfold; about 60 percent of workers faced income tax liability. The steeply progressive tax had a top rate of 88 percent and the income level at which it applied fell from $5 million in 1941 to $200,000 in 1942 (about $2.9 million in today's dollars). The top income tax rate peaked at 94 percent in 1944, and overall federal revenues rose from 7 percent of GDP in 1940 to 20 percent by the war's end. At that point, the income tax constituted 40 percent of federal revenues, up from 15 percent in 1941. In response, policymakers enacted targeted tax deductions to partly offset the burden of higher tax rates, and they implemented administrative changes such as employer withholding of income tax so the government could more efficiently administer a system that now included millions of taxpayers.[8]

World War II was a transformational event in US fiscal history. The fiscal narrative before the war revolved around heavy borrowing during wars and depressions, followed by surpluses and debt repayment. Postwar, the story grew more complicated.

First, as in previous postwar episodes, public debt fell as a share of GDP. The debt-to-GDP ratio fell gradually from the record 106 percent in 1946 to just 26 percent by 1980. But, unlike in previous episodes, the United States did not enact policy changes that paid down the debt and ran surpluses in only eight of those years. Instead, the debt-to-GDP ratio declined due to strong economic growth, a long period of low interest rates in the 1950s that reduced interest payments on the debt, and, in the 1960s and 1970s, rising inflation that pushed taxpayers into higher tax brackets, generating more revenue.

Second, federal policymakers expanded their views of fiscal responsibilities, moving the government more toward Hamilton's views and away from Jefferson's. The 1946 Employment Act embraced Keynesian principles, committing the federal government to manage inflation and unemployment. In the late 1940s and 1950s, policymakers also provided substantial resources to rebuild Europe's economy through the Marshall Plan, finance the Korean War, expand Social Security, establish federal disability insurance, and finance the interstate highway system. The 1964 Kennedy-Johnson tax cuts reduced income tax rates by 30 percent across the board, with the top rate falling from 91 percent to 70.[9]

President Johnson then crafted the "Great Society"—fighting the "War on Poverty," establishing Medicare and Medicaid, expanding Social Security, and creating new education, urban, and transportation programs. With tax cuts, higher domestic spending, and Vietnam-era defense spending, deficits rose, and despite remarkably strong economic growth, policymakers needed to impose a 10 percent income surtax in 1969 to help finance government costs.

Third, the massive wartime spending and revenue increases have proven to be permanent (Figure 2.2). Federal spending and revenues had averaged about 2 percent of GDP from 1901 to World War I, and 6 and 5 percent, respectively, from 1920 to 1940. Between 1950 and 1980, however, they averaged more than 18 and 17 percent, respectively. From the end of the war through the early 1970s, the United States enjoyed strong economic growth. The permanently higher level of taxes and spending did not preclude a robustly growing economy.

Fourth, the composition of spending and taxes shifted substantially (Figures 2.3 and 2.4). Defense spending fell steadily, from about 13 percent of GDP in 1954 (just after the Korean War) to less than 5 percent by 1980 (a few years after Vietnam). The fall in defense spending helped to finance a massive increase in mandatory spending, in particular Social Security and, starting in 1965, Medicare and Medicaid. Combined, these programs rose from less than 1 percent of GDP in 1954 to almost 6 percent in 1980. Payroll taxes also rose to fund Social Security and Medicare. The income tax remained the primary revenue source, but corporate taxes fell markedly relative to GDP due to changes in law and the structure of industry (Figure 2.4).

Fifth, even as the debt-to-GDP ratio was falling from 1945 to 1980, the government created substantial *implicit* debts that don't appear in official budget measures. Social Security expansions through the mid-1970s and Medicare and Medicaid's creation in 1965 (as well as expansions in pensions for government

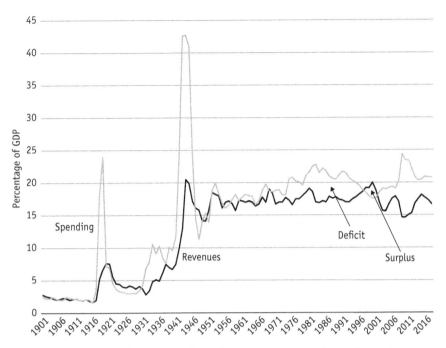

Figure 2.2. Total federal revenues and spending as a percentage of gross domestic product (GDP), 1901–2018. Office of Management and Budget (2018).

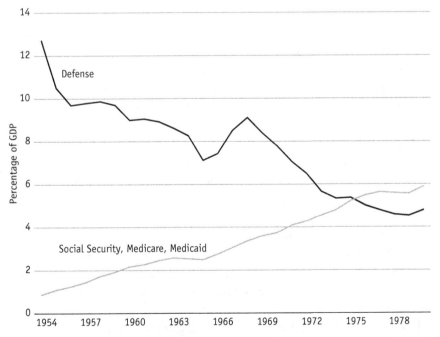

Figure 2.3. Major spending categories as a percentage of gross domestic product (GDP), 1954–1980. Office of Management and Budget (2018).

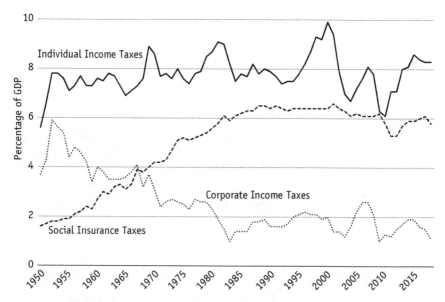

Figure 2.4. Major revenue sources as a percentage of gross domestic product (GDP), 1950–2018. Office of Management and Budget (2018).

workers) created substantial *future* government obligations. The creation and expansion of these programs sowed the seeds of the fiscal problems we face today.

Sixth, the 1945–1980 period witnessed a significant increase in tax expenditures—the deductions, credits, and other preferences that encourage certain activities. Preexisting tax expenditures, like the mortgage interest deduction, grew more important as home ownership rates rose and the income tax applied to more households. In World War II, businesses responded to controls on wages and prices by offering more fringe benefits, such as health insurance. After the war, policymakers made employer-provided health benefits non-taxable.[10] Thus, the growth in tax expenditures raised the scope of federal activity but was not reflected in higher spending.

President Reagan took office in January of 1981 with the economy in "stagflation"—high inflation and high unemployment—amid widespread frustration about taxes. Inspired by the "Laffer curve," the misplaced notion that a broad tax cut could boost the economy so much that it would actually raise revenues, Reagan promised to cut taxes, boost defense, and balance the budget—indeed, to run surpluses. His signature tax cut, which Congress enacted later that year, cut the top personal income rate from 70 to 50 percent, cut other rates, expanded individual retirement accounts, raised the exemption from estate taxes, and provided investment subsidies.

Less well known is that the tax cut also indexed income tax brackets for inflation—meaning that inflation could no longer push taxpayers into higher tax brackets, and Congress would no longer have more or less automatic increases in inflation-adjusted revenues at its disposal. Without that golden goose on the revenue side, we have endured deficit concerns ever since, other than for a few years in the late 1990s.

On the spending side, Reagan hoped that tax cuts would force spending cuts, a theory called "starve the beast." As he put it, "If you have got a kid who is extravagant, you can lecture him all you want to about his extravagance or you can cut his allowance and achieve the same end much quicker."[11] But that's not true when the kid in question—the federal government—has unfettered access to borrowing on world capital markets at risk-free interest rates. In fact, overall spending rose as a share of GDP under Reagan, with the rise in defense spending more than offsetting a cut in social programs.

Reagan's policies marked a major turning point in US fiscal history. Never before had intentional policy decisions, not driven by wars or depressions, caused a sustained rise in the debt-to-GDP ratio. Rather than generate surpluses, his tax cuts and defense buildup generated large deficits "as far as the eye could see," in the words of Reagan's budget director, David Stockman.[12]

These developments set the stage for a remarkable period, 1982 to 1993, in which three presidents and their corresponding Congresses enacted a wide range of reforms that, in combination with economic growth, brought the budget to balance by 1998 and fueled premature predictions of "surpluses as far as the eye can see."

No sooner had the ink dried on Reagan's tax cut than problems emerged. New tax shelters proved embarrassing and revenue losses mounted. The Laffer curve turned out to be too good to be true, excoriated even by Republican leaders. During the 1980 presidential campaign, then-candidate George H. W. Bush had called it "voodoo" economics.[13] After the Reagan tax cut, a bipartisan group of policymakers took numerous steps over the next several years to address burgeoning deficits and debt. They passed, and Reagan signed, tax increases in 1982, 1984, and 1987 so that by the end of the decade the government was recouping almost a third of the annual revenue loss from Reagan's 1981 tax cuts.[14]

Meanwhile, Social Security was running low on cash in the early 1980s. In 1983, a bipartisan commission headed by future Federal Reserve Board chairman Alan Greenspan proposed, and the president and Congress enacted, tax increases and benefit cuts. The plan put Social Security in surplus in every year from 1984 through 2010, thus keeping overall deficits lower than they otherwise would have been. It put the system in overall balance for the subsequent 75 years, but it didn't represent a permanent solution. Now, more than 35 years later, Social Security faces future funding shortfalls again (see Chapter 8).

Long-standing frustration with taxes also came to a head. Liberals, led by New Jersey senator Bill Bradley, didn't like the deductions and shelters that high-income households enjoyed. Conservatives, led by New York representative Jack Kemp, believed high tax rates stymied growth. Everyone thought taxes were too complicated. After years of preparatory work, President Reagan and Congress enacted the Tax Reform Act of 1986, closing dozens of loopholes and cutting tax rates, with the top personal income tax rate falling from 50 to 28 percent and the corporate rate falling from 46 to 34 percent, all in a revenue- and distributionally-neutral manner.[15]

Fiscal policy remained a concern as interest payments on the debt spiked to an unprecedented 3 percent of GDP in 1985 and then 3.2 percent in 1991 (Figure 2.3). Congress tried to impose rules stipulating that the deficit should decline over time, leading to a balanced budget within five years. These rules, commonly called Gramm-Rudman-Hollings after the senators who sponsored them, failed miserably. As deadlines approached, Congress kicked the can down the road, changing underlying budget assumptions and postponing deficit targets.

In response, Presidents George H. W. Bush and then Bill Clinton made politically tough decisions in 1990 and 1993, respectively, to raise taxes and cut spending—another episode inconsistent with "starving the beast." Bush abandoned the "read my lips, no new taxes" pledge of his 1988 campaign, while Clinton abandoned the middle-class tax cut of his 1992 campaign. That Ross Perot, a third-party candidate who spoke incessantly about the deficit, received 19 percent of the vote for president in 1992 highlighted the political potency of the issue and probably helped convince Clinton to address the issue in 1993.

The 1990 budget deal also imposed new budget rules, subjecting total discretionary spending to an annual cap and forcing policymakers who wanted to cut taxes or expand mandatory spending to finance the change by raising other taxes or cutting other mandatory spending. By focusing on factors that policymakers could directly control, these rules were more effective than Gramm-Rudman-Hollings, which focused on the deficit. While the 1990 deal was bipartisan, the 1993 deal received no Republican votes in Congress.

As the 1990s progressed, the fiscal outlook improved. By the end of the decade, revenues were rising due to the 1990 and 1993 tax increases, a strong economy, and a booming stock market. Spending was falling as a share of GDP, fueled by the 1990 budget rules and the "peace dividend" that reduced defense spending after the collapse of the Soviet Union. Clinton confidently declared that "the era of big government is over."[16] The federal government ran a budget surplus in 1998, for the first time since 1969, and then surpluses for three more years in a row, for the longest sustained period of surpluses since the late 1920s.

President George W. Bush assumed office in January of 2001, with fiscal policy looking healthy by conventional measures. In 2000, spending had fallen to 17.6 percent of GDP, a 35-year low; revenues had risen to a postwar high of 20.0 percent of GDP. The debt-to-GDP ratio had fallen from 48 percent in 1993 to 34 percent by 2000. Government and private experts projected growing surpluses over the next ten years (Figure 2.5).[17]

The optimistic fiscal outlook was misleading, however. The surpluses were due entirely to cash-flow surpluses in Social Security, Medicare, and government pensions, and all three programs faced long-term shortfalls. The rest of the federal government was in deficit.[18] Despite those concerns, Federal Reserve chairman Alan Greenspan told Congress in early 2001 that lawmakers should cut taxes. Otherwise, the debt would fall so *low* by 2007 or 2008 that the Federal

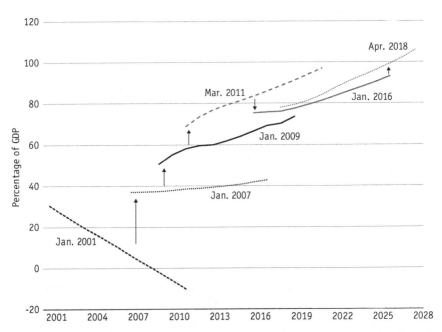

Figure 2.5. The worsening budget outlook: 10-year debt/gross domestic product (GDP) projections, 2001–2028. January 2001: Bush enters office; January 2007: Effects of Bush policies and recession; January 2009: Obama enters office and effects of financial crisis; March 2011: Effects of downturn and stimulus package; January 2016: Effects of budget deals, lower healthcare projections, and a stronger economy; April 2018: Effects of Tax Cuts and Jobs Act (TCJA), budget deals and stronger economy. Auerbach and Gale (2001, 2009a, 2011, 2016); Auerbach, Furman, and Gale (2007); Auerbach, Gale, and Krupkin (2018).

Reserve wouldn't be able to administer monetary policy by buying government bonds. That gave policymakers all the political cover they needed, and Congress enacted President Bush's tax cut that year, providing immediate taxpayer rebates, cutting income tax rates, creating other subsidies, and sharply reducing the estate tax. At President Bush's urging, Congress in 2003 accelerated the phase-ins, provided new rebates, and cut tax rates on capital gains and dividends to 15 percent. All of the provisions were to expire in 2010.

The 2001 and 2003 Bush tax cuts were large and regressive. Along with the 2001 recession, they reduced revenues from 20 percent in 2000 to 15.6 percent in 2004, the lowest share of GDP since 1950. With all provisions phased in, the tax cuts raised after-tax incomes of the top 1 percent by an estimated 6.4 percent (an average of $56,000), compared to just 1.1 percent (an average of $207) for the bottom 40 percent.[19]

If the 1982 to 1993 period showed how policymakers could respond responsibly to rising deficits and debt, the 2001 to 2007 period showed how they could squander surpluses. In addition to passing tax cuts, legislators boosted spending. For the first time since the 1960s, when Democrats controlled the White House and Congress, all three big budget areas—entitlements, defense, and non-defense discretionary spending—rose as a share of GDP. Defense spending rose, largely though not exclusively due to the post-9/11 wars in Afghanistan and Iraq. In 2003, President Bush and Congress created the largest new entitlement since 1965 by adding prescription drug coverage to Medicare, but they did not provide a way to pay for it. Policymakers also abandoned the budget rules that worked so well in the 1990s.

These tax and spending changes added significantly to long-term fiscal challenges.[20] In 2001, forecasters had projected that the debt would approach zero by 2007; in 2007, it was actually 35 percent of GDP and headed higher. Figure 2.5 shows how badly the budget situation deteriorated between 2001 and 2007. And all of that was before the financial crisis and the Great Recession sent short-term budget deficits and debt skyrocketing.

In January of 2009, President Obama inherited the worst economy since the Great Depression. The budget situation had deteriorated significantly in the previous two years as well (Figure 2.5), and the deficit was on track to reach almost $1.4 trillion (almost 10 percent of GDP) for fiscal year 2009.[21]

The first task was reviving the economy, even if that meant letting skyrocketing debt rise even more. Less than a month after taking office, Obama signed the American Recovery and Reinvestment Act, providing about $800 billion in new spending and tax cuts. The bill included federal investments in "shovel ready" infrastructure projects, aid to state and local governments, and tax cuts and transfer payments to individuals. In 2010, President Obama signed a landmark healthcare reform, a temporary payroll tax cut, and a two-year extension of the Bush tax cuts.

Due to Bush-era policies, the Great Recession, and, to a lesser extent, the large but temporary stimulus package, the debt-to-GDP ratio grew dramatically—from 39 percent in 2008 to 70 percent in 2012.[22] After the stimulus package, though, policymakers shifted course by tightening fiscal policy. Mirroring the mistakes of their predecessors in the 1930s, the president and Congress enacted several budget deals that cut short-term deficits during a still-weakened economy and, thus, slowed the recovery.[23] The deals modestly improved the long-term outlook, which also benefited from slowing healthcare cost growth and low interest rates (Figure 2.5).

In the 2010 midterm elections, Republicans regained control of the House, with a particularly strong showing from members of the new "Tea Party" that sought to reduce government spending and taxes. Tea Party members were itching for a budget showdown, and they got one during the summer of 2011, when the budget situation continued to deteriorate (Figure 2.5) and policymakers needed to raise the debt ceiling. The showdown reflected the bitter partisanship that became more common to fiscal policymaking in the ensuing years.

As discussed in Chapter 1, Democratic and Republican presidents and Congresses had raised the debt ceiling scores of times since its inception. Republican opposition to debt limit increases in 2011, however, raised the stakes to a whole new level, with prominent conservatives threatening to block the debt limit increase and thus let the government default.[24] While they may have sought to improve their bargaining position, they were playing with fire. As noted by Adam Posen, president of the Peterson Institute for International Economics, it was the first time a solvent democracy flirted with default simply out of political stubbornness.[25]

President Obama and Republican House Speaker John Boehner hoped to tie a debt ceiling increase to a comprehensive plan to dramatically reduce deficits over the ensuing decade. They were reportedly close to agreement on a "grand bargain," a 10-year, $4 trillion package of tax hikes and spending cuts, but couldn't close the deal. Each side blamed the other.

Instead, the president and Congress agreed to raise the debt ceiling and cut spending by about $1 trillion over the next decade, almost all of it in discretionary programs. Another $1.2 trillion in across-the-board spending cuts ("sequestration") would begin in 2013, split equally between defense and domestic spending, unless a special "Supercommittee" of 12 House and Senate members (six from each party) produced, and Congress approved, proposals to cut deficits by $1.5 trillion over the next 10 years. Sequestration, a mechanical way to cut spending, was generally intended to be a placeholder until a substantive agreement could be reached. But the Supercommittee closed shop without a deal, leaving sequestration to take effect in 2013.

The partisanship, negotiating failures, Supercommittee collapse, brinkmanship, and near default took a toll on US credibility. Standard & Poor's, the influential credit rating agency, downgraded US debt for the first time ever, mostly due to political concerns.[26] Financial markets, however, did not seem to share this concern, as interest rates stayed low.

Afterwards, the partisanship only intensified. At the end of 2012, the country approached the "Fiscal Cliff," when almost all of President Bush's 2001 and 2003 tax cuts (which Obama had extended until 2012) and President Obama's payroll tax cut were set to expire, and the sequestration was scheduled to take effect. Had all of that happened, the still-recovering economy could have fallen into recession. Instead, after a long and acrimonious debate, policymakers enacted the 2012 American Tax Relief Act (ATRA), which extended the Bush tax cuts for all but the top 1 percent.[27] Sequestration took effect because political leaders couldn't agree on a more reasonable set of spending cuts.

In another showdown in late 2013, conservative Republicans refused to raise the debt ceiling unless policymakers enacted legislation to address long-term deficits, but they did not propose any such legislation. As the debt ceiling deadline approached, interest rates on government debt spiked as financial market participants came to believe that the country faced a real threat of default.[28] Facing enormous public pressure and a precipitous fall in their public approval rating, Republicans backed off, and Congress "suspended" the debt ceiling for about four months. But Republicans also refused to enact spending bills to fund the government, letting a host of agencies close during a 16-day government shutdown.

Exhausted by conflict, the two parties cooperated on some smaller budget items in the next few years. In 2013, Senate Budget Committee chair Patty Murray and House Budget Committee chair Paul Ryan negotiated a two-year budget package, easing sequestration's impact on discretionary spending and raising revenues. In 2015, President Obama signed a bill to increase the discretionary spending for 2016 and 2017.[29] While just a small step in economic terms, these deals raised hopes of a new era in which the parties could again reach compromises and make the government run. By 2016, due to the budget deals, an improving economy, and reductions in projected healthcare spending and interest rates, the long-term budget outlook had improved somewhat (Figure 2.5).

Donald Trump entered the White House with the economy riding the crest of a seven-year expansion that had boosted employment by more than 15 million and reduced unemployment to 4.8 percent, the lowest rate since 2007. Amid further (false) Laffer-esque claims that new tax cuts would pay for themselves, the Republican-led Congress passed a regressive tax overhaul in December of 2017, permanently cutting the corporate tax rate from 35 to 21 percent, the lowest level since 1939, and temporarily reducing individual income and estate taxes. And, as if there were any doubt that "starve the beast" policies don't work, a mere two months later, Congress passed and Trump signed a landmark agreement that boosted defense and non-defense spending. As in the 2003–2007 period, a Republican president and Republican-controlled Congress cut taxes, boosted spending, and raised projected deficits and debt, as shown in Figure 2.5, heralding a period when annual deficits seem posed to exceed $1 trillion on a continual basis.

More than 200 years after the nation's founders squared off over debt, its role remains controversial. Debt has enabled our military successes, helped us climb out of economic downturns, and made possible new government investments and social programs. However, it also creates burdens on future generations and is sometimes seen as irresponsible or morally wrong.

We've reversed debt buildups several times. The most striking aspect of today's fiscal challenge is how different it is from the ones we've faced in the past—in magnitude and cause. Before World War I, we ran surpluses to pay off debt after wars by drastically cutting defense spending. We can't do that today, however, because defense spending is already relatively low as a share of GDP. After World War II, we grew our way out of our debt problems. We can't do that today, either, because we won't likely have strong enough growth to duplicate that success any time soon.

The changes implemented between 1982 and 1993 provide the best model for how we can resolve future fiscal policy issues. But the problem is now more serious. The debt-to-GDP ratio is already much higher. The demographic holiday we enjoyed while the baby boomers were in their prime working years in the 1980s is over now; as they retire en masse, they will raise spending on Social Security and Medicare and reduce labor force growth.

How much will policymakers have to raise taxes or cut spending? That depends on how big a fiscal challenge we face in the years and decades to come. That issue—our "fiscal gap"—is where we now turn.

Notes

1. There are a number of excellent analyses of the fiscal history of the United States. See, for example, Bank, Stark, and Thorndike (2008); Brownlee (2004); Brown (1989); Gordon (2010); Hormats (2007); Johnson and Kwak (2012); Makin and Ornstein (1994); Wallis

(2000); and White (2014). Data and events that are easily accessible from these sources are not cited specifically in this chapter.

2. Toynbee (1957).
3. Gordon (2010, page 19).
4. Madison (1790).
5. There is a legal distinction (without a clear economic difference) between a "direct" tax, placed on an individual, and an "indirect" tax, placed on a transaction or business. The Constitution states, "Representatives and direct taxes shall be apportioned among the several States which may be included within this Union, according to their respective numbers." In *Pollock v. Farmers' Loan & Trust Company* (1895), the Supreme Court ruled that the income tax was a direct tax and was unapportioned and thus unconstitutional. The Sixteenth Amendment authorized a "direct" income tax that was unapportioned.
6. Hausman (2016); Romer (2009).
7. A well-known academic paper concluded that sustained fiscal stimulus didn't bring about economic recovery in the 1930s "not because it did not work, but because it was not tried" (Brown 1956). This conclusion focuses on the government sector as a whole, rather than just the federal government. In fact, state and local governments cut their own spending, offsetting some of the gains created by federal spending. See also Thorndike (2008).
8. Taylor (2014). Milton Friedman, the Nobel Prize–winning conservative economist, worked at the Treasury Department during the war and later referred to implementing withholding as a "great mistake" because it made income tax collection easier and hence in his view contributed to the rise of taxes and spending in the postwar period. Withholding for Social Security taxes had been put in place in the 1930s.
9. Oddly, by contemporary standards at least, the tax cut faced significant opposition from Republicans, southern Democrats, and the public—all of whom preferred to balance the budget instead (Bartlett 2014).
10. Tax expenditures rose from 21 percent of federal revenues in 1967 to 35 percent in 1984 (Brownlee 2004).
11. Reagan (1980).
12. Weisman (1983).
13. Krugman (2017).
14. Poterba (1994).
15. Birnbaum and Murray (1987) provide a superb description of how tax reform came about. One of the more interesting aspects of the story is that a major decision—to pursue a top rate around 25 percent—was made in a bar.
16. Clinton (1996).
17. Congressional Budget Office (2001).
18. Auerbach and Gale (2001) estimated that despite the current surpluses, the permanent fiscal gap was about 3 to 4 percent of GDP before the Bush tax cuts occurred. They argued, therefore, that long-term tax cuts were not justified.
19. Gale and Orszag (2004).
20. Auerbach, Furman, and Gale (2007) estimated that the permanent fiscal gap, thought to be 3–4 percent of GDP in 2001, rose to between 6 and 9 percent of GDP by 2007.
21. Auerbach and Gale (2009a).
22. See Auerbach and Gale (2009b), who deconstruct the sources of the growth in debt and show that debt would have been even larger under a continuation of President Bush's policies than under President Obama's.
23. Chapter 4 discusses the stimulus package and its effects. For analysis of the post-stimulus tax increases and spending cuts on economic performance, see Congressional Budget Office (2012), Council of Economic Advisers (2013), and Elmendorf (2013). The massive decline in the full employment deficit from 7.3 percent of GDP in 2009 to 5.1 percent in 2012 (when the stimulus ended) and then to 1.6 percent by 2014 shows the stringency of post-stimulus fiscal policy (Congressional Budget Office 2016).

24. Balkin (2012); Raju and Sherman (2013).
25. Posen (2014).
26. Swann, Chambers, and Beers (2011). Specifically, the report states, "The downgrade reflects our view that the effectiveness, stability, and predictability of American policymaking and political institutions have weakened at a time of ongoing fiscal and economic challenges to a degree more than we envisioned." The authors emphasize the "difficulties in bridging the gulf between the political parties over fiscal policy, which makes us pessimistic about the capacity of Congress and the Administration to be able to leverage their agreement this week into a broader fiscal consolidation plan that stabilizes the government's debt dynamics any time soon" (page 2).
27. It is worth taking a moment to explain how a tax increase could be described as "tax relief." As noted above, all of the Bush-Obama tax cuts were set to expire at the end of 2012. ATRA kept all of the rates at their 2012 level, except the top two rates, which returned to Clinton-era levels. Compared to what would have happened if Congress had done nothing, ATRA represented a tax cut of nearly $4 trillion over 10 years. Compared to what would have happened if 2012 laws were extended into future years, ATRA was a tax increase for high-income households. The "No New Taxes" pledge (formally, the "Taxpayer Protection Pledge," see Chapter 6) that almost all Republican legislators had signed played a key role in the timing of the fiscal cliff resolution. Had they agreed to ATRA before December 31, 2012, they would have been agreeing to a tax increase. By waiting until the wee morning hours of January 1, 2013, after the Bush-Obama tax cuts had expired and rates had returned to their Clinton-era levels, they could say they were voting for tax cuts and not violating the pledge. As a result, the fiscal cliff negotiations went down to the wire, indeed past the wire, and did not get resolved until January 1, 2013.
28. Government Accountability Office (2015).
29. The bill also temporarily "solved" a funding problem in the Disability Insurance (DI) Trust Fund by reallocating revenues from the main Social Security Trust Fund. This extended the date when the DI Trust Fund is projected to run out of money by six years, to 2022. But the bill was an agreement to postpone a problem rather than truly solve it (Social Security Administration 2015).

3

The Challenge

We're on an unsustainable long-term fiscal path. Even under favorable assumptions about future policies and economic factors, the debt will gradually rise from 78 percent of GDP at the end of 2018, to almost 180 percent by 2050, and to even higher levels after that. Under policy assumptions that are more pessimistic but not implausible, the debt will exceed 200 percent of GDP by 2050. As noted, the highest debt-to-GDP ratio we've ever experienced was 106 percent, in the immediate aftermath of World War II.[1] At the projected levels, debt will stymie economic growth and boost interest rates and interest payments. That would create a vicious cycle of even less growth, even more debt, and even higher interest rates.

What's driving these trends? First, rising spending on Social Security, Medicare, Medicaid, and interest. The major entitlement programs will grow because the population is aging and healthcare costs will likely continue to rise faster than other goods and services. Interest payments will rise because the debt (on which interest is paid) will rise and because interest rates may rise as well. All other major categories of government spending—the rest of the safety net, defense, investment—are slated to *fall* as a share of GDP.

Second, tax revenues are not expected to rise anywhere near as rapidly as spending. The *imbalance* between the projections for revenues and spending creates rising debt.

We need to reach a stable and sustainable debt-to-GDP ratio within a reasonable period. The optimal target depends on many factors. Some involve economics—such as the impact of higher debt on economic growth. Some involve value judgments—such as how much of a debt burden each generation should bear. With these considerations in mind, I propose that we stabilize the long-term debt-to-GDP ratio at 60 percent by 2050. That's lower than the current ratio and *much* lower than the projected ratio, but higher than the average ratio in the 50 years before the Great Recession.

What would it take to reach that goal? I estimate that permanent annual tax increases or spending cuts that took effect starting in 2021 would need to equal

4.0 percent of GDP to bring the debt-to-GDP ratio down to 60 percent by 2050. To be clear, this would require an enormous change in fiscal policy. For example, in 2018, that would have been the equivalent of a 24 percent increase in all federal taxes, a 50 percent increase in income taxes alone, or a 21 percent reduction in all non-interest spending. The longer we wait, the larger and potentially more abrupt the changes will have to be to meet that target. Because the *magnitude* of required policies is so large, it is important also to get the *structure* of the changes right—as discussed in the second part of the book.

To show these points, I begin where almost every budget analysis does, with projections from the Congressional Budget Office (CBO). Congress established the CBO as a non-partisan office in 1974 to advise lawmakers about budget issues; no longer would they have to rely on the Office of Management and Budget (OMB), a White House agency that advises the president. Although criticized by both parties on occasion, the CBO has a well-deserved reputation for providing authoritative, non-partisan, objective analysis.

Starting with the CBO's projections, I construct a "baseline" scenario that shows where the budget is headed if we stay on our current path.[2] Think of this as what would happen if Congress follows a "business as usual" approach. Constructing that scenario is part art and part science, and I'll explain the judgments I've made along the way. The projections are based on my work over the last 20 years with University of California economist Alan Auerbach and others.

The key economic assumptions relate to growth and interest rates. Faster growth is good for the budget because it raises revenues and doesn't force as much automatic spending on safety net programs. The CBO assumes the economy will grow steadily but modestly—an average of 1.9 percent per year through 2028 and 2.1 percent after that, adjusting for inflation. That's slower than in the past, when the baby boomers were moving into their prime working years and more women were taking jobs than ever before. Now, the baby boomers are retiring and women's labor force participation has peaked.

Interest rates were extremely low during and after the Great Recession, but the Federal Reserve has raised rates several times in the last few years. Based on information from the CBO and the Social Security trustees, the projected interest rate on government debt, after accounting for inflation, rises over time—from −0.2 percent in 2018 to 0.8 percent by 2028 and then to 1.4 percent by 2050. Projected annual inflation averages 2.6 percent throughout the period.[3]

Turning to the policy side, we need to project taxes and spending. These projections aren't policy recommendations; they're my effort to project "business as usual" among lawmakers. In some cases, it's useful to distinguish between the next 10 years (through 2028 since the projection is based on 2018 data)—the standard period for estimating budget outcomes—and beyond (see Appendix Table 3.1).

For tax policy, I assume that current law continues for the next 10 years, with two exceptions. First, I assume that policymakers make permanent a host of temporary tax provisions, including those in the 2017 Tax Cuts and Jobs Act (TCJA). Second, I assume that policymakers will eventually repeal several of the Affordable Care Act taxes, including the medical device tax, the Cadillac tax, and the health insurance provider tax. They have already delayed such tax increases twice, and they routinely extend temporary tax provisions.[4]

For years after 2028, I assume that income tax revenues will follow current law (with the two exceptions noted earlier) and therefore will gradually rise over time as a result of "bracket creep"—the process by which higher wages push people into higher tax brackets—and because of projected higher withdrawals from retirement accounts, as the baby boomers retire. Most other revenue categories (including corporate taxes, excise taxes, and other taxes) remain constant at their share of GDP in 2028.

I assume that Social Security, Medicare, and Medicaid pay all the benefits to which people are entitled, and that the first two programs receive payroll taxes as expected under current law. Long-term growth projections for Social Security and Medicare taxes and spending come from the annual reports of the trustees of each program.[5] Projections for the growth of Medicaid and other health programs come from the CBO.[6]

Other mandatory programs—for example, unemployment insurance and SNAP—follow current law for the next 10 years and then grow at the rate of inflation plus population growth. For non-defense discretionary programs that policymakers fund each year—education, science, housing, and so on— I assume spending grows at the rate of inflation plus population growth. That reflects the idea that policymakers will maintain current services per person. Additionally, I set emergency funds for hurricanes and wildfires at its historical average for 2019 and then allow the costs to grow with inflation.[7] For defense, I assume that spending grows at the rate of inflation. That means resources devoted to defense will be maintained at their current level in real terms.[8] To be clear, these assumptions are favorable to the budget outlook in that they assume that there will *never* be an increase in current-service spending levels for these categories, even as GDP continues to grow. As a result, all three categories of spending—other mandatory, defense, and non-defense discretionary—fall continuously as a share of GDP after 2028.

Finally, I assume the government continues to pay its interest obligations as they come due and that policymakers raise the ceiling on federal debt as needed. Net interest payments are based on projections of government debt and interest rates.

With these specifications, Figure 3.1 shows debt-to-GDP projections through 2050, coupled with the historical data back to 1940 for perspective. The debt-to-GDP ratio rises from 78 percent in 2018 to 106 percent by 2028, passing the previous all-time high, and reaches 179 percent in 2050 (and continues to rise thereafter, not shown). Both the CBO and the Committee for a Responsible Federal Budget have generated comparable results in recent years.[9]

As the graph highlights, the past is not prologue. After it spiked around World War II, the debt-to-GDP ratio fell rapidly in subsequent years as defense spending fell and the economy grew rapidly. Now, however, defense spending is only one-sixth as large relative to the economy and already slated to fall further as a share of the economy—so there's not much to cut—and economic growth is likely to be slower than in the past. In the 1980s and 1990s, we enacted a series of tax and spending changes to slow and reverse most of the debt increase caused by Reagan's policies. But the problem was easier to solve then: when Reagan took office in 1981, the debt-to-GDP ratio was only 26 percent and baby boomers and women were entering the labor force in droves. Now, debt is three times as high as in 1980 as a share of GDP, the boomers are retiring, and women's labor force participation rates have plateaued. Most important, the demographic forces driving the debt buildup now are persistent and growing, not temporary.

Figure 3.2 shows that the projected annual deficit rises gradually, from 4.0 percent of GDP in 2018 to much higher levels—7.8 percent by 2030 and

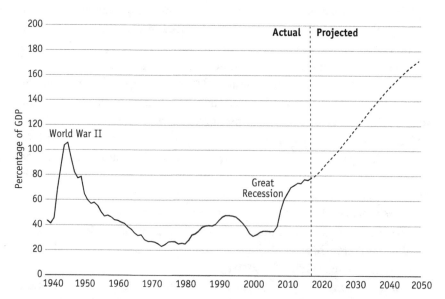

Figure 3.1. Historical and projected debt as a share of gross domestic product (GDP), 1940–2050. Congressional Budget Office (2018a); Office of Management and Budget (2018); Auerbach, Gale, and Krupkin (2018); Author's calculations.

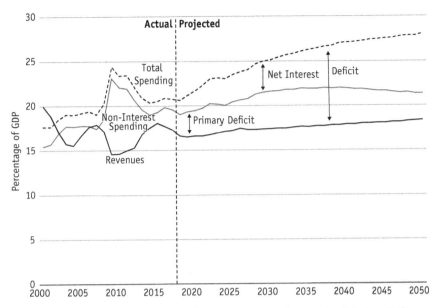

Figure 3.2. Spending, revenue, and deficits, 2000–2050. Congressional Budget Office (2018a, 2018b); Author's calculations.

9.7 percent by 2050.[10] Deficits will rise because spending will rise faster than revenues. Aggregate spending is expected to gradually increase from almost 21 percent of GDP in 2018 to more than 25 percent of GDP in 2030 and more than 28 percent in 2050. Revenues are projected to rise much more slowly, from 16.6 percent of GDP in 2018, to 17.4 percent in 2030, and 18.4 percent in 2050.

It's tempting to think that the rise in government spending reflects an activist, out-of-control government. But a closer look says otherwise. Figure 3.3 shows that more than 100 percent of the rise in spending is driven by interest and three programs—Social Security, Medicare, and Medicaid, not to any new initiatives.

The fastest growing category is interest payments, projected to rise from 1.6 percent of GDP in 2018 to 6.7 percent in 2050—and accounting for 69 percent of the net spending increase as a share of GDP. Rising interest reflects the high and rising path of debt and an expected rise in interest rates. The explosive growth in interest payments, assuming no policy changes, highlights the importance of getting the debt under control sooner rather than later. Much of the overall saving from the budget proposals in this book comes from addressing the problem in the next few years and thus reducing future net interest payments.

Social Security, Medicare, and Medicaid will grow because the population is aging and per capita healthcare costs are rising. Relative to GDP, major federal

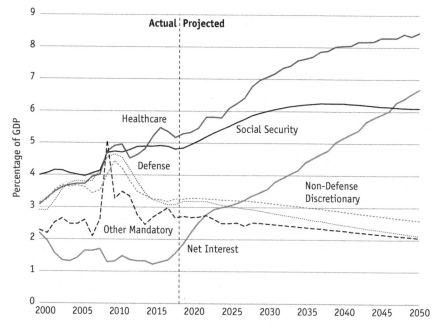

Figure 3.3. Composition of spending, 2000–2050. Congressional Budget Office (2018a); Author's calculations.

healthcare spending is projected to grow by 63 percent (from 5.2 percent of GDP in 2018 to 8.5 percent in 2050) and Social Security by 27 percent (from 4.8 percent in 2018 to 6.1 percent in 2050). Nevertheless, we should keep these increases in perspective.

First, the share of Americans who are 65 or older will grow by about 40 percent (from 16 percent in 2018 to 22 percent in 2050).[11] With more elderly, more people will be eligible for Medicare, Medicaid, and Social Security. Second, healthcare costs per person tend to rise faster than GDP, in both the private and public sectors, and that's expected to continue.[12]

Finally, all other major spending categories—defense, non-defense discretionary, and other entitlements—are projected to shrink by a collective 0.4 percent of GDP through 2028 and then by another 1.9 percent of GDP through 2050. Defense will fall to its smallest share of GDP since before World War II. Non-defense discretionary spending will fall to its lowest GDP share since at least 1962, the earliest year for which we can make consistent comparisons. Other entitlements—largely programs that constitute the "safety net" beyond Social Security, Medicare, and Medicaid—will fall from 2.7 percent of GDP in 2018 to 2.1 percent in 2050, about one-third lower than its average as a share of GDP over the previous 50 years.[13]

We need to stabilize the debt—that is, enact policies to reach a debt-to-GDP ratio at a certain level and prevent that ratio from rising on a permanent basis.[14] That's a prerequisite for nourishing a healthier economy and fairer society.

After all, fiscal policy is not an end in itself; it's a means to higher living standards and a fairer, more robust economy. The issue is balancing the costs and benefits of different debt paths. Debt can serve as Hamilton's "blessing"—facilitating trade, enabling recession-fighting policies, allowing us to defend the country, financing government investment, and giving investors liquid and secure assets. But too much debt can serve as Madison's "curse," bringing slower long-term growth; smaller increases in living standards; stronger limits on government's ability to address recessions, fight wars, and help the poor; and higher burdens on future generations. The problem is that reducing the projected rise in debt will require current generations to bear higher taxes or face lower government spending.

So, what's the right level? Both objective and subjective factors affect the choice. Objectively, the more that debt hurts long-term growth, the lower the optimal level. Higher interest rates raise the cost of financing and make debt less desirable. Higher productivity and labor force growth raise the optimal debt-to-GDP ratio, just as a family that expects its future income to rise can responsibly assume more debt.

Government can contribute to productivity growth by spending more on investments—broadly defined to include infrastructure and research and development, but also education, nutrition, healthcare, and other human capital investments—that yield future returns. So, the more the government invests, the higher the optimal debt can be. This is just another way of saying that there is good debt and bad debt and that we should pay attention not only to the debt level but also to the formulation of tax and spending policies.

Subjectively, the key issue is how much of the debt burden each generation should bear. Generally, the costs of debt reduction come before the benefits fully kick in, since the benefits, namely, stronger economic growth, accumulate slowly over time. As a result, society's willingness to assume current costs for future gains will affect the optimal choice of debt. Average income typically rises with each successive generation, although that may be less likely now than in the past, as discussed in Chapter 5. Moreover, even if average income rises, many people will end up earning less than their parents. We all care about what we bequeath to future generations; creating a stable and affordable fiscal situation for our children and grandchildren is one thing we can do for them.

After balancing these issues, I set a target for long-term debt at 60 percent of GDP. That would be the average over the course of a business cycle; it may be somewhat higher or lower in a particular year, depending on whether the economy is growing or in recession.[15] That target is higher than the 36 percent average of the 50 years before the Great Recession. But there are several reasons to consider a higher debt level than during that period. Most important, the cost of getting to such low levels would be incredibly high because our projected debt levels are so high. Also, there's a good chance that interest rates will be lower in the future than in the past, which would raise optimal debt levels. And if the government makes the investments proposed in subsequent chapters, the nation will benefit from productivity growth that can justify additional debt.

To be clear, the goal is not a balanced budget. Balanced budgets may have symbolic value in politics, but they are not necessary. As long as the economy grows and the deficit is not too big, the debt-to-GDP ratio will fall. Indeed, the proposals I offer don't generate a balanced budget through 2050, but they put debt on a stable and sustainable path. And balanced budget requirements create a number of problems—they make recessions deeper and longer by forcing spending cuts or tax increases during hard times, and they can be manipulated through budget gimmicks, which means they are no guarantee against long-term debt problems. Indeed, almost all the states have balanced budget rules, but many of them face long-term fiscal shortfalls focused on healthcare and retirement spending, just as the federal government does.[16] Reaching a stable debt-to-GDP ratio of 60 percent will be challenging enough without adding obstacles like balanced budget rules.

How quickly should we reach our target? After the Civil War, World War I, and World War II, we cut the debt-to-GDP ratio in half in about 10 to 15 years. Taking just 15 years to reach the 60 percent target now, however, would be overly optimistic. For one thing, the problem is bigger than it was then. For another, the factors that caused most debt run-ups in the past—wars and recessions—eventually ended. In contrast, our rising debt is driven largely by demographic factors that will only grow in importance. Thus, aiming to reach our target by 2050 seems more realistic than a 10- to 15-year time frame.

There's no drop-dead date by which we must have a plan in place. That gives us time to tackle issues and phase in sensible solutions. Without a drop-dead date, however, policymakers will be less inclined to impose the necessary tax increases and spending cuts. Enacting reforms sooner and phasing them in slowly would give people more time to adjust to them. The longer we wait to phase in changes, the larger and more abrupt they will have to be. To balance those concerns, I assume fiscal reforms begin in 2021, and I subsequently also show how much larger the policy changes would have to be if they were not implemented until 2025. If the economy is in recession, though, the appropriate fiscal policy would be to stimulate first and return to full employment, before policies that address long-term fiscal issues take effect.

The "fiscal gap" measures how much policy would have to change on net for us to reach our 60 percent target by 2050.[17] As shown in Table 3.1, reaching our target would require a combination of tax increases and spending cuts that equal 4.0 percent of GDP per year if the changes start in 2021. That's about $810 billion per year in today's dollars, with the dollar figure rising at the same rate as GDP in future years. There are many ways to make those changes, but they all involve enormous changes in policy. In 2018, for example, $810 billion represented a 50 percent increase in income tax revenues, a 24 percent increase in all federal taxes, or a 21 percent cut in all non-interest federal spending. If we wait until 2025, however, the required policy changes would rise to 4.6 percent of GDP per year (Table 3.1).

While the fiscal gap shows the required changes as a constant share of GDP, policymakers will likely make changes more gradually, "back-loading" the changes so that the annual adjustment starts small and rises over time. Back-loading, which my policy proposals reflect as well (Figures I.1–I.4 in the Introduction), gives the government time to phase in policies, gives people and

Table 3.1. **Fiscal Gap Projections with a 60 Percent of GDP Target Starting in 2021**

| | *Fiscal Gap (% of GDP)* | *Required Percentage Change (in 2018 Terms) If Just Through* | | |
		Income Tax	*All Tax*	*Non-Interest Spending*
Central Estimate				
Baseline	4.0	50	24	21
Alternative Options				
Start in 2025	4.6	57	28	24
Higher Defense, Non-Defense Discretionary, and Safety Net Spending	4.8	59	29	25
Current Law Taxes	2.9	36	18	15
Alternative Trustees' Medicare Assumptions	4.2	52	26	22
CBO Medicare Assumptions	4.3	52	26	22
Constant Low Interest Rates	3.0	37	18	16

Source: Author's calculations.

firms time to adjust to them, and gives all of us time to see how uncertainties pan out and thus what adjustments we might need to make down the road. But back-loading also carries risks. The biggest is that elected officials may not follow through on the needed changes for future years, and thus they may fail to meet debt-reduction goals. And if events turn out worse than expected, additional policy adjustments will be needed on top of the already substantial long-term changes built into a back-loaded solution.

Nobel laureate and *New York Times* columnist Paul Krugman once wrote that budget projections are "an especially boring genre of science fiction."[18] He may have overstated things a bit, but his point remains valid; we should take all projections with a grain, if not a barrel, of salt. At best, they're the educated guesses of informed people. Not surprisingly, previous projections by the CBO and others (including me) have been too optimistic in some cases, too pessimistic in others.[19]

Still, we should have some confidence that the long-term budget situation is a problem. The major factor driving long-term budget projections is demographic change, and that is relatively easy to predict, compared to, say, interest rates or growth rates. If we know how many 50-year-olds we have today, we can make fairly well-educated guesses as to how many 70-year-olds we will have in 20 years.

Uncertainty can cut both ways, though. For example, the policy assumptions outlined earlier may be too *optimistic*. They assume no new US wars for the indefinite future—or none that require additional spending. They expect extreme political discipline from policymakers, assuming they will never raise real, per capita spending for non-defense discretionary and other mandatory programs and never raise real defense spending. If, instead, we assumed that as our society grows richer after 2028, we will demand the same share of our income in the form of the goods and services that these programs provide, the debt-GDP ratio by 2050 would rise to 200 percent in the absence of corrective action, and the fiscal gap, with adjustments starting in 2021, would rise to 4.8 percent of GDP (Table 3.1).[20]

On the other hand, the projections could be too pessimistic, since they assume that the president and Congress will make temporary tax cuts permanent. If, instead, current tax laws remain in place and temporary tax cuts expire as scheduled—for example, the temporary tax cuts of the 2017 TCJA—projected revenues would be higher, and the 2050 debt-to-GDP ratio would equal 148 percent. The fiscal gap would fall to 2.9 percent of GDP. Even this scenario, however, would require substantial changes in taxes and spending to meet the 60-percent-of-GDP debt target for 2050 (Table 3.1).

Healthcare spending constitutes a sizable share of the budget, so uncertainty about its path can have a significant impact on budget projections as well. Increases in healthcare costs, which have outstripped overall inflation for decades, have slowed considerably in recent years. But we don't know how long and to what extent that will last. I use the mid-range projections of Medicare costs from the program's trustees, but projections from the trustees' illustrative alternative scenario or from the CBO yield higher healthcare spending.[21] Through 2050, the differences in the fiscal gaps implied by the different healthcare scenarios are relatively small. Using the alternative trustees' assumptions raises the fiscal gap to 4.2 percent of GDP, while using the CBO Medicare projections raises the fiscal gap to 4.3 percent of GDP. Over longer periods, however, the differences are larger.[22]

The economic assumptions behind the budget projections also merit scrutiny. The CBO's growth assumptions are mainstream and reasonable.[23] Growth flows from increases in the labor force's size and productivity. Higher productivity would help reduce the long-term debt, but not by much. The CBO estimates that if productivity growth were 0.5 percentage points higher than it assumes— which would be an enormous change, given that annual productivity growth averaged 1.5 percent from 1950 to 2017—the projected debt-to-GDP ratio would decline by only about 30 percentage points by 2050. Thus, the debt picture isn't that sensitive even to substantial variations in productivity. *In other words, we can't grow our way out of the problem.*[24]

Two additional caveats related to growth are warranted. First, the projections above ignore the negative long-term effects of higher debt on the economy, which—if they were accounted for—would raise the debt-to-GDP ratio further by reducing future economic growth (as explained in Chapter 4). Second, although faster economic growth would help the long-term fiscal outlook, *tax cuts* that generate some economic growth usually make the fiscal situation worse. For example, the CBO estimates that the 2017 tax act will increase cumulative budget deficits by $1.9 trillion through 2028, even though it will also raise the size of the economy during that period.[25] The tax bill will not come close to "paying for itself," despite the administration's claims that it would.[26]

Interest rates affect the budget outlook significantly, especially because the debt is already high. Historically, the interest rate on government debt tends to be lower than the economy's growth rate, and my projected interest rates are below projected growth rates in every year through 2050.[27] The CBO expects interest rates to rise from the historically low levels of recent years, in part because debt will rise. It is hard to predict how much rates will rise, but we have a lot riding on the answer. If, for example, interest rates didn't rise at all through 2050, the debt-to-GDP ratio would be 132 percent in 2050, and the fiscal gap would be 3.0 percent of GDP.[28] Even so, it would require a 37 percent increase in income tax revenues, or an 18 percent increase in all taxes, or a 16 percent cut in spending to reach the debt target of 60 percent of GDP by 2050 (Table 3.1).

This favorable adjustment due to the possibility of lower interest rates comes with three qualifications, though. First, assuming no increase at all in interest rates seems extreme, given that debt is projected to rise by 100 percentage points relative to GDP through 2050. Extrapolating the results of careful studies suggests that such a change would raise interest rates by about 3 percentage points, which is actually more than assumed in the baseline projections.[29] Second, if interest rates stayed so low for so long, that would probably reflect underlying economic weakness, which would cause an increase in the debt-to-GDP ratio, offsetting some of the gains from lower interest rates. Third, if interest rates turn out to be *higher* than we assume, rather than lower, the debt may well explode.[30]

How should uncertainty affect when and how we make policy changes? Some argue that it means we should wait before doing anything. "Given how uncertain we are about what the world will look like in 25 years," Krugman wrote in 2013, "there's a pretty good case for letting the future of entitlements take care of itself."[31] Former treasury secretary Larry Summers said that given low interest rates, we should see what the next decade brings in terms of economic performance before acting.[32]

Uncertainty can cut both ways, however. Things could get worse, which would require even bigger, more disruptive changes. Confronting the problem sooner rather than later would let us "buy insurance" against a particularly bad long-term outcome and would reduce the growth in interest payments.

Many people will be tempted to look away from the politically difficult choices, hoping that the future will take care of itself or assuming they won't have to bear any of the burden. For example, in 2013, the Republican House Ways and Means Committee chairman Dave Camp and the Democratic Senate Finance Committee chairman Max Baucus took a listening tour to learn about citizens' views regarding tax reform. One person said that policymakers should "get rid of the deductions that don't affect me."[33] While such a policy would be great for that person, it obviously can't work for everyone!

Two policy actions that many other countries have taken—when they had to, and at great cost—will not solve the fiscal problem in the United States. First, defaulting on the debt might seem like a clever alternative. After all, it would impose much of its burden on foreigners, who own a significant share of our debt. But I am horrified by the idea—it is what we are trying to *avoid* and there are several reasons for this. First, it's unconstitutional. Second, it would not solve the problem—it would only eliminate our current net debt. It would do nothing to help us pay for Social Security, Medicare, and Medicaid in the future. Third, it would dramatically raise the price of future borrowing. In 1979, an inadvertent default on a small batch of Treasury securities caused by a computer error spooked investors enough to raise interest rates that the Treasury was required to pay, costing the government about $40 billion (in today's dollars) in higher interest payments.[34] An intentional, large-scale default could prove an unmitigated disaster, and we should do everything we can to ensure that we never have one. Even flirting with default can create uncertainty, hurt the economy, and drive up interest rates and government costs.[35]

Nor will inflating the currency and thus devaluing the debt work well. Inflation is a kind of partial default. It reduces the value of government bonds whose payoffs are denoted in nominal terms—for example, a bond that pays $30 per year in interest and then returns principal of $1,000 five years after purchase. Inflating away debt works best when the debt is composed of long-term nominal bonds. But most of our bonds are short-term, so investors would require higher interest rates on new bond issues as soon as it was clear that the United States was trying to inflate away the debt. And most of our long-term debt takes the form of obligations that are explicitly or implicitly indexed to inflation, namely, payments to Social Security, Medicare, and Medicaid participants. Inflation would not reduce their real—inflation-adjusted—value.

One final point: in our projections, we assume that Social Security and Medicare continue to pay all the benefits they're scheduled to pay, even though their trust funds will lack the money to do so at some point. By law, however, the trust funds can pay benefits only from current payroll taxes or trust fund surpluses (with a few minor exceptions). That implies that unless policymakers act, Social Security would have to cut benefits by 21 percent starting in 2034 and Medicare Part A by 9 percent starting in 2026.[36] Some analysts argue that the budget projections should reflect the letter of the law in this case and that, absent policy changes, we should assume that the benefit cuts take effect to ensure that the trust funds don't overspend. In fact, due to this provision of law, some conclude that we really don't face a debt problem at all.[37]

That's misleading, though. The fiscal gap, or the size of the *overall* policy changes that Americans will need to face, is not affected by assuming that the Social Security and Medicare shortfalls will be met by spending cuts within those programs. That assumption just places *some* of that burden on the beneficiaries of those two programs. At the broadest level, the "debt problem" means that policymakers have promised more government spending in general—implicitly or explicitly—than they're willing to raise in taxes. Thus, the required cuts in Social Security and Medicare benefits that would occur by law are *one potential way* to address part of the problem—not evidence that the problem doesn't exist. Whether policymakers choose that route or take other action, Americans face tough choices.

We have a big challenge: taking a national debt that's now 78 percent of GDP and projected to hit 179 percent in 2050, reducing it to 60 percent, and stabilizing it at that level while also making substantial investments in human and physical capital. But we have no choice other than to address the problem head-on because letting the debt continue to rise will have adverse consequences for our economy, our children, and their future. And so, in the next chapter, we turn to those long-term consequences.

Notes

1. State and local governments face similar long-term shortfalls. Those issues are not addressed here, but they will make dealing with federal debt harder rather than easier. See Government Accountability Office (2015b).
2. See Auerbach, Gale, and Krupkin (2018). In budget parlance, I develop a "current policy" baseline here. In contrast, a "current law" baseline aims to show the effects if Congress does (almost) nothing in the future. The major differences between the Congressional Budget Office's current law baseline (Congressional Budget Office 2018a) and my current policy baseline are that the CBO's current law baseline (a) allows most temporary tax provisions to expire, including those from the TCJA; (b) allows several healthcare taxes to be implemented as scheduled; (c) lets defense spending follow the caps in the Budget Control Act of 2011 through 2021, as amended, and then rise with inflation rather than rise with inflation in the entire 10-year window; (d) lets non-defense discretionary spending follow the caps in the Budget Control Act of 2011 through 2021, as amended, and then rise with inflation rather than rise with inflation and population growth in the entire 10-year window; and (e) extrapolates non-defense emergency funding over time instead of letting it fall to its historical average.
3. See Congressional Budget Office (2018a, 2018b) for the economic assumptions. GDP growth does not incorporate macroeconomic feedback effects. The Congressional Budget Office uses the GDP price index to calculate real GDP growth. I use a combination of the employment cost index for wages and salaries (ECI) and the price index for GDP to report inflation for real interest rates.
4. For example, policymakers extended the life of a "temporary" tax credit that businesses receive for research and development (R&D) expenses (the so-called R&D credit) 16 times after creating it in 1981 before they made it permanent in 2015 (Malakoff 2014; Joint Committee on Taxation 2015).
5. Board of Trustees (2018); Boards of Trustees (2018).
6. Congressional Budget Office (2018b).
7. In their baseline, the Congressional Budget Office extrapolates additional funding related to Hurricanes Harvey, Irma, and Maria and recent wildfires into future years.
8. Congress has placed statutory caps on discretionary programs through 2021. The assumptions made above imply that Congress will raise the caps periodically, as they have done several times in the past few years.
9. The Committee for a Responsible Federal Budget (2018) estimates that under one plausible scenario, the debt could rise to 192 percent of GDP by 2048. Before the enactment of the 2017 tax cuts and the 2018 budget deal—both of which will raise debt—the

Congressional Budget Office (2015) projected a debt-to-GDP ratio of 220 percent by 2050 under their "alternative fiscal scenario."

10. These projections assume the economy is running at near capacity for the whole period through 2050, so the projected deficits are best compared not to actual historical deficits but to previous "cyclically adjusted" deficits, which show what the deficit would be if the economy were at full employment. The weighted average full-employment deficit was just 2.6 percent from 1965 to 2017, so the projected deficits are substantially higher than those that occurred in the past, once one controls for the state of the economy (Congressional Budget Office 2017).

11. US Census (2014).

12. Boards of Trustees (2018); Congressional Budget Office (2018b).

13. Programs in this category include SNAP (food stamps), Temporary Assistance to Needy Families, housing assistance, unemployment insurance, Supplemental Security Income, and the "refundable" parts of the earned income tax credit and the child tax credit, among others (Congressional Budget Office 2018a).

14. Publicly held debt is by no means a perfect measure of the financial status of the government, but it is a clear, understandable, and verifiable measure. It is also the most commonly used benchmark. Scaling debt by GDP makes sense, since a growing economy has more capacity to finance debt. For example, all recent budget commissions have used the debt-to-GDP ratio as a measure of fiscal sustainability (National Commission on Fiscal Responsibility and Reform 2010; Debt Reduction Task Force 2010; Peterson Pew Commission 2010). The chief concern with using publicly held debt as a measure of the government's financial status is that it does not account for implicit future obligations such as Social Security and Medicare benefits. This shortcoming can be addressed—as in this chapter—by examining the long-term public debt-to-GDP ratio. In the long term, the implicit future liabilities created by Social Security and Medicare obligations (which don't show up as publicly held debt now) eventually turn into future benefit payments (which do affect publicly held debt).

15. There is a broad—but certainly not universal—consensus in the policy community around similar figures. In a 2012 book, MIT economist Simon Johnson and University of Connecticut law professor James Kwak suggest a 50 percent target (Johnson and Kwak 2012). The Bowles-Simpson Commission aimed for 40 percent, while the Domenici-Rivlin commission aimed for 60 percent (Debt Reduction Task Force 2010; National Commission on Fiscal Responsibility and Reform 2010). Analysis by the Obama administration implicitly used a 75-percent-of-GDP debt target (Office of Management and Budget 2011). Each of these targets is far below the 179 percent debt-to-GDP currently projected for 2050 and would "bend the curve" in Figure 3.1 dramatically. Reaching any of these targets will require significant and sustained policy changes.

16. Government Accountability Office (2015b).

17. The fiscal gap methodology was developed by Auerbach (1994) and has been used extensively. For a recent exposition, see Auerbach, Gale, and Krupkin (2018).

18. Krugman (2013b).

19. For recent discussions of uncertainty and fiscal projections, see Aaron (2014); Auerbach (2014); Auerbach, Gale, and Krupkin (2016, 2018); and Kamin (2014).

20. This is not an unreasonable assumption. Discretionary spending was roughly the same as a share of GDP in 2015–2016 as it was from 1996 to 1997 (Congressional Budget Office 2018a).

21. Boards of Trustees (2018); Congressional Budget Office (2018b).

22. Auerbach, Gale, and Harris (2014); Auerbach, Gale, and Krupkin (2018).

23. Some experts see reasons for optimism in the growth of productivity, citing gains from information technology, lower energy costs, and more demand for exports due to the historic growth of the middle class in China and India. Others, notably Northwestern University economist Robert Gordon, argue growth will likely slow considerably in the future

compared to our past due to trends in education, globalization, and other "headwinds" (including higher debt) (Gordon 2016).

24. Congressional Budget Office (2018b).
25. Congressional Budget Office (2018a).
26. US Department of the Treasury (2017).
27. Ball, Elmendorf, and Mankiw (1998); Kogan et al. (2015). Those who think rates will stay low note that the world is awash with savers seeking places to invest, the demand for safe assets (such as US Treasury debt) has increased in recent years, and financial market participants don't seem to expect high interest rates in the future. Those who believe rates will rise note the projected increase in public debt, the potential fall in saving among a population with more retirees and fewer workers, and other factors (Hamilton et al. 2015; Irwin 2015).
28. The 2018 implied nominal interest rate of 2.2 percent is used for every year through 2050.
29. Engen and Hubbard (2005); Gale and Orszag (2004); Laubach (2009).
30. Burman et al. (2010).
31. Krugman (2013a).
32. Summers (2013).
33. Weisman (2013).
34. Zivney and Marcus (1989).
35. Government Accountability Office (2015a).
36. Board of Trustees (2018); Boards of Trustees (2018).
37. Aaron (2015); Goss (2016).

Appendix Table 3.1. **Budget Category Assumptions**

	10-Year Window	*Beyond*
Interest Rate	as implied in CBO 10-year outlook	CBO Long-Term Budget Outlook through 2048, gradually rises through 2050 based on Social Security Trustees Report
Growth Rate	as reported in CBO 10-year outlook	CBO Long-Term Budget Outlook through 2048, constant thereafter
Income Tax	current law + extension of temporary tax provisions and TCJA provisions	current law + extension of temporary tax provisions and TCJA provisions
Corporate Tax	current law + extension of temporary tax provisions and TCJA provisions	constant share of GDP
Payroll Taxes	current law	grow using assumptions in the Social Security Trustees report
Other Taxes	current law + repeal of certain healthcare taxes	constant share of GDP
Social Security Benefits	current law	grow using assumptions in the Social Security Trustees report
Medicare	current law	grows using assumptions in the Medicare Trustees report
Medicaid	current law	grows using assumptions in CBO Long-Term Budget Outlook
Other Mandatory	current law	grows with inflation and population
Defense	grows with inflation	grows with inflation
Non-Defense Discretionary	grows with inflation and population, emergency spending falls to historical average	grows with inflation and population
Net Interest	as reported in CBO 10-year outlook + adjustments from above policy changes	calculated from debt and interest rate

Note: 10-year outlook refers to Congressional Budget Office (2018a); Long-Term Budget Outlook refers to Congressional Budget Office (2018b); Trustees reports refer to Board of Trustees (2018) and Boards of Trustees (2018); TCJA refers to the Tax Cuts and Jobs Act of 2017.

4

Termites and Wolves

If left unaddressed, rising deficits and debt will cause significant, long-lasting economic problems, curtailing growth and limiting the rise of living standards for our children and grandchildren. They will also hamper government's ability to address other issues and reduce America's global standing.

To be clear, rising debt probably will *not* trigger a financial crisis. US government debt remains the world's safest asset, and we have the resources to pay interest on the debt for decades.

Rather, we face a problem that's more gradual and less dramatic, but that's real nonetheless. In the words of Charles Schultze, who served as President Johnson's budget director and chairman of President Carter's Council of Economic Advisers, the deficit isn't the wolf at the door; it's termites in the woodwork.[1] Rising debt won't blow your house down; it will eat away at its foundation. Over the course of decades, the house gets shakier and slowly disintegrates.

Despite public controversy about fiscal policy, there is a well-established consensus among experts that our current path is unsustainable and will do long-term damage to the economy.[2] It is imperative that policymakers put fiscal policy back on a sustainable course.

In Hemingway's *The Sun Also Rises*, one person asks another, "How did you go bankrupt?" The second replies, "Two ways. Gradually, then suddenly."[3] That aptly describes how debt can matter in the long term. A nation with too much debt can suffer gradually, and it can suffer suddenly. Either way, the costs can be substantial. So, let's look more closely at the two scenarios, starting with the gradual one.

The gradual scenario is the termites in action. Here's how it works: the more we invest as a society, the more our economy grows. Investment can come from the private sector and from the government. Businesses that invest more in factories, equipment, computers, and the like are more productive and, hence, can pay their workers more. People who invest more in their own education, skills, and job training are more productive and can earn more. Governments that invest more in infrastructure, science, research, education, and job training can make businesses and workers more productive. All these investments can raise future living standards for American households.

Those investments must be financed, of course, and the financing comes from two sources—national saving and foreign capital. National saving is the sum of saving by domestic businesses, households, and governments. Capital from abroad represents the amount that foreigners lend to participate in our economy—buying Treasury securities, investing in our businesses, and so on.

When the government runs a deficit and borrows money, it is saving *negative* amounts. Figure 4.1 shows what happens next. (For now, let's assume the government spends the funds it borrows on consumption or gives the money to its citizens, who spend it on consumption.)

In response to a higher budget deficit, private saving will likely rise somewhat, but not by the full amount of the higher deficit. For example, if policymakers cut taxes, people will likely save some, but not all, of their tax cut. This means that national saving—the sum of government and private saving—falls because government saving falls more than private saving rises.[4] *The decline in national saving is why higher deficits ultimately hurt the economy over the long run.* The decline in national saving can reduce future income through various channels. But, one way or another, the decline in national saving leads to a decline in future national income. This is exactly analogous to the idea that a family that saves less now will have less future income.

For example, if government borrowing does not generate an increase in capital inflows from abroad (see the first column of Figure 4.1), the fall in national saving means we'll face a shortage of funds to finance investment. Competition for the smaller amount of national saving among those who want to invest will drive up interest rates, which in turn will weaken the economy by raising borrowing costs for families and businesses and reducing investment. The decline in investment reduces future output and future income. It slows growth in the economy, wages, and living standards.

At the other extreme, suppose that, in response to higher deficits, enough additional capital flows in from abroad to fully offset the fall in national saving (as shown in the second column of Figure 4.1). Then interest rates don't rise and national investment doesn't fall. Thus, future domestic economic *output* doesn't decline, but the future *income* attributable to US households and businesses will still fall.[5] That's because more of the proceeds of our future production goes to the foreigners who supplied the capital and less is left for our own welfare.

In reality, neither of the extreme scenarios in Figure 4.1 will hold; the result will be somewhere in the middle. In either extreme case—and in an intermediate situation—though, future US national income will fall if current national saving falls.

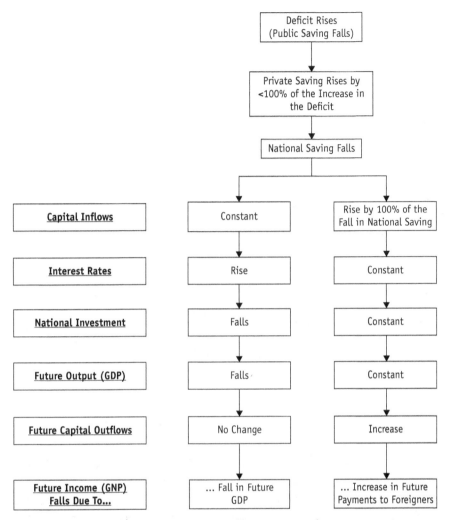

Figure 4.1. Effects of deficits on the economy (gradual scenario). GDP = gross domestic product, the output produced within the United States. GNP = gross national product, the income accruing to Americans.

An abundance of evidence is consistent with the logic above—and shows how long-term debt reduces long-term economic growth by reducing national saving and investment and raising interest rates and exchange rates.

In a 2015 study, two International Monetary Fund (IMF) researchers used data from a sample of 79 countries from 1970 to 2007 (Figure 4.2) and found that an advanced country with a higher initial debt-to-GDP ratio of 10 percentage points had slower subsequent annual growth by between 0.10 and 0.20 percentage points.[6] The researchers also found that the slower growth was largely due to lower investment, which generated a smaller capital stock and

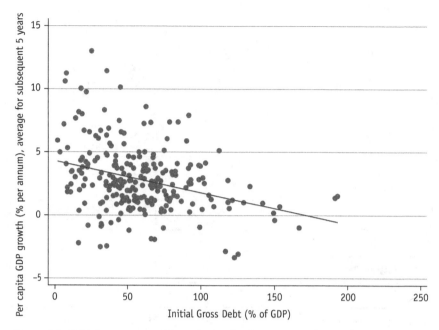

Figure 4.2. Initial government debt and growth of per capita real gross domestic product (GDP) over subsequent five-year periods. Woo and Kumar (2010).

lower labor force productivity—all of which is consistent with the reasoning shown in Figure 4.1.

In Chapter 3, we discussed the trade-offs in choosing an optimal debt level: higher debt slows future economic growth but allows for more current consumption. The IMF study helps put a number on the costs, implying that with a debt ratio close to 180 percent of GDP in 2050 (where we're headed under current policy), the annual growth rate would be between 1.2 and 2.4 percentage points lower than if the debt-to-GDP ratio were 60 percent (the target that I propose). This is an "out of sample" calculation, as few of the countries in the IMF study had debt-to-GDP ratios around 180 percent, and it should be treated as a rough approximation. But even if the impact on growth is somewhat smaller, it would still be huge, relative to other policies. By comparison, the effect of the 2017 tax cut on the long-term annual growth rate is an order of magnitude smaller—0.1 percentage points or less.[7]

Several other researchers have reached similar conclusions about debt and growth. While they've tended to show that low debt levels aren't harmful, higher debt levels reduce economic growth by economically significant amounts.[8] Thus, our main point: America's projected debt buildup would have a gradual but substantial negative impact on economic growth.

Models that simulate the economy, which offer another way to examine the evidence, generate consistent findings. Douglas Elmendorf, former director of the Congressional Budget Office, and Greg Mankiw, former chairman of President George W. Bush's Council of Economic Advisers, found that higher debt reduces the size of the economy. Specifically, they found that reducing the debt-to-GDP ratio by 50 percentage points of GDP would raise gross output by 4.75 percent.[9] That, in turn, would raise GDP by about $2,800 per person in 2018 terms. The Congressional Budget Office obtained similar results when it used a much more sophisticated model. In one study, the CBO found that raising debt by 45 percent of GDP by 2046 would reduce national income by 3 percent in that year.[10] In another study, raising the debt-to-GDP ratio by 40 percentage points would reduce national income by between 3 and 7 percent depending on other policies.[11]

The two CBO studies imply that GDP would be higher by 8 percent and by 9 to 21 percent, respectively, in 2050 if the debt-to-GDP ratio were 60 percent rather than 180 percent. The Elmendorf-Mankiw study implies that the impact on GDP would be more than 11 percent. As with the IMF study, cautions about out-of-sample results are relevant, but even if the impacts were significantly smaller, they still indicate a sizable negative effect of debt on the economy.

US historical data also show that higher deficits are associated with lower national saving and national investment. Figure 4.3, for example, shows that federal saving (that is, the opposite of federal deficits) correlates closely with national saving and national investment. Controlling for the business cycle, raising deficits by 1 percent of the economy reduces both national saving and national investment by about 1 percent of the economy.[12]

As noted, a rise in interest rates isn't necessary for deficits to impair long-term growth, but it's one way that deficits can hurt the economy. Examining the relationship between deficits and interest rates is complicated because each factor can affect the other. But studies that take this into account show that federal borrowing raises interest rates.[13] Studies also suggest that higher US budget deficits generate more borrowing from abroad, with 10 to 50 percent of deficit increases reflected in higher capital inflows.[14]

All these results tell a story that's consistent with Figure 4.1. Deficits reduce national saving, which reduces future national income. That effect can come through higher interest rates, which reduce investment and thus reduce future output and income. And it can come from more borrowing from foreigners, which helps preserve future output but raises the amount we owe them in the future and, thus, still reduces future national income. None of this story depends on deficits creating a financial crisis.

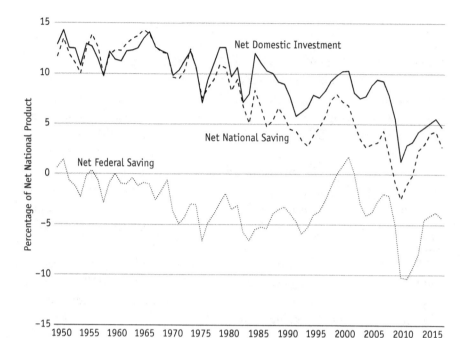

Figure 4.3. National saving, federal saving, and net domestic investment, 1950–2016. Bureau of Economic Analysis (2018).

Notwithstanding such evidence, some question whether our long-term deficit path poses a concern because "we owe the money to ourselves." They mean that public debt is money that one generation borrows and owes to another. How, they ask, can we become poorer by owing money to ourselves?

The answer is that the historical evidence discussed above on how deficits affect growth, saving, investment, and interest rates refers—at least in the US case—to debt that we, indeed, largely owed to ourselves. Those deficits and debt did affect economic performance, through the channels described above. In addition, future generations will have to finance that debt or repay it with higher taxes or lower spending, and those steps will cause pain, especially if we design the policies poorly.

Also, we increasingly don't owe it to ourselves. We owe it to investors around the world. As of early 2018 foreign investors held 41 percent of US government debt, an amount equal to 31 percent of our annual GDP.[15] That's way up from 1981 when foreign investors held about 17 percent of US debt, or about 4 percent of GDP at that time.

Skeptics also ask why, if deficits and debt are so harmful, interest rates have been so low over the past decade even though federal debt rose substantially. Many factors affect interest rates, however, not just deficits. The economy struggled for several years, reducing demand for investment and encouraging the Federal Reserve to keep interest rates low; the world has been awash in capital; and more capital has been attracted to safe assets—namely, US government bonds. As the economy grows stronger and government debt keeps rising over the coming years, we should expect interest rates to rise. In any case, we must remember that interest rates don't have to rise for debt to have deleterious long-term effects on national income, as explained above.

Skeptics also point to several countries that have sustained high debt. The examples show that the relationship between debt and economic growth is complex, but not that we should ignore the implications of high and rising debt. Japan, for example, has had high debt and low interest rates for more than two decades, seemingly contradicting the notion that higher debt causes higher interest rates. In this case, however, several factors have affected both interest rates and the debt. Japan has had a persistently weak economy, driving down demand for investment. Unlike the United States, Japan has a very high saving rate, and its investors tend to keep their assets at home in safe accounts.[16] All these factors tend to reduce interest rates on government debt.

Likewise, in the early 1800s, the United Kingdom had high debt—a whopping 250 percent or so of GDP—but low interest rates.[17] But the country was a dominant world power that extracted resources from colonies around the globe. That may have worked then, but it can't work now.[18]

Finally, the US debt-to-GDP ratio peaked at 106 percent in 1946, followed by robust economic growth. Why didn't our high debt choke off growth at that point? Because the United States dominated the globe both economically and politically, with much of Europe and Japan devastated by World War II. The situation is much different today. First, in 1960, the United States accounted for about 40 percent of world output, compared to 20 percent today.[19] Second, our debt-to-GDP ratio fell steadily after World War II. Now, however, it is slated to rise in the coming years. For perspective, we also had top personal income tax rates reaching 94 percent at that time, but no one suggests that we can go back to those rates without hurting the economy. The world and America's role in it are different now.

If one looks beyond the specific examples above and takes a broader view of the experience of other nations as well as our own history, it seems that countries intuitively understand that too much debt is a problem. Governments do not tend to voluntarily run up their debt. This would be odd if debt were costless, because, after all, politicians and citizens love lower taxes and the benefits of higher spending. Yet countries avoid high and rising debt-to-GDP ratios whenever they can. In 2007, for example, before the financial crisis—which boosted debt levels everywhere—only three of 30 countries in the OECD (Greece, Italy, and Japan) had net financial liabilities in excess of our current debt-to-GDP ratio of 78 percent, and each of those was a special case. Greece ended up in a financial crisis. Japan, as discussed, had been mired in a slowdown lasting over two decades. Italy has had a long history of fiscal imprudence. None of these countries creates a fiscal example that we should want to follow.

Besides their economic effects, high and rising debt can have other harmful consequences for our economy and politics. High deficits and debt will make it more difficult for the government to implement policy, for the understandable reason that some policymakers will feel reluctant to raise deficits to even higher levels.[20] This will make the government less likely to make routine investments in people and the economy. Indeed, some have argued that a conservative government would want to run up debt specifically as a way to constrain the choices of future governments.[21] Rising red ink will also make the government more reluctant to respond fully to emergencies like recessions or wars.

More broadly, high debt may reduce America's global standing in political and military terms. In 2011, the Joint Chiefs of Staff chairman, Admiral Mike Mullen, said "the single, biggest threat to our national security is our debt."[22] As Harvard's Benjamin Friedman noted 30 years ago, "World power and influence have historically accrued to creditor countries. It is not coincidental that America emerged as a world power simultaneously with our transition from a debtor nation . . . to a creditor supplying investment capital to the rest of the world."[23] Adam Posen, president of the Peterson Institute for International Economics, argues that unsustainable fiscal policy will make it harder for the United States to maintain its standing in global trade talks and disputes.[24]

As for the "sudden scenario"—in which debt foments a financial crisis—when a government runs a deficit, it borrows money from investors, including individuals, pension funds, and foreign governments. To those investors, the most important thing about our debt is that it's safe (backed by the world's richest economy and most stable democracy) and liquid (easy to resell because the demand for it is so strong).[25]

Under the sudden scenario, something quickly makes government debt seem risky. Something might lower people's confidence in the government's willingness to pay its debt (e.g., if it defaulted on some of it) or in the government's ability to pay its debt (e.g., if someone discovered that the country was cooking its books to hide a financial problem). Either way, investors would grow much less willing to hold government debt.

It's hard to predict what would trigger an event like this. Some countries have faced crises with debt as low as 40 percent of GDP. Others have not faced crises despite debt that topped 200 percent of GDP. A range of factors presumably matters: the country's repayment history, its projected debt trajectory, the state of its economy, the strength of its legal and political system, whether it is-sues debt in its own currency, what share of its debt is held by foreigners (since countries may be more likely to default on debt owed to foreigners than on debt owed to domestic residents[26]), and so on.

Nevertheless, we know what happens in the aftermath. When investors rap-idly sell off government bonds, interest rates on those bonds rise quickly—as the government needs to pay more to coax investors to buy its debt—and cap-ital flees the country. The resulting financial crisis can trigger a deep recession with a long, slow recovery and large increases in debt as the economy tanks and revenues dry up.[27]

That's basically what happened in Greece in 2009. A new government re-vealed that Greece had been fudging its books and the fiscal situation was worse than previously believed. This sharply reduced investor confidence that Greece could pay its debts, which led to a rapid sell-off of Greek debt, a swift flow of cap-ital from the country, and a spike in interest rates. By May 2010, Greece needed a group of European countries and the IMF to provide loans to avoid defaulting. In return, Greece promised to significantly cut spending and raise taxes. The finan-cial crisis, spending cuts, and tax increases severely weakened Greece's economy.

In recent decades, top economists and leading Wall Street figures of both po-litical parties have expressed concern that America could experience a kind of sudden scenario, or "hard landing," similar to what dogged Greece.[28]

If a sudden crisis were to arise, it could spread quickly. Global financial markets can respond to events virtually instantaneously, and policymakers can lose control of things just as quickly. As the late Massachusetts Institute of Technology (MIT) economist Rudiger Dornbusch said of Mexico's financial crisis of the 1990s, "The crisis takes a much longer time coming than you think, and then it happens much faster than you would have thought. . . . It took forever and then it took a night."[29]

Nevertheless, I doubt that we'll see a sudden scenario in the United States in the foreseeable future. The nation remains the world's safest place to invest; even after the financial crisis that began here in 2007 and spread across the world, investors flooded US markets in search of safe assets, helping to keep interest rates low. We undoubtedly have the resources to pay our debt for decades to come. We issue bonds in our own currency (as do Britain and Japan), giving us an important lever of control over our own debt. The dollar is the world's reserve currency.

To be sure, policymakers could create an emergency by forcing a default on the country's debt, as right-wing leaders and commentators threatened to bring about in debt ceiling standoffs in 2011 and 2013.[30] An intentional default would be a big mistake, for reasons explained in Chapter 3.

A financial crisis would turn out badly, of course, and would make the need to address the fiscal challenge even more compelling. The key point, though, is that even if a crisis does not materialize, the United States still faces a debt problem. It's just one that's growing gradually. This may be less exciting than a crisis, but it can be plenty damaging.

Despite all these issues, not all debt is bad. As Alexander Hamilton explained in the 1790s, debt helps governments establish credit and trade with other nations. It gives investors a safe and liquid asset, provided the government stays solvent. It helps nations finance their responses to emergencies, such as wars and recessions, and finance investments that will raise future living standards. When interest rates are low, borrowing gives government the chance to take advantage of cheap funding to undertake policies that need to be done at some point.

Deficits can also provide a boost when the economy falls into recession. When our economy is weak, some people can't find work and some businesses don't operate at full capacity, which creates a kind of vicious circle. Businesses are reluctant to hire new workers or make new investments because consumers, who are hurting while their breadwinners are out of work or working fewer hours, are reluctant to spend money for their products. Businesses retrench, consumers retrench, businesses retrench further, consumers retrench further, and so on, making a weak economy even weaker. Meanwhile, states, which face falling revenues during a recession, must then raise taxes or cut spending to meet their balanced-budget requirements, making the vicious cycle still worse.

That leaves the federal government as the only major force to pump money into the economy. The Federal Reserve can cut interest rates and take other steps. The president and Congress can cut taxes and boost benefits in programs like SNAP or unemployment insurance, giving families and businesses more resources. More federal spending on infrastructure projects and other programs can put people back to work. As families, businesses, and government spend more, the demand for workers grows, jobless workers return to work, and business operations can return to full capacity.[31]

The idea that government spending and tax cuts can stimulate a weak economy in the short term is associated with the great British economist John Maynard Keynes, who called for these policies in response to the Great Depression, saying, "The boom, not the slump, is the right time for austerity at the treasury." The idea is typically associated with liberal views, but politicians of all stripes often become Keynesian when faced with a slowdown. Under President George W. Bush, for example, policymakers provided stimulus in 2001, 2003, and 2008 via tax rebates.

In February of 2009, with the economy mired in the Great Recession, President Obama and Congress enacted the American Recovery and Reinvestment Act, providing $800 billion in tax cuts for workers, home buyers, college students, and small businesses, and higher spending for states, SNAP beneficiaries, and infrastructure projects.[32] That temporary stimulus clearly helped move the economy from recession to recovery.[33] It raised long-term debt by no more than 4–5 percent of GDP, which was well worth the price of helping to rescue such a weak economy.[34]

How can higher deficits and debt be part of the short-term solution for a weak economy but part of the long-term problem in a strong economy? In both cases, after all, higher deficits raise current consumption and reduce national saving.

In a weak economy, the economy expands by *utilizing* more of its existing capacity—by putting individuals back to work and getting businesses to run at their full speed. Deficits—and the tax cuts and spending increases that generate them—stimulate economic activity by tapping unutilized resources without crowding out private activity.

In a strong economy, in which all resources are already utilized, the economy expands by *raising* its capacity—by investing more in plant, equipment, human capital, and so on. In those circumstances, higher government borrowing crowds out private investment (or leads to borrowing from abroad) and so will reduce future income. For these reasons, the stimulus contained in the 2017 tax cut, which President Trump and Congress enacted when the economy was already at full employment, was the wrong medicine at the wrong time.

Thus, all else being equal, deficits and larger debt reduce long-term national saving and, in turn, future national income to a significant extent. But all else isn't always equal. The effects of fiscal policies on the economy depend not only on the size of the deficits but also on the specific policies that generated those deficits. For example, spending $1 on public investment projects or cutting taxes by $1 would boost the deficit by $1, but the effect on future income also would depend on the returns on the investment project or taxpayers' response to the tax cut.

That reminds us that debt can be good or bad, depending on what it's funding. Debt used to finance productive long-term investments, offset temporary revenue shortfalls, or cover temporary spending needs will likely have very different effects than debt that finances transfer spending on a long-term basis.

That we must address our long-term fiscal challenge is clear, for we will otherwise suffer the serious consequences. *How* we do so, however, is a different question, one with potentially profound implications for Americans at different socioeconomic levels. To control our long-term debt, some Americans will pay more in taxes while others will get less in benefits and services. The question of who shall bear the burden of debt reduction raises profound issues of fairness, particularly at a time of rising inequality in America. And it is to the issue of fairness that we turn next.

Notes

1. Schultze (1989).
2. All conventional economic models suggest that high and rising debt-to-GDP ratios will hamper long-term growth. A 2013 survey of leading academic economists of varying political affiliations asked for reactions to this statement: "Sustained tax and spending policies that boost consumption in ways that reduce the saving rate are likely to lower long-run living standards." More than two-thirds strongly agreed or agreed. The rest either were uncertain or had no opinion. Remarkably, not a single one disagreed (IGM Forum 2013a).
3. Hemingway (1926, chapter 13).
4. There is a school of thought that says that deficits don't reduce growth under certain conditions. In particular, the theory behind so-called Ricardian Equivalence is that a deficit that is created by a temporary lump-sum tax cut today that is followed by a temporary lump-sum tax increase in the future will not have any impact on national saving, investment, growth, or interest rates. The reason is that taxpayers will anticipate that their future tax liabilities will rise, by the exact amount of the tax cut they receive, and so they will save the entire tax cut in order to pay the future tax increase. Thus, the reduction in government saving due to the tax cut would be exactly offset by the increase in private saving, and there would be no change in national saving. "Ricardian Equivalence" is named after the nineteenth-century British economist David Ricardo, who did not actually believe in the idea but raised it as a conceptual possibility. It was revived intellectually by Harvard economist Robert Barro (1974) in a famous (in academia, at least) article. While the theory is intellectually elegant, there is significant evidence against it (Bernheim 1989; Elmendorf and Mankiw 1999), and, in any case, it does not apply to the situation facing the country—namely, rising long-term deficits and debt-to-GDP ratios. Virtually all economists, including Barro (2012), agree that if current budget projections play out, they will cause long-term economic harm.
5. GDP measures the output produced in the country. Gross national product (GNP) measures the income that accrues to Americans. GNP equals GDP less the income earned in the United States by foreigners plus the foreign income earned by Americans.
6. Woo and Kumar (2015).
7. Barro and Furman (2018); Congressional Budget Office (2018); International Monetary Fund (2018); Joint Committee on Taxation (2017); Page et al. (2017); Tax Foundation Staff (2017); University of Pennsylvania (2017); Zandi (2017).
8. See, for example, Caner, Grennes, and Koehler-Geib (2010), who use data from 79 countries from 1980 to 2008; Cechetti, Mohanty, and Zampolli (2012), who use data from 18 OECD countries for 1980 through 2005; Ursua and Wilson (2012), who use data on several advanced and emerging countries from 1950 to 2010. Each of these studies finds negative effects of added debt on growth in the range found by Woo and Kumar (2010). Chudik et al. (2015) and Baum, Checherita-Westphal, and Rother (2013) find significantly larger effects. These studies cover different time periods and different (large) collections of countries and they employ a variety of statistical techniques to test for robustness. In recent years, there was a short-lived controversy over whether the effects of debt on growth became bigger as the debt-to-GDP ratio exceeded 90 percent. This has been proven to be a false threshold. A dollar of added debt when debt is at or above 90 percent of GDP reduces economic growth, but not by a different amount than a dollar of debt when debt is between 60 and

90 percent of GDP. See Reinhart and Rogoff (2010); Herndon, Ash, and Pollin (2014); and Egert (2013) and the studies cited above.

9. Elmendorf and Mankiw (1999). As they note, this estimate probably overstates the negative impact of debt because of some technical issues, but they examine those factors and argue that the extent of any overstatement is small.

10. Congressional Budget Office (2016).

11. Page and Santoro (2010). See also Macroeconomic Advisers (2013) for similar results.

12. This statement is based on regressions using annual data on GDP and net national product (NNP) from 1950 to 2016 (Bureau of Economic Analysis 2018), controlling for the unemployment rate. These effects are particularly strong in the 1980–2016 period, during which the impact of federal saving/NNP on national saving/NNP is 1.43 and the impact on investment/NNP is 0.98. All of the effects are highly statistically significant. Similar findings hold using GDP instead of NNP.

13. See Engen and Hubbard (2005); Gale and Orszag (2004); Krishnamurthy and Vissing-Jorgensen (2012); Laubach (2009). Gale and Orszag (2004) provide a comprehensive review of the literature on deficits and interest rates, emphasizing the crucial distinction that studies that look at anticipated deficits' effects on future interest rates tend to find effects. In contrast, studies that look at current deficits' impact on current interest rates tend not to find an effect, presumably because it is harder to tease out cause and effect among current variables.

14. Chinn and Ito (2005, 2008); Chinn, Eichengreen, and Ito (2011). Huntley (2014) surveyed the economic literature and finds that, as far as central tendencies are concerned, for every dollar increase in the deficit, national saving falls by 57 cents (with a range of 39 to 71 cents), capital inflows offset between 30 and 60 percent of the decline in national saving, and, as a result, national investment falls by 33 cents (with a range between 15 and 50 cents).

15. US Department of the Treasury (2018). This does not mean foreigners own 31 percent of our economy; it just means that the public debt they hold is equal in size to 31 percent of our economy.

16. Ito (2014). Domestic investors in 2014 held 92 percent of Japanese debt. In the United States, as noted earlier, domestic investors held only about 55 percent of US debt.

17. Abbas et al. (2010); Hills, Thomas, and Dimsdale (2010).

18. Feinstein (1981).

19. World Bank (2018).

20. Romer and Romer (2017).

21. Persson and Svensson (1989).

22. Marshall (2011).

23. Friedman (1988).

24. Posen (2014).

25. Krishnamurthy and Vissing-Jorgensen (2012).

26. Reinhart and Rogoff (2011).

27. Recessions following financial crises tend to be both more severe than others and take longer to recover to pre-recession levels of employment (Reinhart and Rogoff 2009).

28. They have included Greg Mankiw, chairman of the President's Council of Economic Advisers under President George W. Bush; Peter Orszag, director of the Congressional Budget Office and then director of the OMB under President Obama; Robert Rubin, chairman of the National Economic Council and treasury secretary under President Clinton; and even fiscal doves like Paul Krugman, a Nobel laureate and *New York Times* syndicated columnist, who warned of a "fiscal train wreck" in 2003, when our debt-to-GDP ratio was a far less worrisome 35 percent (Ball and Mankiw 1995; Rubin, Orszag, and Sinai 2004; Krugman 2003).

29. Dornbusch (1997).

30. Bartlett (2013); Weisman (2013).

31. An alternative school of thought argues that fiscal tightening during a recession is stimulative (Alesina and Ardagna 2010), but the results are contested and controversial (International Monetary Fund 2010).

32. Congressional Budget Office (2015).

33. See Chodorow-Reich et al. (2012) and Wilson (2012). The Congressional Budget Office (2015) suggests that the law boosted the size of the economy by between 0.5 percent and 2.4 percent between 2009 and 2011. A comprehensive study and simulation by Alan Blinder, a leading Princeton economist who served in the Clinton administration, and Mark Zandi, co-founder of Moody's www.Economy.com, found that fiscal stimulus increased the size of the economy by 3.6 percent by 2010 (Blinder and Zandi 2015). Indeed, there was agreement stretching from prominent conservatives like Harvard economist and former Reagan adviser Martin Feldstein (2009) to liberal economist Paul Krugman (2011) that the stimulus package was too small and the economy could have benefited from a larger boost.

34. Based on the CBO's (2015) estimates of the impact of the stimulus on the economy, and assuming an 18 percent share of revenues in new growth, the package raised the debt-to-GDP ratio by between 4 and 5 percentage points through 2011. DeLong and Summers (2012) argue that the long-term impact on the debt-to-GDP ratio could be smaller and possibly negative because the package could have permanently boosted the economy out of the doldrums. Auerbach and Gorodnichenko (2017) provide further evidence for the view of DeLong and Summers.

5

Solving the Debt Problem Fairly

Fairness has always played a key role in American public policy. From the earliest cries of "no taxation without representation" to recent debates about healthcare, Americans have strong feelings about economic justice. Are we "soaking the rich," or should they pay more to cover their "fair share?" Do the poor need more opportunities, or are they "moochers"?

Fairness should be a central goal of fiscal reform as well. Most people would reject a policy that solved the debt problem by exempting the rich from any sacrifice and imposing the costs on everyone else. But even if we can see what *isn't* fair, deciding what *is* fair isn't always easy. Some issues, like the effects of debt on growth, can be resolved with evidence. Notions of fairness, however, are firmly in the eyes of the beholder, dependent on values, ethics, and judgments.

Meanwhile, current debates about social equity are playing out against a 40-year backdrop of rising income inequality and stagnating market incomes for lower- and middle-class families. Not all inequality is bad, of course. The prospect of differential rewards creates incentives for people to work hard and take risks that are crucial to a modern economy. But the enduring trends in inequality raise fundamental concerns about the fairness of our society and prospects for our economy.

An overwhelming majority of Americans believe that inequality is a major problem and a smaller majority believe the government should do something about it, but there are extreme partisan splits. For example, in one poll conducted by the Pew Research Center, 86 percent of "steadfast conservatives" said they thought the poor had a good life, whereas 86 percent of "solid liberals" thought the poor had a hard life.[1]

These issues matter because they affect attitudes about who should pay to reduce the debt. When it comes to fairness, the fundamental question about the debt is which generation(s) should bear the burden of addressing the fiscal challenge. But since paying down the debt requires changes to specific tax and spending policies, we also need to consider who within each generation should face the costs. What should policymakers do?

- *First, recognize that too much debt is a burden on future generations.* We not only have good economic reasons to address debt issues sooner rather than later but also strong moral obligations to pass down a stable fiscal system to our children—reflecting a broader American ethic that each generation should leave the next one better off.
- *Second, use fiscal reform to expand opportunity and reduce inequality within each generation.* While we shouldn't (and can't) use public policy to offset the entire increase in inequality, we shouldn't exacerbate it, either. We should narrow inequality in ways that are economically productive and fiscally sound and that distribute opportunities and outcomes more fairly.

What's a fair society? What role should government play in creating one? These questions bring no easy answers, despite centuries of thinking by philosophers and economists.

Different views on fairness start from reasonable positions. But they don't always provide practical guidelines, and they often conflict with one another. As a result, pursuing fairness often becomes an exercise in balancing different objectives, each of which is desirable. Even a taste of the alternatives shows how tricky fairness issues can be.

Some concepts of fairness focus on *outcomes*. Utilitarianism suggests that social justice occurs when policy choices maximize the sum of everyone's well-being—the "greatest good for the greatest number." Another approach—associated with philosopher John Rawls—would provide the greatest well-being possible to the least-well-off people, consistent with maintaining each individual's liberty.[2] A third approach argues that society's obligation ends with ensuring that each person has access to at least a minimal level of income or necessities.

Other approaches to fairness focus on the *process* by which outcomes emerge rather than the outcomes themselves. Some people believe that letting people keep the income they earn is fair, as long as markets are competitive and legal rules are enforced. And almost everyone supports equal opportunity, perhaps because it means different things to different people.[3] While truly equal opportunity for all people in all ways would be impossible to achieve, reducing disparities in opportunity in key respects—access to good education, safe neighborhoods, mentors, and job networks—would improve the economy's equity and efficiency.

Another approach focuses on the *burdens* people face to pay for government. Some believe that people should make equal sacrifices to finance government (in whatever dimension those sacrifices are measured). Others think that burdens should differ across people. For example, we might want to base taxes on people's ability to pay, which is how the progressive income tax works. Alternatively, we might want to have those who benefit from a program pay for it, such as when governments use gasoline taxes to pay for road repairs.

Each of these approaches has obvious merit. But each also has shortcomings as well as differing implications for policy. They all implicitly ask two questions: how society should treat people in different situations (vertical equity), and how it should treat people in equivalent situations (horizontal equity). For vertical equity, the key question is how much the rich should pay relative to the middle class and the poor. For horizontal equity, the key issue is the extent to which people in similar circumstances (however those are defined) should bear similar burdens and receive similar benefits.

Views about fairness often relate closely to views about luck. Everyone agrees that hard work and education are important to getting ahead and achieving success.[4] But even if people like to attribute their own success to hard work and skill, luck, broadly defined as things a person can't control, surely plays a key role in determining one's economic success as an adult.[5]

One's income as an adult depends to a remarkable degree on one's luck as a child, as it depends on parents' income, marital status, education, and occupation; genetic inheritances like IQ, personality, health, and looks; and neighborhood and community characteristics, like the quality of public schools. The best single predictor of a child's relative income ranking in his generation is his parents' relative income ranking in their generation.[6]

Billionaire investor Warren Buffett describes all this luck as the "ovarian lottery"—children can't predict or change the circumstances of their birth. "You could be born intelligent or not intelligent, born healthy or disabled, born black or white, born in the United States or in Bangladesh," and those circumstances dramatically affect your chance to succeed.[7] In his thinking, the liberal Buffett is joined by Richard Posner, a leading conservative scholar and judge, who wrote, "I think that ultimately everything is attributable to luck, good or bad. Not just the obvious things . . . but also the characteristics that cause a person to make critical decisions that may turn out well or badly."[8] Nevertheless, feelings about luck illustrate a striking philosophical divide among the public. When asked why people are poor, conservatives are likelier to blame a lack of effort, while liberals are likelier to highlight luck.[9] These differences translate naturally into divergent views of appropriate public policy.

Moving from views of what the government *should* do, let's explore what it *actually* does. The Congressional Budget Office provides the most comprehensive analysis of income distribution and government redistribution. It defines "market income" as what people get from the private market (including government employment)—that is, all income other than government benefits. It defines "income before transfers and taxes" as market income plus social insurance benefits and "after-tax income" as income before transfers and taxes plus means-tested transfers and minus federal taxes.[10] We also consider "pre-tax income," the sum of market income, social insurance benefits, and means-tested transfers.[11]

Measuring the redistributional impact of fiscal policies can be tricky. For example, the person sending the tax check to the government is not always the one who becomes worse off. A tax on a business is ultimately borne by someone—a customer, worker, owner, and so on—not by the business itself. And the burden of a tax change depends on how the resulting revenues are spent. The CBO assumes that income taxes, excise taxes, and spending programs affect the people who directly pay the tax or receive the benefits, and workers bear the burden of both the employer and employee share of the payroll tax. Another assumption is that 75 percent of the corporate income tax is borne by all owners of capital (not just shareholders) and 25 percent by workers. These are reasonable assumptions in economic analysis and are consistent with a wide body of literature (Chapter 12).

Table 5.1 shows the CBO's measures of federal taxes and transfers (but not direct spending like education or infrastructure investment) by income group in 2014. This is the most recent comprehensive data available. Table 5.1 does not incorporate the 2017 TCJA, but the main trends toward inequality in after-tax income would only be accentuated if it did.[12] Both taxes and transfer payments (e.g., Social Security) are progressive. They give more, as a share of income, to the poor, and they take more, as a share of income, as income rises.[13] Households in the bottom two-fifths of the income scale get much more from the federal government than they pay in. That's not surprising, since this group includes disproportionate numbers of the poor, the unemployed, students, and the elderly. These groups don't have much of their own income and receive significant amounts of government benefits. Households in the middle get, on average, slightly more in transfers than they pay in taxes.[14] Households in the top two-fifths, and those in the top 1 percent in particular, pay more in taxes than they get in benefits. As a result, the distribution of after-tax income is less extreme than that of market income.[15]

Although we often hear that the rich get all sorts of breaks and that some high-income individuals pay little tax, the tax system as a whole is progressive. Table 5.1 shows that average tax rates (as a share of pre-tax income), again not including the effects of TCJA, rise from about 1 percent in the bottom income quintile, to 13 percent in the middle quintile, to 27 percent in the top quintile, and to 34 percent in the top 1 percent.[16]

Table 5.1. Average Income, Taxes, and Transfers by Income Group, 2014

Income Group	Market Income	Social Insurance	Means-Tested Transfers	Pre-Tax Income	Federal Taxes	Post-Tax Income	Average Tax Rate (%)	Average Tax Rate Net of Social Insurance and Transfers (%)
Lowest Quintile	14,800	4,300	12,300	31,400	400	31,100	1.3	−109.5
Second Quintile	30,600	11,500	6,200	48,300	3,800	44,500	7.9	−45.4
Middle Quintile	56,400	12,200	3,200	71,800	9,600	62,300	13.4	−10.3
Fourth Quintile	92,200	12,200	1,800	106,200	18,600	87,700	17.5	5.0
Highest Quintile	270,800	10,600	1,100	282,500	75,100	207,300	26.6	23.4
Top 1 Percent	1,764,200	9,400	1,200	1,774,800	596,200	1,178,600	33.6	33.2

Notes: Subject to rounding, pre-tax income is market income plus social insurance plus means-tested transfers. Post-tax income is pre-tax income minus federal taxes. Average tax rate is defined as federal taxes as a share of pre-tax income. Average tax rate net of transfers is defined as the ratio of (a) taxes minus social insurance and transfers to (b) market income. A negative average tax rate net of social insurance and transfers indicates a net benefit, whereas a positive average tax rate net of social insurance and transfers indicates a net loss. Households are ranked by size-adjusted market income plus social insurance benefits.

Source: Congressional Budget Office (2018).

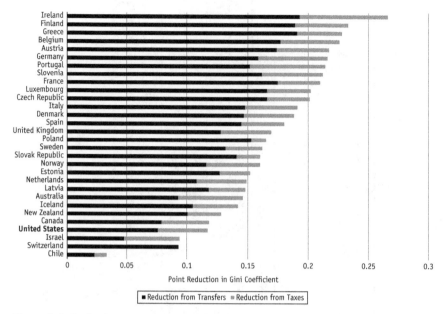

Figure 5.1. Reduction in income inequality due to taxes and transfers, 2013. Australia data are for 2014. New Zealand data are for 2012. OECD (2016b).

Considering both taxes and transfers, America has less redistribution than most other advanced countries. We ranked 27th out of 30 OECD countries in 2013 (Figure 5.1). Our tax system scores relatively high, as the 12th most re-distributive. As the figure shows, however, most redistribution in every country occurs on the spending side, and our spending system ranks 28th out of 30.[17] That reflects the finding (in Chapter 1) that OECD countries spend significantly more on social programs than we do. The relative lack of US redistribution is particularly surprising in that our pre-tax income distribution is one of the most unequal among advanced countries.[18]

Just as taxes and spending redistribute resources, so does government debt. Within one generation, debt redistributes wealth from low- to high-income households. That's because, as shown in Chapter 4, higher debt raises interest rates and reduces wages. As a result, low- and middle-income households, who get most of their income from wages, are hurt relative to high-income households, who save more and thus get more of their income from interest.

More important, debt transfers resources from future to current generations. "Blessed are the young," Herbert Hoover once said, "for they shall inherit the national debt."[19] Deficits don't eliminate the need to pay for current spending; they merely *postpone* the payment. Because current spending generally benefits only current generations (with notable exceptions such as government investment and defense), future generations bear the burden when that spending is eventually financed by spending cuts or tax increases.

Debt hurts younger households, due to the lower wages and higher interest rates that it creates. Younger households receive almost all their income in wages, and they're typically borrowers who pay interest—for college, homes, and cars. Older households are generally savers, and they receive interest payments as income and thus benefit more from debt, especially if policymakers postpone the steps needed to repay the debt until after they die.[20]

In a 2011 study, International Monetary Fund researchers found that under the policies in place in 2010, all living US generations will receive positive transfers (transfers in excess of taxes) from the federal government over the course of their lifetimes.[21] That means future (unborn) generations will bear the burdens—receiving less in transfers than they pay in taxes. The average tax rate— taxes paid minus transfers received—on future generations was an estimated 10 to 17 percent of lifetime labor earnings. These are substantial burdens. By way of comparison, the combined employer and employee payroll tax is 15.3 percent of earnings up to a capped amount.

We can't devise a fair approach to address our debt challenge without acknowledging a 40-year trend of growing economic inequality, coupled with stagnating market income for low- and middle-class households. From the end of World War II to the early 1970s, incomes generally grew robustly for the rich and poor alike.

Since the 1970s, however, income has grown much more unequal, as shown in Figure 5.2. The richest households have seen dramatic income growth while the market incomes of low- and middle-income households have generally stagnated. For those in the middle income quintile and the quintile just below it, average market income barely budged from 1979 to 2014. Their meager increases reflected increases in female employment, not living standards.[22] Market income in the bottom 20 percent grew at a stronger pace—totaling 51 percent over the period. Households in the top 40 percent enjoyed more significant gains.[23] Average market income for the top 1 percent grew by a whopping 222 percent,[24] with that increase driven predominantly by wage growth through 2000 and by income from actively managed businesses since then.[25] People in the top 20 percent received 80 percent of all gains in market income—with the top 1 percent alone receiving 37 percent of all gains. The bottom 60 percent of the population received only about 6 percent of the gains.

Federal tax and transfer policies offset some of these trends. As noted earlier, federal taxes and transfers are progressive, so after-tax income is less unequal than market income. Including all federal taxes and transfers, income grew by 40 percent in the second income quintile and 36 percent in the middle income

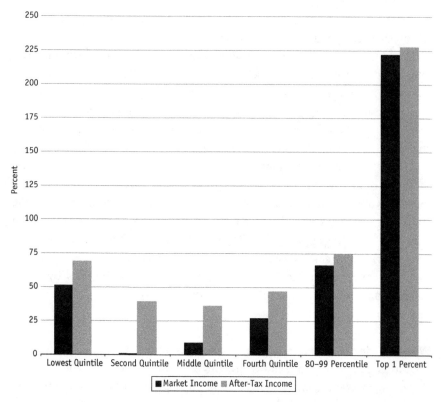

Figure 5.2. Growth of average income by income group, 1979–2014. Households are ranked by size-adjusted market income plus social insurance benefits. Congressional Budget Office (2018).

quintile, even though market income was virtually stagnant (Figure 5.2). Thus, the vast bulk of income increases among these groups was due to government tax and transfer programs, not increases in market income. After-tax income grew by 69 percent for the bottom quintile, showing faster growth than market income.

In some ways, however, taxes and transfers became less progressive. In a progressive tax system, the average tax rate should rise as income rises. The only way this can happen is if after-tax income rises by less than before-tax income. However, for the top 40 percent, after-tax income rose by more than pre-tax income. For the top 1 percent, after-tax income grew by 228 percent, exceeding the 222 percent increase in market income. As a result, most of the gains in after-tax income went to high-income households. The top 1 percent received 23 percent of the growth in post-tax income. Households in the top 20 percent received 59 percent of the gains. Households in the bottom 60 percent received only 24 percent of the gains.

Widening inequality has appeared in many other contexts—such as consumption, life span, health, and exposure to crime—and has occurred in almost all advanced countries, though the changes have been more extreme in the United States.[26]

Growing income inequality has multiple causes. Perhaps the most important is "skill-biased technological change." The revolution in computing and information technology raised the productivity of, and demand for, high-skilled workers compared to low-skilled workers. At the same time, the growth of highly educated workers in America slowed.[27] That's partly because baby boomers had fully entered the labor market by the end of the 1980s and subsequent birth cohorts were smaller, providing fewer workers; it's also partly because of slower increases in educational attainment.[28] As a result, skilled workers enjoyed wage increases relative to unskilled workers because technological changes raised the demand for their services just as population and education trends slowed the rate of increase of such workers.

Globalization also played an important role. Transformational changes in communications and transportation costs and (until the Trump administration's spate of tariffs) lower trade barriers have dramatically broadened the reach of markets. Hundreds of millions of workers in China, India, and other countries now participate in global markets. Some American workers benefited as the demand for what they produce rose in world markets, and many American consumers benefited from low-cost imports. But many workers fell behind as the demand for their products fell or low-wage competition in other countries rendered them overpriced. Their wages stagnated, or they lost their jobs entirely. That's especially true for unskilled laborers, who already were at the bottom and hurt by the rising demand for more highly skilled workers due to technological innovation.

Declines in the share of workers belonging to a union, which fell by almost half between 1983 and 2017, and in the minimum wage, which fell by one-third between 1968 and 2017 on an inflation-adjusted basis, have further fueled inequality.[29] Trends in family formation reinforced these factors. The rise in single-parent families raised the number of relatively low-income families, and the rise in "assortative mating" (basically, educated people marrying each other) raised the number of high-income households.[30] Increasing disparities in profits across firms have played a role as well. Some firms are doing quite well, some not, and the gap between them has risen. Firms with higher profits tend to share some of them with their workers by paying them more.[31] Finally, some experts now believe that the increasing concentration of market power within many industries has raised employers' bargaining power and curtailed wage growth.

While all these factors fueled rising income inequality, they don't fully explain the explosive growth of income at the top. What else is happening? Globalization lets executives, entertainers, and others meet the demands of global markets and audiences much more easily. The growth in "winner-take-all" markets, where a small difference in performance or timing can translate into extremely large differences in rewards, has fueled the trend. Likewise, technological advances have raised the optimal size of businesses, and not surprisingly, the executive of a company with 10,000 workers has a bigger job and gets more compensation than one in a company with only 1,000 workers.

In addition, "rent-seeking" suggests that some of the income gains at the top came *at the expense of* lower-income groups. In economics, rent-seeking is an effort to gain income or wealth by appropriating it from others rather than creating new resources. Rent-seeking is unproductive for the economy; it just transfers money from one person or group to another. As a potential cause of increased income inequality, it has particularly important implications. To the extent that the gains by the top 1 percent were due to rent-seeking, the gains came at the expense of other income groups. Lawmakers could take back that income through higher taxes without reducing the effort that the top 1 percent put into constructive management and investment.

Certainly, the incentive for high-income Americans to seek rent has risen. Top federal income tax rates have fallen considerably—from 70 percent before Reagan to 28 percent after tax reform in 1986 and about 41 percent now.[32] By letting high-income earners keep more of their next dollar of earnings, policymakers intended for the tax rate cuts to boost work effort, saving, and investment. But they also raised the return on rent-seeking.

We have evidence, though it's not conclusive, that rent-seeking among high-income households has risen significantly. In one study, in a sample of 18 countries over 50 years, lower top income tax rates caused higher concentrations of income among the rich but not more economic growth; the pie did not expand, the rich were just claiming a larger slice.[33]

Broad, deep, and enduring changes in income distribution have had profound effects on everything from the pursuit of the American Dream and the growth of the economy to the nature of our political system. America has always prided itself as the land of opportunity, a dynamic place where everyone gets a fair shot, where effort generates success. In the past, our nation has tolerated substantial inequality as the supposed price of an upwardly mobile society. But that relationship has changed for the worse.

Economists distinguish two types of mobility, both of which are closely related to the rise in inequality. *Relative mobility* refers to a child's standing (as an adult) in the income distribution of his generation compared to his parents' standing in the income distribution of their generation. It focuses on questions like how frequently people raised in poor families can become well-off as adults, and whether a "glass floor" keeps the children of rich families rich as adults.[34] *Absolute mobility* refers to whether children (as adults) have higher real income than their parents did. It addresses whether a generation is better off than the one preceding it.

The decades-long increase in inequality has not raised relative mobility.[35] Instead, America now has more inequality than almost all other advanced nations, but *less* relative economic mobility than they do. Contrary to popular belief, if you grow up in a disadvantaged family, it's harder to get ahead in America than in many other advanced countries. If you start in a family at the top, it's easier to stay there than in other countries.[36] In fact, higher income inequality and lower relative mobility seem to go hand in hand, in analyses across countries and across US metropolitan areas.[37] Higher inequality could reduce relative mobility in many ways—by increasing inequality of opportunity at every stage of a person's development and thus increasing the disparities in what determines adult success.[38] What's notable—along with the direct negative effects of inequality on children's welfare—is the vicious cycle it creates: inequality restricts relative mobility, which widens inequality, and so on. With inequality rising over time and relative mobility not changing, the economic consequences of being born rich versus poor matter more than ever.

The increase in inequality has reduced absolute mobility as well. The likelihood that a child has higher income as an adult than his or her parents has fallen from over 90 percent for people born in 1940 to less than 60 percent for those born in 1960 to 50 percent for those born in 1980. The main reason for the decline is not the slowdown in GDP growth but rather the widening distribution of income over time, which left many people behind.[39]

Inequality also can impair overall economic performance. But the links between inequality and economic growth are numerous and complex. Different sources of inequality can affect growth in different ways, and growth likely affects inequality as well.

The traditional view posits a trade-off between equality and growth.[40] Arthur Okun famously framed the trade-off by imagining that society transferred resources from rich to poor via a "leaky bucket"—that is, the process of transferring resources, through taxes and transfers, reduces the total amount of resources available even as it makes the distribution of resources more equal.[41] The trade-off between equality and growth is also inherent in supply-side economics, through the notion that lower tax rates on the rich will spur growth by inducing more productive activity—working harder, investing more, taking more risks. At the same time, lower tax rates on high-income households raise inequality.

The problem with the supply-side notion, however, is that lower marginal income tax rates have not fueled significantly higher growth either in the United States or in other countries (see Chapter 11).[42]

Despite these trade-offs, recent cross-country studies find that more equality and more growth can go hand in hand.[43] How can we, in the United States, better achieve both through public policy? Programs that help low- and middle-income children attend college make outcomes more equal and boost economic growth. And programs that offer food (SNAP), early education (Head Start), or children's healthcare (Medicaid, CHIP) help lower-income households and produce future adults who are more productive (see Chapter 9).[44] Likewise, work incentives such as the EITC that target low- and moderate-income households can help the economy and reduce inequality.

More economic inequality can also mean more political inequality, which then reinforces and extends the economic inequality. At the low end, groups that are economically marginalized or don't think they have a stake in economic growth are less likely to vote and participate in the political process.[45] At the high end, the vast shift in relative income over the last 40 years raises concerns that it's affecting the one-person, one-vote ideal that pervades our democracy. With the share of income going to higher-income households in general and the top 1 percent in particular rising so much since the late 1970s, we'd be surprised if these groups did *not* buy more of everything, including political influence.[46]

The 2010 *Citizens United* case, in which the Supreme Court prohibited limits on corporations' funding to support or oppose a candidate, only exacerbates these concerns. Political contributions come heavily from the very richest Americans.[47] Concerns about the extremely rich in American politics are exacerbated by the high cost and private financing of elections. Political officeholders, especially members of Congress, depend heavily on private contributions to finance their campaigns.[48]

There is little reason to believe that recent trends in inequality, and the impact on mobility, growth, and politics, will cease or reverse in the absence of policy actions. Indeed, increasing automation of the workforce could further widen income inequality by replacing human labor with machines, and the growth of the contingent workforce could also erode the market power of labor. If inequality is growing, imposing increasingly harmful impacts on our economy, our society, and our politics, what does that mean for fairness and the debt? I see two main conclusions.

First, we—the current generation of Americans—should not shirk the challenge of addressing our long-term fiscal problems. That's true even though future generations, on average, could well be more prosperous than we are and, thus, better positioned to absorb the needed tax increases and spending cuts. That doesn't mean we shouldn't, or won't, pass *some* of our debt to future generations. After all, as an economic matter, we don't need to eliminate the debt but rather to reduce it as a share of the economy to manageable levels. Moreover, debt is part of a larger package that we bequeath to future generations—including a knowledge base, a physical environment, and so on. Nevertheless, on purely economic grounds, we should address the fiscal challenge in the coming years. Higher debt will hurt our future economy, which, in turn, will impair the ability of future generations to improve their own standards of living and address the fiscal problem. The longer we wait, the greater and more disruptive the required tax increases and spending cuts will have to be. The evidence on declining absolute mobility suggests that many people will not be better off than their parents, so appealing to the idea that future generations will have higher income and thus should bear more of the debt burden is not as sure a thing as it used to be.

Apart from the economics, the "Golden Rule" applies. We should not do to future generations what we wouldn't have wanted earlier generations to do to us. If previous generations had passed down more debt, we would have been materially worse off than we are today. That our living standards today still would have been higher than those of, say, a century ago wouldn't be much consolation as we struggled unnecessarily. Likewise, America's history and values are rooted in the idea that each generation faces a moral imperative to leave a better world to future generations.[49]

The second policy implication for fairness is that we should treat the fiscal challenge as an opportunity to address inequality and mobility issues. In fact, addressing inequality and mobility can help solve the fiscal problem. For instance, we can invest more in early education and expand access to college, increase monthly nutrition benefits through SNAP, expand access to healthcare for more low- and middle-income Americans, and improve work incentives (see Chapter 9). By boosting spending, these policies will force tax increases to offset the cost. But, as discussed in Chapter 11, increases in tax levels, if designed well, don't seem to impede economic growth, whereas sustained deficits will hurt growth.

We should also collect more revenue from the rich for multiple reasons. In a progressive tax system, increases in income should raise average tax rates. However, the average tax rate for the rich hasn't risen even though their real income has skyrocketed since 1979. Moreover, if the main benefit of fiscal reform is economic growth, and if the fruits of growth continue to go mainly to those at the top, those high-income households should bear the greatest burden of fiscal reform. The public supports the idea; higher taxes on the wealthy are one of the few consistently popular ideas over time (see Chapter 6).

Finally, the only substantial way to have the wealthiest households share significantly in reducing the fiscal burden is to raise their taxes. Although rich elderly people receive Social Security and Medicare, even eliminating those benefits would create only a small dent in their lifetime income.

Taxing the rich more would have several ancillary benefits as well. It would reduce the chances that fiscal reform will exacerbate inequality, which has been a concern in other countries.[50] It need not restrain economic growth and it could well reduce rent-seeking, which would help other income groups. It need not raise the risk that taxes on high-income households go anywhere near the "soak-the-rich" tax rates during World War II; tax rates on the rich were much higher for most of the 20th century than they are today.[51] Last, it would help mitigate the very substantial role of luck in the economic system.

Both of the major implications drawn above have to do with good versus bad use of debt. Good debt will finance investments in our people and economy and thus make the future economy stronger and fairer. Bad debt will squander valuable resources, breeding inefficiency and inequity.

Notions of fairness can help guide a comprehensive plan that addresses our long-term fiscal challenge and, at the same time, narrows inequality, expands opportunity, fuels growth, and helps our children. But the issues are not just about policy design; politics plays a key role. The political realities that surround deficit reduction are no small problem, and that is where we turn next.

Notes

1. Pew Research Center (2014a).
2. Rawls reasoned that is how people would design a society if they didn't know what their own status in it would be. A premise of this argument is that people's views about fairness are purer when they don't know their own status in the system. There is evidence that people's views change as their status changes. Lottery winners, for example, become more conservative after they have won big pots of money (Powdthavee and Oswald 2014).
3. In a 2011 Gallup poll, 88 percent said it is at least somewhat important that the government increase "equality of opportunity for people to get ahead if they want to" (Newport 2011).
4. In a 2014 Pew poll, 92 percent of parents ranked hard work as an especially important trait to teach children (Parker 2014).
5. See Frank (2016) and Kleinbard (2014). Kleinbard writes that "the pervasive hand of fortune—of simple luck—[is] at work everywhere," urging the reader to think carefully about which traits are considered lucky in our society, how they are meted out, and how they might influence policy decisions.
6. Inherited factors can explain half or more of the variation in adult income (Chetty et al. 2014a; Reeves and Sawhill 2016; Sacerdote 2007). People's adult outcomes can be predicted not just from their parents' status, but to a remarkable extent, also from their great-grandparents' status (Clark 2014).
7. Kass (2013).

8. Posner (2012). When asked how he accounted for his success, even the economist Milton Friedman—a Nobel Prize winner and the free market's great apostle—answered, "Luck. Chance." (Academy of Achievement 1991).

9. In a 2014 Pew poll, 39 percent of respondents blamed lack of effort if a person was poor, while 50 percent blamed circumstances beyond the person's control. But 61 percent of "steadfast conservatives" pointed to lack of effort, while 83 percent of "solid liberals," highlighted "circumstances beyond control" (Pew Research Center 2014a, Q53). About 81 percent of "steadfast conservatives" believed that most people who want to get ahead can do so if they are willing to work hard, but only 29 percent of "solid liberals" did (Pew Research Center 2014a, Q25k). See also Pew Research Center (2014b).

10. Market income consists of labor income, business income, realized capital gains (profits from the sale of assets), capital income excluding capital gains, income received in retirement for past services, and other sources of income. A household is a group of people sharing a housing unit. CBO adjusts income for inflation and the number of people in the household. Social insurance benefits include Social Security, Medicare, unemployment insurance, and workers' compensation. Means-tested transfers include cash payments and in-kind services provided through federal, state, and local government assistance programs. Federal taxes in this case include individual income taxes, payroll taxes, corporate income taxes, and excise taxes, but not estate and gift taxes (Congressional Budget Office 2018). Omitting the estate and gift tax has a tiny effect on distributional estimates because these taxes are small relative to the economy and are concentrated among very wealthy households.

11. Previous Congressional Budget Office reports analyze this measure (Congressional Budget Office 2016).

12. Gale et al. (2018). The Congressional Budget Office (2018) ranks households by market income plus social insurance benefits.

13. Auerbach, Kotlikoff, and Koehler (2016) present evidence that the tax system is even more progressive if examined over the remaining portion of individuals' lives.

14. In 2014, taxes for this group on average were $9,600 and the sum of social insurance and means-tested transfers was $15,400. Before 2008, though, this group paid more in taxes than it received in benefits (Congressional Budget Office 2018).

15. In 2014, the top 1 percent received 19 percent of market income, but 13 percent of after-tax income. The bottom income quintile received just 3 percent of market income, but 7 percent of after-tax income (Congressional Budget Office 2018).

16. Congressional Budget Office (2018). This is the total average federal tax rate, which takes into account individual income taxes, payroll taxes, corporate taxes, and excise taxes.

17. Economists measure the inequality of income with a measure called the Gini coefficient. A Gini value of zero implies that every household has the same income. A Gini value of one implies that one household has all of the income. Figure 5.1 reports the point difference in the Gini coefficient due to taxes and transfers, not the percent difference.

18. OECD (2016b).

19. Hoover (1936).

20. Policy changes also can redistribute resources across generations in ways that don't show up in official debt figures. An immediate, permanent increase in Social Security benefits, financed by an immediate, permanent increase in payroll taxes could be designed to not affect the deficit in any year. But it would help current retirees and those near retirement, since the increase in their benefits would swamp the few years of higher taxes they would have to pay. Who pays for the benefits for older generations? Younger and future generations. It is also possible to change the official debt and deficit figures without redistributing resources (Kotlikoff 1986).

21. Batini, Callgegari, and Guerreiro (2011). The study developed measures of generational accounts, which aim to keep track of the many ways that government policies redistribute resources across generations (Auerbach, Kotlikoff, and Gokhale 1991, 1994). Gokhale (2012) provides alternative estimates based on earlier data. Generational accounts start

from the notion that someone has to pay for existing debt and for government purchases, like defense and infrastructure. If one generation pays less, via lower taxes or higher transfer payments received, others have to pay more. The accounts show the net taxes—the difference between transfer payments received and taxes paid—for each generation under current policies. The accounts do *not* show the net benefits received from all government policies because they do not attribute the benefits of government purchases to the various generations.

22. The labor force participation rate among 25- to 54-year-old women rose from 62 percent in 1979 to 74 percent in 2013 (Bureau of Labor Statistics 2016).

23. Reeves (2017) focuses on the role of the top 20 percent of the income distribution, arguing that it has pulled away from the rest of society and is using its political power to reinforce its newfound status. Rose (2016) shows that the "upper middle class," defined as households with incomes ranging between $100,000 and $349,000 in 2014, experienced a 62 percent gain in real income from 1979 to 2014.

24. The Gini coefficient for market income rose from 0.47 in 1979 to 0.60 in 2014 (Congressional Budget Office 2018).

25. Piketty, Saez, and Zucman (2017); Smith et al. (2017).

26. See Aguiar and Bils (2015); Case and Deaton (2015); Keeley (2015); Kelly (2000); Piketty (2013). Winship (2014) and Burkhauser, Larrimore, and Simon (2012) critique the income inequality trends, but the basic results are supported by other analyses (including Piketty and Saez [2016] and Piketty, Saez, and Zucman [2017]) and related trends. The gap in wages for college graduates relative to those with just a high school education more than doubled from 1963 to 2012 (Autor 2014). The share of national income going to capital owners increased relative to laborers (Bureau of Economic Analysis 2016), implying a more unequal distribution of income because capital income is highly concentrated among high-income households. The share of income going to the top 400 tax filers more than doubled from 1992 to 2013 (Statistics of Income Division 2015). The distribution of wealth became more unequal after the late 1970s (Bricker et al. 2016; Kopczuk 2015; Saez and Zucman 2016). The share of wealth accounted for by the Forbes 400—the 400 wealthiest Americans—has more than doubled in the last 30 years (Board of Governors 2016; Kroll 2015; Kaplan and Rauh 2013; Schwartz 1982).

27. The college-educated population grew at a rate of 3.9 percent annually between 1960 and 1980, falling to 2.3 percent annually between 1980 and 2005 (Goldin and Katz 2009).

28. In the United States, 41 percent of those who are aged 55 to 64 have a tertiary education (post-secondary education), compared to the OECD average of 23 percent. For those aged 25 to 34, the gap is much closer. In the United States, 42 percent of the younger cohort completed tertiary education, compared to the OECD average of 38 percent. Moreover, the United States is in the bottom half of the OECD with respect to education enrollment rates of 15- to 19-year-olds (OECD 2016a).

29. Union membership fell from 20 percent of the workforce in 1983 to 11 percent in 2017. Unions raise the wages of middle- and lower-middle-class workers, and they boost wages for their members as well as for non-union workers. The fall in union membership reduced unions' bargaining power as well as wage growth, particularly among middle- and low-income workers (Bureau of Labor Statistics 2017; Card 2001; Council of Economic Advisers 2015). On the minimum wage, see United States Department of Labor (2009). For contrasting views on the effect on employment, see Card and Krueger (1995) and Meer and West (2016). For the impact on the labor market generally and income inequality, see Kearney and Harris (2014); Congressional Budget Office (2014); and Autor, Manning, and Smith (2016).

30. Sawhill (2014).

31. Bloom (2017); Furman and Orszag (2015).

32. For the highest earners, this includes the 37 percent top income tax rate plus an additional 3.8 percent tax, representing either the net investment income tax for capital income, or the 2.9 percent Medicare payroll tax plus the 0.9 percent Medicare surtax for labor income.

33. Piketty, Saez, and Stantcheva (2014). In addition, CEO pay appears to be higher in countries with lower marginal tax rates and with weak corporate governance rules—places where CEOs have more incentive and more opportunity to seek rents.

34. Reeves (2017).

35. Chetty et al. (2014b) find that percentile rank measures of intergenerational mobility have been extremely stable for the 1971–1993 birth cohorts. Hauser (2010), Hertz (2007), and Lee and Solon (2009) find no trend in intergenerational income mobility over the last few decades. Aaronson and Mazumder (2008) and Putnam, Frederick, and Snellman (2012) find that income mobility has declined.

36. Causa and Johannson (2010); Corak (2013a); Corak, Lindquist, and Mazumder (2014); Reeves and Sawhill (2016). At least one measure of relative mobility is almost twice as high in Canada as in the United States. The probability that child raised in a household in the bottom 20 percent of the income distribution rises, as an adult, to a household in the top 20 percent of the income distribution is 13.5 percent in Canada compared to 7.5 percent in the United States (Chetty et al. 2014a; Corak and Heisz 1999).

37. Chetty et al. (2014a). Princeton University and Obama administration economist Alan Krueger (2012) labeled this relation the "Great Gatsby Curve," based on research by Miles Corak (2013b).

38. Poorer children grow up in households with fewer resources spent on them, in particular on education and enrichment expenses—books, computers, camps, and so on (Corak 2013a; Miller 2015). Relative to low-income youth living in areas with less inequality, youth who grow up in low-income households in areas with more inequality have worse outcomes—girls are more likely to give birth at a young age, and boys are more likely to terminate schooling early. This may be because these youths perceive from their surroundings that economic success is not available to them and that there is a lower return to investing in their human capital (Kearney and Levine 2014, 2016). Increased inequality in an area raises violent crime and incarceration rates and reduces children's academic achievement (Kelly 2000; Reardon 2011). Inequality leads to increased residential segregation across economic groups. This result, combined with the finding that the qualities of the neighborhood in which one grows up significantly affect one's chances for economic success, suggests another clear way through which inequality reduces economic mobility (Chetty, Hendren, and Katz 2016; Chyn 2016; Kneebone and Holmes 2016). Inequality raises mortality rates, a relationship found in the United States, Canada, and the United Kingdom (Case and Deaton 2015; Galea et al. 2011; Kaplan et al. 1996; Kennedy, Kawachi, and Prothow-Stith 1996; Marmot 2015; Tjepkema, Wilkins, and Long 2013).

39. Chetty et al. (2014b). Another study finds that between 1967 and 1983, the median lifetime income of men entering the labor force fell by between 10 percent and 19 percent, with almost no increase at all in the bottom three-quarters of the income distribution. At that same time, median earnings for women rose by between 22 percent and 33 percent but started from a very low base. For both groups, inequality in lifetime income has increased significantly (Guvenen et al. 2017).

40. The earliest economic thought on the subject hypothesized that inequality rose in the early stages of growth and then fell as growth became more widely shared, but the empirical support for this view is not strong (Fields 2001; Kuznets 1955).

41. Okun (1975).

42. Gale and Samwick (2017); Piketty, Saez, and Stantcheva (2014).

43. A recent OECD statistical study of 19 countries concluded that "income inequality has a negative and statistically significant impact on subsequent growth" (Cingano 2014). The study implies that the growth rate in the United States would have been more than one-fifth higher between 1990 and 2010 if the rise in inequality between 1985 and 2005 had not

occurred. Likewise, a recent IMF study finds that more equality generates more long-term growth, concluding that "lower net inequality is robustly correlated with faster and more durable growth, for a given level of redistribution" (Ostry, Berg, and Tsangarides 2014). Taking a longer view, another study tracked nine advanced countries from 1830–1850 to 1970–1985 and found that per capita income growth falls as the share of personal income going to the top 20 percent rises (Persson and Tabellini 1994). Furthermore, the effect is economically significant: an increase by one standard deviation in the income share of the top 20 percent lowers the average annual growth rate by almost half a percentage point. Alesina and Rodrick (1994) and Alesina and Perotti (1996) also find that inequality leads to less growth in panels of countries using data since the 1960s. In contrast, Forbes (2000) finds a positive relationship between inequality and growth in high- and middle-income countries. Barro (2000) finds a positive relationship in rich countries and a negative relationship in poor countries.

44. Aizer et al. (2014); Brown, Kowalski, and Lurie (2015); Deming (2009); Hoynes, Schanzenbach, and Almond (2016).

45. Solt (2008).

46. Reeves (2017).

47. Those in the top 0.01 percent (fewer than 32,000 people) accounted for 29 percent of all political contributions in the 2014 federal election cycle. From 2010 to 2014, 60 percent of super-PAC spending was financed by just 195 donors—about the top 1 percent of the top 1 percent of the top 1 percent. As of early 2016, the figures were even starker: a mere 50 individuals and their relatives had given 41 percent of all super-PAC contributions through the end of February (Gold and Narayanswamy 2016; Norden, Ferguson, and Keith 2016; Olsen-Phillips et al. 2015).

48. Prat, Puglisi, and Snyder (2010).

49. Friedman (1962).

50. Agnello and Sousa (2014) studied 18 industrialized countries from 1978 to 2009 and found that income inequality rises during times of fiscal consolidation. "Austerity packages are, overall, regressive in nature." Spending cuts seem to be particularly regressive in nature. When the focus is on tax increases, the consolidation packages seem to equalize the distribution, especially when above 0.57 percent of GDP. This suggests that "properly designed tax-based consolidation plans could be an effective tool for reducing income inequality." They conclude that "reducing the government debt and deficit could be achieved in an equitable way via tax-hikes."

51. Scheve and Stasavage (2016).

6

The Politics of Deficits,
the Deficits of Politics

Sooner or later, every discussion of fiscal policy reform turns to politics and the numerous challenges it creates. Politicians find it easy to put off hard fiscal choices that impose costs on current voters and mainly benefit future generations. To the extent that the public pays attention at all, it does not present a clear mandate: Americans want less red ink but not the higher taxes or lower benefits needed to get there. By creating a governing system that's designed to make big changes hard to enact under the best of circumstances, the Founding Fathers didn't make life easy for today's policymakers. The increasing partisanship of recent years only makes it more difficult to build consensus.

Despite these obstacles, fiscal reform remains possible. We've addressed similar—though smaller—problems as recently as the 1980s and 1990s, with the same governing system. And, at least in principle, fiscal responsibility aligns with the goals of both conservatives and liberals. In the absence of a fiscal crisis that can galvanize the nation, however, we'll need both political leadership as well as a campaign to educate and energize the public to build support for reform.

Fiscal problems are not new. They contributed to the fall of several great societies, from the Romans to the Ottoman Empire.[1] America, as noted, has wrestled with fiscal questions since its founding. But today's fiscal challenge may prove particularly hard to address.

For starters, neither conservatives nor liberals make debt reduction their top priority. Conservatives are more interested in lower taxes, liberals in addressing current social needs. Republicans and conservative leaders decried deficits during the Obama administration, but when President Trump was elected, they said that deficit concerns were just a "talking point" and proceeded to pass a large tax cut and a major spending package. Democrats and liberal leaders argued that long-term debt did not need to be addressed in the latter years of the Obama administration but criticized Republicans for raising the debt via their recent legislative actions.[2]

When they do focus on long-term debt, the parties don't agree on the source of the problem. Conservatives point to rising spending on Social Security, Medicare, and other programs; liberals point to low tax burdens compared to other countries, particularly on the wealthiest Americans.

Resolving fiscal issues will pit some Americans against others. It would probably be easier for the country to pull together if, instead, we were facing a foreign enemy. But in the words of Pogo, "We have met the enemy and it is us."[3] To address the fiscal problem, we will need to make choices that hurt some groups of Americans and sacrifice some short-term benefits in the name of long-term gains.

In addition, rising deficits and debt do not constitute an immediate, tangible emergency that will force action. That's a recipe for inaction, especially when politicians already have incentives to postpone hard choices and often don't look past the next election. The Bowles-Simpson Commission in 2010 tried to market the fiscal problem as a "Moment of Truth," but, due to the gradual nature of the problem (discussed in Chapter 4), we do not face a *moment* when we must act.[4] Instead, we face the slow weakening of our economy over the course of years.

A key obstacle to fiscal reform is that the benefits—a stronger, fairer economy, and higher living standards—are not easy to see. They accrue mainly to future generations, and only over a period of time. Nor is the connection between fiscal reform and better outcomes self-evident. Cause and effect are obvious when an earthquake reduces a building to rubble, but it's not easy to discern that a building never got built in the first place because high government debt crowded out private investment opportunities.

In contrast, the potential costs of reforms—spending cuts or tax hikes—are clearly visible and more immediate. Those who would bear those burdens tend to object passionately, lobby lawmakers heavily, and contribute generously to political campaigns, capturing the attention of political leaders and distracting them from the broad gains that fiscal reform can create.[5] As Charles Schultze, President Lyndon Johnson's budget director, once said, elected leaders often act as if they were complying with a political version of the Hippocratic Oath: "Never be seen to do obvious harm."[6] At the same time, special-interest groups lobby for preferential tax and spending programs that often make the long-term debt problem worse.

The structure of our government makes a solution even harder to enact. Legislation must work its way through congressional committees, obtain passage in the House and Senate, and be signed by the president. If the president vetoes it, Congress can override the veto only with a two-thirds vote in both the House and Senate.

Recent political trends have further complicated matters. Each political party used to be home to a wide diversity of positions, with Democrats ranging from liberal to fairly conservative and Republicans ranging from conservative to fairly liberal (Figure 6.1). In recent years, however, the political parties have become

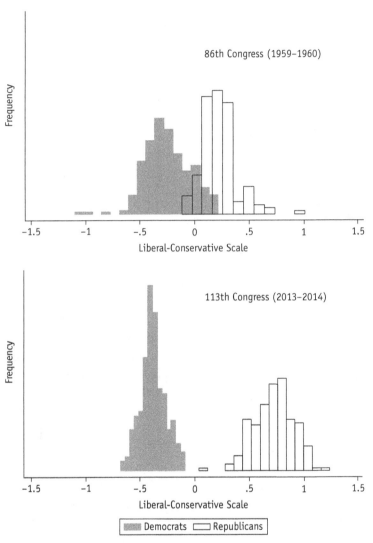

Figure 6.1. Ideology in the House of Representatives. (a) 86th Congress (1959–1960). (b) 113th Congress (2013–2014). Each bar contains the data points within its width. Height represents proportional frequency where the sum of each bar's area is equal to one. N(D86)=283. N(R86)=156. N(D113)=205. N(R113)=239. The X-axis is the first dimension in Carroll et al. (2015) and can be interpreted in most periods as government intervention in the economy or liberal-conservative in the modern era. Carroll et al. (2015).

more polarized—the center of gravity has shifted to the right for Republicans and to the left for Democrats—and they have "sorted" or become more uniform—the diversity of views within each has declined.[7] As a result, ideological overlap across the parties has all but disappeared. Conservative southern Democrats and liberal Rockefeller Republicans—who in the past could build coalitions with like-minded members of the other party—are largely creatures of the past.[8] By standard measures, polarization in Congress has risen to its highest level since the end of the 19th century.

The causes of polarization include rising income inequality, increased housing segregation, and splintered media markets. Political redistricting has also played an important role, creating "safe" districts where incumbents worry more about facing challenges in primaries by more extreme members of their own party than losing to the other party in the general election.[9]

Polarization and sorting have made compromise more difficult. Things have gotten so bad that American Enterprise Institute political scientist Norm Ornstein says we are now facing what he calls "tribalism"—the idea that "if you are for it, I am reflexively against it, even if I was for it yesterday."[10] As one of many examples, Ornstein notes that in 2010, Republican senator John McCain and then minority leader Mitch McConnell opposed a bipartisan debt reduction commission once President Obama supported it. Earlier that year, McConnell had endorsed the very same commission, and McCain had signed on as a co-sponsor of the proposed legislation authorizing it.

Ornstein and former Brookings Institution political scientist Thomas Mann have excoriated Republicans in general, and the Tea Party in particular, on this issue, referring to recent versions of the party as "insurgent outliers."[11] Numerous other commentators, including many Republicans, agree that conservatives have come to see compromise as caving.[12] A 2014 Pew survey found that among consistently conservative respondents, 63 percent would prefer leaders to stick to their positions, compared to 32 percent who favor compromise. In contrast, 82 percent of consistently liberal respondents believed political leaders should compromise, compared to 14 percent who opposed it.[13]

With all its checks and balances, our political system requires a willingness to compromise, an understanding that governing is the art of the possible. For example, in the 1980s, President Reagan, a classic conservative, and House Speaker Tip O'Neill, an old-school liberal, disagreed fundamentally about the role of government, but they came together on several issues including a land-mark Social Security reform. Those days are long gone. Major legislation—like the 2017 tax cut under President Trump or the 2010 Affordable Care Act under President Obama—now routinely attracts support from only one party.

The lack of collaboration and trust is a particular problem for long-term fiscal policy because reaching a solution will entail phasing in significant policy changes that remain in effect for a long time. Each party must not only be willing to compromise; it must also trust that the other will carry out the agreement. No one wants to be left holding the bag, watching the policy changes they oppose be implemented on time while the ones they support are tossed aside.

In the category of making governing difficult, a special citation should go to the "No New Taxes" pledge. Created by the lobbying group Americans for Tax Reform, which is headed by Grover Norquist,[14] the pledge says:

> I, _____, pledge to the taxpayers of the _____ district of the State of _____ and to the American people that I will: One, oppose any and all efforts to increase the marginal income tax rates for individuals and/or businesses; and Two, oppose any net reduction or elimination of deductions and credits, unless matched dollar for dollar by further reducing tax rates.[15]

In the 114th Congress of 2015–2016 (the most recent Congress for which we have such data), 89 percent of Republicans had signed the pledge, including almost all the party's leaders. Only one Democrat had signed it.

It's a remarkable statement, implying that *no* economic problem or situation *ever* merits higher income tax rates, and *no* public policy goal other than cutting tax rates merits cuts in deductions. It obviously flies in the face of logic and reality. Every reasonable person understands that there are situations in which the country needs to raise taxes. World Wars I and II come to mind. Every budget commission proposes a package with both tax increases and spending cuts. The public strongly favors a fiscal solution that combines spending cuts and tax increases (discussed later). Even Ronald Reagan saw fit to raise taxes several times.[16] The pledge makes fiscal negotiation next to impossible. If one side refuses even to consider raising taxes, how can the other side be expected to negotiate on spending cuts?

The pledge is also deceptive. It cynically focuses on taxes, since no one enjoys paying them. But Norquist's real goal, in his own words, is "to cut the government in half in 25 years, to get it down to the size where we can drown it in the bathtub."[17] So, why not pledge never to raise spending? Because voters—and pledge signers—like government spending.[18] Indeed, most Republicans who voted for the 2018 budget deal that substantially increased spending (as well as, of course, for the 2017 tax cut) are pledge signers.[19]

The pledge is based on the notion that lower revenues will generate lower spending—the "starve the beast" theory, discussed in Chapter 2.[20] US experience disproves this idea. In 1964, 1981, 2001, 2003, and 2017, major tax cuts did not lead to lower spending; instead, spending rose. Formal analysis confirms these impressions and shows that tax cuts that are designed to reduce the size of government do not succeed and may actually lead to increases in government spending.[21] In contrast, effective budget discipline tends to work only when it's imposed on both taxes and spending at the same time. In the 1983 Social Security reforms and the 1990 and 1993 budget deals, Congress and the White House did just that, slashing spending and raising taxes.

The pledge's cynicism and irresponsibility have been highlighted by the left, of course, but also by the right. Glenn Hubbard, who served as chair of President George W. Bush's Council of Economic Advisers and an adviser to Mitt Romney in 2012, wrote (along with Tim Kane) that "what is left in the hardened anti-tax stance of the Republicans is not a defense of limited government but simply low taxes alongside rising debt." Former senator Tom Coburn, a stalwart conservative, called the starve-the-beast strategy a disaster.[22]

Unfortunately, Democrats have played the pledge game, too, but not as seriously as Republicans. Barack Obama and Hillary Clinton promised not to raise taxes on those with incomes below $250,000.[23] In 2013, 44 House Democrats wrote to President Obama, stating they "will vote against any and every cut to Medicare, Medicaid and Social Security benefits."

In a 2015 Washington Post–ABC News poll, only 23 percent said the next president should pledge never to raise taxes, compared to 72 percent who opposed that step.[24] The bottom line is that a fiscal solution would be easier to reach if political leaders simply pledged not to make any more pledges regarding fiscal policy.

Public opinion on deficits is decidedly a mixed bag. "In my years of polling," Andrew Kohut, who for many years directed the Pew Research Center, wrote in 2012, "there has never been an issue such as the deficit on which there has been such a consensus among the public about its importance—and such a lack of agreement about acceptable solutions."[25] After sifting through mountains of polling data, here's my take on how Americans view fiscal policy solutions:

• *Deficits and debt are important problems but not the most important matters.*

Former vice president Dick Cheney once exclaimed, "Reagan proved deficits don't matter" to the public.[26] A more accurate view is that Americans have long been concerned about deficits and debt but accept them in certain situations. While the deficit consistently appears in polls as an important economic issue, it's rarely listed as the top concern.[27]

In Gallup polls in the mid-1980s, more than 80 percent of respondents thought the deficit was a "fairly serious" or "very serious" problem. Between 2011 and 2014, a period when fiscal policy was often front-page news because of numerous showdowns between congressional Republicans and President

Obama, Gallup polls show that more than 80 percent said they worried a "great deal" or a "fair amount" about federal spending and the budget deficit. Recent polls continue to show the deficit and debt as issues that concern a substantial share of Americans, though the share has fallen as the economy has recovered.[28]

- *Sustained deficits will hurt our children.*

Americans link fiscal policy with concerns about their family and children. In a CBS/*New York Times* poll in 2011, 90 percent of respondents were "very" or "somewhat" concerned "that deficits would create hardships for future generations."[29] In an NBC/*Wall Street Journal* poll that year, 80 percent were concerned "a great deal" or "quite a bit" with how the deficit would affect their family's future.[30]

- *Concern over fiscal policy has a distinctly partisan tilt.*

Concern about debt generally varies depending on which party holds the White House. Typically, Republicans care more about the debt than Democrats when a Democrat holds the White House, and vice versa. When Barack Obama was president in 2014, 80 percent of Republicans wanted to reduce the deficit, compared to 49 percent of Democrats. When George W. Bush was president, the ordering was reversed.[31]

- *Much government spending is waste, but policymakers shouldn't cut any specific program, especially not Social Security or Medicare.*

For decades, Americans have said that they think a large share—usually 40 to 50 percent—of government spending is wasted.[32] But support for spending cuts evaporates when people are asked about specific programs. In 2017, a Pew poll asked people about 14 budget items that, collectively, covered virtually all non-interest spending (see Table 6.1). In every area, more than half of respondents wanted to *increase or maintain* spending. The only area with even close to a third of respondents supporting cuts was the usual suspect, foreign aid. Support for cutting major programs was weak. Twenty percent wanted to cut military defense; less than 10 percent would cut Medicare or Social Security.[33]

- *Taxes should be more progressive, and policymakers should scale back tax expenditures in general—but no specific ones.*

Even before the 2017 tax cuts—which were tilted toward high-income households and slashed corporate taxes—most people thought that taxes on

Table 6.1. **Pew Poll Results about Spending Category Preferences**

"Would you increase, decrease or keep spending the same for . . ."

		Republicans (%)	Democrats (%)	Total (%)
Veterans' benefits	Decrease	6	1	3
	Increase	70	78	75
Education	Decrease	15	4	9
	Increase	52	78	67
Rebuilding highways, bridges	Decrease	7	7	7
	Increase	55	61	58
Medicare	Decrease	15	5	9
	Increase	35	61	51
Healthcare	Decrease	35	4	18
	Increase	28	71	50
Scientific research	Decrease	20	6	12
	Increase	33	60	48
Military defense	Decrease	8	27	20
	Increase	71	31	46
Environmental protection	Decrease	38	6	19
	Increase	23	61	46
Anti-terrorism in the United States	Decrease	7	15	11
	Increase	61	33	46
Social Security	Decrease	10	3	6
	Increase	36	53	46
Assistance to needy in United States	Decrease	37	6	21
	Increase	26	63	45
Assistance to unemployed	Decrease	44	10	24
	Increase	13	41	29
Assistance to needy in the world	Decrease	56	13	31
	Increase	13	41	29
State Dept. and embassies	Decrease	29	17	23
	Increase	10	20	15

Source: Pew Research Center (2017b).

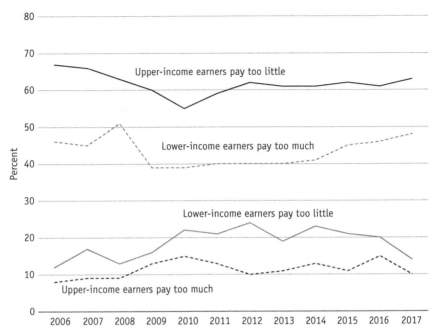

Figure 6.2. Views on the taxes paid by high- and low-income people. Gallup (2017).

the wealthy were too low and taxes on the poor were too high (Figure 6.2).[34] In fact, people were more concerned that corporations and the wealthy don't pay their fair share (62 percent and 60 percent, respectively) than they were about what they themselves are paying or how complex the tax code is, according to a 2017 Pew poll.[35] As noted earlier, tax expenditures act like spending programs in the tax code. Unsurprisingly then, people have views about tax expenditures that are similar to their views on spending. They support cuts to tax expenditures in general, but not cuts to specific provisions.[36]

- *A fiscal solution should include both spending cuts and tax increases, especially tax increases on high-income households, but it should preserve Social Security and Medicare benefits as they are, except for the wealthy.*

Polls show strong support for combining tax increases and spending cuts to address the fiscal challenge. In a 2013 Pew poll, 63 percent favored such a combination, compared to 20 percent who would only "cut major programs" and 7 percent who would only "increase taxes."[37] Most Democrats, Independents, and non–Tea Party Republicans favored the combination, as did 44 percent of Tea Party members.

Where does that leave us? Do we have any hope of reaching agreement on these issues? I believe the answer is yes. Our history shows that what seems politically impossible one day can become politically feasible the next. Former senator Bill Bradley, a chief architect of the 1986 Tax Reform Act, once said that tax reform was impossible until 15 minutes before it happened.[38] Let's remember: we have a lot to gain from fiscal reform—a more productive economy, a fairer distribution of income, a better future for our children, a more secure retirement, better healthcare, a stronger social safety net, and so on. So we can't simply surrender to the political obstacles of the moment. Instead, let's look at how and why a creative and responsible solution to our fiscal challenge may spring forth.

First, some historical perspective: our fiscal problem was fairly manageable as recently as 2000, with the budget on track at that time to produce short-term surpluses and distant long-term deficits.[39] Although the obstacles within the structure of our government are real, they haven't proven insurmountable in the past. We'll likely try many different options first—deny the problem, hope it disappears, look for painless (albeit inadequate) solutions like eliminating foreign aid, and debate ideological proposals that have no prospects of being enacted, like privatizing Social Security or raising the top income tax rate to 80 percent. Only after that will our leaders and the public be ready to make the necessary compromises that will impose new burdens on tens of millions of people all over the country.

A broader perspective on societal conflict is also constructive. Recent political trends in the United States are real and troubling, but such issues tend to ebb and flow over time. The increased polarization and dysfunction of recent years could well generate a backlash.[40] We've been here before, with bitter divisions over major policy issues—for example, slavery in the 19th century, isolationism in the 1930s, and civil rights in the 1950s and '60s. Our debates can be bitter, our rhetoric ugly. But we've often made progress, even during times of polarization.

The ground may, in fact, be shifting a bit. Republicans, for instance, are pushing back against the no-tax pledge. While about 98 percent of Republicans in the 112th Congress (2011–2012) signed it, new members in the 114th Congress (2015–2016) were more reluctant to do so, with only 75 percent signing on.[41] In addition, several prominent signers—including former and current senators Tom Coburn, Lindsey Graham, and John McCain—have said that they don't feel bound by it and that their fundamental pledge is to serve their country.[42]

The fiscal changes that policymakers enacted in the 1980s and early 1990s to address the deficits of that period share much in common with the fiscal changes that we must enact in the future, although the problem is bigger now. That political leaders of that period successfully addressed fiscal problems should provide some optimism and a model of how to get things done.

What would it take to achieve major fiscal change?[43] In the past, it often took a crisis. Wars have prompted our leaders to enact significant changes in borrowing, spending, and taxing. A crisis, of course, need not be as dramatic as a war. Fiscal or economic deadlines, real or imagined, have spurred changes. President Reagan and Congress enacted major reforms to Social Security in 1983 as its trust fund faced a serious cash-flow crisis; it would have run out of money in a few months, leaving it unable to pay full benefits to eligible recipients. The 2011 budget deal, which helped chip away at current and projected deficits, was spurred by an artificial crisis—Republicans' refusal to raise the debt ceiling as a potential default loomed. This is not meant to condone the manufacturing of artificial crises, of course; as it turns out, policymakers have reversed a significant share of the severe cuts in discretionary spending enacted in 2011.

But it does not always take a "back-to-the-wall" crisis. The budget agreements in 1990 and 1993 occurred in the presence of very high government interest payments, which worried many people, but policymakers did not face a specific deadline, just a concern that the fiscal situation was moving in the wrong direction.

Absent a crisis, which could bring people together, the key imperative is to break through the "chicken and egg" problem that plagues public discourse on long-term fiscal policy. Voters don't focus on the problem because their leaders don't raise the issue. And their leaders don't talk about it because the voters don't focus on it.

Let's start with the public. We have good reasons to doubt the power of public opinion to influence fiscal policy choices. First, Americans often don't know key aspects of spending and tax policy. They vastly overestimate spending on foreign aid and, to a lesser extent, defense, food and nutrition assistance, education, and public broadcasting.[44] Consequently, they tend to think we can address our fiscal challenge by targeting only those programs for cuts. If they don't understand the facts, they are less likely to be able to exert concerted pressure on policymakers to reach real solutions. The same is true if they have contradictory views about fiscal policy, as noted earlier.

Second, people often don't recognize the positive role that government plays in their lives on an ongoing basis. A 2012 Cornell University study indicated that 96 percent of survey respondents had benefited from a federal social program at some point in their lives. Yet only 43 percent of those surveyed believed they had used such a program. To be sure, many may not recognize a certain federal provision, such as the tax subsidy for employer-provided health insurance, as a "government program." But even among recipients of two major programs—Social Security and unemployment insurance—more than 40 percent said they had never received a benefit from a federal social program.[45] A constituent's comment at a 2009 town hall meeting in South Carolina that political leaders should "keep your government hands off my Medicare"[46] highlights the strong public disconnect between the government assistance that people actually receive and the government assistance they think they receive.

Third, in at least one recent policy change, policymakers essentially ignored public opinion. In the months before passing the 2017 tax bill, policymakers discussed proposals that were extremely unpopular with the public.[47] Yet the Republicans pushed ahead, reducing taxes for high-income households and for corporations, two groups that strong majorities of the public consistently thought should pay more, not less. Why weren't Republicans conforming to public views? Because they were responding to their donors. Representative Chris Collins said that donors pressured him to "get [the tax bill] done or don't ever call me again," and Senator Lindsey Graham warned that "financial contributions [to Republicans] will stop" if they did not pass tax legislation.[48]

Nevertheless, public opinion can still have an important impact on our elected leaders' behavior. Nothing short of a major campaign to inform and inspire the American public is needed, though. Ross Perot's 1992 presidential campaign, in which he hammered relentlessly on fiscal issues and drew 19 percent of the popular vote, is the best example in the last several decades, and it probably played an important role in President Clinton's willingness to raise taxes the following year. It is not hard to imagine that as deficits and debt continue to rise and increasingly constrain the government's ability to address problems, long-term fiscal issues will become more salient to the American public.

Political leadership will be crucial, too. Leaders have fundamentally changed the nation's fiscal course, from Alexander Hamilton to Franklin Roosevelt to Ronald Reagan. White House leadership is particularly important because the president can best address a national audience and provide "cover" for lawmakers to make the fiscal policy compromises that serve the national interest but may hurt particular constituencies. By blessing the general goal of tax reform in the 1980s—which took benefits away from many groups—Reagan showed how presidents can lead and gave lawmakers the political room to make sometimes painful compromises. More generally, in the 1980s and 1990s, congressional leaders assumed the fiscal challenge as their cause and made significant headway.

Leadership would be easier under a unified government, with the White House and both houses of Congress controlled by the same party, but it would be more *effective* in a split government. Divided government has usually been a requisite for addressing fiscal problems. All but one of the fiscal deals in the 1980s and 1990s occurred under split government. That is, when the center of gravity of each party was closer to the political middle and when each had a wide diversity of views within its membership, each party was well positioned to reach a compromise. Each party would get some of what it sought, but each would also accept a bit of what the other side sought and it had opposed. Republicans would get domestic spending cuts but also accept tax increases; Democrats would secure tax increases but also accept domestic spending cuts. Each party could boast about what it secured and blame the other for what it was forced to accept. Unfortunately, the new political dynamics make such compromise between the parties less likely.

With a unified government, the party in charge can enact its own fiscal solution as long as it maintains the support of enough of its own members. But, historically, unified governments tend to *raise* long-term deficits, not lower them. Democrats in the 1960s, Republicans in the early 2000s, Democrats in 2009–2010, and Republicans in 2017–2018 cut taxes and increased spending, boosting short- and long-run deficits. The one exception was in 1993, when President Clinton worked with congressional Democrats, who controlled both chambers, to craft a deficit-reduction agreement and enact it with only Democratic votes.

A fiscal solution that a unified government passes would likely be more partisan than a compromise reached by the two parties. As a result, it may prove less stable. Even if, say, an all-Democratic government enacted legislation that would truly address the long-term fiscal challenge, if Republicans did not support it they could repeal major elements of it once they returned to power. In 2001, for example, an all-Republican government cut taxes across the board, notably reducing the top income tax rate that President Clinton and a Democratic-controlled Congress raised in 1993. In 2010, President Obama and congressional Democrats enacted health reform without a single Republican vote, and Republicans partially reversed this legislation in 2017.

These political concerns highlight the beneficial role of a strong "center" in American politics. Though the center has hollowed out in recent years, a centrist coalition would likely be more stable with respect to changing political winds than a group on either extreme of the political spectrum.

The stability of a fiscal deal depends not just on whether it stems from a centrist or bipartisan coalition but also on its contents. To be long lasting, it must include *both* spending cuts and tax increases. Conservatives won't agree to a solution that doesn't rein in spending, certainly on the domestic side and perhaps for defense as well. Liberals won't agree to a solution that doesn't raise taxes, particularly on high-income households, in order to help reduce inequality and also to minimize domestic spending cuts.

Such a long-term solution won't likely eliminate our major tax and spending programs. These programs have been around a long time, in part because they enjoy broad public support. Thus, the nation will likely need to establish new taxes to raise more revenue. I propose a value-added tax and a carbon tax in subsequent chapters. Either new tax, of course, would face political obstacles, but either may prove a more viable political alternative to raising income tax rates sharply or scaling back popular spending programs.

In recent years, some budget experts and organizations have sought a sweeping "grand bargain" among conservatives and liberals that would simultaneously address the long-term fiscal challenge; restructure Social Security, Medicare, and Medicaid; reform taxes; raise revenues; and fix the budget process to better control deficits in the future. But our political leaders won't likely address all of those issues in one fell swoop and they don't need to. To do everything at once is simply too complicated. If the problem is too big, politicians will respond by ignoring it. Each issue will require a separate, intensive, time-consuming effort by the White House, Congress, and the public. This may generate the need to enact simultaneous tax and spending changes, as in 1983, 1990, and 1993. For example, legislators might enact a value-added tax whose revenues were earmarked to finance healthcare spending.

From 1982 to 1993, policymakers enacted an extraordinary series of measures—raising taxes significantly in 1982 (and, to a less extent, in subsequent years); reforming Social Security to solidify its financing in 1983; reforming the tax code in 1986; and enacting significant budget agreements in 1990 and 1993 that controlled spending while raising taxes. Together, these actions helped change the nation's fiscal trajectory, turning deficits into surpluses, while addressing other pressing issues. But they required 11 years of effort and a series of agreements, not one all-encompassing measure.

Some people believe that a key element of fiscal reform is changing the budget process—the steps lawmakers take to pass a budget—or budget rules—which specify permissible outcomes and how policy must change if those outcomes are not attained.[49] This process often fails, leaving important spending programs in a state of uncertainty.[50] If they can't even "walk" through the annual budget process, policymakers will never be able to "run" toward sophisticated solutions to the complex long-term problems we discuss throughout the rest of this book.

My general view is that reform of process and rules is neither a panacea nor a substitute for making hard choices. As Rudy Penner, former director of the CBO, has said, "The process isn't the problem, the problem is the problem."[51] Still, there is a limited but useful role for process and rule changes.

Good rules make the government function more effectively, without biasing choices. For example, for reasons discussed in Chapter 1, it would make sense to get rid of the debt ceiling, or at least stipulate that if Congress has voted for a spending program it has also authorized the government to pay for that program.[52]

Likewise, to avoid the costs of a government shutdown, Congress should enact a rule that if appropriations bills are not passed on time, a continuing resolution that funds the government at the previous year's inflation-adjusted levels would *automatically* occur.[53] The frequent failure to ratify a budget in a timely manner breeds uncertainty about whether programs will continue. This makes the operation of government agencies more difficult. Shutdowns are expensive: the 2013 shutdown reduced GDP by $24 billion.[54] The confidence-sapping effect on the public was probably far larger.[55] Moreover, the notion that the government should shut down because of relatively small disagreements in the desired funding in one or a few areas defies logic and common sense.[56]

Budget rules tend to work best when they apply to things that policymakers can control and when they are used to enforce agreements that have already been reached. For example, the PAYGO rules enacted in the 1990 budget deal and extended through the early 2000s required policymakers to pay for new mandatory programs.[57] Since taxes and mandatory spending are handled by the same committees in each chamber, the rules applied to items policymakers could control. The rules also enforced an agreed-upon bipartisan framework for tax increases and spending cuts.

In contrast, rules cannot force lawmakers to do things they don't want to do. Nor do they work if they stipulate limits on items—such as the overall deficit—that political leaders cannot control in the first place. The inability of the Gramm-Rudman-Hollings legislation to make Congress reach deficit targets in the 1980s is a good example of both points.

Finally, there's the prospect of setting up a commission to make a long-term fiscal reform proposal. Normally, that's what Congress does when it *doesn't* want to deal with an issue—such as with the Bowles-Simpson Commission in 2010. Indeed, there is a long history of failed commissions on all sorts of policy issues. But a commission might work under two conditions. First, policymakers should guarantee that the commission's proposals (assuming they are supported by a specified share of the commission members) will receive an up-or-down vote in Congress with no amendments in a timely manner or that the commission's proposals will be enacted unless Congress explicitly votes them down. This would reduce Congress's ability to create a commission as a way to avoid the issue. Second, each party should get to choose some members of the *other* party to be on the commission. This would bring in members who are less partisan and more willing to compromise. For example, in a commission of 16 members, Republicans should be able to choose four Democrats and Democrats choose four Republicans, with the rest being appointed by their own party.

At this point, we're left with several basic realities that will shape our path ahead. We face a long-term fiscal shortfall, an imbalance between what we expect from government and what we are willing to pay. We face a shortage of investment in people and in the economy. We cannot duck these challenges. Left unaddressed, they surely will weaken our economy and limit the living standards of our people.

We collect our revenue mostly from a few key sources (personal income taxes and the payroll tax), and we spend the money mostly on a few key items (Social Security, Medicare, Medicaid, defense, and interest). These major tax and spending pieces have been in place for decades because they enjoy broad public support, and policymakers will be hard-pressed to radically revamp them. However, as much as Americans would like to, we can't address our long-term fiscal challenges just by cutting unpopular items, like foreign aid or congressional salaries, because they represent tiny shares of the budget.

We've faced other fiscal challenges in our past, periods in which deficits were rising and debt was accumulating. But we can't hope to address today's fiscal challenge as we addressed so many of our previous ones because today's projected fiscal shortfall is different. It's not driven by a weak economy or a war. Instead, it's the result of an aging population, rising healthcare costs, and limited revenue growth, and it is occurring against a backdrop of rising inequality and political partisanship. In the absence of action by policymakers, the problems will get worse.

We can't realistically address our fiscal challenge without taking a hard look at the entitlement programs. At the same time, however, we need to look at every other area of spending for potential cuts, to raise taxes to meet spending needs, and to remember to make sound investments in infrastructure, research, and children.

With all of that in mind, we now turn to the specific policy changes that will reduce the debt-to-GDP ratio from the projected 179 percent in 2050 under current policies to 60 percent at that time and that also will invest in our nation and its people—all of which is a prerequisite for preparing the nation for a healthy economic future.

Notes

1. Hubbard and Kane (2013).
2. In 2012, then-Senate Minority Leader Mitch McConnell called the debt the nation's "most serious long-term problem." That same year, Paul Ryan, in a speech at the Republican National Convention, stated that "in this generation, a defining responsibility of government is to steer our nation clear of a debt crisis while there is still time" (O'Keefe 2012; Ryan 2012). In 2017, Representative Mark Walker, chairman of the conservative Republican Study Committee, stated that "it's a great talking point when you have an administration that's Democrat-led. It's a little different now that Republicans have both houses and the administration" (Kaplan 2017). On the liberal side, in October 2016, just before the presidential election, economist Paul Krugman (2016) wrote that "putting the debt question aside, we are not in any way making the future worse." But just three months later, with the

economy in the same position as before, but with President Trump having won the election, Krugman (2017) criticized the proposed Trump tax cut proposals on the grounds that "they're going to blow up the deficit. . . . In fact, by crowding out investment it will somewhat reduce long-term economic growth."

3. Kelly (1970). This quote was featured in a 1970 comic strip, called *Pogo*. It was originally intended to call attention to humans' role in climate change.

4. National Commission on Fiscal Responsibility and Reform (2010).

5. Olson (1965); Rauch (1994).

6. Schultze (2010).

7. Studies suggest that Republicans have moved further to the right than Democrats have moved to the left (Hare and Poole 2014; Mann 2014).

8. For example, southern Democrats, who were about halfway between Republicans and northern Democrats in the 1940s, are now almost indistinguishable from northern Democrats. Moreover, in the late 1930s, more than 70 percent of members of Congress were moderates. That share has declined steadily to less than 7 percent in 2013–2014 (Poole and Rosenthal 2015).

9. Dews (2017); Orszag (2011).

10. Ornstein (2014).

11. Mann and Ornstein (2012).

12. Garver (2014); Rauch (2013).

13. Pew Research Center (2014b). Other polls by Pew and Gallup generally show consistent results.

14. Americans for Tax Reform (2012). The pledge is formally known as the "Taxpayer Protection Pledge."

15. Americans for Tax Reform (2013).

16. Bartlett (2011). As Reagan said in 1982: "The single most important question facing us tonight is: Do we reduce deficits and interest rates by raising revenue from those who are not now paying their fair share—or do we accept bigger budget deficits, higher interest rates and higher unemployment?" (Reagan 1982).

17. Norquist (2003).

18. In 2003, about 86 percent of members of Congress who had signed the pledge voted for the prescription drug benefit under Medicare, the biggest new entitlement since the creation of the Medicare program in 1965, creating a $16 trillion long-term liability with no intent or ability to pay for it (Boards of Trustees 2004, Table II.c23; Kelly and Gale 2004).

19. This compares the database in Americans for Tax Reform (2013) to the voting record in Congress.gov (2018).

20. Bartlett (2007).

21. Romer and Romer (2009).

22. Coburn (2012); Hubbard and Kane (2013, page 285).

23. Tankersley (2015).

24. *Washington Post*/ABC News (2015).

25. Kohut (2012).

26. Dickerson (2004).

27. Thorndike (2018).

28. Thorndike (2018).

29. CBS News/*New York Times* (2011).

30. Hart and McInturff (2011).

31. Pew Research Center (2014a).

32. Bowman, Rugg, and Marsico (2013).

33. Pew Research Center (2017b). Republicans were more willing to cut spending than Democrats, but even among Republicans, only foreign aid generated majority support for cuts. Only 10–15 percent of Republicans wanted to cut Social Security or Medicare, and more wanted increases in these programs than cuts.

34. Since 2006, 55 to 67 percent of respondents have said upper-income people pay too little, compared to 8 to 15 percent who say they pay too much. Between 39 and 51 percent say the poor pay too much, compared to 12 to 24 percent who say they pay too little (Gallup 2017).

35. Pew Research Center (2017a).

36. For instance, in 2012, Pew found that 54 percent of respondents supported limiting the amount of itemized deductions as a way to reduce the national debt (Pew Research Center 2012b). In a different poll, Pew found an almost even split on whether to limit the mortgage deduction as a way to reduce the deficit and national debt (Pew Research Center 2012a). But in 2011, Gallup found that large majorities oppose eliminating the mortgage interest deduction, deductions for state and local taxes, and deductions for charitable contributions (asked separately), either to lower income tax rates or reduce the deficit (Jones 2011).

37. Pew Research Center (2013).

38. Wyden (2010).

39. Auerbach and Gale (2000) reported a fiscal gap of just 0.3 percent of GDP through 2070 assuming that discretionary spending grew at the same rate as GDP. Note that this assumption is different from the baseline described in Chapter 3.

40. For opposing views on whether political dysfunction is here to stay, see Mayhew (2011) and Mann and Ornstein (2012).

41. "New Republicans" are defined here as senators or representatives who had not previously served in Congress. In the Senate, one of five new Republicans abstained from signing the pledge. In the House of Representatives, nine of 35 new Republicans abstained. Information on pledge signers comes from the Americans for Tax Reform database.

42. Associated Press (2008); Coburn (2012); Sullivan (2012).

43. Wholesale political reform is beyond the scope of the book, but it could contribute to fiscal reform. Political redistricting could reduce polarization and political leaders' unwillingness to compromise. Campaign finance reform could reduce the role of special interests and donors in the political process, a role that is usually corrosive with respect to long-term debt.

44. Opinion Research Corporation (2011).

45. Mettler and Koch (2012).

46. Rucker (2009).

47. Enten (2017).

48. Marcos (2017); Savransky (2017).

49. Altering the budget presentation—by presenting a capital budget or what are called generational accounts—is another "process" proposal that receives attention. But there is already plenty of information available if policymakers and the public choose to avail themselves of it. The United States does not have a capital budget, but the Office of Management and Budget annually releases a summary of federal investment as a supplement to the budget. Many states use a capital budget since capital spending is not subject to the balanced budget requirements they face. But several commissions and studies have recommended against a federal capital budget (Congressional Budget Office 2008; Government Accountability Office 1983; President's Commission on Budget Concepts 1967; and President's Commission to Study Capital Budgeting 1999). The reasons ranged from the concern that policymakers might define "capital expenses" too broadly to the confusion that would arise from mixing accrual accounting in the capital budget with cash-flow accounting in the operating budget. Other countries have experimented with capital budgeting, but its prevalence has decreased, and there are currently only a few countries with a distinct capital budget (Jacobs 2008). For discussion and critique of generational accounting, see Auerbach, Kotlikoff, and Gokhale (1991, 1994) and Congressional Budget Office (1995).

50. In theory, the budget process works in three stages. First, the president submits a budget to Congress in February, proposing levels for discretionary programs, and changes to the laws regarding taxes and mandatory spending, as well as detailed budgets by program.

Administration officials justify the president's budget at congressional hearings. Second, by April 15, Congress adopts a budget resolution that sets aggregate targets for taxes, mandatory spending, and each of 12 discretionary spending categories, such as defense, transportation, and agriculture. Third, consistent with the budget resolution, each chamber of Congress debates and passes 12 "appropriations bills" for discretionary spending as well as any bills that change mandatory spending or revenue. The House and Senate reconcile the bills in conference, each chamber passes the conference report, and the president signs it into law—all before the fiscal year starts on October 1.

51. Posner (2015). Or, as Jim Nussle (R-IA), former House Budget Committee chair, said, "Leadership is more important than process" (Nussle 2011).

52. Plumer (2013). Under the so-called Gephardt rule that was in place intermittently between 1979 and 2005, the House of Representatives automatically approved any new debt needed to finance the proposals in its budget resolution. Employing that rule—for both the House and Senate—and applying it to all legislation, would solve much, but not all, of the need for debt ceiling debates. It would cover changes in debt due to legislation, but not debt changes due to economic conditions.

53. Senator Rob Portman (R-OH) introduced bills in 2013 and 2015 that would make continuing resolutions automatic. His bill would initially fund government programs at their nominal levels. If Congress failed to pass a new appropriations bill, funding would be cut by one percentage point after 120 days and an additional percentage point each subsequent 90 days (Portman 2015). The problem with this proposal is that it builds in spending cuts. This is a good example of a rule that biases the solution in a particular direction, in this case toward spending cuts.

54. Perlberg (2013).

55. After the government shutdown, 33 percent of Americans cited dissatisfaction with government and elected officials as the nation's top issue—the highest percentage in Gallup's history since it began in 1939—and double the 16 percent figure from the previous month (Newport 2013).

56. Continuing resolutions have become vehicles for all sorts of unrelated issues. In 2016, a continuing resolution was held up because of a disagreement on whether to include funding to combat the water crisis in Flint, Michigan. There is a legitimate issue about whether and when the federal government should step in to help states and localities, but it is hard to believe it is worth disrupting the operations of the entire federal government to have that debate over one intervention. And that was just to keep the government open for about two months, at which point Congress had to act again (DeBonis 2016).

57. Specifically, the Budget Enforcement Act (BEA) introduced caps on discretionary spending and a "pay-as-you-go" (PAYGO) rule under which changes to tax and mandatory spending, taken together, could not add to the deficit. The BEA rules helped limit spending growth over the next decade (Auerbach 2008). But as deficits turned to surpluses in the late 1990s, lawmakers' resolve faded, and BEA expired in 2002. In 2010, President Obama and a Democratic Congress reestablished PAYGO rules. Budget deals in 2011, 2013, and 2015 updated caps on discretionary spending (Keith 2010; Rivlin and Dominici 2015).

7

Reforming Healthcare

Healthcare reform must be a central part of the fiscal solution. Healthcare programs already account for a quarter of the federal budget, and they will grow significantly as the population ages and medical technology evolves. Almost half of Americans get their health insurance through public programs, including Medicare for the elderly and Medicaid for the some of the poor, disabled, and elderly. Other programs serve low- to moderate-income children, members of the military, and veterans; provide tax subsidies for healthcare insurance; and subsidize insurance purchases for low- and moderate-income families in the private market.

We like to think that we have the world's best health system, and in some ways we do. Our doctors and hospitals use state-of-the-art technology, and we're a world leader in pharmaceutical innovations and in treating heart conditions, hypertension, cancer, and other major diseases. But too many people lack health insurance, which impairs their health and causes economic hardship. And our costs are too high. Healthcare spending has been rising for several decades, and, counting both public and private outlays, we spend far more than any other country with little difference in health outcomes. Slower spending growth would free up resources for other uses, which would help the economy grow faster, boost wages, and raise living standards.

Notably, these are issues with the *healthcare system*, not just government programs. Our policies, therefore, must induce change in both private and government healthcare. Fortunately, precisely because it plays such a large role in health insurance, the federal government can induce private-sector changes by reforming its own programs.[1]

In 2010, President Obama and a Democratic-controlled Congress enacted the Affordable Care Act (ACA, also known as "Obamacare"). It required people to obtain adequate insurance coverage, created online marketplaces ("exchanges") that centralized information about private insurance plans, stopped insurance companies from refusing coverage or raising premiums due to applicants' pre-existing conditions, heavily subsidized states that expanded their Medicaid programs, slowed Medicare spending, and provided incentives for better medical care. The law has raised coverage, slowed healthcare spending growth, and improved the quality of care.

Despite these gains, President Trump and a Republican-controlled Congress undid parts of the ACA in 2017 and 2018. That's the wrong direction for policy. Policymakers should reinstate the ACA provisions that were removed. To raise coverage further, they should convince the states that have not expanded Medicaid to do so, and they should create a "public option" for health insurance in the exchanges. To curtail costs, the government should pay medical providers based on the quality of care they provide and the patient outcomes they secure, not the services they provide. Medicare should expand its use of competitive bidding, and it should get the same drug price discounts as other government programs. Policymakers should limit tax subsidies for health insurance and adjust taxes on alcoholic beverages to better account for their social costs.

These reforms would raise insurance coverage, improve care, and make people healthier. They would take a big bite out of the fiscal shortfall, reducing the debt-to-GDP ratio by about 18 percentage points by 2050 (Appendix Table 7.1).

The two broad problems noted earlier—low access and high costs—help frame the discussion. Regarding access, most Americans believe the federal government should ensure that people have health insurance.[2] About 91 percent of Americans had private or public health insurance in 2018.[3] The remaining 9 percent were disproportionately young adults (aged 26–34), minorities, or those with low incomes. Among them, some don't want to pay for coverage they think they don't need, but most cite cost as a barrier. The failure of 17 states to expand Medicaid under the ACA explains why many poor people remain uninsured.[4]

About 175 million people received health insurance through employer-sponsored plans in 2018.[5] Health insurance is the most popular fringe benefit among workers and it's not subject to income tax, even though it's a form of income that workers receive. That tax exemption reduces the cost of buying healthcare by a third for middle-income families and by half for high-income families.[6] But it also encourages families to use more health services than they need and it costs the government lots of money—a whopping $341 billion in forgone revenues in 2017, almost as much as federal spending on Medicaid.[7]

About 24 million people bought private insurance directly in 2018.[8] About 40 percent of them used the ACA's federal- and state-run exchanges. The federal government subsidizes purchases in the exchanges through progressive refundable tax credits for individuals with household incomes between 100 and 400 percent of the poverty line, or up to $97,200 in income for a family of four in 2018.[9] The other 60 percent bought insurance directly or went through an insurer or broker.[10] Individual and small-group plans are typically more expensive than employer-provided plans because the smaller group size means that overall costs are more variable and thus costlier to insure.

Medicare provides insurance for people aged 65 and over.[11] In 2018, it covered about 60 million people and, after Social Security, was the largest federal program, costing $583 billion in net spending. Medicare accounts for 20 percent of all national healthcare spending. The program has four parts. Everyone who is at least 65 years old is eligible for Part A, often called traditional Medicare, which is free and covers care in hospitals, homes, nursing homes, or hospice centers. Part B, called supplementary medical insurance, is voluntary but requires participating individuals to pay premiums. Like private insurance, it covers physician services, outpatient care, lab tests and preventive visits; participants pay a monthly premium and face deductibles and copayments. Part D—jumping out of order for a moment—subsidizes prescription drugs for Medicare enrollees and is available only through private insurance plans. Part C—called Medicare Advantage—lets beneficiaries receive Medicare benefits (Parts A, B, and often D) by joining a private insurance plan. Medicare Advantage covers about one-third of all Medicare beneficiaries.[12] To supplement Medicare coverage, some elderly buy "Medigap" policies, private insurance plans that typically cover deductibles and copayments that Medicare does not cover and sometimes cap lifetime out-of-pocket payments as well.

Medicaid provides health insurance for some low-income children, families, and individuals; the aged; and the disabled. People move on and off Medicaid as their economic status changes. In any given month in 2018, the program financed healthcare services for about 68 million people. Over the year, though, it reached about 100 million individuals, or roughly 30 percent of Americans.[13] Medicaid is a crucial part of children's healthcare across the country. Children make up almost half of all recipients, and Medicaid covers an astonishingly large share of young children—about 45 percent—nationwide. Medicaid is a federal-state program, with the federal government paying half the costs in the richest states, rising to 75 percent in the poorer states.[14] In 2018, Medicaid accounted for 17 percent of national healthcare spending, including federal spending of about $380 billion, making it the third largest federal program.[15]

In 2018, the Children's Health Insurance Program provided insurance to roughly 7 million children and pregnant women in families with incomes that are too high to qualify for Medicaid but too low to afford private plans.[16] Eligibility and programs vary by state. Most states cover children who live in families with income up to 200 percent of the poverty line. Like Medicaid, CHIP is a federal-state program. States can use CHIP funds to expand their Medicaid programs for children, create their own CHIP program, or have a combination of the two.[17]

The Veterans Health Administration (VHA) provides an integrated network of healthcare facilities for almost 9 million veterans, including medical centers, outpatient clinics, and nursing homes.[18] The military provides care—through a network of facilities and a health insurance plan called Tricare—to more than 9 million people around the world, including active duty and retired service members, their families, and surviving family members.[19]

Having health insurance improves people's health and financial status and reduces death for preventable reasons.[20] Moreover, better health for any partic-ular individual can lead to better health for others by reducing the spread of dis-ease. Of course, personal choices and social factors affect health, too, suggesting that the social spending programs advocated in Chapter 9 could well help to improve health in addition to their other positive impacts.

Medicare substantially raises access to health insurance and reduces financial risks among the elderly.[21] Medicaid makes people more likely to use health serv-ices, reduces the chances of having unpaid medical bills and catastrophic out-of-pocket medical spending, reduces rates of depression, improves self-reported ratings of good health, and reduces the incidence of low-birthweight infants and infant mortality.[22] Children enrolled in Medicaid or CHIP are more likely to have annual check-ups and flu shots, and less likely to have unmet medical needs (such as reading glasses).[23] They're more likely to complete high school and col-lege, and less likely to participate in risky behavior.[24] From a pure budgetary per-spective, a significant portion of Medicaid spending pays off in the long run via higher tax receipts and lower EITC payments.[25]

Turning to cost issues, healthcare spending averaged more than $11,000 per person in 2018 and is distributed very unevenly. The 50 percent of patients with the lowest spending accounted for just 3 percent of overall costs, while the top 5 percent accounted for half of all costs.[26] Most of the high spending is driven by patients who face a significant medical procedure (like treatment for a heart at-tack), have a chronic condition (like hypertension or diabetes), or are in the last year of life.[27] As a result, significant cost savings will come from reducing the in-cidence and severity of extremely expensive cases. Getting the 50 percent of the population with the lowest costs to reduce costs further won't save much money.

Healthcare spending—both public and private—has grown dramatically over time, from about 5 percent of GDP in 1960, to about 9 percent by 1980, and more than 18 percent by 2018 (Figure 7.1). Over the past 25 years, spending per beneficiary in inflation-adjusted terms rose at about the same rate in the private sector as in Medicare. Medicaid per-beneficiary spending grew more slowly.[28]

The long-term rise in healthcare spending stems from several factors that interact with each other in complex ways. Five items—technological

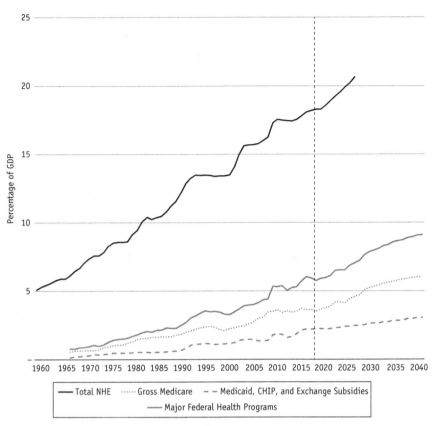

Figure 7.1. Health spending over time (1960–2040). Projections of Medicaid include only the federal share. Major federal programs include gross Medicare, Medicaid, Children's Health Insurance Program (CHIP), and exchange subsidies. Author's calculations; Boards of Trustees (2018); Centers for Medicare and Medicaid Services (2018a, 2018b); Congressional Budget Office (2018b).

innovation; health insurance expansion; fee-for-service plans; trends in income, aging, and health; and administrative costs—are worth a closer look.[29]

Technological innovations are the single biggest factor in boosting healthcare spending.[30] Many are expensive, raising overall healthcare spending (in part by making new procedures and services possible). They include imaging technologies, surgical procedures, cancer drugs, and surgical robots. Many have greatly improved the quality of healthcare.[31]

Health insurance is a big part of the story as well. It spread dramatically after World War II. Insurance reduces healthcare costs for consumers, encouraging them to use more healthcare services—perhaps more than they need. Out-of-pocket healthcare spending has stayed constant at about 2 percent of GDP over the last 60 years even though total healthcare spending rose substantially.[32]

The form of insurance has also boosted spending. Insurance companies, Medicare, and Medicaid in the past used a fee-for-service approach, with healthcare providers receiving payments for the services they perform, not the quality of the outcome.[33] That incentivizes doctors, hospitals, and other medical providers to provide too many services for which they are well compensated and too few that are poorly compensated. To put it bluntly, a significant amount of medical spending—as much as one-third in some studies—is unnecessary. For example, there is significant variation in healthcare treatments and expenses across the country without discernible differences in outcomes.[34]

Over the past 50 years, income, aging, and health trends have raised the demand for healthcare as well. Per-capita GDP has risen substantially, giving more Americans the resources to afford insurance and health treatments. The aging of the population has greatly boosted Medicare's rolls, with the share of the population over age 65 rising from less than 10 percent in 1970 to 16 percent in 2018. The share of Americans over age 85 has also risen dramatically, and Medicare spends twice as much annually per enrollee aged 85 to 94 as it does for those aged 65 to 74. Similarly, the share of Americans with a chronic health condition—for example, obesity or type 2 diabetes—has risen substantially.[35] Some 38 percent of adults were clinically obese in 2014, up from 15 percent in 1980,[36] and 60 percent of adults had at least one chronic disease in 2014, up from 45 percent in 2005.[37] The one-quarter of Americans with at least three chronic conditions accounts for two-thirds of all health spending.[38]

Administrative costs have risen dramatically.[39] Doctors deal with numerous insurance companies, each of which may have different billing procedures and requirements. Patients who deal with their providers and insurers face numerous filing issues.

Collectively, the factors above help explain why US healthcare spending has grown so much and point to why American healthcare spending is so much higher than in other countries. Whereas healthcare spending in the United States grew from 11 percent of GDP in 1990 to 17 percent in 2016, it grew from 7 percent of GDP to 11 percent in the rest of the G7 countries (Figure 7.2).[40] Public spending on healthcare as a share of the economy is about the same in the United States as in other advanced countries, but private spending here is much higher.[41]

Differences in healthcare spending between the United States and other advanced countries have grown dramatically since 1980 and are plausibly related to a variety of factors: the push toward deregulation in the 1980s and the absence of healthcare price controls, the greater increase in income inequality in the United States, and lower social spending in the United States.[42]

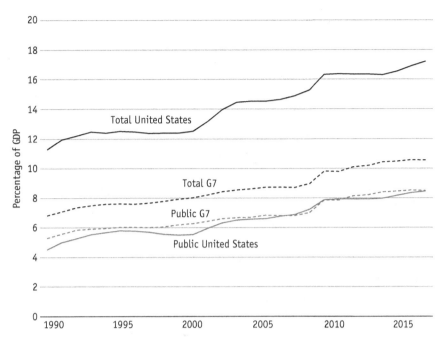

Figure 7.2. Total and public healthcare spending, United States vs. G7, 1990–2016. G7 average excludes the United States. OECD (2017).

Many of the trends driving US healthcare spending—including technological innovation, the spread of health insurance, and trends in aging and health—also occurred in other advanced countries. The other G7 countries have some form of national health insurance and/or control costs directly. This blunts some of the impact of the common trends. For example, the incentive to use new, expensive technology may be stronger when consumers have fee-for-service plans, in which doctors are paid for the services they provide, and when fees are determined in the private market, rather than under national health insurance plans, where doctors are paid salaries or are paid fees that are subject to government control.

A second factor—also related to the spread of private fee-for-service systems versus national health insurance—is the higher level of administrative costs in the United States. Fragmented private healthcare markets generate higher administrative costs than healthcare systems with a single payer. By one count, such costs are 8 percent of health expenditures in the United States compared to 1 to 5 percent in other high-income countries.[43] Medicare, which is a single-payer system, has far lower administrative costs than the US private healthcare sector.[44]

The third factor driving divergent healthcare spending trends is that the prices of almost everything health-related are higher in America than elsewhere. General physician salaries average over $218,000 in the United States compared to a range of $86,000 to $154,000 in other advanced countries.[45] On average, retail brand-name drug prices are 10 to 15 percent higher in the United States than in Canada, France, and Germany and 50 percent higher than in the United Kingdom.[46] The average cost of hospital stays is more than 60 percent higher in the United States compared to other OECD countries.[47]

In principle, spending more on healthcare need not be a problem. We have higher incomes than other countries, and people naturally demand more healthcare as their income rises.[48] In practice, however, we have less access to health insurance than other advanced countries and we do not generate better health outcomes along a wide variety of dimensions ranging from infant mortality rates to obesity and life expectancy. A 2014 Commonwealth Fund study found that the United States is "last or near last on dimensions of access, efficiency, and equity" among 11 advanced countries.[49]

The analysis above points to several major approaches to policy reform—restructuring provider payments, reducing administrative costs, limiting prices of healthcare services and products, and improving access to health insurance. We return to these issues below.

How much healthcare spending will continue to rise will greatly affect the budget outlook. Even with the overall rise in healthcare spending of the last several decades, the nation experienced two periods when such spending either rose at a reduced rate or fell as a share of GDP. In the 1990s, the emergence of health maintenance organizations drove down costs, but a consumer backlash spurred the spread of less restrictive health plans and healthcare spending resumed its earlier trend. Another slowdown began around 2003 and has persisted more or less to date.[50] Why it occurred and whether it will continue is unclear. The Great Recession of 2007 to 2009 helped limit spending because people consume less when they have less income.[51]

Some of the slowdown, however, is related to more permanent changes in how Americans provide and use healthcare. The share of insurance plans with high deductibles has risen, inducing patients to use less healthcare. Providers are replacing fee-for-service systems with those that pay on a per-patient basis or on outcome-based criteria. Healthcare is increasingly provided by nurse practitioners, physicians' assistants, and other health professionals, rather than doctors, further reducing costs. Healthcare delivery organizations that can provide less expensive service—for example, patient centers and minute clinics—are increasing. Digital recordkeeping is spreading quickly, with the potential to reduce paperwork and administrative costs.

All of these trends can help dampen future spending growth, but population aging will almost inexorably raise healthcare spending. Total healthcare spending is projected to rise from 18.3 percent of GDP in 2018 to 20.6 percent of GDP in 2026.[52] About half of the increase will come in major government programs. The rise in spending is projected to continue beyond 2026. By 2050, federal spending on the major programs is slated to reach 8.5 percent of GDP, about 87 percent of the projected deficit in that year.[53] About 40 percent of this increase is due simply to population aging, with the rest owing to higher incomes, new drugs, and technological advances.

Paying for healthcare spending will be an increasing challenge. General revenues finance Medicaid and, along with participant premiums, Medicare's Part B, C, and D. But traditional Medicare benefits (Part A) are financed out of a trust fund. The trust fund receives the 2.9 percent Medicare payroll tax on all earnings, split between employers and employees and the additional 0.9 percent tax on earnings above $200,000 ($250,000 for couples). Part A benefits can be financed only from the trust fund balance or new payroll taxes. The trust fund balance is slated to hit zero by 2026, leaving only dedicated tax revenue (mainly payroll taxes) to finance benefits. As a result, either payroll taxes must be raised, the financing will have to change, or benefits will have to be cut by approximately 9 percent in 2026 and 15 percent in the long term.[54] The changes proposed later will help extend the date at which the trust fund is exhausted, but in any case policymakers should simply cover any shortfall in Part A financing by using general revenues, which is what is assumed in the baseline projections in Chapter 3.

Moving forward, we need to build on the ACA. As the nation's most comprehensive healthcare reform since Medicare and Medicaid in 1965, it took an essentially conservative approach to healthcare reform, aiming to disrupt the existing system as little as possible. To ensure that significant and effective healthcare insurance was available to all legal residents regardless of income or health status, the ACA tapped the private market to make it easier to buy insurance rather than adopting a single-payer plan that covers all individuals.[55] The mandate and subsidy structure were modeled on a plan that Mitt Romney pushed through as governor of Massachusetts—a plan based on a proposal by the conservative Heritage Foundation.[56] To slow healthcare spending growth and increase the value in healthcare, the ACA created new incentives for private insurers to compete, and it made changes to Medicare that increased the rewards to providing value rather than just services. The key to the plan was the triumvirate of (1) the individual mandate to obtain adequate insurance or pay a penalty, (2) subsidies to help households pay for insurance, and (3) the requirement that insurance companies issue policies and set premiums without regard to pre-existing conditions. *Together*, these policies create a viable and functioning market with near-universal coverage. However, each provision is needed to ensure that the others work properly. Without the mandate that everyone must obtain coverage, for example, some healthy people would drop out of the market, making insurance more expensive for everyone else, and making it harder for people to buy policies. Likewise, without the provision blocking insurance companies from considering pre-existing conditions, premiums for some people would be so high that they could not afford to buy insurance.

To help implement these changes and facilitate comparisons across insurance policies, the ACA created marketplaces where insurance companies bid on standardized health insurance packages. The act also heavily subsidized states to expand Medicaid for the poor and children, added measures to control spending and reform provider payment systems, and raised several taxes to pay for the changes.

The ACA has produced positive results. It was projected to reduce deficits by $350 billion in its first decade and $3.5 trillion in its second.[57] It raised health insurance coverage (Figure 7.3); after hovering between 12 and 15 percent for

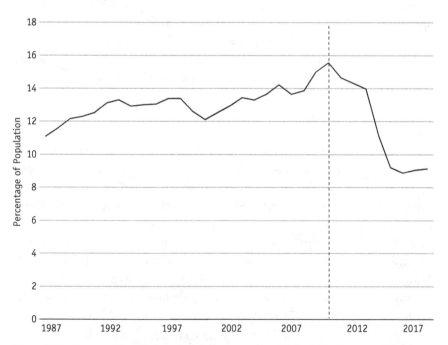

Figure 7.3. Uninsured rate before and after enactment of Affordable Care Act (ACA). Centers for Medicare and Medicaid Services (2018a, 2018b).

many years, the percentage of Americans who are uninsured fell below 9 percent in 2016.[58] The increase in coverage reduced income inequality and personal bankruptcies.[59] The ACA also boosted the quality of healthcare in some ways, which, in turn, has reduced costs. For example, the changes in Medicare policy have led to lower hospital readmission rates and patient infection rates.[60]

Nevertheless, President Trump and Congress moved to undo aspects of the ACA. The 2017 tax bill effectively eliminated the individual mandate, which will raise the number of uninsured individuals by an estimated 8 to 9 million by 2027.[61] The Trump administration also altered cost-sharing reduction subsidies that help low-income earners pay for healthcare, slashed the budget for advertising enrollment in exchange-based insurance plans, approved waivers that let states make it harder for their residents to receive Medicaid, and lowered barriers to buying bare-bones insurance plans that don't comply with the ACA. The net result of all these changes is that healthier people will drop out of the exchanges, which in turn will raise the cost of healthcare insurance for the remaining, less healthy pool of applicants and thus cause fewer of them to buy insurance as well.[62]

Instead of repealing and replacing part or all of the ACA, we should recognize it as the most promising way to expand access, improve the quality of care, and control costs. Building on the ACA, we should emphasize two themes: (1) harness the power of competition and consumer choice to cut costs, and (2) use the public sector to ensure that coverage is as broad as possible and that private insurance markets function well.

For starters, policymakers should reinstate and enforce the penalty for the individual mandate—or impose a similar penalty, such as eliminating the use of the standard deduction and itemized deductions in the income tax, for those who do not have qualified coverage.[63] That would bring healthier people back into the market, raise coverage, and reduce healthcare insurance premiums. The Internal Revenue Service should have the power to collect the penalty as it would any other tax, and the funds to do so.[64]

In addition, policymakers should appropriate funds for the cost-sharing reduction payments that help low-income families pay for healthcare insurance.[65] This would, on net, improve the fiscal situation.

Policymakers also should make it easier for working families to get affordable healthcare insurance.[66] People with access to "affordable" employer-sponsored health insurance aren't eligible for federal tax credits to help them buy coverage in the ACA exchanges. But because of a drafting error in the 2010 legislation, the so-called family glitch, the law is too restrictive with respect to the definition of "affordable," and many families who should get subsidies do not. By loosening up the law, policymakers can help millions of families pay for healthcare insurance.[67]

As of August 2017, every county in America had at least one insurer participating in its exchange, though about 3 million people had *only* one available insurer.[68] Policymakers should boost the supply of insurers on the exchanges; increased competition would give consumers more choices and hold down prices. To do that, they should take three steps:

- First, they should provide a stronger financial backstop for insurers. ACA redistributes funds to protect insurers on the exchanges against unpredictable costs that arise from the requirement that they not reject customers.[69] But extremely high-cost enrollees still introduce significant risk into the market. Initially, the ACA had a reinsurance program that provided a backstop to address this problem, but it expired in 2016, at which point premiums rose significantly.[70] Reinstating this program could help stabilize insurer participation in the exchanges, leading to lower premiums for households.[71]
- Second, policymakers should create a public option for health insurance on the exchanges, raising coverage and creating competition for private plans to reduce costs. It would be based on Medicare but updated to improve its cost-sharing structure and account for differences in the population it would serve.[72] That would *save* the government significant amounts through lower spending on exchange subsidies and increased tax revenue.[73]
- Third, all states should expand Medicaid, as they can under the ACA with substantial federal subsidies. As of this writing, 17 states haven't done so, leaving millions of low-income households without health insurance and without access to federal subsidies to buy a policy on the exchanges. States that expanded Medicaid have boosted healthcare coverage dramatically within their borders and have experienced lower premiums on their exchanges. Having all states expand Medicaid would increase state spending by about $60 billion over a decade, increase Medicaid coverage for more than 4 million people, and improve the health and finances of those who gain coverage.[74]

These changes will raise coverage and increase consumer choice. But we can do much more to cut costs. The traditional fee-for-service approach wastes money, rewarding providers for the services they provide, not the medical outcomes of these services. Provider payment reform offers the potential to reduce costs and increase the quality of care. Medicare, which has long been a pioneer in developing new payment systems, has piloted over 20 new types of alternative payment models, as the ACA authorizes.

The most promising alternative payment model is "bundled care," through which insurers define large "episodes of care"—for example, a hip replacement and 90 days of post-surgery care—and pay a set amount that's divided up among the providers involved.[75] Bundled payments encourage coordinated, cost-effective medicine since the payment depends on the medical situation, not the treatment. In a government-sponsored experiment in the 1990s, hospitals receiving a bundled care payment for a certain heart surgery cut costs by 10 to 40 percent and reduced patient mortality.[76] Private efforts to develop bundled care have also shown considerable success in reducing costs and raising the quality of care.[77] The government should adopt a policy that bundles services during a patient's hospital stay plus any post–acute care that's provided within 90 days thereafter.

Expanding competitive bidding in Medicare will reduce government spending while preserving beneficiaries' options to get Medicare at no additional cost. There's already a significant amount of competitive bidding in government health programs. In the ACA exchanges, insurers announce the prices at which they will offer a standard benefit package. In Medicare Part D, insurers announce the price at which they will provide a drug benefit package that meets certain minimum standards. In Medicare Advantage, insurers submit bids to provide beneficiaries with a wide range of Medicare standard and supplemental benefits.

I propose that we implement "premium support," which is a form of competitive bidding. Medicare and private insurers would announce how much they would accept to provide Medicare benefits (Parts A and B) to a beneficiary in average health in each region of the country. Those eligible for Medicare would then choose a plan. For each enrollee in a plan, the federal government would pay the insurance company the average bid in the region less a standard premium that beneficiaries owed.[78] The standard premium would roughly equal one-quarter of the cost of Part B services, about what beneficiaries currently pay. Beneficiaries who choose a plan that costs more than the government contribution plus the standard premium would pay the difference. Those who choose a less expensive plan would receive a partial rebate. This plan would generate significant government savings because private insurers' bids would generally be lower than the cost of traditional fee-for-service Medicare. Beneficiaries' total payments for Medicare premiums and cost sharing would be lower than projected under current law.[79]

Curtailing drug prices would help many people afford the drugs they need and reduce overall healthcare costs.[80] US drug prices are higher than those in similar advanced countries with well-developed drug markets. The United States spends much more than any other country on prescription drugs. Drug spending has risen rapidly relative to overall healthcare spending since the 1980s, and that's expected to continue over the next decade.[81]

At the same time, we should preserve incentives for drug companies to develop new therapies, which often requires large upfront costs for research, development, and testing. If the law doesn't protect newly developed drugs to some extent, any company could produce a drug without paying the upfront costs, undercutting the profits of the company that put in the work and offering little incentive for it to invest in the first place.[82] Patents appropriately give drug manufacturers some protection for new drugs;[83] once the monopoly ends, generic drugs can enter the market and tend to reduce prices dramatically.[84]

We should change the way Medicare pays for drugs. The nation's largest prescription drug buyer, it has no authority to negotiate which drugs it covers and at what prices.[85] Medicaid must cover all approved drugs, but it receives at least a 23 percent rebate on drug prices and doesn't face price increases that exceed inflation. The Department of Veterans Affairs (VA) receives at least a 24 percent rebate, can negotiate prices, and can reject certain drugs.[86] Medicare should be able to negotiate drug prices and reject certain drugs with the same authority as the VA.[87]

The tax exclusion for employer-sponsored health insurance is expensive and regressive, encourages gold-plated health insurance plans, and raises healthcare spending. With these considerations in mind, the ACA created a "Cadillac tax" on high-cost, employer-sponsored plans that's supposed to take effect in 2022. Taxing health insurance is the right approach, but a different tax would work better. Policymakers should replace the Cadillac tax by eliminating the income tax exclusion for the benefits from employer-sponsored insurance plans that exceed the cost of the median healthcare plan. Among its other benefits over the Cadillac tax, this policy would make healthcare costs more transparent to beneficiaries.[88]

The federal government imposes "sin" taxes on purchases of alcohol and cigarettes. By raising the price of these products, the taxes reduce smoking and alcohol consumption.[89] That improves people's health and reduces the costs that smoking and drinking impose on others, such as drunk-driving accidents. In light of the 2009 tax increase from $0.39 to $1.01 per pack of cigarettes, studies suggest that cigarette taxes are now high enough to offset the societal costs of smoking.[90] But taxes on alcohol should be raised to incorporate the full social costs of drinking, including drunk-driving accidents, increased violence and domestic abuse, and higher medical costs.[91] Moreover, alcohol is taxed inconsistently. Beer and wine are taxed by liquid volume, whereas distilled spirits are taxed based on alcohol content. Raising the excise tax on all alcoholic beverages to $16 per proof gallon (or to about 25 cents per ounce of alcohol) would standardize the rate for all alcohol, reduce alcohol consumption, improve health, reduce drunk-driving deaths, and raise revenues. That roughly translates to a tax increase of 50 cents per six-pack of beer or 60 cents per bottle of wine.[92]

The changes I advocate would produce (near) universal coverage and lower prices in both the over-65 and under-65 markets. But healthcare reform will be a process, with a lot of experimentation, not a single event. There are many additional promising approaches.

To raise access further, policymakers could let individuals buy into Medicare or Medicaid even if they are not eligible by current standards. To deepen consumers' choices on the exchanges, policymakers could require that all non-employer insurance be sold on exchanges rather than through private brokers.

To reduce costs, policymakers could limit monopoly power among providers, hospitals, insurers, and drug makers; cut administrative costs; reform malpractice rules;[93] and encourage greater use of non-physician providers (physician assistants, nurse practitioners, clinical nurse specialists, etc.). Policymakers could also consider "rate setting," a policy under which the government directly limits how much hospitals and doctors can charge.[94]

To reduce drug prices, Medicare could stipulate that a generic drug that is approved in other advanced countries is by default approved in America and could prohibit manufacturers from charging higher prices here than in those other countries. Under "reference pricing," Medicare could group drugs based on their therapeutic effects and set a price per group. This could simultaneously regulate prices of existing drugs while giving incentives to produce new ones.[95]

When drug makers charge what can only be described as obscenely high prices, due to their monopoly power, the federal government should step in. Drugs for hepatitis C, for example, can cost tens of thousands of dollars for a 12-week treatment, prompting insurers (including Medicaid) to restrict patients' access to them. The government has the power to pay patent holders "reasonable and entire compensation" and then produce the drug itself or let others do so.[96]

Further provider payment reform could help reduce the cost of the expensive episodes that account for such a large share of healthcare costs. "Pay for performance" programs—or value-based payments—offer financial rewards to providers who achieve pre-established quality benchmarks. The ACA created Accountable Care Organizations (ACOs), groups of providers that are collectively responsible for the health and payment outcomes of a specific population, that have grown rapidly.[97]

Finally, we should encourage the states, as "laboratories of democracy," to experiment with alternative systems as long as they do not reduce coverage or raise costs.

While policymakers have plenty of options to pursue, there are a few they should steadfastly avoid. For starters, they should not convert Medicaid to a block grant to the states. With a block grant, the federal government gives states a set amount of funds each year to address a problem (e.g., healthcare, hunger) and, in exchange, states get more leeway in how to spend the money. If, however, a state's costs for its Medicaid program exceeded its federal Medicaid funds—because, for instance, healthcare costs went up more than expected or a weak economy put more struggling people on Medicaid—that state would have to cover all of the additional costs itself or cut Medicaid services. Under this scenario, because states often lack the capacity to raise taxes or cut other popular programs, they would likely have to scale back Medicaid services or throw some low-income people off the rolls. Block grants have led to substantial reductions in welfare payments over the past 20 years, disproportionately affecting lower-income households (Chapter 9).

Nor should policymakers raise the age of Medicare eligibility. This would shift healthcare costs from Medicare to the individuals who would no longer be eligible, but it wouldn't do anything to strengthen the healthcare system. It wouldn't save Medicare much money either. The youngest elderly (e.g., 65- or 66-year-olds) are the least expensive people to cover in Medicare. Among the downsides of this policy, costs would rise for the seniors affected as well as for employers who provided coverage for employees who could no longer receive Medicare.

Policymakers do not need to provide new incentives for high-deductible (HD) healthcare plans or health saving accounts (HSAs), which give consumers a tax-preferred way to save money that they can then use, if needed, for their healthcare expenses.[98] High-deductible plans have been on the rise in recent years. They have lower premiums but larger out-of-pocket costs. Proponents argue that high deductibles prompt patients to make wiser, more cost-effective choices when deciding on their care. In practice, however, consumers tend to "throw the baby out with the bathwater" by reducing all forms of care, including high-value care like preventative screenings.[99] Meanwhile, HSAs cost the government a lot in forgone revenue, and they mostly benefit those with high incomes who least need the help. And the potential for HD/HSA plans to reduce healthcare costs more than they have already is limited, as so much of aggregate healthcare spending is dominated by a relatively small number of people with extreme health episodes whose costs far exceed even very high deductibles.

On a final note, a "single payer" system, in which the government finances healthcare for everyone, is the holy grail for many reformers, especially for Democrats. Many countries have a single-payer system, though they vary a bit. In Britain, the government finances and provides healthcare; in Germany, it finances private insurers; in Canada, it pays for national health insurance, while private providers supply the care. In the United States, Medicare is a single-payer system for the elderly.

A single-payer system brings big potential advantages. Coverage is universal; costs are generally lower because the government can set rates for doctors, hospitals, and drugs; and administrative and advertising costs are minimized. I'm very sympathetic to those goals, and a single-payer system might be what we'd want if we were starting from scratch.

But we're not. We're starting from a system that accounts for a sixth of the economy, with entrenched government programs, insurance companies, and physicians, and 175 million people who get employer-sponsored insurance. The switch to a single-payer system would generate immense transition costs for the government and private sector, and people would face massive "sticker shock" as the program would greatly expand the size of government.

Three states have considered and rejected single-payer systems in recent years. Vermont, among the nation's most liberal states, rejected it in 2014 in part due to its tax burden.[100] California, where it would have cost more than the entire state budget at the time, rejected it in 2017.[101] In Colorado, about 80 percent of voters rejected it in a referendum in 2016.[102] Thus, in America, single-payer healthcare seems to be more of a slogan than a solution.

Healthcare reform is central to the fiscal outlook and to the lives and livelihoods of our citizens. We have the opportunity to make enormous gains along all of those dimensions if we embrace reform.

Notes

1. Medicare reforms, such as changing the way providers are compensated, tend to make their way to the private sector relatively quickly (Clemens and Gottlieb 2013).
2. Kiley (2017).
3. Centers for Medicare and Medicaid Services (2018b). Slightly over one-quarter of adults in the United States were "underinsured" as they had large out-of-pocket payments and deductibles relative to their income (Collins, Gunja, and Doty 2017).
4. Finegold et al. (2015). Among the uninsured in 2016, about 43 percent were eligible to receive Medicaid or discounted coverage in the marketplace. Approximately 10 percent fall into what is called the coverage gap: they would be eligible to receive Medicaid, but they live in a state that did not expand it under Obamacare and their income is too low to receive a federal subsidy on the exchanges. About 17 percent were offered a plan from their employer but did not accept it, and 11 percent had incomes too high to receive financial assistance for the marketplace. The remaining 20 percent of the uninsured population are undocumented immigrants who are not eligible for coverage under ACA (Garfield et al. 2016).
5. Centers for Medicare and Medicaid Services (2018b). Employer-provided health insurance is a bit of a historical accident. When the government instituted wage and price controls during World War II, firms offered health insurance as a way to compete for workers. Employer-sponsored group insurance offers an effective way to pool risks. Because workers are usually not hired based on health status, the set of employees at a firm often provides a stable and average risk profile (controlling for age and sex). This allows insurance companies to offer policies at lower premiums than otherwise.

6. For an individual facing a 12 percent federal income tax rate, a 5 percent state income tax, and payroll taxes, an extra $107.65 generates $75.35 in available resources after taxes, so the ability to buy health insurance with pre-tax dollars reduces the price by 30 percent $(= 1 - (75.35/107.65))$. For an individual earning above the Social Security limit, facing a 35 percent income tax rate, the 3.8 percent Medicare tax and a 7 percent state tax, the ability to pay with pre-tax dollars reduces the cost by about 50 percent.

7. Congressional Budget Office (2018b); US Department of the Treasury (2018).

8. This includes people whose employers do not offer health insurance or who are not eligible for their firm's plan (or do not like the benefits they are offered), are self-employed, or do not work. It also includes so-called Medigap policies that households over 65 purchase to supplement their Medicare coverage.

9. In addition, individuals cannot be eligible for other types of health insurance coverage (including affordable coverage from their employer), must file federal income tax returns, and enroll in an insurance plan through a healthcare marketplace.

10. Hamel et al. (2016). This includes "Medigap" coverage.

11. Individuals under the age of 65 can also receive Medicare if they meet one of the following criteria: received Social Security disability benefits for 24 months, have Lou Gehrig's disease, or have permanent kidney failure that requires dialysis or a transplant.

12. Curto et al. (2017); Miller and Capretta (2014); Newhouse and McGuire (2014).

13. Center on Budget and Policy Priorities (2016). About 10 million elderly and disabled Americans receive both Medicare and Medicaid and are called "dual eligibles." Medicare coverage provides hospital and physician care, while Medicaid fills in the gaps (such as long-term care and nursing homes). Over two-thirds of dual eligibles are fully dual eligible, meaning that they receive full Medicaid benefits in addition to Medicare. The remainder are partially dual eligible, in that they receive full benefits from Medicare and some cost sharing and premium assistance from Medicaid (Mitchell, Baumrucker, and Herz 2014). Dual eligible individuals tend to have more extensive medical needs than other beneficiaries, leading to disproportionately higher healthcare costs.

14. This matching amount is called the Federal Medical Assistance Percentage and is determined by per capita incomes in the state.

15. Congressional Budget Office (2018a).

16. Centers for Medicare and Medicaid Services (2018b).

17. Rudowitz, Artiga, and Arguello (2014).

18. The Veterans Health Administration does not provide health insurance. Rather, it is a government-owned and -run source of care for veterans and active duty service members. This is different from Medicare or Medicaid, where the government reimburses private providers for care they provide to beneficiaries. Veterans pay no premiums or enrollment fees and out-of-pocket costs are low. Half of the VHA beneficiaries are enrolled in Medicare or Medicaid, and many others have supplemental private insurance (Rovner 2014; Congressional Budget Office 2014a).

19. Defense Health Agency (2016); Rovner (2014).

20. Chua and Sommers (2014); Finkelstein et al. (2012); Garfield et al. (2016); Mazumder and Miller (2016); Sommers et al. (2017); Sommers, Gawande, and Baicker (2017).

21. Finkelstein (2007).

22. Baicker et al. (2013, 2014). A series of papers published by the Oregon Health Study Group details the effects of the Oregon Medicaid expansion experiment. They find that Medicaid coverage did not impact the prevalence or diagnosis of high blood pressure or cholesterol in recipients but did increase the probability of their being diagnosed with diabetes and using diabetes medication. It also reduced their probability of having depression. Having Medicaid essentially eliminated the prevalence of catastrophic medical expenses (over 30 percent of income) for recipients. It also increased their use of preventative care and screening services. Medicaid does not have any impact on employment or earnings, but is associated with increases in SNAP receipts.

23. Kenney and Coyer (2012).
24. Cohodes et al. (2016) examine how Medicaid expansions in the 1980s and 1990s impact educational attainment. The authors find that a 10-percentage-point increase in a person's Medicaid eligibility as a child decreases the possibility of being a high school dropout by 4 to 5.9 percent and increases the chances of getting a bachelor's degree by 2.3 to 3 percent.
25. Brown, Kowalski, and Lurie (2015) analyze administrative tax data and find that the government recoups 56 cents for every dollar spent on a child's Medicaid coverage by the time the child reaches 60. Children who received Medicaid tend to have lower EITC payments, and women have higher cumulative earnings by age 28.
26. Berk and Fang (2017); National Institute for Health Care Management (2012).
27. National Institute for Health Care Management (2012).
28. Center for Medicare and Medicaid Services (2018a, 2018b); Congressional Budget Office (2018a, 2018c). Excess cost growth is the growth rate of healthcare spending per person (after demographic changes are removed) relative to the growth rate of potential GDP per capita. From 1990 to 2014, average annual excess cost growth was 1.2 percent for Medicare, 0.6 percent for Medicaid, and 1.3 percent for other sectors (including private insurance and out-of-pocket payments). For all sectors combined, average annual excess cost growth was 1.2 percent.
29. The rise in healthcare spending can be thought of as an example of what is called "Baumol's cost disease." This idea traces back to Princeton economists William Baumol and William Bowen, who studied the performing arts in the 1960s and noted that it took as many musicians as much time in the 20th century to perform a Beethoven string quartet as it would have in the 19th century. That is, there has been no productivity growth in this regard. Nevertheless, wages for musicians were higher in the 20th century than in the 19th century—that is, costs in the music industry have risen. Why is that? They argued that increases in productivity and hence wages in some sectors—like manufacturing—drive up wages in other sectors, since otherwise too many workers would leave the sectors with low productivity growth. Healthcare (as well as education and many other public services) exemplifies this trend. Healthcare depends heavily on labor, and the productivity of doctors and nurses has not changed very fast. It takes a similar amount of time to treat a patient now as it did decades ago. While Baumol's cost disease implies that healthcare costs should be rising over time, it is still the case that reforms could reduce the growth of healthcare spending (Baumol 2013).
30. Cutler (1995); Newhouse (1992); Orszag (2008); Smith, Heffler, and Freeland (2000).
31. Economists Amitabh Chandra and Jonathan Skinner (2012) distinguish three types of technological innovations: changes that are cost-effective and help nearly everyone (e.g., antibiotics, washing of hands before surgery); changes that are cost-effective for some people but not for others (antidepressants, imaging technology); and changes that are technically feasible but may not be worth the costs or resources used (arthroscopic surgery for osteoarthritis of the knee). They estimate that the third type of spending has played a significant role in the rise of healthcare costs.
32. Centers for Medicare and Medicaid Services (2018a).
33. Medicaid can be offered as fee-for-service, managed care, or a combination of the two. Approximately three-quarters of the Medicaid population are enrolled in managed care plans, but fee-for-service incurs the majority of Medicaid costs.
34. Cutler (2018); Lallemand (2012). Evidence from the Dartmouth Atlas Project shows that areas of the country with more resources per capita (i.e., more hospital beds, more specialists and physicians) will have higher spending as well. A higher supply of resources leads to a higher provision of care, and thus higher costs, though not necessarily better outcomes. This pattern is especially prevalent in the Medicare system (Fisher et al. 2009; Fisher, Bynum, and Skinner 2009). For example, the variation in resources explains why areas such as Miami, Florida, have average Medicare spending per enrollee of over $16,000 compared to $6,700 in Rochester County, Minnesota, where the world-renowned Mayo

Clinic is located. And, it explains why an individual who moves from a low-treatment area to high-treatment area can face higher costs for the same procedures. Other studies point to differences such as patient health, consumer preferences, differences in the utilization of types of care, and differences in prices negotiated by different health plans (Cassidy 2014; Finkelstein, Gentzkow, and Williams 2016; Sheiner 2014). Health economist Atul Gawande (2009) provided a well-known example of wasteful spending by observing that in 2005 and 2006, McAllen County, Texas, spent almost double what neighboring El Paso County did on healthcare, even though the counties had similar health and demographic characteristics and the same available treatments and technology. He argued that utilization differences arose because the medical industry in McAllen County was highly fragmented and driven by profit rather than the well-being of patients. Doctors had incentives to recommended more treatments, leading to larger associated costs. They were able to act on this incentive because they were reimbursed for each service rather than on a per-patient basis or on quality of the medical outcomes.

35. A chronic health condition is a "physical or mental health condition that lasts more than one year and causes functional restrictions or requires ongoing monitoring or treatment" (Buttorff, Ruder, and Bauman 2017).

36. Ogden and Carroll (2010); Ogden et al. (2015).

37. Bodenheimer, Chen, and Bennett (2009); Buttorff, Ruder, and Bauman (2017).

38. Buttorff, Ruder, and Bauman (2017). Almost half (46 percent) of Medicare spending goes to the 14 percent of enrollees with over five chronic conditions (Lochner et al. 2012). Obesity-related health conditions (e.g., hypertension, type 2 diabetes, and high cholesterol) raise costs by an average of $3,600 per year for each affected person (Cawley and Meyerhoefer 2012). Thorpe et al. (2004) estimated that a quarter of per capita healthcare spending growth between 1987 and 2001 was due to obesity. Hammond and Levine (2010) also note that beyond directly affecting healthcare costs, obesity can also affect the economy through labor market effects such as lost productivity at work, increased absenteeism, premature death, and increased disability payments.

39. As noted earlier, precise estimates of administrative costs in healthcare are hard to come by. The Centers for Medicare and Medicaid Services (2018a) reports a measure of administrative costs that rises from about 0.2 percent of GDP in 1960 to 1.4 percent of GDP in 2016.

40. These data are for cross-country comparisons and are not directly comparable to the National Health Expenditure numbers presented in this chapter.

41. OECD (2017).

42. Frakt (2018a, 2018b).

43. Papanicolas, Woskie, and Jha (2018). Other countries include Germany, the Netherlands, Switzerland, Canada, Australia, the United Kingdom, Sweden, Denmark, France, and Japan.

44. Archer (2011); Jiwani et al. (2014).

45. Papanicolas, Woskie, and Jha (2018). The other countries include Japan, Germany, the United Kingdom, France, Canada, Australia, the Netherlands, Sweden, Switzerland, and Denmark.

46. Kanavos et al. (2013).

47. Koechlin, Lorenzoni, and Schreyer (2010).

48. Hall and Jones (2007).

49. Davis et al. (2014, p. 7).

50. Center for Medicare and Medicaid Services (2018a).

51. Hartman et al. (2010); Martin et al. (2011); Martin et al. (2012). Sheiner (2015) shows that states with slower per capita income growth during the recession also experienced slower growth in real per capita health services.

52. Centers for Medicare and Medicaid Services (2018b).

53. After a couple decades, the projections of various government agencies—CBO, GAO, the Centers for Medicare and Medicaid Services (CMS)—begin to diverge due to differences

in assumptions about costs, population growth, and other factors. In Chapter 3, I use estimates from the Medicare Boards of Trustees (Boards of Trustees 2018). See Chapter 3 for more details.

54. Boards of Trustees (2018). The 3.8 percent net investment income tax is not dedicated to the Medicare trust fund. The supplementary insurance in Part B and the prescription drug benefit in Part D are primarily financed through the Supplemental Medical Insurance (SMI) Trust Fund, which is funded by general revenues and monthly premiums that beneficiaries pay. The SMI Trust Fund is not in immediate danger of running out of money because general revenues are added every year to cover expected costs. The government pays for a pre-determined amount of Medicare Advantage enrollees' Part A and B benefits using funds from those programs' dedicated trust funds. If the insurance costs exceed the government contribution, enrollees pay the difference in the form of a monthly premium. If the plan's costs are lower, the insurer gives the funds back to enrollees through lower premiums or higher benefits.

55. "Significant and effective health insurance" means that all Americans have access to a quality insurance plan that provides a minimum set of benefits, as specified in the ACA, at an affordable rate. The opposite of this would be a plan with an extremely high deductible and very little coverage above that level. While the latter would technically be "health insurance," its prohibitive cost and lack of benefits mean that enrollees would receive little real gain.

56. Butler (1989); Kaiser Family Foundation (2012).

57. Congressional Budget Office (2015); Furman (2017). The analysis runs from 2016 to 2025.

58. Massachusetts saw similar changes when the state converted to a similar system (Kaiser Family Foundation 2012).

59. Furman (2017).

60. Agency for Healthcare Research and Quality (2016); Zuckerman et al. (2016).

61. Congressional Budget Office (2018b).

62. Congressional Budget Office (2018b); Rampell (2018).

63. Congressional Budget Office (2017b). In 2017, if an individual chose not to purchase insurance, he or she was charged a monthly fee equal to the greater of 2.5 percent of household income (up to the total yearly premium for the average price of a Bronze plan) or $695 per adult and $347.50 per child in the household, up to $2,085. The fee was adjusted for inflation each year. Individuals were exempt if their income was below the taxable threshold, if they would have to pay over 8.13 percent of their income to purchase insurance, if they experienced certain hardships, if they were members of certain religions, or if they were undocumented immigrants (Healthcare.gov 2017).

64. Even when the mandate was in place, the government did not enforce it seriously, and about 40 percent of the people who should have paid a penalty did not (Congressional Budget Office 2014b).

65. Hall (2018).

66. Brooks (2014). The law states that if one member of a family receives insurance coverage through his or her employer that is deemed an "affordable" share (less than 9.66 percent) of his or her income, then the whole family is ineligible to receive subsidized care on the exchange, even if the price of the employer-provided insurance for the whole family is greater than the affordability threshold. For example, consider an employee who is offered an insurance plan that totals 9 percent of his income. The cost of that plan goes up to 14 percent when including the cost for his family of four. Even though the total cost of the insurance is unaffordable for the family, they would be ineligible for federal subsidies, since the determination of affordability is based only on the cost of insurance for the individual.

67. Buettgens, Dubay, and Kenney (2016).

68. Soffen and Uhrmacher (2017).

69. It appears as if risk adjustment is working as intended. In 2016, the program transferred about 11 percent of premium dollars toward plans with less healthy beneficiaries, underscoring its importance in maintaining marketplace stability.

70. Jost (2017); Trish (2017).

71. For example, a reinsurance program could compensate insurance companies for 60 percent of the costs for enrollees who incur over $1 million in costs in a given year, financed by fees on insurers. Such a program would not have any budgetary effects since collections from insurance companies would be directly offset by payments to them, as evidenced by ACA's initial reinsurance program.

72. The proposal for a public option builds on that outlined by the Congressional Budget Office (2013).

73. Congressional Budget Office (2013). The presence of a public option may push more people onto the exchanges, including those who previously received insurance from their employers. If employers are less inclined to offer health insurance, taxable wages, and thus income tax revenue, will increase. The downward pressure on premiums from enhanced competition will reduce government expenditures on subsidies.

74. Dorn and Buettgens (2017). The authors estimate the potential federal budget effects through 2027 if all 19 states that did not expand Medicaid as of 2017 did so. The vast majority of cost increase is due to increased Medicaid caseloads. This spending is offset by reduced spending on marketplace subsidies (since some people would plausibly move off the exchanges into Medicaid) as well as a small amount of reduced spending on uncompensated care (federal expenditures for healthcare provided to those who are unable or unwilling to pay for care).

75. An episode of care is defined on the basis of a major condition or procedure and includes a number of pre-determined services related to this issue over a period of time. For more on bundled payments, see Romley and Ginsburg (2018).

76. Cromwell et al. (1998).

77. Porter and Kaplan (2016). In the private sector, the Geisinger health system, an integrated health delivery organization headquartered in Pennsylvania (serving over 1 million patients annually), implemented a bundled payment method under its ProvenCare system. Initial results showed that this method increased the percentage of patients receiving all recommended processes of care from 59 percent to 100 percent and decreased the mean length of hospital stay for certain heart disease patients by 16 percent (Shih, Chen, and Nallamothu 2015). Another interesting development has been the creation of the Prometheus payment system. This payment method generates single, risk-adjusted payments given to providers, plus an additional post-care redistribution to providers based on patient outcomes. The current system has the potential to impact payment for almost 30 percent of the entire adult population, showing that it can be further expanded for an even wider group (Hussey, Ridgely, and Rosenthal 2011).

78. The federal payment to insurers would be adjusted for the health of beneficiaries.

79. Congressional Budget Office (2017a).

80. A 2016 Kaiser Family Foundation poll found that among Americans who take a prescription medicine, a quarter have trouble affording the medicine they need (Kirzinger, Wu, and Brodie 2016).

81. Centers for Medicare and Medicaid Services (2018a, 2018b).

82. While manufacturers frequently argue that the price of their drugs reflects the research and development costs involved to create them, evidence shows that this is not true. Rather, drugs tend to be priced based on what the market can bear (Kesselheim, Avorn, and Sarpatwari 2016).

83. Patent protections last 20 years beginning from the filing date and are issued by the US Patent and Trademark Office. The Food and Drug Administration (FDA) offers its own form of protection through offers of market exclusivity, which prevents drug competitors from entering the market for a certain period. Currently, small molecule drugs receive

5 to 7 years of guaranteed protection, and biologic drugs receive 12 years of protection before generic versions can be sold. Patents and market exclusivity can occur at the same time but do not necessarily have to. Companies can apply to have patents extended to compensate for the time spent in regulatory review (up to 5 years) or clinical trials (up to 14 years), and they receive an additional 6 months of market exclusivity if they test the drugs on children.

84. Food and Drug Administration (2015). When two generic manufacturers enter the market, the price of a drug falls on average to 55 percent of the original branded price. It continues to decrease to one-third of the price with the entrance of 5 manufacturers and to 13 percent with 15 manufacturers.

85. For most classes of drugs, Medicare is required to cover at least two types. The six classes of drugs for which Medicare is required to cover all or substantially all drugs are immunosupressants (for prophylaxis of organ transplant rejection), antidepressants, antipsychotics, anticonvulsants (for seizures), antiretrovirals (for HIV/AIDS), and antineoplastic (cancer) classes (Centers for Medicare and Medicaid Services 2008). One study found that these drugs account for 17 to 33 percent of total outpatient drug spending in Part D and that these drugs are, on average, priced 10 percent higher than they would be without this requirement (Kipp and Ko 2008).

86. Specifically, under Medicaid, drug manufacturers are required to provide rebates on drugs equal to the lesser of 23.1 percent of the average price paid by other buyers or the lowest price paid by other buyers. States are also allowed to further negotiate with drug manufacturers to lower drug prices. The VA and the DoD require that drug manufacturers offer them rebates of 24 percent or the lowest price paid by other non-federal buyers. They can negotiate directly with drug manufacturers, either alone or together, and they can reject drugs from their formularies (Blumenthal and Squires 2016).

87. Gagnon and Wolfe (2015). The authors estimate Medicare Part D savings if the program used the same pricing strategy as the VA. They estimate that in 2010, the VA paid 46 percent of official manufacturer prices for drugs and Medicare Part D paid 83 percent (for a total of $36 billion to brand-name manufacturers). Using these data, the authors estimate a ratio of the Medicare to VA discounts to roughly estimate what Medicare would have saved if it had used VA pricing. They find the following: $36 billion—([46/83]*$36 billion) = $16 billion. Frakt, Pizer, and Feldman (2012) obtain very similar results. They estimate that retail VA drug costs are 40 percent of those paid by Medicare, and each beneficiary cost Medicare $1,275 in 2009. If Medicare received an additional 40 percent savings per beneficiary, it would have saved 40 percent*$1,275 = $510 per enrollee each year.

88. However, because limiting the deduction would make insurance more expensive, it could raise the number of uninsured individuals by an estimated 1 million (Congressional Budget Office 2016, Health Option 18).

89. A 10 percent increase in price reduces cigarette consumption by 3–7 percent and alcohol consumption by 5–11 percent (Chaloupka et al. 1993; Chaloupka et al. 2002; Chaloupka and Warner 2000; Congressional Budget Office 2012; Cook and Durrance 2011; International Agency for Research on Cancer 2011; Gallet and List 2003; Lowry 2014; Roodman 2015).

90. Furman (2016); Viscusi (1995). Cigarette consumption creates secondhand smoke, which is detrimental to those exposed to it. It also leads to higher public and private healthcare costs in the short term, since smoking is associated with a host of various diseases and cancers. However, since cigarettes also cause people to die earlier, baseline long-term health costs may be lower than what they would be if the smoking rate were lower.

91. Looney (2017).

92. Congressional Budget Office (2016). The 2017 tax act temporarily reduced excise taxes on alcohol through 2019.

93. To avoid malpractice lawsuits, healthcare providers sometimes use "defensive medicine," ordering tests and other services that they don't really think are necessary but can protect

them against a lawsuit. The standard way to address malpractice is to limit liabilities, but a better way might be to provide a "safe harbor" so that a provider who can show that he or she used best-practice protocol could not be sued (Orszag 2013).

94. Rate setting has been experimented with at the state level. Evidence from Maryland shows that state-based rate setting can slow price increases but not necessarily overall cost growth (National Conference of State Legislatures 2017). Under one proposal in California, a new state board would have the authority to regulate the prices of medical procedures that private health plans charge, using Medicare's rates as a baseline. On the international front, Switzerland and Germany use rate setting in their health systems (Kliff 2018).

95. Frakt (2015).

96. Committee on a National Strategy for the Elimination of Hepatitis B and C (2017); Kapczynski and Kesselheim (2016).

97. Muhlestein, Saunders, and McClellan (2017).

98. Kaiser Family Foundation (2016). For 2018, the HSA contribution limit was $3,450 for an individual and $6,900 for a family (Internal Revenue Service 2017).

99. Chandra, Holmes, and Skinner (2013); Fronstin and Roebuck (2016).

100. Wheaton (2014).

101. Mason (2017).

102. Ingold (2016).

Appendix Table 7.1. **Healthcare Reform Policies**

Policy	2050 Spending Change	2050 Revenue Change	2050 Debt Effect
Reinstate the individual mandate	0.15	−0.02	4.2
Appropriate cost sharing reduction payments	0.02	0.04	−0.9
Fix the family glitch	0.06	—	1.4
Create a public option	−0.04	0.08	−3.2
Expand Medicaid	0.26	—	6.4
Bundle Medicare payments	−0.06	—	−1.4
Install a premium support system	−0.24	—	−6.0
Allow Medicare drug negotiation	−0.42	—	−7.8
Change tax treatment of employer-sponsored health insurance	0.02	0.45	−10.3
Increase alcohol tax	—	0.01	−0.6
Total	−0.26	0.57	−18.2

Notes: All numbers are referenced as a percentage of GDP. Total may not equal sum due to rounding. Installing the mandate, fixing the family glitch, costs associated with the public option, changing the tax treatment of ESI, and Medicaid expansion all grow with major healthcare costs. Revenue from the public option grows with GDP. Drug negotiation grows with Medicare drug costs. Premium support and bundled payments grow with Medicare costs. Alcohol proposal revenue falls as a share of GDP over time. Several policies mentioned in the text are budget neutral or do not yet have fully developed cost estimates, and thus do not appear in the table. They include reinsurance, reference pricing, reducing administrative costs, malpractice reform, and increasing the use of non-physician practitioners.

Sources: Buettgens, Dubay, and Kenney (2016); Centers for Medicare and Medicaid Services (2018a, 2018b); Congressional Budget Office (2013, 2016, 2017a, 2017b, 2018a, 2018c); Dorn and Buettgens (2017); Hall (2018); Gagnon and Wolfe (2015).

8

Saving Social Security

Social Security is one of the nation's most popular and successful programs, providing a crucial foundation of income support every year for tens of millions of beneficiaries, including retirees, surviving spouses, dependents, and the disabled. The program covers almost all current workers and is mostly financed with payroll taxes. But Social Security is financially unsustainable as it's now constituted, making it a big part of our overall budget problem. Policymakers have not reformed Social Security since 1983, when it was facing a financing crisis. It needs an overhaul to address its coming shortfall and to modernize its features.

The financing problem arises because Social Security is largely a pay-as-you-go system—the taxes that today's workers pay go mainly to cover the benefits of today's retirees. As a result, the coming rise in the number of retirees relative to workers will wreak havoc on the system, eventually leaving the program with too little revenue to pay all of the owed benefits. With reserves that accumulated in previous years and annual payroll taxes, Social Security can pay, through 2034, all of the benefits that workers earn and claim. After that, the reserves will be depleted and projected revenues will only cover about three-quarters of the benefits to which workers are entitled, leaving the program with a significant shortfall. Policymakers will need to enact some combination of higher payroll taxes, lower benefits, or a new revenue source.

To address this shortfall and modernize the program, policymakers should enact a reform package crafted in 2016 by a commission established by the Bipartisan Policy Center (of which I was a member).[1] It would raise taxes and reduce benefits in a progressive manner, protecting the poor, encouraging people to work longer, and fixing the way Social Security calculates the impact of inflation.

Enacting the proposal as of 2021 would mitigate a significant part of the overall long-term fiscal problem, reducing the debt-to-GDP ratio by about 22 percentage points in 2050 and by larger amounts in later years. Fixing Social Security would also preserve and enhance a social compact that links generations, and it would provide momentum for other reforms: if we can modify a program as popular as Social Security, then surely we can modify others as well.

Created in 1935 as part of Franklin Roosevelt's New Deal, Social Security originally covered a modest fraction of the workforce and required employers and employees to pay a small dedicated payroll tax. FDR wanted taxes that were explicitly earmarked to finance the program because, in his words, "with those taxes in there, no damn politician can ever scrap my Social Security program."[2] Benefits were payable at age 65 (at a time when life expectancy was 66 for 20-year-olds) and were first paid in 1940. Over the next several decades, successive presidents and Congresses expanded the program's size and scope.

Today, Social Security, which is formally known as Old-Age, Survivors, and Disability Insurance (OASDI), consists of two linked programs. Old-Age and Survivors Insurance (OASI)—which is what most people regard as Social Security—provides benefits for retirees and their survivors and dependents. Disability insurance (DI) provides income for working-age people who can no longer work, given their skills and physical abilities. The programs cover almost all Americans except for a minority of state and local government employees.[3]

More than 60 million Americans—almost a fifth of the population—receive benefits in a given year, mostly through the retirement program.[4] Retirement benefits average about $16,000 per year, less for widows and the disabled.[5] Social Security kept as many as 26 million Americans out of poverty in 2016, including 17 million people aged 65 and older.[6] Although its designers never meant for it to provide all of the resources people need in retirement, it now provides more than 90 percent of income for more than a third of the elderly and more than half of income for about two-thirds of the elderly.[7]

Social Security's operating rules are straightforward. Workers pay a 6.2 percent tax on their wages (and employers pay the same 6.2 percent tax on each employee) up to an income cap, which was $128,400 in 2018 and which rises each year with average wage growth across the economy.[8] Most experts believe that workers bear the economic burden of the entire 12.4 percent tax because employers compensate for their share by holding down wages. About 85 percent of Social Security payroll tax revenues go to OASI, the rest to DI.

A worker's monthly retirement benefit depends on his or her average lifetime wages, adjusted for national wage growth and other factors.[9] In 2018, the basic monthly benefit (the "primary insurance amount" or PIA) was 90 percent of the first $895 in career average monthly earnings, plus 32 percent of average earnings between $895 and $5,397, plus 15 percent of average earnings above $5,397, up to the taxable earnings cap (Figure 8.1).[10]

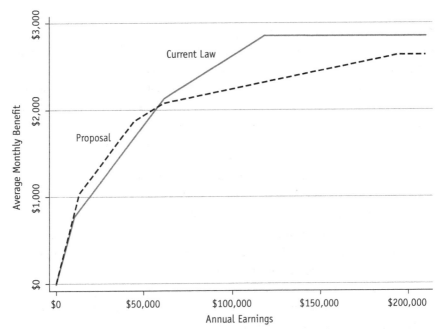

Figure 8.1. Social Security benefit paths. The graph depicts the benefit schedule in 2016 and in the reform package developed in this chapter (2016 dollars). Commission on Retirement Security and Personal Savings (2016).

Benefits are 100 percent of the PIA for workers who first claim benefits at the "full retirement age" (FRA), less if they claim benefits earlier, and more if they claim benefits later. The FRA was 65 for Social Security's first several decades. Under the 1983 reforms, it rose gradually to 66 as of 2017 and will continue to rise, reaching 67 by 2027. At that point, someone who claims benefits at age 62 (the youngest eligible age) will receive only 70 percent of their annual PIA. Someone who first claims benefits at age 70 (the latest eligible age) will receive 124 percent of their annual PIA.[11] These adjustments to monthly benefits are meant to give people about the same expected value of benefits over their lifetimes, regardless of when they choose to start claiming them.[12]

Besides offering retirement income, Social Security offers several forms of social insurance, most of which are hard to buy in the private market. Benefits rise each year to offset inflation, and they last for the beneficiary's lifetime. Benefits are allocated under a progressive formula, through which those who earned relatively low wages during their working years receive relatively more in retirement benefits compared to high-income earners.

Survivor, spousal, and dependent benefits provide life insurance. Qualifying spouses and former spouses of retirees can choose between their own benefits and 50 percent of the retiree's payments. A retiree's children also may be eligible for dependent benefits if they are under age 18 and unmarried, or in certain other circumstances. When a beneficiary dies, surviving spouses are eligible for payments that are usually at least 75 percent of the retiree's benefits.[13]

Disability benefits provide further protection against income loss and play a valuable, but often overlooked, role in the economy. Disability is a significant economic risk for many people. Workers face about a 1-in-4 chance of becoming disabled at some point, and the consequences—including lower income and higher medical expenses—can be substantial.[14]

DI aims to protect people against these risks without unduly reducing their willingness to work. Private markets for disability insurance do not always work very well in providing adequate coverage at affordable rates, in part because disability is hard to define and measure—especially with regard to hard-to-verify conditions like back pain or mental health, each of which has been the source of a rising number of claims in recent decades.

DI provides benefits to workers who suffer from a medical condition that's expected to last at least one year (or result in death) and that prevents the individual from working. To be eligible, an individual must have worked a sufficient number of years and have an impairment that the Social Security Administration (SSA) determines is severe enough to qualify. The benefit formula is similar to that of OASI. An individual who earns more than $1,180 per month while disabled loses DI eligibility. The program does not cover partial or short-term disability. Like OASI, DI plays a critical role for its beneficiaries, providing at least half of income for more than two-thirds of recipients and at least 90 percent of income for almost one-half of recipients.[15]

As noted, Social Security's annual benefits are progressive, with low-income earners receiving relatively more than high-income earners. The ratio of retirement benefits to average earnings—called the replacement rate—falls as average earnings rise (Figure 8.1). As the Social Security Administration calculates it, the average replacement rate for workers who earn average wages and claim benefits at the FRA is about 40 percent.[16] That's about two-thirds of the average in industrialized countries, whose Social Security programs are generally larger than America's.[17]

Due to the cap on taxable wages, Social Security payroll taxes are regressive; the average payroll tax rate that a worker pays falls as his or her wages grow above the cap. For most lower- and middle-class households, as noted in Chapter 1, payroll tax burdens (including Medicare payroll taxes and the employers' share of them) exceed income tax payments. Combining the progressive annual benefits and the regressive taxes, Social Security as a whole is progressive for workers of a given age. As discussed below, however, higher-income households tend to live longer and thus receive benefits for longer periods, making the program less progressive.

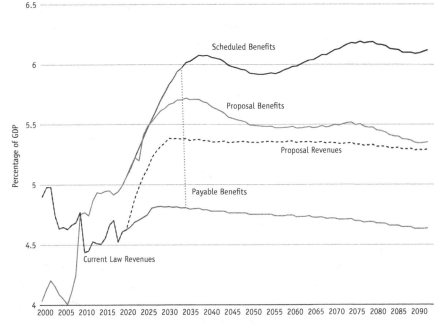

Figure 8.2. Social Security benefits and revenues, current law vs. reform package. Board of Trustees (2016, 2018); Goss (2016).

To most people, Social Security may look like a bank account or a 401(k) plan—you put in money while you're working and get the money back in retirement. Unlike a bank account or 401(k), however, the Social Security program *as a whole* doesn't generally save the contributions that people make. Rather, it's largely a pay-as-you-go system; the payroll taxes that workers contribute in a given year go mainly to cover the payments that current beneficiaries receive in that same year. If taxes exceed benefits in a given year, the Social Security Administration uses those excess revenues to "build up the trust fund"—that is, to buy special Treasury bonds, which pay interest that the Social Security program earns. When benefits exceed taxes in a given year, the balances in Social Security's trust fund and the interest payments help pay current benefits.

The 1983 reforms, which policymakers enacted to prevent an imminent financing crisis, raised payroll taxes and cut benefits. In every subsequent year from 1984 to 2009, tax revenues exceeded benefits and the excess revenue generated a higher balance in the trust fund, making Social Security a partially pre-funded system rather than a pure pay-as-you-go system. At the end of 2018, the combined trust fund held almost $2.9 trillion in Treasury bonds.[18] Yearly benefits now exceed yearly taxes, however, and that annual difference will grow in the future (Figure 8.2), which will drain trust fund balances.

The headline-grabbing fact is that Social Security's trust fund is slated to run out of money by 2034.[19] Despite popular misconceptions, however, Social Security will *not* disappear at that point. Workers will still be paying payroll taxes, but under current law the taxes won't be sufficient to pay *all* the benefits owed at that time. By law, Social Security benefit payments can come only from payroll taxes or the trust fund (or the income tax on the benefits of higher-income Americans, which is a tiny source of revenue), not from general tax revenues. So, in the absence of any policy changes, benefits would have to fall by about 21 percent in 2034 and 26 percent in the long run. That is, future retirees would not receive all of benefits they had earned.

While the trust fund's depletion naturally gets the public's attention, Social Security experts generally focus on Social Security's financial outlook over a 75-year period and in the 75th year, with the latter serving as a window into the program's fiscal sustainability (or lack thereof) in subsequent years. Social Security's average shortfall over the next 75 years is roughly 1 percent of GDP. The annual shortfall grows over time, making the shortfall larger in the 75th year, at 1.5 percent. In that year, workers will have earned benefits equal to 6.1 percent of GDP (compared to 4.9 percent in 2018), but program revenues from payroll taxes and taxes on Social Security benefits will be only 4.6 percent of GDP (Figure 8.2). These are sizable, but manageable, shortfalls. As with any projection, the long-term estimates are uncertain and outcomes could be better or worse.[20]

Why does Social Security face a long-term shortfall? Because in a pay-as-you-go system, demography is destiny. We face a substantial increase in beneficiaries relative to workers (Figure 8.3). The number of retirees will rise rapidly as life spans increase and as the baby boomers—the huge cohort of Americans born between 1946 and 1964—move fully into retirement (the youngest boomers turn 65 in 2029). At the same time, the number of workers will grow more slowly than in the past because fertility rates have fallen.[21]

In the future, each worker will support more retirees than in the past, and that will have profound effects on Social Security. With roughly 5 retirees for every 10 workers (as projected for 2070), payroll taxes have to be two-thirds higher, or benefits 40 percent lower, than with 3 retirees for every 10 workers (as in 2010).[22] The nation benefited greatly when the baby boomers moved through their working years, supporting Social Security with all the taxes they paid. Now that's ending, and current payroll tax rates and benefit formulas are not sustainable for future decades.[23]

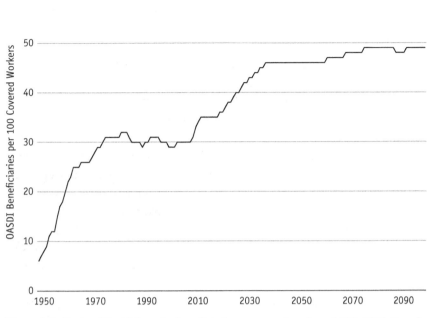

Figure 8.3. Ratio of Social Security beneficiaries to covered workers, 1950–2095. Board of Trustees (2018, Table IV.B3).

An effective Social Security reform plan should meet seven criteria:

- First and foremost, it should restore the program's long-term solvency, eliminating its 75-year shortfall and putting Social Security on a sustainable basis thereafter. The 1983 reforms addressed the first issue, but not the second, which is the main reason we again face a long-term shortfall.[24]
- Second, it should finance the reforms through changes in Social Security itself.[25] Although using more revenues from the income tax to support Social Security would be progressive, it raises other concerns. While it would reduce the Social Security shortfall, it would not reduce the size of the government's overall shortfall. It would muddy the political waters, as Social Security has always stood on its own.
- Third, it should protect vulnerable Americans and enhance the social insurance and anti-poverty features that make Social Security so successful. It should not cut benefits significantly for low- and middle-income retirees. These beneficiaries depend critically on Social Security, and cutting their benefits may not save much money anyway because it could push them into other federal means-tested programs such as Supplemental Security Income. In addition, the rise in the full retirement age that's already occurring through

2027 is equivalent to a reduction in benefit growth for later generations. Given the increase in inequality and stagnant wage patterns shown in Chapter 5, we shouldn't add insult to injury by substantially reducing benefits for low- and moderate-income households.

- Fourth, it should reflect changes in the economy since the 1983 reforms. For one thing, widening income inequality, coupled with the way Social Security calculates increases in the payroll tax cap, means that a smaller share of total wages is now subject to the Social Security payroll tax. For another thing, growing life expectancy for high-income households, coupled with Social Security retirement ages that haven't changed much in recent years, means that high-income retirees will receive benefits for increasingly longer periods but low-income households will not. Before they raise Social Security's retirement age any further, policymakers must consider the fact that life expectancy has not grown significantly for low-income households. Also, women's involvement in the labor force has changed dramatically over the past four decades, suggesting a reexamination of how Social Security provides spousal benefits.

- Fifth, it should treat workers in each generation fairly. The first generation of Social Security recipients received benefits but paid little in taxes because the program started in the middle or end of their careers. Similarly, each time that policymakers expanded the program to cover new groups of Americans, it created a new set of people who were "first generation"—that is, the value of their benefits exceeded their payroll taxes. Policymakers may have good reason to treat first-generation recipients this way; for example, many first-generation beneficiaries of the original Social Security program were veterans of World War I, and the Great Depression caused crippling rates of poverty among the elderly. But this generous treatment of first-generation recipients imposes the costs of their retirement on subsequent generations. Going forward, each generation of workers should pay for the benefits of the retirees of their day plus some of the inherited burden, and those workers should then receive their own retirement benefits from the workers of the next generation.[26]

- Sixth, it should respect public opinion. While any reasonable overall reform will contain both tax increases and spending cuts, the public seems to favor maintaining Social Security benefits over keeping payroll taxes low, as noted in Chapter 6, so the package should tilt toward tax increases.

- Seventh, it should address Social Security's problems sooner rather than later. For Social Security to remain the cornerstone of Americans' retirement security, people should know what benefits they will receive and what taxes they will pay so that they can plan ahead. While 2034—the date of trust fund exhaustion—may seem far away, policymakers typically reform Social Security only gradually. Because no one wants to cut current benefits and because many reform proposals exempt people who are 55 and older from benefit cuts, the effective window for reform is shorter than it may first appear. We shouldn't wait until the last minute, which would force substantial and abrupt tax increases or benefit cuts.

To address these issues, I support the 2016 reform package crafted by a commission sponsored by the Bipartisan Policy Center and led by former Senate Budget Committee chairman Kent Conrad and James B. Lockhart III, former Social Security deputy commissioner under President George W. Bush.[27] Because Social Security is complex, the package contains a significant number of proposals. The main ones are described below. Appendix Table 8.1 lists each element's contribution to the long-run financing solution. As originally unveiled, the package would have taken effect in 2017. All implementation dates (and revenue estimates) here are delayed for four years, so the revised package would take effect in 2021.

Raise the Payroll Tax Cap

The 1977 reforms to Social Security set the payroll tax cap to cover 90 percent of wages in the economy and indexed it to grow with the average increase in wages across the economy. Since then, however, average wages have grown only modestly while high-income wages have grown substantially. Consequently, by 2016, Social Security taxes covered about 83 percent of total wages.[28]

Under the proposal, the taxable earnings cap would quickly rise so that Social Security taxed 86 percent of economy-wide wages by the end of 2024. After 2024, it would index the payroll tax cap for growth in the average wage index plus 0.5 percentage points. The cap would grow faster than average wages over time to strengthen the program's finances and respond fairly to decades of strong income growth among higher-income households.

Several recent bipartisan commissions have proposed similar policies.[29] The change would help restore program finances, would be progressive, and would respond to the widening wage inequality of the past several decades.

Tax More Social Security Benefits of High-Income Households

Currently, people with income above $25,000 if single ($32,000 if married) may owe income taxes on some of their Social Security benefits, with the taxable share of their benefits peaking at 85 percent. The commission proposes that *high-income* households (singles with overall income above $250,000 and married couples with income above $500,000) face income tax on *all* of their Social Security benefits. That would be a small increase in taxes for those households, but it would help make the program more progressive.

Raise the Payroll Tax Rate

The proposal would raise the payroll tax rate by 0.1 percentage points each year for the next decade to eventually reach 13.4 percent. That is, employees and employers would each eventually pay 6.7 percent of wages below the taxable cap, up from 6.2 percent today. The first two tax changes listed above focus on high-income households. Raising payroll taxes would help bring about financial balance and ensure that low- and middle-income earners share some of the burden of higher taxes.

Raise the Full Retirement Age

The package would raise the full retirement age by one month every two years starting in 2027 until it reaches 69 for those turning 62 in 2074. Like raising the payroll tax cap, raising the retirement age is a central element of several other bipartisan plans in recent years.[30] The rationale is simple. People are living longer. For example, 20-year-olds in 2014 were expected to live to age 80, while 20-year-olds in 1950 were expected to live to age 71.[31] To ensure that the balance between working years and retirement years is not tilted excessively, policymakers should respond by raising the full retirement age. Evidence shows that raising the FRA prompts people to delay retiring and claiming benefits, perhaps because it sends a signal that the cultural norm for retirement is changing.[32]

But make no mistake—raising the full retirement age is a benefit cut. Each one-year increase in the full retirement age represents about a 5 percent cut in annual benefits. The cut would hurt the poor more than the rich because the poor rely on Social Security for a greater share of their annual retirement income.

Moreover, life expectancy has risen faster for higher-income people than for others.[33] That's due to many factors, including poorer healthcare and nutrition among lower-income households as well as widening income equality, which directs a growing proportion of resources to the wealthy. Divergent trends in life expectancy make Social Security less progressive because they raise the total lifetime benefits that the rich receive as opposed to the poor.

Consequently, as we raise the full retirement age and, thus, cut annual benefits, we should *not* raise the age, now 62, at which retirees can begin to take *early* retirement benefits. Raising the early retirement age would disproportionally hurt beneficiaries who would find it hard to work past age 62, including, for instance, manual laborers who can no longer do their jobs. Further, we should pair any full retirement age increase with measures to help low-income retirees, such as those discussed next.

Protect Low-Income Beneficiaries and Make Retirement Benefits More Progressive

Because low-income workers would experience benefit cuts resulting from a raised retirement age, the commission's reform package includes several provisions to help protect these beneficiaries. First, it would make the benefit formula more progressive (Figure 8.1). In 2018, PIAs replaced 90 percent of the first $895 in average monthly lifetime earnings. That ratio would rise to 95 percent and apply to a wider band of earnings. Second, it would raise minimum benefits. For example, for a single person with a monthly benefit of $500, the benefit would rise by 57 percent to $784. The benefit boost would decline as benefits rise, and it would disappear as monthly benefits for a single beneficiary reached about $900 per month ($1,360 for couples).

The proposal would make the overall benefit structure more progressive not only by boosting low-income benefits, as above, but also by reducing high-income benefits. The top marginal replacement rate would fall to 5 percent (down from the current 15 percent) on average monthly earnings between $5,397 and the cap (see Figure 8.1).

In addition, the cap on spousal benefits for high-income households would fall below current levels. Currently, each member of a married couple (or of a divorced couple that was married for at least 10 years) is entitled to his or her own benefit or a benefit half as big as the spouse's. In an earlier era of one-earner families, the spousal benefit provided insurance to families across the income spectrum. Over the last half century, though, women have entered the workforce in increasing numbers, and one-worker families are now increasingly concentrated among high-income families. The proposal would scale back and cap benefits for non-working spouses in high-income households.

Support Vulnerable Populations

The package would bolster benefits for vulnerable populations. Currently, a surviving spouse is entitled to the benefit that is greater: his or her own benefit or that of the deceased spouse. The proposal would give survivors 75 percent of their deceased spouse's benefits *in addition to* his or her own benefit. It would reestablish benefits for college-age children of deceased beneficiaries, which were discontinued in 1981. Children (under the age of 23) of disabled or deceased workers would be eligible for benefits if they are full-time students.

Improve Work Incentives for Near-Retirees by Changing the Benefit Formula to Reward Continued Work

Many people will be willing and able to work to older ages in the future than in the past due to longer life expectancies, better health, and shifts in employment toward white-collar jobs. Social Security should encourage this trend, since it will strengthen the program's finances and raise individuals' retirement security by reducing the number of years they are retired. To do this, the commission proposes to change the PIA calculation. The PIA is now determined by lifetime average earnings—that is, wages are averaged over each year in a career. For example, someone who earns $80,000 per year for 10 years (and nothing in the other years) earns the same benefit as someone who makes $40,000 a year for 20 years, even though the former generally had higher lifetime income prospects. The commission would have a PIA calculated for each year's earnings, and then add up the PIAs to obtain the overall retirement benefit. That would boost benefits for the second worker relative to the first and encourage people to work longer.

Change the Way Social Security Calculates Inflation

Experts agree that the consumer price index (CPI) used to calculate cost-of-living increases in Social Security retirement benefits overstates inflation; it doesn't adequately account for people choosing to buy fewer of the things that are rising in price and more of the things that are falling. An alternative measure—the chained CPI—accounts for these issues, providing a more accurate gauge of changes in the cost of living.

The 2017 tax cut changed the indexation of income tax brackets to use the chained CPI. Social Security should use the chained CPI as well. It would reduce the growth rate of benefits very slightly.[34]

Together, these changes would reform Social Security in a way that meets all seven criteria outlined earlier. The package would restore 75-year solvency to Social Security as a whole and to each of its separate programs (OASI and DI) and sustain that solvency further into the future (Appendix Table 8.1). It would also reduce the debt-to-GDP ratio by 22 percentage points by 2050 and by more in subsequent years.

In describing the package's impact, we must distinguish *scheduled benefits*— the benefits that workers will earn under the current system—from *payable benefits*—the benefits that Social Security can legally pay if the trust fund were depleted in 2034. As noted earlier, payable benefits are about 26 percent lower than scheduled benefits over the long run. Relative to payable benefits, low-income beneficiaries would receive a 53 percent increase, middle-income beneficiaries would receive about a 31 percent increase, and high-income households would lose 2 percent. Relative to scheduled benefits—which, we must remember, are unsustainable under current law—low-income households would see a 17 percent increase, middle-income households would see a 2 percent cut, and higher-income households would see a 26 percent cut.[35]

The package would raise benefits for the most vulnerable retirees and reduce poverty rates among the elderly by 49 percent compared to currently payable benefits and by 25 percent compared to scheduled benefits.

By building up trust fund balances to above 150 percent of annual costs, the package would restore equity across generations. Workers in the next few generations would pay not only for the retirement of the generation that preceded them but also for some of the inherited debt.

To be sure, this plan isn't the only way to strengthen Social Security, and policymakers will undoubtedly consider other ideas as well. But whatever they do, they should avoid two prominent ideas.

The first involves investing Social Security's surpluses in the stock market. Proponents say it would help strengthen the program's finances because stocks yield higher average returns than the Treasury securities in which Social Security invests under current law. Higher stock market returns could, in fact, reduce the need for painful benefit cuts or tax increases.[36] But stock market investing isn't the free lunch that its proponents sometimes suggest. The stock market is a riskier investment for Social Security's surpluses than Treasury bonds for an obvious reason: stocks go up, but stocks also go down. If the market falls at a time when Social Security needs its surpluses to pay benefits, the program could find itself without the needed resources, leaving policymakers with the tough choice of cutting Social Security benefits, raising taxes, or borrowing more money.

The second, and bigger, mistake would be to privatize part or all of Social Security—that is, to divert some of workers' payroll taxes into individual accounts that work like individual retirement accounts (IRAs) or 401(k) plans. Privatization would replace some Social Security benefits—which are adjusted for inflation, last for a retiree's lifetime, and are immune to stock market fluctuations—with individual accounts that have none of those positive features. Private accounts would probably reduce the program's progressivity as well.

Proponents claim that people can do better financially with their own private investments than they do when you consider the Social Security payroll taxes they pay and the benefits they will receive. That's a classic apples-to-oranges comparison, though. As noted, stocks go up and stocks go down, making private accounts riskier than today's guaranteed benefits. Under Social Security, people get the money when they need it most—in survivorship, dependency, or disability situations. That wouldn't be true under private accounts if workers needed benefits early in their careers (before assets were built up) or at just the time the market tanked. Moreover, if Social Security were converted—all or in part—to private accounts, the program would still need to pay currently promised benefits. Proponents often ignore this burden when they tout the benefits of a private system. Finally, Social Security operates with extremely low overhead. Privatization would generate administrative costs of managing tens of millions of private accounts.

To be clear, encouraging people to save more in private accounts *outside* of Social Security—so-called add-on accounts—could help people better prepare for retirement. Policymakers could establish automatic enrollment in individual retirement accounts and expand automatic features in 401(k) plans. Or they could establish mandatory add-on accounts to which workers and employers would contribute 1 percent of pay and the government would make a progressive contribution. Workers could withdraw funds from these accounts beginning at age 62 to match what their Social Security benefits would be. They would have to exhaust funds from these accounts before claiming Social Security benefits. This would allow people to claim Social Security at later ages, raising their annual benefit payments and reducing poverty rates among the elderly.[37]

In any case, in the words of Peter Diamond, MIT economics professor and Nobel Prize winner, and Peter Orszag, former director of the Congressional budget office and Obama's Budget Office, we don't need to destroy Social Security to save it.[38] Progressive reforms would restore sustainability, maintain the program's vital role in providing retirement income and social insurance, and improve the program's design.

Notes

1. Commission on Retirement Security and Personal Savings (2016).
2. DeWitt (2005).
3. At the inception of Social Security, policymakers were concerned whether the federal government was constitutionally permitted to impose taxes on state and local governments.
4. Currently, about three-quarters of state and local government workers are covered by Social Security, and all of them are covered by Medicare (Gale, Holmes, and John 2015).
5. Center on Budget and Policy Priorities (2016).
6. Fox (2017).
7. Social Security Administration (2016).
8. Self-employed workers pay both the employee and employer share—the full 12.4 percent. In 2018, payroll tax revenue accounted for 96 percent of all Social Security tax–related funding (Board of Trustees 2018). Social Security benefits are subject to the income tax, which contributes the rest of the revenue.
9. To calculate benefits, the Social Security Administration adjusts a worker's earnings in each year for nationwide wage growth, averages the highest 35 years, and converts that average to a monthly figure called "average indexed monthly earnings" (AIME). For someone with more than 35 years of earnings, the highest 35 years are included. For someone with fewer than 35 years of earnings, all years' earnings are included and earnings are deemed to be zero for any years fewer than 35.
10. Figure 8.1 depicts the benefit schedule in 2016 and in the reform package developed in this chapter (2016 dollars).
11. Social Security Administration (2015).
12. The benefit is reduced further for people who retire early and who earn above a certain income threshold. This is known as the "earnings test." In 2018, payouts for beneficiaries below the FRA were reduced by $1 for every $2 over $17,040 in earnings. The penalty is offset by a compensating benefit increase once the beneficiary reaches the full retirement age, which is calculated to be actuarially fair given one's expected life span.
13. Spouses can receive old-age or disability benefits if they are at least 62 years old (or caring for a child who is younger than 16 or disabled). Divorced spouses who are unmarried and 62 or older can receive old-age benefits if the marriage lasted at least 10 years and the benefit they would receive based on their own work is less than what they would receive based on their spouse's work. Children can generally receive benefits until they reach 18 if they are unmarried. Disabled children can generally receive benefits even if they are older than 18. Spouses with low earnings can receive up to 50 percent of the worker's benefit. This share is lower for those who receive benefits before the full retirement age. Total family old-age benefits are limited to around 150–180 percent of the retiree's benefit. Each family member can receive up to 50 percent of the disabled worker's DI benefit, up to the same limit.
14. Social Security Administration (2017a).
15. Fichtner and Seligman (2016). Beyond fiscal balance, DI reform should focus on getting DI beneficiaries to stay in or return to the workforce. Only about 1 percent of DI beneficiaries return to the workforce each year. Research implies that a sizable minority of DI recipients could plausibly return to work. Numerous policies could help achieve this goal, including giving employers better incentives to retain or hire disabled workers, giving states less incentive to transfer indigent citizens from state welfare programs to federal disability

insurance, and allowing for partial or temporary disability payments. The single most important change would be to ensure that the Social Security Administration has enough funding to conduct reviews of the status of existing beneficiaries. Funds for reviews have been restricted with the discretionary spending cuts and sequestration in recent years, and there is now an enormous backlog of cases. The Social Security Administration estimates that each dollar it spends doing reviews saves $10 in future benefits (Autor and Duggan 2006, 2010; Bipartisan Policy Center 2015; Liebman 2015; Liebman and Smalligan 2013).

16. Board of Trustees (2018, Table V.C7). Others estimate the replacement rate to be higher. The difference occurs because the Social Security Administration adjusts prior years' wages by national wage growth whereas other calculations adjust prior years' wages by price inflation. See, for example, Pang and Schieber (2014).

17. OECD (2017); Ruffing (2013).

18. Board of Trustees (2018).

19. This is the combined OASI and DI Trust Fund. When looking at each component separately, the OASI Trust Fund is expected to be depleted in 2034, whereas DI is expected to become insolvent in 2032. Because the programs are so closely related, it makes sense to think of them as a combined whole. Focusing on the 2034 date implicitly assumes that when the DI Trust Fund balance hits zero in 2032, policymakers will shift funds from the OASI Trust Fund to the DI Trust Fund. In similar situations, policymakers enacted similar changes in 1994 and 2015.

20. The current law projections in Figure 8.2 are based on calculations by the Social Security Trustees (Board of Trustees 2018). Projections by the Social Security Technical Panel of Advisors and by the Congressional Budget Office (2018) show even higher shortfalls. The different projections are due to differences in assumptions about interest rates, wage growth, income distribution, life expectancy, birth rates, immigration, and other factors.

21. National Center for Health Statistics (2016).

22. The rise in beneficiaries per worker coincides with a decline in young people per worker, so that the overall population dependency ratio—the number of people younger than 18 or older than 64 compared to the number of people aged 18–64—will be lower in the future than it was in the 1960s and 1970s (Ortman and Velkoff 2014). This could help free up societal resources for the elderly.

23. Demographic patterns would not affect the viability of a fully pre-funded system—where each worker pays for his or her own retirement by building up a fund, like a 401(k) plan. But converting from a pay-as-you-go system to a fully funded system would require the transitional generation to pay for both its own retirement and the retirement of the generation preceding it.

24. About 70 percent of the decline in Social Security's 75-year outlook since 1983 is due to the change in the projection period. The rest is due to patterns of wage growth, income distribution, immigration, disability claiming, and other factors that turned out differently from what had been projected in 1983 (Munnell 2017).

25. There are a few exceptions. Most recently, during the payroll tax holiday of 2011 and 2012, general revenues were used to partially finance Social Security. This made it so that the rate reductions would not have a large effect on the overall trust fund. General funds also paid for special Social Security benefits to military personnel from 1957 to 2001 and a payroll tax credit in 1984 (Committee for a Responsible Federal Budget 2014).

26. For discussion and estimates of the inherited debt, also called the "legacy debt," see Board of Trustees (2018, Table VI.F2) and Diamond and Orszag (2005). Which future generations pay for the legacy debt is a question of fairness. If, for example, we set payroll taxes for the next several decades sufficiently low that they just cover benefits in each year, the trust fund would remain at zero (after 2034) and the burden of legacy debt would be pushed further into the future. If, instead, we set payroll taxes high enough that we could continue to pay current beneficiaries and we had enough revenue as well to convert Social Security to a fully funded system—where each worker's contributions went into a saving account like

a 401(k) plan—then one generation (or a few, until all current beneficiaries died) would end up paying twice—for the previous generation's retirement and for building up its own retirement. Policies that embody generational fairness fall between those two extremes. An equitable approach would provide a significant trust fund buildup relative to the zeroing out projected in 2034, but it would not require any single generation to pay fully for two generations' retirement.

27. Commission on Retirement Security and Personal Savings (2016).
28. Board of Trustees (2018); Commission on Retirement Security and Personal Savings (2016).
29. Debt Reduction Task Force (2010); National Commission on Fiscal Responsibility and Reform (2010).
30. Debt Reduction Task Force (2010); National Commission on Fiscal Responsibility and Reform (2010).
31. Arias, Heron, and Xu (2017).
32. Aaron (2013); Manchester and Song (2011). Working longer and claiming benefits later would also make it easier for households to accumulate adequate amounts of overall saving for retirement since people would have more years to save and fewer in retirement.
33. National Academies of Sciences, Engineering, and Medicine (2015).
34. Social Security Administration (2017b). The package would also amend some anomalies in the treatment of government workers.
35. In this example, beneficiaries are assumed to work 35 years and be part of a two-earner couple with equal earnings. Similar results apply for single taxpayers.
36. It is not a crazy idea—state pension plans hold private assets, and some other countries invest their Social Security trust funds privately. Governance problems, such as how the government would vote as a stockholder, and policy complications—the government would want to take into account the effect of any new legislation on the stock market and its impact on the trust fund—could be managed.
37. Koenig, Fichtner, and Gale (2018); Gale, Iwry, and Orszag (2005); Iwry and John (2009).
38. Diamond and Orszag (2005).

Appendix Table 8.1. **Effects of the Proposal on the Social Security Trust Fund**

	Percent of 75-Year Gap[1]	Percent of Gap in 75th Year[1]
Provision[2]		
Encourage Work		
Raise retirement age	18.8	30.8
Change benefit formula	8.6	8.7
Make System More Progressive		
Raise payroll tax cap	21.1	14.5
Add new bend point	1.5	2.3
Raise minimum benefit level	−7.1	−5.5
Raise survivor benefits	0.8	−4.8
Reinstate benefits for college-aged children	−2.3	−1.4
Limit spousal benefits for high-income households	4.1	4.8
Increase taxation of benefits for high-income households	0.4	0.2
Correct Inflation Calculation		
Use chained CPI-U	17.7	14
Other		
Raise payroll tax rate	33.1	23
Change treatment of government workers	2.3	2.1
Subtotal Including Interactions	104.1	95.4
Interest Income	NA[3]	34.5

Notes:

1. Percent of the gap reported in Board of Trustees (2016). Estimates are for the proposal as written, updated for the 2016 Social Security Trustees Report.

2. Does not include interaction effects.

3. Interest income is embedded in the 75-year estimates for each component.

Source: Goss (2016); Author's calculations.

9

Investing in People

Economic growth used to be an effective anti-poverty program that helped everyone climb the economic ladder. That's what President Kennedy meant when he said, "A rising tide lifts all boats." Over the past 40 years, however, the economy more than tripled in size but wages stagnated for low- and middle-income workers, showing that growth alone won't necessarily boost incomes and reduce poverty anymore. We need better policies.

The federal government invests in people in two main ways. Through safety net programs, it promotes economic security by providing a helping hand for those who face temporary or long-term hardship. Through education and training programs, it helps people expand knowledge and develop skills to improve their economic opportunity.

Although many people say that government programs don't work, growing evidence shows that investing in people has significant benefits. Many major safety net programs benefit adults and their children by reducing poverty, improving educational outcomes, raising future earnings, improving health, and reducing crime. More education makes workers more productive, boosts their future earnings and tax payments, and helps the economy as a whole.

We can exploit these findings to grow the economy and make it fairer at the same time. We should provide an additional 1 percent of GDP per year through 2050 to finance initiatives in five areas: patching holes in the safety net, investing in children, raising educational attainment, providing jobs and job training to people who need them, and making work pay better. That would be a sizable increase in these programs. But it's not an unreasonable one; it is only about a fifth of what we spend on Social Security and an eighth of income tax revenues. These investments would raise the debt-to-GDP ratio in 2050 by 28 percentage points before considering the multitude of benefits noted above. They would be financed by tax increases described in later chapters.

Poverty is surprisingly widespread in the richest nation known to history. About 14 percent of Americans (45 million people), including 15 percent of children

(11 million), were poor in 2016. For context, the poverty line for a family of four that lived in rental housing was about $24,300 that year.[1]

But many more people are poor for at least part of their lives than in any single year. Over half of working-age Americans will spend at least a year in poverty.[2] Half of all children will live in a household that benefits from food assistance programs such as the Supplemental Nutrition Assistance Program (SNAP) or the Special Supplemental Nutrition Program for Women, Infants and Children (WIC) at some point when they're children.[3] These programs provide crucial support at the time it is needed most.

More troubling, poverty can be persistent for many people, over time and across generations, due to a complicated web of self-reinforcing constraints. Growing up poor adversely affects children's future health, education, and adult earnings.[4] These effects are strongest for the children of families in "deep poverty"—with incomes at less than half of the poverty line—and children who are poor early in life or who remain poor for extended periods.[5]

The safety net plays a key role in protecting many of our most vulnerable people, including children, the elderly, the disabled, the unemployed, and the poor (Appendix Table 9.1). It provides a basic level of economic security and insurance against many major economic risks while, at the same time, preserving or creating incentives for people to work, save, and invest—that is, it provides a "hand up," not a "hand out."[6] Medicare, Medicaid, CHIP, Social Security, and Disability Insurance are key elements of the safety net, as discussed in earlier chapters. Among the other major safety net programs, two provide cash:

- Temporary Assistance for Needy Families (TANF) provides cash assistance and other benefits such as childcare to low-income earners. The program seeks to encourage the transition from welfare to work. Benefits are time limited, and recipients also must engage in work or work-related activity such as training or seeking work. Monthly benefits come from federal and state governments and vary widely, ranging from $1,021 in New Hampshire to $170 in Mississippi for a single-parent family of three in 2017. TANF benefit levels don't come close to lifting households out of poverty in any state.[7]
- Supplemental Security Income (SSI) provides income to the elderly, blind, and disabled. Originally designed to supplement Social Security for the low-income elderly, it's grown into a broader anti-poverty program. Unlike in TANF, beneficiaries don't face benefit time limits.

The tax code is home to several major safety net programs. Here are the two largest:

- The Earned Income Tax Credit (EITC), which provides benefits through income tax reductions and refunds, is larger than TANF or SSI and is one of the nation's most effective safety net programs. The tax credits that it provides to low- and moderate-income earners are "refundable," meaning they can reduce one's tax liability below zero, at which point the taxpayer receives a net payment from the government. For a single parent with two children in 2018, the credit is 40 percent of the first $14,290 of earnings, tops out at $5,716 when earnings are between $14,290 and $18,660, and then phases out as income rises to $45,802.
- The child tax credit (CTC) provides a partially refundable tax credit for working families with children. The 2017 tax overhaul temporarily expanded the credit so that as of 2018, it's equal to 15 percent of earnings above $2,500 up to a maximum value of $2,000 per child (the maximum refundable portion is only $1,400). The credit phases out as income exceeds $200,000 ($400,000 if married filing jointly).[8] More than 80 percent of families with children received at least some portion of the credit in 2018.[9] To receive the full credit, families must earn over $30,000.

Several other federal programs provide "in-kind" transfers, either by providing vouchers with which recipients can pay for particular items or by providing particular goods or services directly. For example, two major programs help people buy food:

- SNAP, the successor to food stamps, is widely available to low-income households. Federally funded and state administered, the program provides benefits based on family size to those in or near poverty. In a typical month, SNAP helps nearly 20 million children, or one in four children in America. Two-thirds of SNAP benefits go to children.
- WIC provides food and healthcare services to low-income pregnant women and their children. It's funded federally but administered by state and local governments.

The federal government also provides subsidies for housing and home energy costs:

- Housing assistance subsidizes low-income families' rental costs and the building of affordable rental housing, mainly by providing vouchers with which such families can pay their rent. About 75 percent of households that get federal housing assistance live in privately owned properties. Public housing grew very unpopular in recent decades because it fueled segregation, concentrated poverty, and crime, prompting policymakers to opt more for rental subsidies.

- The Low-Income Home Energy Assistance Program (LIHEAP) provides federal grants to states to help households below 150 percent of the poverty line pay for home heating and cooling costs. Lower-income households typically face higher energy bills as a share of their income because energy is a necessity and because they live in older buildings that are less energy efficient.

The programs described above serve a broad swath of Americans. In 2012, the most recent year for which comprehensive data are available, about 106 million people, or a third of the population, received benefits from at least one of these eight programs.[10] In addition, tens of millions more received benefits from Medicare, Medicaid, Social Security, or Disability Insurance.[11]

The stereotype of the "welfare queen" who sits idly and collects welfare checks remains a common image, implicitly if not always explicitly, but it's highly misleading. Over 80 percent of households that received assistance under one or more of the programs listed above had earned income, and most of the other 20 percent included individuals who were blind, elderly, or disabled.[12]

Two other programs round out the federal government's major social safety net programs:

- Unemployment insurance (UI) pays benefits for up to 26 weeks to unemployed workers, and it's financed by a small payroll tax that employers pay for each of their employees.[13] To qualify for UI benefits, recipients must have lost their jobs through no fault of their own, be actively looking for work, and have earned a specified minimum income during a prior period.
- Veterans' benefits provide financial support and other services to veterans who were wounded in combat or subsequently disabled as a result of their combat duty. Veterans' pensions and survivors' benefit programs provide financial support to elderly low-income veterans.

The safety net has evolved over time in accordance with societal resources and values, changing from an original system that largely provided outright, unconditional assistance to the needy to one today that provides less help for the extremely poor and more for the working poor.

President Franklin D. Roosevelt initiated the safety net in the 1930s with his New Deal, when lawmakers created Social Security, Aid to Families with Dependent Children (AFDC, the predecessor to TANF), public housing, a temporary food stamp program, and other initiatives.

In the 1960s, President Johnson launched the War on Poverty not just to insure people against risk but also to break the cycle of poverty. Under his leadership, policymakers created Medicare, Medicaid, Head Start, Job Corps, and many other initiatives. He also made food stamps a permanent part of the safety net.

As AFDC caseloads rose in the 1960s and 1970s, concerns grew that welfare was reducing incentives to work because families could receive benefits while idle. In response, policymakers created the Earned Income Tax Credit (EITC), which raises people's incentives to work by boosting the incomes only of working households. Since then, policymakers have expanded the EITC several times on a bipartisan basis.

These changes set the stage for welfare reform. The 1996 welfare law would, in the words of President Clinton, "end welfare as we know it" by replacing AFDC with the TANF block grant, which gave states a certain amount of money each year to provide poor families with cash and work-related assistance. Unlike AFDC, TANF set limits on the amount of time during which recipients could receive benefits.

Since then, the safety net system has continued to move toward assistance for the working poor, with recent expansions of EITC and CTC and a simultaneous decline in TANF cash assistance (Figure 9.1). President Trump and

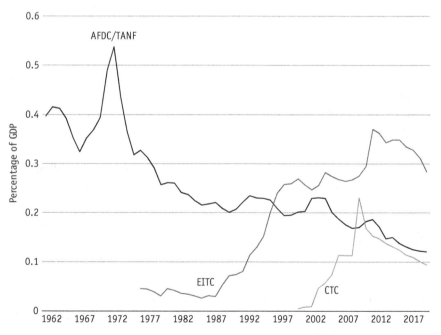

Figure 9.1. Changing composition of cash assistance, 1962–2018. Temporary Assistance for Needy Families (TANF) spending also includes family support payments. Earned income tax credit (EITC) and child tax credit (CTC) values represent only the refundable portions. Office of Management and Budget (2018).

the Republicans in Congress have pushed for increased work requirements for TANF, SNAP, and public housing recipients.[14]

Safety net programs provide numerous economic benefits for the people they reach. Most prominently, they reduce poverty. In 2016, the programs discussed above lifted as many as 36 million people (including about 7 million children) above the poverty line.[15] Cash assistance alone doesn't often do the job because only a small share of eligible families receive any support and the amounts provided are small.[16] But SNAP lifted more than 8 million people out of poverty, including almost 4 million children; together, the EITC and CTC did the same for almost 10 million people, including more than 5 million children.[17] SSI did so for more than 5 million people, and vouchers and other housing policies did so for 4 million people, including 1.5 million children.

The safety net has reduced the poverty rate over time as well. In 1967, as President Johnson was launching the War on Poverty, the poverty rate was 26.4 percent when calculated only on people's privately earned income. That rate was about the same as of 2015. But after accounting for all federal safety net programs—including Social Security and the programs listed above—the poverty rate fell from 25 percent to 14.7 percent over the same period.[18]

Safety net programs also combat deep poverty, though this effect appears to have declined over time with the shift of focus from unconditional assistance to conditional programs in recent years. In 2015, SNAP fueled the largest drops in deep poverty (4.5 million people, including 2 million children), followed by SSI (4.3 million people, including 800,000 children). TANF, the EITC, and housing subsidies also had significant impacts.[19] But the "deep poverty" rate has actually increased since the 1980s.[20]

Beyond reducing poverty, safety net programs help children, families, and the economy in other ways. They often generate positive long-term effects for people's health, educational attainment, and earnings potential.

For instance, mothers on SNAP during pregnancy gave birth to fewer low birthweight babies. Children whose families receive SNAP have higher reading and math skills (especially among girls) and greater chances of graduating from high school.[21] Children with SNAP benefits from conception through early childhood tend to have lower rates of child obesity, lower blood pressure, and less heart disease and diabetes. Access to SNAP early in life gives women more economic self-sufficiency as adults.[22]

Women on WIC give birth to healthier babies with higher average birthweights and lower infant mortality.[23] Children on WIC have comparable immunization rates to higher-income children and may have greater access to healthcare services.[24] Children with mothers on WIC while pregnant have higher cognitive development by age two, and those benefits extend into early school years.[25]

The EITC boosts the employment of single mothers, especially those with multiple children and lower skill levels.[26] It may be, says one expert, "the single most important policy measure for explaining the decrease in welfare and the rise in work and earnings among female-headed households."[27] Within families that receive the EITC, health outcomes tend to be better for both children and mothers. Infants whose mothers receive the credit are less likely to be born at a low birthweight.[28] The CTC has similar effects on recipients, albeit smaller in magnitude than the EITC.

Vouchers and other housing policies reduce rent costs for recipients, allowing them to spend their limited funds on other necessities. Households with children that receive vouchers are less likely to end up homeless or live in crowded conditions and move less frequently.[29] Housing policy can also influence lifetime outcomes through neighborhood effects. The Moving to Opportunity (MTO) experiment found that adults reported feeling safer and more satisfied with their housing and neighborhoods and were less likely to be obese after moving to communities with higher average income.[30] Children in these programs who moved when they were younger than 13 were more likely to attend college and have higher incomes. [31]

There is even evidence that safety net programs reduce crime. Children who grow up in families that receive food stamps engage in less criminal behavior—particularly violent acts and felonies—later in life.[32] Head Start (discussed below) also reduces crime by participants and children whose parents were in the program.[33]

Critics complain that safety net programs can reduce incentives to work, but if so, the effects tend to be small. And some programs, especially the EITC, CTC, and TANF, encourage work. In fact, for the EITC, the earnings gains from employment may be as large as government spending on the credit.[34]

Education and training programs are the other main way that the government invests in people (Appendix Table 9.2). State and local governments finance most public education at the elementary and secondary level, while the federal government plays a larger role in supporting pre-kindergarten programs and higher education. Through federal funding:

- Head Start provides pre-school programs for three- and four-year-olds in low-income families, helping to develop school readiness, giving health services to the pre-schoolers, and offering various services to their parents. A smaller program called Early Head Start provides similar services to infants and toddlers under three years of age. In 2017, about 4 percent of children five years old and younger were enrolled in a Head Start program.[35]

- The National School Lunch (NSLP) and School Breakfast (SBP) programs give federal assistance to schools to provide free and subsidized meals to children from low-income families.

- Pell Grants help students cover the costs of two-year and four-year, for-profit and non-profit post-secondary institutions. Students must demonstrate a financial need and meet certain academic requirements.[36] In 2018, 7.5 million recipients received grants of up to $6,095.

- The Direct Student Loan Program provides loans to undergraduate and graduate students and their parents to help pay for undergraduate and graduate degree programs. In 2018, 16.2 million new loans were granted, about 40 percent of which were subsidized. The average undergraduate loan in 2018 was around $3,600.

The tax code also offers a plethora of higher education subsidies. Participation in one of these programs often precludes participation in others.

- The American Opportunity Tax Credit (AOTC) provides a maximum credit of $2,500 a year to students for up to four years while they are enrolled in an undergraduate degree program, and it's partially refundable. The Lifetime Learning Credit (LLC) provides a non-refundable (that is, the value is capped at tax liability) 20 percent credit up to $2,000 a year per taxpayer for qualifying tuition and expenses. Both programs phase out as income rises.

- Tax-preferred saving accounts—Coverdell Education Saving Accounts and Qualified Tuition plans (QTPs, also called 529 plans)—help households save for educational expenses. Although contributions are not tax deductible, the assets accumulate tax free and account holders can withdraw them tax free to pay for education. Coverdells have income limits, contribution limits of $2,000, and can go for elementary and secondary schooling as well as college. QTPs have no income limits, higher contribution limits, and must go toward postsecondary education.[37]

The federal government also provides job training that's focused on low-skilled workers and displaced workers. One Stop Career Centers offer job postings, workshops on résumé writing and interview skills, counseling, and other services. Participants can get vouchers to buy training through an approved list of providers (including community colleges and private companies). Youth programs include tutoring, alternative schools, mentoring, leadership development, and summer employment. The Labor Department also sponsors Job Corps for disadvantaged youth and young adults.

Early childhood education can shape the rest of a child's life and thus can generate high returns, both for the child and for society. The skills that children learn in pre-school help them develop into more responsible, healthier, higher-earning adults. The gains to the public include a more productive, healthier workforce and less crime—all of which generate higher tax revenues and less public spending. Head Start enrollees, for example, experience substantial long-term gains on a wide variety of education, earnings, and mental and physical health measures. These results are consistent with those of other pre-school programs.[38]

College is, on average, undoubtedly a very good investment for the individual and society. As of 2016, college degree holders earned $25,000 more per year than those with only a high school diploma.[39] Over the course of a lifetime, the earnings difference is $590,000 for men and $370,000 for women in present value, after accounting for tuition costs.[40]

Current tax credits to help families afford college generally do not raise college attendance or affect college choice.[41] One reason is that most recipients would have attended college anyway. Other than Pell Grants, education subsidies aren't targeted enough on low-income students who need the most help with college costs and are least likely to acquire post-secondary education. That's particularly true for 529 plans, whose participants are almost exclusively high-income families. A second reason is that taxpayers receive their credits after filing tax returns in the winter or spring rather than when tuition is due in the fall, limiting the ability of cash-constrained households to exploit the opportunity in the first place.[42] A third reason is complexity: applications are so complicated and programs so numerous that many people forgo aid, complete the forms incorrectly, or don't know of the opportunities.[43]

Vocational training boosts employment and earnings for low-skilled workers. Workers can raise their per-quarter earnings between $300 and $900 on average by enrolling in a job training program—more than enough to outweigh the costs.[44] Results are less encouraging for dislocated workers, however, because many who start the programs don't complete them and those who complete them often struggle to find a job that matches the new skills they learned and pays as much as their previous skilled job.[45]

Community college attendance, often funded through Pell Grants, has been rising among unemployed workers, and many programs teach the skills needed for new careers. For youth, intensive jobs training programs are the most effective because disadvantaged teens face a myriad of problems beyond unemployment. Job Corps is extremely effective because it removes children from environments that are often troubled, raising their educational attainment and earnings and reducing their criminal activity for several years after program completion.[46]

Federal investments in people aren't budget busters. In 2018, federal spending on all of the safety net, education, and training programs cited above was just 2.5 percent of GDP. Counting the non-refundable portions of the EITC and CTC, the total equaled 2.75 percent. That's slightly less than all of Medicare, and it's substantially less than defense or Social Security.

The United States spends less on comparable social programs as a share of GDP than the average across the OECD.[47] It also spends significantly less than other countries on job training programs. The United States, however, ranks among the highest for total education spending when taking both private and public sources into account and across all levels of schooling. Nevertheless, it ranks near average in reading and math test scores.

As we allocate an additional 1 percent of GDP per year in federal investments in people, we should take guidance from a bipartisan task force of experts that provided three guiding principles for such investments.[48] First, society should offer people as much *opportunity* as possible to improve themselves and live freely, regardless of the circumstances of their birth. Second, people should take *personal responsibility* for their actions, and public policies should strengthen their ability to do so. Third, society has a *collective responsibility* to provide economic security, especially to provide particular goods and services and at particular times and places when private markets cannot do so.

We should also be cognizant of the ubiquitous role of luck in the economic system, as discussed in Chapter 5. Children don't choose their parents, but parents' genetic, social, and economic characteristics have an enormous impact on the lives and welfare of their children, as do the neighborhoods and schools the children experience.

Reflecting these ideas, I propose a fivefold strategy for investing in people: patch holes in the safety net, invest in children, raise educational attainment, provide job training and jobs to people who need them, and make work pay better. This strategy represents the themes we should address in reform; many particular program options are consistent with those themes.

Patch Holes and Strengthen the Safety Net

We could significantly help low-income households simply by ensuring that people receive all the benefits for which they qualify. Only 23 percent of eligible families—all of whom are poor families with children—receive TANF benefits. Only a quarter of eligible households receive federal rental assistance.[49] Only 16 percent of families eligible for energy assistance receive it.[50]

We need to boost core benefits. Average TANF benefits have shrunk by 20 percent in inflation-adjusted terms since TANF's creation in 1996 and now equal less than half of the poverty line in every state except New Hampshire.[51] Energy assistance covered just 10 percent of home energy bills of eligible households in 2014.[52]

We need to do more for childless adults, who receive very limited SNAP and EITC benefits and may not be eligible to receive SSI even if they are elderly or disabled. The EITC provides no more than $300 a year for a childless worker, compared to more than $3,000 for one with children. An expanded EITC for childless adults not only would increase work incentives for those adults, it may help children as well. That's because many people who are considered "childless" are actually non-custodial parents with child-rearing responsibilities.[53]

We also need to provide better protection to people during recessions. During the Great Recession, TANF caseloads did not increase (whereas SNAP and UI did), causing extreme poverty for those with the lowest incomes and limiting TANF's potential to help those it was intended to support.[54]

Invest in Children

A significant national effort to invest more in the education and care of children would enhance their outcomes as adults and provide significant benefits for society. Children who attend pre-school are better prepared for kindergarten than their peers, setting them up for later success in school. But currently, higher-income children are more likely to attend pre-school than lower-income children. While most states have pre-K programs, the federal government should continue to set and enforce quality standards and expand its Head Start program both in funding and enrollment.

The CTC provides parents with more income, which has positive long-run benefits for children. But only families with earnings above $2,500 can receive its refundable portion, even though the lowest-income families need it the most. Policymakers could eliminate the minimum earnings threshold for refundability, or they could go further and replace the credit altogether with a refundable Universal Child Allowance that would provide benefits to all families with children.

Better, more affordable childcare would help children, their parents, and the businesses where such parents work. But good childcare is expensive. The average cost of full-time childcare is about $10,000 per year or higher.[55] In fact, when childcare costs for a single-parent family with two kids and earnings equal to half of the average wage are compared among developed nations, the United

States ranks last on childcare affordability.[56] To help cover childcare costs for low-income parents, the government could deposit funds into special accounts, with the amount deposited each year dependent on the child's age and the associated average cost of care.[57]

Raise Educational Attainment

A simpler financial aid process would make it likelier that students would go to college and receive more financial aid.[58] The government should focus college subsidies on households that are most sensitive to price and deliver the benefits at the time that households have to cover schooling expenses.[59] Policymakers should consolidate all higher education credits and Pell Grants into a single federal program. The IRS could send family income data to the Education Department, which would then deliver the funds directly to the applicable institution. To apply, students or their families could check a box on their tax returns.[60]

And for student loans, policymakers should establish an income-based repayment system that lets borrowers spread out their repayments over a longer period of time and conform them with recipients' ability to pay.[61]

Though states and localities finance most K–12 education, federal funds and policies certainly have an impact. Declining levels of federal aid to states put more pressure on state education budgets, and state funding shortfalls potentially hurt student performance.[62] The federal government should increase its K–12 funding, targeting additional funding toward low-income school districts to help narrow the educational funding disparities between well-to-do and struggling communities.[63]

Provide Training and Jobs

If the government requires work as a condition for eligibility for safety net programs, it should guarantee that jobs are available to those who want them. During the Great Depression, the government created public service jobs—though program eligibility was not conditioned on working. Today's economy is increasingly skill-based, so workers without the needed skills can be left at a disadvantage in trying to find good jobs. While funding for traditional job training programs has shrunk significantly over the past several decades, community colleges are providing, and Pell Grants are funding, an increasing amount of technical training. In addition, states have been experimenting with programs that allow disadvantaged teens and adults to learn skills and enter a particular sector in their local economy. To expand these efforts, the federal government can increase its funding to community colleges and target it on technical training.

The federal government can also work with state and local governments to introduce students to technical career pathways from an early age.[64] Federal policymakers could provide incentives for community colleges to offer such programs, or the federal government could promote apprenticeship programs that train students for jobs in high demand.[65]

Make Work Pay Better

For work to be the centerpiece of anti-poverty efforts, it must actually lift people out of poverty. We need a range of policies that, together, would give hard-working, low-earning families a hand up.

In 2018, a full-time minimum wage worker earned $15,080, which would leave a one-parent family with two children more than $4,000 below the poverty line. The federal minimum wage was $7.25 in 2018 (although some states and cities have set higher minimums).[66] Because policymakers haven't raised it since 2009, it has shrunk in inflation-adjusted value by 15 percent since then and by 36 percent since its peak value in 1968. Policymakers should raise it to $10.10 and set it to rise automatically with inflation. That would raise wages directly for 16.5 million people, indirectly for 8 million more, and lift 900,000 people out of poverty.[67] And with higher incomes, the families in question would need less public assistance.[68] It would have modest effects on employment.[69]

The United States is the only OECD country without a paid maternity leave policy, and most advanced countries also have paternity leave policies. In Europe, children whose mothers used maternity leave programs ended up with more education, less teen pregnancy, higher IQs, and higher earnings as adults.[70] Paid parental leave also makes it likelier that women return to work after giving birth, fueling higher long-run earnings and employment.[71] In the United States, the Family Medical Leave Act allows for 12 weeks of *unpaid* leave for covered workers who give birth or need to care for another family member.[72] Many parents, however, can't afford to take time off, and less than 40 percent of workers have access to paid parental leave.[73] We need a federal paid leave program that's cost-effective, encourages parents to return to work, is gender-neutral, ensures access for the poorest workers, minimizes labor market disruptions, and is funded through employer and employee contributions.

Unemployment insurance helps work pay better because it enables jobless workers to search longer and more effectively for jobs, raising the chances that they'll find positions that capitalize on their skills and, thus, pay more. Reforms, however, would make UI even more effective. For example, policymakers could pair UI benefits with entrepreneurial training programs, providing assistance while the unemployed take internships or temporary jobs that may lead to full-time work. Those who participate in job training programs could receive extended UI benefits.

Another option is to provide a tax subsidy for two-earner couples. The income tax, coupled with government transfer programs, creates high effective tax rates on the wages of a second earner in a couple. While the marginal tax rate for the primary worker starts at zero on the first dollar of earnings (and the effective marginal tax rate is negative because of the Earned Income Credit), a second earner's wages can be taxed at high rates because the earnings are added on top of those of the primary earner when calculating income taxes. These costs can add up quickly and make it impractical for the second earner to work.[74]

In their efforts to improve the safety net, policymakers should avoid two options that some experts promote. The first is block granting, often a cause célèbre among conservatives, through which the federal government would provide a set amount of funds each year to the states to address a problem (e.g., healthcare, hunger) and give them far more leeway in how to spend the money. As noted, policymakers converted AFDC into the TANF block grant in 1996, empowering states to provide welfare assistance to poor families. The problem, as TANF has shown, is that with a finite amount of federal funds each year, states don't have the money to respond to rising needs, such as those that occur during a recession. More people suffer during hard times, which is unfortunate in itself and prolongs the economic downturn.

The second is universal basic income (UBI), often hailed as a cure-all among both conservatives and liberals, through which the federal government would eliminate all safety net programs and replace them with a basic level of income that the government would provide to every family. Conservatives like the idea of ending government programs; liberals like the notion of guaranteed incomes.[75] But a UBI that's financed by eliminating all programs other than Social Security, Medicare, and Medicaid would provide only about $1,600 per person,[76] which would boost poverty and hurt many low- and moderate-income families. Besides, a UBI probably wouldn't eliminate the demand for programs that provide such benefits as food assistance, education, and housing.

Fairness and economic growth are key components of a responsible fiscal plan. There is no better way to achieve both simultaneously than to invest in people.

Notes

1. Fox (2017). The measures of poverty reported in this chapter are based on the Census Bureau's supplemental poverty measure (SPM) rather than the official poverty measure. After decades of concern that the official poverty measure did not fully account for a household's income situation, the Census began to publish an SPM in 2009 in addition to official poverty measures. The official poverty measure classifies households by their pre-tax, market income. The SPM provides a more accurate measure of the number of Americans living in poverty as well as the importance of the government's role in alleviating poverty. The SPM measures a household's cash income and non-cash benefits, less taxes, and out-of-pocket medical, work, and child support expenses. The SPM poverty threshold is calculated as the average of a family in the 33rd percentile's spending on food, clothing, shelter, and utilities multiplied by 1.2, and adjusts for family size and composition, and geographic location. The SPM measure of poverty tends to be higher on average than the official measure on an overall basis but tends to be lower for children and for those living in female-headed households (likely because of the inclusion of non-cash benefits, which tend to target these groups).

2. Rank and Hirschl (2015).

3. Rank (2013).

4. Engle and Black (2008); Hair et al. (2015); Moore et al. (2009). Also see the discussion of economic mobility in Chapter 5.

5. For more information, see Chapter 4 of the 2016 Economic Report of the President, which describes inequalities in early childhood and public policies to address it (Council of Economic Advisers 2016).

6. Sawhill and Thomas (2001).

7. Floyd (2017).

8. If Congress does not act, the CTC will return to its previous levels after 2025. That is, the credit would be equal to 15 percent of earnings above $3,000, with a value of up to $1,000 per child and would begin to phase out as income exceeds $75,000 ($110,000 for married people filing jointly). The credit would be refundable for earnings over $3,000.

9. Maag (2018). The tax law also created a new non-refundable $500 tax credit for other qualifying dependents.

10. Government Accountability Office (2015). There is significant overlap in program usage. Among recipients of the eight largest assistance programs, almost two-thirds of beneficiaries received assistance from two or more programs in 2012.

11. In 2018, there were roughly 59 million Medicare beneficiaries (including Medicare Advantage). About 74 million individuals were enrolled in Medicaid or CHIP. There were about 50 million beneficiaries of Social Security and an additional 11 million individuals with Disability Insurance. There is significant beneficiary overlap between the programs.

12. Government Accountability Office (2015).

13. The federal government and states also provide additional weeks of benefits during times of high unemployment, such as during the Great Recession.

14. Bowden (2018); Executive Order 13828 (2018); Golshan (2018). In addition to work requirements, the administration has also proposed increasing the cost of rental assistance for low-income earners.

15. Center on Budget and Policy Priorities (2018a).

16. Moffit and Scholz (2010); Ziliak (2008).

17. Center on Budget and Policy Priorities (2018a). Studies that include employment incentives and the resulting effect on earnings show that the anti-poverty effect of the EITC could be even greater (Hoynes and Patel 2015).

18. Furman (2017). Given that the supplemental poverty measure is a relatively new measure, the Census does not have published data for historical patterns. Instead, researchers such

as Wimer et al. (2016) have created a modified "anchored" SPM threshold that carries back today's expanded definition of poverty to the past, allowing us to compare historical trends.

19. Center on Budget and Policy Priorities (2018a).

20. Furman (2017).

21. Frongillo, Jyoti, and Jones (2006) estimated the effects of food stamp participation between kindergarten and third grade. They found that among female students, food stamp receipt was associated with a one-third of a standard deviation increase in math and reading test scores compared to similar low-income students who stopped receiving food stamps during that time. They also found that children in these households had slightly less weight gain compared to those in households without food stamps, though this result was not statistically significant. The authors suggest that these results occurred because food stamps may reduce the stress resulting from food insecurity, which in turn may increase cognitive performance.

22. Hoynes, Schanzenbach, and Almond (2016). The authors examined the long-run impacts of the introduction of the food stamp program on adults who were born between 1956 and 1981 into low-income families.

23. Bitler and Currie (2005) compared pregnant women on Medicaid who received WIC to those who did not (yet were still eligible) and found that mothers who received WIC were 6 to 7 percent more likely to have begun prenatal care in the first trimester, and the probability that a baby would be born at a low birthweight decreased by 29 percent. The impacts are larger for the more disadvantaged groups. Hoynes, Page, and Stevens (2009) found that when WIC was made available by the third trimester of pregnancy, average birthweights increased by 10 percent among children borne by low-income, poorly educated mothers. Rossin-Slater (2013) found that access to a WIC clinic was associated with a .8 percent increase in the birthweight of babies born to WIC mothers, a 6 percent increase in the likelihood that the infant was being breastfed upon release from the hospital, and increases in pregnancy weight gain among mothers. Khanani et al. (2010) found that prenatal WIC participation led to decreases in disparities in infant mortality rates between African American and white infants due to significant decreases in infant mortality for African Americans.

24. Carlson and Neuberger (2015); Thomas et al. (2014).

25. Jackson (2015).

26. Much of the research on the labor force impacts of the EITC examined how the 1993 EITC expansion impacted employment. Meyer and Rosenbaum (2001) estimated that the EITC and other tax changes that encouraged work in 1993 increased annual employment by 7.2 percentage points among mothers between 1984 and 1996 compared to childless women. Grogger (2003) found that a $1,000 increase in the maximum credit caused a 3.6 percentage point increase in employment among single mothers and a $610 increase in earnings. Hoynes and Patel (2015) found that a $1,000 increase in the EITC caused a 7.3 percentage point increase in employment and a 9.4 percentage point reduction in the share of families with post-tax income below the poverty line. These effects were most concentrated at incomes slightly above and below the poverty line.

27. Grogger (2003).

28. Hoynes, Miller, and Simon (2015). A $1,000 increase in the EITC leads to a 2 to 3 percent decline in low birthweight due to greater maternal access to prenatal care and fewer negative health outcomes. Currie and Cole (1993) found a positive association between AFDC receipt and birthweights, further suggesting the importance of cash assistance for families with children.

29. Wood, Turnham, and Mills (2008).

30. MTO was a decade-long experiment that began in 1994. Researchers randomly assigned almost 5,000 low-income families from the most distressed public housing projects to three groups: one group receiving a voucher that could be redeemed only in a low-poverty neighborhood, one group receiving a traditional section 8 voucher, and a control group. In the interim (4 to 7 years after the start of the study), adults receiving either type of voucher

reported feeling safer and more satisfied with their housing and neighborhoods and were less likely to be obese; there was no effect on employment or earnings. For children, MTO had positive effects on female mental health but negative effects on male risky behavior and no impact on academic achievement (Orr et al. 2003). These results also extended into the long term (10 to 15 years), though the differential effects on male and female children decreased.

31. Chetty, Hendren, and Katz (2015); Sanbonmatsu et al. (2011).
32. Barr and Smith (2017).
33. Barr and Gibbs (2017); Carniero and Ginja (2014).
34. Hoynes and Patel (2015).
35. Kids Count Data Center (2017).
36. To qualify for federal aid, students must complete a complex form called the Free Application for Federal Student Aid (FAFSA). The Department of Education then uses the FAFSA to award aid in the form of Pell Grants, loans, and work-study funds.
37. Also, traditional IRS account holders can withdraw funds from their IRAs before the normal retirement age without incurring penalties if they use the money for college expenses.
38. Garcia et al. (2016). See also Bauer and Schanzenbach (2016); Carniero and Ginja (2014); Cascio and Schanzenbach (2013, 2014); Council of Economic Advisers (2016); Currie and Thomas (1995); Deming (2009); Heckman, Pinto, and Savelyev (2013); and Lipsey et al. (2013).
39. Shambaugh, Bauer, and Breitweiser (2018).
40. Autor (2014). Oreopoulos and Petronijevic (2013) found that higher education yields present value benefits, net of costs, for both the average and marginal student. Benefits are positive for each degree type. Starting but not completing a college degree yields results similar to being only a high school graduate.
41. Dynarski and Scott-Clayton (2018).
42. Baum and Scott-Clayton (2013); Bettinger (2004); Bulman and Hoxby (2015); Government Accountability Office (2012); Hansen (1983); Hoxby and Bulman (2015); Kane (1995); Long (2003); LaLumia (2012); Seftor and Turner (2002); Turner (2011).
43. For example, 14 percent of taxpayers who were eligible for education tax benefits didn't claim them, and 40 percent of those who chose the tuition deduction would have benefited more from a different program (Government Accountability Office 2012). Dynarski and Scott-Clayton (2006a) noted that the complexity of student aid has a high cost and little marginal benefit. In another study, Bettinger et al. (2012) randomly assigned students to either a group where tax professionals helped them fill out their financial aid forms and advised them of their aid options or a group that only received information on aid but no help completing the forms. They found that students who received assistance with their financial aid forms and information about available aid received more aid than those who did not receive help with the forms and were more likely to enroll in college. Receiving information alone had no impact.
44. Card, Kluve, and Weber (2010); Heinrich et al. (2013); Hollenbeck (2009).
45. A study of the Workforce Investment Act's Adult and Dislocated Worker Program found that only 40 percent of voucher recipients worked in the field they received training for (Perez-Johnson, Moore, and Santillano 2011). Another study of a similar program for dislocated workers found that four years after being laid off their initial jobs, 37 percent of participants held a job in the occupation they had trained for (Schochet et al. 2012; Hollenbeck 2009).
46. McConnell, Perez-Johnson, and Berk (2014); Schochet, Burghardt, and McConnell (2008).
47. This was calculated by subtracting Social Security and health programs from the gross total OECD social spending accounts. The OECD average is a weighted average. The items included in our measure of social spending include family, labor, and unemployment and housing programs.

48. American Enterprise Institute/Brookings Institution Working Group on Poverty and Opportunity (2015).

49. Fischer and Sard (2017).

50. Department of Health and Human Services (2016).

51. New Hampshire's average TANF benefits are indexed to cover 60 percent of the federal poverty line.

52. Department of Health and Human Services (2016).

53. Marr et al. (2016).

54. Bitler and Hoynes (2016).

55. Whitehurst (2017).

56. OECD (2017).

57. Whitehurst (2017).

58. Dynarski and Scott-Clayton (2006b). Receiving financial aid has been shown to reduce barriers to a student's enrollment and reduce attrition once in college under certain circumstances. Dynarski (2003) examined how the elimination of a Social Security grant for college affected enrollment. She found that offering $1,000 in aid increased educational attainment by 0.16 years and the probability of attending college by 4 percentage points.

59. For example, the IRS could automatically compute students' eligibility for available tax credits via information provided on tax returns when the child turns 17 so that families are made aware of potential aid while considering college options. The IRS could then send the credit to the institution the child attends and institutions can deduct this amount from tuition to make the lower college cost more salient (Hoxby and Bulman 2015).

60. Dynarski and Scott-Clayton (2007).

61. Dynarski and Kreisman (2013).

62. Leachman et al. (2016).

63. Lafortune, Rothstein, and Schanzenbach (2016) found that historic school finance reforms that reallocated resources reduced inequities in achievement between districts over time, but not among students within those districts.

64. American Enterprise Institute/Brookings Institution Working Group on Poverty and Opportunity (2015).

65. Holzer (2018).

66. National Conference of State Legislatures (2017). As of 2018, 29 states plus the District of Columbia have a minimum wage higher than the federal level. Fourteen states have minimum wages equal to the federal level, and seven states have no minimum wage or one set below the federal rate. In this case, the federal rate prevails. Eighteen states plus DC index their rates to inflation. Forty-one localities set minimum wages higher than their state minimums. Because of these higher rates at the state and local levels, the average effective minimum wage in states, the wages that workers in a state actually face, is slightly over $8 (Furman 2017).

67. Congressional Budget Office (2014).

68. Cooper (2016).

69. Cangiz et al. (2017); Card and Krueger (1995); Meer and West (2016).

70. Rossin-Slater (2017).

71. Rossin-Slater, Ruhm, and Waldofgel (2011); Waldfogel, Higuchi, and Abe (1999).

72. Department of Labor (2016). Covered workers include those who work for an employer with more than 50 employees, has worked for that employer for over a year, and has worked for 1,250 hours the previous year. Employees can take leave for the birth or adoption of a child, or to care for an immediate family member who is sick or has a serious health condition. Once an employee returns to work, he or she must have the same job and wage.

73. Gault et al. (2014).

74. For example, suppose that a second earner would face a 15 percent federal income tax on all earnings, a 5 percent state tax, the payroll tax, childcare expenses of $15,000 per

year and work expenses of $3,000. The second-earner would net virtually nothing out of his or her first $25,000 in earnings, if the family has one child. If there are two children, the second earner would net zero out of the first $45,000 of earnings. To mitigate these disincentives, we could implement a 20 percent secondary-earner tax deduction for secondary earnings up to $60,000 that would phase out once family income reaches $110,000 (Kearney and Turner 2013). Under such a plan, two-earner families with both parents working at or near minimum wage would see up to a 4 percent increase in their disposable income. Federal income and payroll tax revenues would fall by $18.5 billion in 2019 ($227 billion over a decade, or 0.09 percent of GDP), but incentives to work would improve and working low- and middle-income families would obtain more economic security.

75. Matthews (2016).
76. Dolan (2014).

Appendix Table 9.1. **Major Federal Safety Net Provisions**

	Program[1] Type	Eligibility	Beneficiaries[2]	Average Benefit[3]	Poverty Effect (# lifted above Federal Poverty Line [FPL] in 2015)[4]	Cost ($)[5]
TANF	Mandatory	Federal guidelines: (1) Time limit of up to 60 months. (2) Be engaged in work or work-related activity for at least 30 hours/week. (3) Maintenance of effort requirement that states spend at least 75–80% of what it spent on welfare programs in 1994.	3.6 million monthly average	$429 median state benefit per month for family of three	1.2 million	$16.5 billion
SSI	Mandatory	Blind, aged, or disabled with little to no income and assets of up to $2,000 for individuals ($3,000 for couples).	8.3 million	$542 per month	5.3 million	$54.7 billion
EITC	Tax	Working families with children that have annual incomes ranging from $40,320 to $54,884 and working poor with no children and incomes below $15,270.	26.4 million families	$3,176 for family with children or $295 for family without in 2016	5.8 million	$64.8 billion
CTC	Tax	Incomes between $3,000 and $400,000	35 million families	$1,060 in 2015	2.7 million	$54.6 billion

SNAP	Mandatory	(1) Gross monthly income at or below 130% of FPL and net monthly income at or below FPL unless elderly or disabled. (2) Net monthly income below FPL. (3) Assets below $2,250 for households without elderly or disabled ($3,250 for households with elderly or disabled). (4) Most unemployed childless adults limited to three months unless they work 20+ hours/week or are in a job training program (can be waived for areas with high unemployment).	40.9 million	$125 per person monthly	8.4 million	$69.2 billion
WIC	Discretionary	Income at or below 185% of FPL. Automatically eligible if already receiving SNAP or TANF. Must be deemed "at nutritional risk" by a professional.	7.3 million	$61.24 food value per individual per month	400,000	$5.6 billion
Housing	Discretionary	Public housing: Income cannot exceed 80% of local area median income (AMI). At least 40% of tenants admitted by each agency must be extremely low income. Vouchers: Income up to 80% of AMI; 75% of new households admitted annually must be extremely low income. Low-income housing tax credit: Awarded to developers for projects if 20% of tenants have income below 50% of AMI or 40% of tenants have incomes below 60% of AMI.	10 million (~5 million households) in one of the three major programs	$7,600 per household annually in 2013	4 million	$46.5 billion

(continued)

Appendix Table 9.1. **(Continued)**

Program[1]	Type	Eligibility	Beneficiaries[2]	Average Benefit[3]	Poverty Effect (# lifted above Federal Poverty Line [FPL] in 2015)[4]	Cost ($)[5]
LIHEAP	Discretionary	Household income is the higher of less than 150% of poverty line or 60% of state median income.	6.3 million households	$336 for cooling, $301–$366 for heating (2014)	340,000	$3.4 billion
UI	Mandatory	Must lose a job through no fault of your own, be able to work, available to work, and actively seeking work. Must earn a certain base amount before becoming unemployed.	5.4 million	$348 per week	2.7 million in 2012	$28.7 billion
Veterans' Benefits	Mandatory	Disability benefits are given to veterans with diseases or illness due to military service. Veterans' pensions are available to low-income veterans who are 65 or older and are eligible for SSI or DI.	Disability: 4.7 million; Pensions: 273,000	$14,862 annually in 2018 for disability benefits; $12,086 for pensions	—	$81.6 billion

Notes:

[1] This table does not include the government's largest social spending programs—Social Security (Old Age and Survivors Insurance and Disability Insurance), Medicare, and Medicaid. See other chapters in this book for the details of these programs.

[2] Participation data are for individuals unless otherwise stated. EITC, CTC, SSI, and housing participation data are for 2014. SNAP, UI, and Veterans' benefits are for 2018. TANF and WIC are 2017. Sources include Center on Budget and Policy Priorities (2017b); Congressional Budget Office (2017, 2018); Department of Health and Human Services (2016, 2018b); Maag (2017); Social Security Administration (2017).

[3] EITC, CTC, and SSI benefits are for 2016. Note that the average CTC benefit will increase after 2018 because of the new tax law. LIHEAP benefits are for 2014, the most recent year for which data are available. Housing assistance benefit amounts are for 2013 and represent the average subsidy received by households that receive a housing choice voucher, project-based rental assistance, or public housing (Congressional Budget Office 2015). TANF and WIC benefits are for 2017. SNAP, veterans' benefits, and UI benefits are for 2018. Sources include Center on Budget and Policy Priorities (2017a, 2018b); Social Security Administration (2017); Tax Policy Center (2016); Congressional Budget Office (2017); Department of Health and Human Services (2016).

[4] Effects on poverty are shown for 2015, the most recent year for which data are available, unless otherwise noted. Combined, the EITC and CTC would reduce poverty for 9.9 million people (more than the sum of the two above) because the two tax credits put together would lift some people over the poverty line, a result that wouldn't have happened with just one of the credits. EITC and CTC poverty effects are for 2016. Veterans' benefits certainly impact the poverty level of affected households, though comparable calculations have not been done to show their magnitude. Estimates for the anti-poverty effects of UI, LIHEAP, and WIC are for 2012. Sources include Center on Budget and Policy Priorities (2018a, 2018b); Government Accountability Office (2015).

[5] Program costs are for 2018 unless otherwise stated. TANF costs reflect federal spending via the State Family Assistance Grant. Under what is termed the maintenance of effort requirement, states must contribute a level of spending based on their AFDC spending prior to welfare reform in 1996. State and federal governments each contribute roughly half of total TANF funds (Falk 2017). EITC costs only include the refundable portion (Joint Committee on Taxation 2017). CTC costs include the refundable and non-refundable portions. The refundable portion totaled $32.7 billion in 2018. LIHEAP costs are for 2014, the most recent year for which data are available. Veterans' benefits costs include the sum of outlays for disability compensation ($76.5 billion) and veterans' pensions ($5.1 billion). Sources include Congressional Budget Office (2018); Department of Health and Human Services (2016); Falk (2017); Office of Management and Budget (2018, Table 8.7).

Appendix Table 9.2. **Major Federal Education and Training Programs**

	Program Type	Beneficiaries[2]	Cost ($)[3]
Head Start	Discretionary	899,374 children	$9.2 billion
Child Nutrition[1]	Mandatory	Lunch: 30 million students; Breakfast: 14.7 million students	$23.2 billion
Pell Grants	Mandatory and Discretionary	7.5 million students	$29.7 billion
Student Loans	Credit Subsidy	42.3 million students	$15.3 billion
American Opportunity Tax Credit	Tax Credit	10.1 million tax units	$17.5 billion
Lifetime Learning Credit	Tax Credit	3.8 million tax units	$2.6 billion
Coverdell Education Savings Account	Savings Account	—	$100 million
Qualified Tuition Plans (529 Plans)	Savings Account	12.9 million	$1.1 billion
IRA Deductions for Education	Tax Deduction	—	—
Exclusion of Scholarships and Grants from Income	Income Exclusion	Almost all scholarship recipients	$3.9 billion
Tuition and Fees Deduction	Tax Deduction	1.7 million tax returns	$400 million
Student Loan Interest Deduction	Tax Deduction	12.4 million returns	$2.4 billion
Job Training	Discretionary	6.1 million disadvantaged adults, 334,310 youth, 533,843 dislocated adults	$5.4 billion

Notes:

[1] The National School Lunch and School Breakfast programs make up the vast majority of the child nutrition category. The Special Milk Program and commodity costs are also included in this estimate.

[2] Pell Grant participation is for 2018. Head Start, child nutrition, student loan, American Opportunity Tax Credit, and Lifetime Learning Credit participation is for 2017. 529 plan and student loan interest deduction participation is for 2016. Tuition and fees deduction and job training participation is for 2015. Sources include: US Department of Agriculture (2018a, 2018b); Department of Education (2018); Department of Health and Human Services (2018a); Department of Labor (2018a); Investment Company Institute (2017); Internal Revenue Service (2017); Tax Policy Center (2017).

[3] Child nutrition funding, Pell Grant funding, and all tax deductions and exclusions (except the AOTC and LLC) are for 2018. Pell Grant funding includes mandatory ($6 billion) and discretionary ($23.6 billion) components. Student loan costs are based on CBO projection of all federal loan outlays for 2018 using a fair value estimating procedure. Head Start funding, AOTC, and LLC costs are based on projections by Tax Policy Center (2017) and include the refundable portions. Funding for jobs training includes the sum of services provided by the Department of Labor's Employment and Training Administration, Job Corps, and community service programs for low-income elderly individuals in 2018. Sources include Congressional Budget Office (2017, 2018); Department of Health and Human Services (2018a); Department of Labor (2018b); Joint Committee on Taxation (2017); Tax Policy Center (2017).

10

Investing for Growth and Security

Along with investing in its people, the federal government makes critical investments in the nation's infrastructure and scientific research and provides resources for our national defense and security.

Federal funding for infrastructure and research and development (R&D) plays a key role in the economy, but it has fallen significantly in recent years. Simply restoring the quality of current roads, bridges, and the rest of our infrastructure will require significant new funding. Generating additional economic growth from public investments in new infrastructure and a stronger flow of new ideas and products from R&D will require even more commitments.

To that end, the federal government should address the infrastructure needs identified by the American Society of Civil Engineers (ASCE) through 2040 and maintain the elevated level of spending thereafter to address maintenance and new projects. Although the federal government funds only about one-quarter of all infrastructure projects currently, with state and local governments funding the rest, I propose that the federal government cover half the costs of meeting the ASCE infrastructure needs through 2050 because this is such an important national priority and because there are spillover benefits to the federal government and the nation as a whole that are not captured by state or local governments. In addition, I propose doubling non-defense R&D spending in 2021 relative to its projection to about 0.7 percent of GDP and maintaining that share of GDP through 2050. We should also eliminate recently enacted tax rules that would make R&D more expensive for firms.

National defense is the government's most fundamental responsibility. Our military is the world's strongest, with skilled troops, state-of-the-art technology, and a worldwide network of alliances. But the defense budget was significantly restricted earlier in the decade, and it is only now beginning to recover relative to earlier projections. To meet the nation's defense and security needs, we should provide the funding necessary to enable the Defense Department to carry out its plans, as suggested by President Obama's final Future Years Defense Program (FYDP), and extend this through 2032.[1] After that, the defense budget would grow 1 percent per year in inflation-adjusted terms. This would allow for continued US presence overseas, but it assumes no new major conflicts. The proposal does not represent President Trump's long-term plans, which would call for even sharper spending increases. A key caveat, though, is that we shouldn't shape defense spending mainly on how it fits with our fiscal goals. If the world grows more unstable, the government may have to spend more to ensure our security.

The entire investment package in this chapter would increase the debt-to-GDP ratio in 2050 by about 32 percentage points (though that figure doesn't account for the added economic benefits of increased infrastructure and R&D, which reduce the increase in debt). As a share of GDP, spending on infrastructure and R&D would be significantly higher in 2050 than today. Defense would be smaller as a share of GDP but significantly larger in inflation-adjusted terms. The programs would be funded by tax increases described in later chapters.

Government investment can help the economy grow by providing goods or services that generate returns to the public or that make individuals and businesses more productive, but that the private market would undersupply on its own.[2] These investments are often for public goods—that is, items that everyone can use free of charge once they're developed.

Better infrastructure allows for cheaper transportation and communication of goods, services, and ideas, and it can directly raise the productivity of businesses and individuals. But the societal return to infrastructure projects is probably underestimated because a portion of the return takes non-financial or otherwise unconventional forms that are often hard to measure.[3] A well-designed transportation system can reduce congestion, pollution, and damage to vehicles. Expanded broadband services can make it easier for seniors and people with disabilities to connect with their families and their doctors. These effects do not show up in traditional measures of economic activity.

The overall economic effects will also depend on how the investment is financed. Debt-financed projects, as discussed in Chapter 4, leave less capital available for private investment. The effects can depend, too, on whether the economy is in a recession. In a weak economy, infrastructure can be an important part of a stimulus package that can help return the economy to full employment.[4]

What is clear is that the rate of return can vary dramatically across projects. Building, maintaining, and repairing highways can provide high returns.[5] But projects that are undertaken as political payoffs—such as the famous "Bridge to Nowhere" in Alaska—won't likely be worth the costs.[6]

The government has a long tradition of successful investments in the economy. In the 1800s, New York State funded the Erie Canal, sparking westward migration and providing a supply route that helped turn New York City into an economic powerhouse. Through the 1862 Pacific Railway Act, the federal government provided land grants that facilitated the building of transcontinental railroads. Under President Franklin D. Roosevelt's New Deal, the government hired millions of jobless individuals to build public infrastructure—roads, dams, bridges, buildings, schools, and airports. In the 1950s, President Eisenhower and Congress authorized the interstate highway system, which changed the face of commerce and leisure in America by making it easier to move people, goods, and services.

Today, federal investment in infrastructure comes in two forms: (1) direct spending projects, which account for about 30 percent of the total and focus on aviation and water resources; and (2) federal grants to state and local governments, which account for 70 percent and focus on highways and public transit. Counting all levels of government, the United States spends somewhat less on public infrastructure as a share of GDP than other OECD countries.[7]

Gross federal investment was about 2.5 percent of GDP in 1980. It rose dramatically as a share of the economy in the Reagan years (largely due to defense) and then fell under George H. W. Bush and Bill Clinton (Figure 10.1). Investment rebounded modestly under George W. Bush and somewhat more

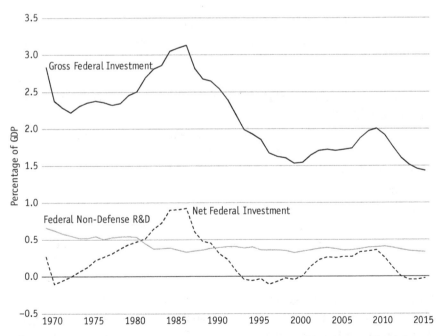

Figure 10.1. Federal investment and non-defense research and development (R&D) as a share of GDP. Bureau of Economic Analysis (2017); Office of Management and Budget (2018).

under Barack Obama's economic stimulus package in 2009, but then fell rapidly after that and is now at its lowest share of GDP since 1947.

Over time, physical investments depreciate—that is, they decline in economic value due to wear and tear and other factors. Notably, *net* federal investment—gross investment minus the depreciation of the existing capital stock—has almost vanished, averaging just 0.1 percent of GDP since the mid-1990s, compared to 0.5 percent in the preceding 20 years (Figure 10.1). Combined federal, state, and local government net investment in non-defense infrastructure is at its lowest level in more than six decades.[8]

These trends confirm what our eyes see. Problems in the nation's infrastructure are all around us. The Army Corps of Engineers' faulty construction and testing of levees led to the breaches that made Hurricane Katrina so damaging to New Orleans in 2005.[9] In 2007, a Minneapolis bridge collapsed during rush hour, killing 13 and injuring another 145, due to insufficient oversight by the Federal Highway Administration and the Minnesota Department of Transportation as well as a faulty design.[10] Shortages of runways and airport gates, as well as outdated air traffic control systems, make US air travel extremely congested.[11] Major airports like New York's JFK International and LaGuardia are in constant disrepair.[12] Things have gotten so bad that Domino's Pizza (whose workers drive on roads to deliver pizza) has donated money to 20 cities to help patch potholes and fix roads.[13]

Clearly, the nation's infrastructure badly needs repair and further development. The Government Accountability Office, Obama administration, and Trump administration have made this case forcefully.[14] The American Society of Civil Engineers (ASCE) periodically evaluates the country's infrastructure. In its most recent "Report Card for America's Infrastructure" of 2017, the United States received a D+. That reflects the reality that one in 11 bridges are classified as structurally deficient and over 40 percent of major urban highways are congested (costing the economy $160 billion a year in wasted time and fuel).[15] The Federal Transit Administration and its equivalent state agencies struggle to maintain aging fleets of buses and trains in the face of funding cuts. Students attend classes in deteriorating buildings as state and local school construction funding shrinks. Americans increasingly rely on an aging electric grid to power their homes, while many inland waterways haven't been updated in over half a century.

In 2016, the ASCE estimated that the country would need $10.8 trillion in federal and state funds from 2016 through 2040 to maintain or rebuild existing infrastructure and build new infrastructure sufficient for the demands of future populations.[16] The systems that need the most funding are surface transportation ($7.6 trillion), electricity ($2.5 trillion), and airports (almost $400 billion).

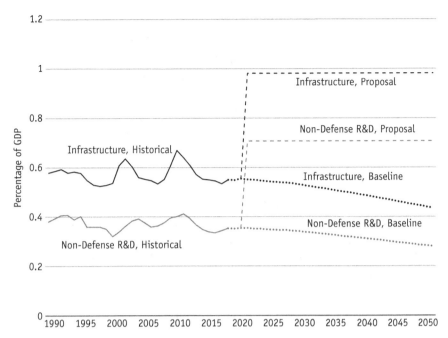

Figure 10.2. Infrastructure and non-defense research and development (R&D) projections through 2050. Author's calculations; Congressional Budget Office (2015b); Congressional Budget Office (2018); Office of Management and Budget (2018).

I propose that we provide this investment between 2021 and 2040. To cover maintenance of the newly built projects and any new projects deemed worthwhile, I propose that we maintain the higher level of spending after 2040. Under this proposal, the federal government would fund half of the estimated infrastructure need, as compared to the one-quarter share of all US infrastructure investment that it currently undertakes, signaling the national importance of this investment.[17] To meet the full ACSE requirements, state and local governments would need to pick up the other half.[18]

Under the proposal, total federal investments on infrastructure would equal about 1 percent of GDP per year, starting in 2021. That represents an increase in projected infrastructure spending of 0.4 percent of GDP in 2021, rising to 0.5 percent of GDP by 2050 (Figure 10.2).

To help keep financing decisions free of political consideration, policymakers could create a national infrastructure bank, structured like the Federal Reserve Board as an independent agency. The bank would help the nation fund the most socially beneficial projects. The bank also could more easily direct large projects that involve multiple states and jurisdictions and could helpfully keep infrastructure projects focused on urban areas, where they are most needed.[19] To reduce costs, it could also encourage pooled procurement—across projects and jurisdictions—and competition among potential suppliers.[20]

Surface transportation is currently funded by gas taxes that go into the highway trust fund. My proposal to increase infrastructure spending includes funding the added spending with tax increases described in later chapters.[21] Raising gas taxes wouldn't be ideal if we implement a national carbon tax (as proposed in Chapter 14), since the carbon tax would raise taxes on gasoline.

R&D projects can generate economic growth, as the basic knowledge and technological innovations they create spur the production of new goods and services and improvements in existing ones.

Private sector R&D, fueled in part by federal tax breaks, focuses on the development stage, which capitalizes on previous discoveries to bring new products and technologies to market. Federal government R&D, in contrast, focuses more on basic and applied research, which may well provide larger overall social benefits than the development of new products. Private firms will likely supply too little basic research from a societal perspective because the benefits of such projects are often available to everyone, making it harder to make the investments worthwhile from the companies' perspective.[22] But there's no bright line between private and public R&D. Over time, large firms have increasingly relied on start-ups for research. The start-ups in turn depend in part on university funding, much of which comes from the National Institutes of Health (NIH) or the National Science Foundation (NSF).

Federal investment in R&D has a decorated history. The projects have helped develop modern medicine, from spreading the use of penicillin in World War II to facilitating the Human Genome Project. More than 80 Nobel Prizes have been awarded for research funded by the NIH. The internet—created with funding from the Defense Department and the NSF—has transformed our lives, businesses, and society. Government technology investments have led to fluorescent lights; the recording technology behind all music, video, and data storage; water purification techniques; batteries for electric cars; and so on. Even Google was founded by two Stanford PhD students who were initially funded by an NSF grant.[23]

Federal non-defense R&D spending—consisting of direct outlays for federal laboratories as well as grants to universities, non-profits, and private firms—peaked around 1 percent of GDP in the mid-1960s but fell to about 0.34 percent of GDP by the late Reagan years. It increased slightly to about 0.4 percent of GDP by the mid-1990s, but then fell to 0.32 percent by the end of the Clinton administration. It has remained at or slightly above that point ever since (Figure 10.1). As a whole, the United States ranks 10th in the world in combined private and public R&D spending as a share of its economy, behind Germany, Israel, Japan, South Korea, and several Nordic countries.[24]

About half of federal non-defense R&D goes to healthcare, and the rest to areas such as science, space exploration, technology, energy, the environment, natural resources, transportation, and agriculture. Health investments rose in the early 2000s due to a funding surge for the NIH. But in recent years, funding for the NIH and the NSF shrank to their 2001 level as a share of GDP, making it harder for researchers to establish or continue projects and, in turn, curbing innovation and economic growth.[25] In the face of these declines, some studies suggest that the socially optimal level of R&D spending could be two to four times higher than current levels.[26] Emerging areas such as artificial intelligence offer particularly compelling cases for more R&D spending to fuel innovation.[27]

Moreover, the 2017 tax overhaul reduced the tax benefits of private R&D spending. Starting in 2022, firms must amortize their R&D expenditures over five years (15 years for offshore R&D) instead of immediately deducting them. The change, coupled with the lower corporate rate, may reduce private R&D since it dampens the incentive for firms to engage in research activity, leaving a larger hole for the government to fill.

To that end, I propose to repeal this reduction in tax benefits for R&D expenditures and to double non-defense R&D spending as a share of GDP relative to what would otherwise occur in 2021 and maintain spending at that share through 2050.[28] Since the baseline described in Chapter 3 provides about 0.35 percent of GDP in non-defense R&D spending in 2021, the federal government would spend about 0.7 percent of GDP on non-defense R&D per year under the proposal (Figure 10.2).[29] Altogether, the R&D policy would increase the debt in 2050 by about 12 percentage points.

To enhance the payoff from R&D spending, the government should offer contests with prizes for those who meet (or are the first to meet) specified criteria. The government could identify national priorities (for example, clean energy standards or a cure for cancer) and offer prizes to the first group to achieve a carefully described goal.[30]

The nation has long debated the relative merits of funding for military versus domestic needs. As President Eisenhower said, "Every gun that is made, every warship launched, every rocket fired signifies, in the final sense, a theft from those who hunger and are not fed, those who are cold and are not clothed."[31] We must address the defense budget carefully, though, with broader strategic goals in mind. If ever there were a budget category where merely "bean counting" is a bad idea, it's defense. The consequences of an unprepared military would surely not be worth the budget savings.

Fiscal status and military power are inextricably linked. As former defense secretary Robert Gates said, "At some point, financial insolvency at home will turn into strategic insolvency abroad."[32] An unsustainable debt path hurts prospects for long-term growth, which in turn limits the economic resources and political will needed to maintain a robust national defense. Thus, addressing the fiscal problem is important for defense, just as making the most of every defense dollar is important for addressing the fiscal challenge.

The federal government devotes substantial resources to defense. In 2018, defense accounted for 15 percent of spending and 3.1 percent of GDP, and that doesn't include the security-related activities of the Departments of Homeland Security and Veterans' Affairs.[33] Defense spending is more than twice as large a share of GDP in America as in the rest of the G7. The United States accounts for more than a third of all global military spending, allocating almost three times as much to it as the next highest spender, which is China.[34] Nevertheless, that does not give the United States as much superiority as it might seem to imply, since other powers concentrate their military resources in particular geographic areas.

Defense spending peaks in wars, of course. Over the long term, however, it has fallen substantially as a share of GDP (Figure 10.3). Comparing periods of peace, defense spending was roughly 10 percent of GDP in the late 1950s but

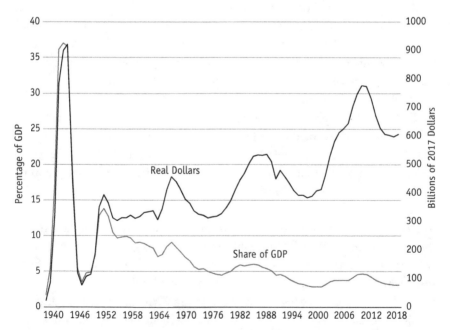

Figure 10.3. US defense outlays, 1940–2018. Congressional Budget Office (2018); Office of Management and Budget (2018).

just 3 percent in the late 1990s. It rose to almost 5 percent in 2010 during operations in Iraq and Afghanistan before falling again.[35]

Although it makes sense to evaluate many programs relative to the size of the GDP, it also makes sense to evaluate the defense budget in real (inflation-adjusted) terms. A doubling of the size of the economy, for example, would not require a doubling of defense spending.

Though generally falling as a share of GDP, defense spending has generally risen since the 1950s in inflation-adjusted terms (Figure 10.3). Using that metric, it grew rapidly under President Reagan and then fell almost as much in the 1990s after the Soviet Union's collapse. It rose again under President George W. Bush and in the early Obama years, as the United States fought wars in Iraq and Afghanistan. But the 2011 Budget Control Act (BCA) and the additional sequestered budget cuts reduced defense spending sharply. These cuts reflected a budget strategy, though, not the funding required by the Defense Department to carry out its military strategy. Over the last few years, Congress subsequently raised the defense spending caps, with the latest increase occurring in 2018 for fiscal years 2018 and 2019. While that legislation provided substantial funding, the resulting caps were still about $17 billion (2.6 percent) lower than what was projected for those years under a 2011 baseline.[36]

Defense Department spending consists of a "base budget," which records spending for regular, ongoing functions, and "overseas contingency operations (OCO)," the costs of active wars.[37]

In 2018, the base budget was capped around $600 billion, and OCO and related emergency spending was about $70 billion.[38] Of the base budget, roughly two-thirds funds operations, maintenance, personnel, and healthcare (the fastest growing category since 2000). Procurement (i.e., weapons) accounts for 20 percent. Research, development, testing, and evaluation of weapons and military vehicles account for about 14 percent. Research dollars focus on defense needs, but advances have helped lead to more broadly consumed goods, including the internet, microwave oven, laser technology, and global positioning systems.[39]

Wars raise current as well as future obligations for veterans' health and disability spending, and these costs can be substantial.[40] For example, OCO spending rose dramatically when the United States engaged in multiple overseas military operations after the terrorist attacks of September 11, 2001. The OCO budget itself totaled about $2 trillion (in 2017 dollars) from 2001 through 2018. Troop withdrawals reduced OCO spending in recent years, but operations continue in Afghanistan and Iraq. Looking forward, one estimate suggests that from 2019 to 2056, the United States will spend about $1 trillion on veterans' programs related to the post-9/11 wars.[41]

Under the baseline described in Chapter 3, the Defense Department would not receive enough funding to carry out its long-term plans or develop new options.[42] The need for moderately higher defense spending stems from several sources. The United States faces multiple threats, from actors ranging from China and Russia, to ISIS and al Qaeda, to Iran and North Korea. Multiple wars since September 11, 2001, have depleted the military's resources. Budget deals earlier in the decade forced large, indiscriminate cuts to defense that were motivated by the fiscal situation rather than military strategy.[43]

I propose to provide enough funding to cover the Defense Department's plans, as described by the 2017 FYDP and extended through 2032. After that, I propose that the base DoD budget rise by 1 percent per year, adjusted for inflation, while OCO and related non–Defense Department programs such as the nuclear programs in the Department of Energy grow only with inflation, emphasizing the assumption of no new wars.[44] Raising real defense spending in the base budget is important because most of its major costs—for personnel, healthcare, equipment maintenance, and others—generally rise faster than inflation.[45] Modest real growth would better prepare the United States to confront both current and future threats.[46]

The 2017 FYDP was President Obama's final FYDP. It does not represent the long-term plans of the Trump administration, which would call for even larger spending increases.[47] Under my proposal, defense spending would fall relative to the baseline for a few years but then ultimately rise above the baseline projections. Although the proposal meets defense plans as described in the 2017 FYDP and creates real growth in the defense budget, it would ultimately leave defense spending at its lowest share of GDP since before World War II, equaling 2.6 percent of GDP in 2050. Still, this is about 0.5 percent of GDP greater than the projection under the baseline described in Chapter 3 (Figure 10.4).

This does not imply that every detail of the Obama defense plan should remain fixed. There will undoubtedly be areas where the military can economize and other areas where more resources will be productive. Within this framework, the military could improve its efficiency, and thus save money, in numerous ways—a goal that Pentagon leaders share.[48] In 2014, a study commissioned by the Defense Department found that the military could save $125 billion over five years by relying more on early retirement, relying less on outside contractors, and modernizing its information technology and other systems.[49] By realigning some military bases and closing others, it could consolidate services, scrap excess infrastructure, and reduce overhead and maintenance costs. The military has asked Congress to create another process, like previous ones, to close bases, but lawmakers have declined. Reforming the military's healthcare system by aligning patients' costs with those in civilian plans also could save substantial sums.[50] In addition, the government could scale back some acquisitions, such as

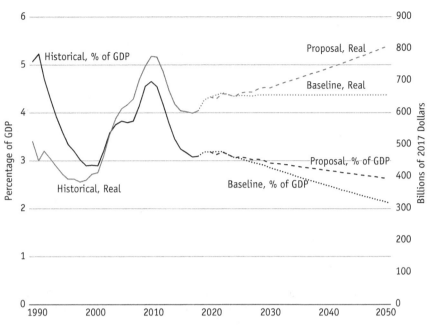

Figure 10.4. Defense spending projections through 2050. Historical data use the gross domestic product (GDP) price index to measure inflation, while projections use the average of the GDP price index and the employment cost index (ECI). All real values are billions of 2017 dollars. Author's calculations; Congressional Budget Office (2018); Office of Management and Budget (2018).

the F-35 fighter—an expensive stealth jet designed to perform air and ground defense missions, for which unmanned or other aircraft may well be a feasible substitute.[51]

Government investments in infrastructure, R&D, and defense are critical for our nation's success. We should support these needs even as we aim for fiscal sustainability. Indeed, by improving the economy and our national security, these programs can put us on a better path toward fiscal sustainability and would have other long-lasting benefits.

Notes

1. Congressional Budget Office (2017b).
2. See Aschauer (1989); Bom and Ligthart (2014); Congressional Budget Office (2016a); Fernald (1999); Gramlich (1994); Holtz-Eakin (1995); International Monetary Fund (2014); Munnell (1992); Romp and de Haan (2007).
3. For further discussion, see Congressional Budget Office (2016a); Summers (2016); Deshpande and Elmendorf (2008).

4. Congressional Budget Office (2015a); Elmendorf (2014).

5. Gramlich (1994).

6. Alaska's infamous "Bridge to Nowhere"—a $400 million project from 2005 that would have connected the small town of Ketchikan to Gavina Island, which housed 50 residents and a tiny airport—became a symbol of politically motivated, wasteful government spending and was eventually shuttered (Dinan 2015).

7. OECD (2017). The United States spends 0.6 percent of GDP on inland transport infrastructure (including highways, rail, and inland waterways) compared to a G7 average expenditure of 0.8 percent of GDP.

8. Burtless (2016).

9. Rogers et al. (2015).

10. National Transportation Safety Board (2008); Schaper (2017).

11. Kroft (2014).

12. McCartney (2016). The Federal Aviation Administration does have a plan in place to update this inefficient radar-based flight control system. But its new and improved automatic system, called "NextGen," is decades behind schedule, costing billions of unnecessary dollars and frustrations with complex bureaucracy. When implemented, this new technology will have the potential to reduce travel times, minimize flight costs, and improve safety (Winston 2013).

13. Smith (2018).

14. Government Accountability Office (2012); National Economic Council and President's Council of Economic Advisers (2014); Office of Management and Budget (2017).

15. American Society of Civil Engineers (2017).

16. American Society of Civil Engineers (2016). Values are in 2015 dollars.

17. Congressional Budget Office (2015b). Baseline spending projections from 2016 to 2020 across all levels of government are subtracted from each infrastructure category's funding need from 2016 to 2040 (in real dollars, provided in the ASCE report), where state and local infrastructure spending is assumed to be three times federal spending. The baseline assumes that federal infrastructure spending represents about 17 percent of non-defense discretionary spending, equal to its historical average share (Congressional Budget Office 2015b). Half of the remaining need is distributed such that the resulting shares of GDP from 2021 to 2040 are equal. The resulting percentage of the GDP spending goal is then continued through 2050.

18. Enforcement mechanisms would have to be in place to ensure that the states do not reduce their investment in the wake of rising federal investment.

19. Like the Federal Reserve, an infrastructure bank would function as an independent, government-owned corporation, with a CEO and board of directors appointed by the president and confirmed by the Senate to fulfill the bank's mission and a permanent professional staff to analyze proposed projects and dispense advice to developers (Istrate and Puentes 2009).

20. Klein (2018).

21. Other alternatives are possible, though. Charging fees for using infrastructure, such as tolls during rush hour, would be possible and helpful. Re-creating "Build America Bonds," which offer subsidized debt to investors, could help as well. Public-private partnerships offer some possibilities, but, at the very least, they are not well suited to the major maintenance work that we need on roads, bridges, and schools. Converting the gas tax to a vehicle-miles-traveled tax would be more efficient but might not raise much revenue. Congressional Budget Office (2011); Engel, Fischer, and Galetovic (2011); Government Accountability Office (2012); Schanzenbach, Nunn, and Nantz (2017); Winston and Langer (2004).

22. Council of Economic Advisers (2016). Federal R&D investments make up 24 percent of all R&D spending in the United States. Private industry makes up 67 percent, and non-profits, academia, and other government institutions make up the remainder (Boroush 2017).

23. Pool and Erickson (2012).

24. Industrial Research Institute (2016).
25. Congressional Budget Office (2014a); Korn et al. (2002). Prior to the spending surge in the late 1990s, the NIH budget was set on a funding path for the prior four decades such that its budget doubled every 10 years in that period.
26. Council of Economic Advisers (2016); Jones and Williams (1998).
27. West and Allen (2018).
28. The Joint Committee on Taxation (2017) provides cost estimates for this policy through 2027, after which I assume a constant annual cost of $6.3 billion, equal to the cost in 2027.
29. As a simplification, baseline non-defense R&D spending is calculated as non-defense discretionary spending multiplied by the 30-year average historical ratio of non-defense R&D spending to non-defense discretionary spending (about 11 percent).
30. Kremer (2000a, 2000b).
31. Eisenhower (1953).
32. Federal News Service (2012).
33. Congressional Budget Office (2018). Spending by these agencies clearly is related to national defense issues but is placed under different classifications in the budget. In 2018, DHS outlays were 0.3 percent of GDP, while VA spending was about 0.9 percent of GDP.
34. Stockholm International Peace Research Institute (2017).
35. These figures include all defense spending, not just the Department of Defense budget. Other defense spending includes nuclear energy programs in the Department of Energy and other national defense–related programs across various agencies. This type of spending is typically 3 to 5 percent of all national defense outlays (Daniels and Harrison 2018; Office of Management and Budget 2018).
36. Driessen and Labonte (2018).
37. For political reasons, Congress and DoD sometimes misclassify base budget expenditures as OCO costs. In the presence of an active war, an OCO budget has an urgency to it that will make Congress more likely to accept spending. Moreover, shifting base budget spending to the OCO category allows DoD to boost its base operations above the Budget Control Act spending caps since OCO spending is not subject to the discretionary limits. One estimate suggests that about $20 billion of annual OCO spending in recent years went toward expenditures that should have been in the base budget (Harrison 2016).
38. The $600 billion figure adjusts the $629 billion cap from the Bipartisan Budget Act of 2018 by removing defense spending from agencies other than the Department of Defense, which is roughly $30 billion per year (Daniels and Harrison 2018).
39. Congressional Budget Office (2014b, 2017b); National Academy of Sciences (2013).
40. Congressional Budget Office (2010).
41. Crawford (2017).
42. Every year, the Department of Defense produces an FYDP that lays out how its base budget would evolve over the subsequent five years if DoD were to execute its current plans. The spending caps in the BCA do not permit these funding levels, however. CBO reestimates the budgetary costs and extends the period another 10 years. The Congressional Budget Office (2017b) projects that in the 10 years beyond the 2017 FYDP period, procurement and research costs will be relatively flat. However, health costs will rise by 32 percent from 2022 to 2032. Historical experience suggests that the costs of current plans will be higher than DoD anticipates, especially costs to develop and purchase weapon systems, compensation costs including those for healthcare, and operations and maintenance costs. CBO projects that costs would be about 3 percent higher on average through 2032 if several broad areas were to experience growth similar to that in the past (Congressional Budget Office 2017b).
43. O'Hanlon (2013, 2016).
44. Maintaining constant real OCO spending also accounts for the uncertainty in future world conditions. I also adjust spending projections to account for the difference between budget authority and outlays. This difference is projected to be about 3 percent per year,

according to the Congressional Budget Office (2018). Since the Cold War, the US military has operated in a framework structured to handle two large-scale concurrent wars. Over the last several years, however, the need for this structure has become less clear, and experts have proposed alternative frameworks. One of those alternatives, favored by Brookings defense expert Michael O'Hanlon (2015), calls for a "1+2" framework where the military is prepared to fight one large-scale war and two smaller "missions" at the same time. For decisions like these, I defer to whatever strategies DoD deems appropriate to protect this country and its interests.

45. Congressional Budget Office (2014b, 2017b).
46. O'Hanlon (2016).
47. Congressional Budget Office (2017a).
48. Gates (2010); Whitlock and Woodward (2016).
49. Whitlock and Woodward (2016).
50. Congressional Budget Office (2017c).
51. O'Hanlon (2013); Congressional Budget Office (2016b).

11

Taxing People

To address the fiscal challenge, we need to raise taxes substantially. That will require adjusting existing taxes and creating new ones. This chapter covers income and estate taxes. Later chapters cover business taxes (Chapter 12), a new national consumption tax (Chapter 13), and a new national carbon tax (Chapter 14).

The goals of tax policy are clear: raise the revenues needed to finance government as simply, as equitably, and in as growth-friendly a manner as possible.[1] Nevertheless, tax policy remains controversial. People may disagree on what each goal means, the best way to achieve it, or what to do when the goals conflict.

The income tax plays a central role in these debates. Created in 1913 as a niche tax on high-income households and converted from a "class tax" to a "mass tax" to help finance World War II, it's the centerpiece of the federal tax system—raising almost half of all federal revenues, providing a key source of progressivity, and housing many economic incentives and social programs. As a result, income tax debates are often proxies for deeper issues. Arguments to cut income taxes, for example, are sometimes disguised efforts to shrink government policies. Since the income tax is the most direct and frequent way that people interact with the federal government, the tax is often related to debates about citizens' rights and responsibilities.[2]

This chapter summarizes the income tax, provides evidence that moderate increases in the tax do not hurt economic growth much, and discusses issues related to fairness, simplicity, and compliance. I then propose that we undo the tax rate cuts enacted in 2017, let various temporary provisions expire, close loopholes related to capital gains, replace the mortgage interest deduction (MID) with a first-time home buyers tax credit, and enforce the tax law more fully. I also propose that we convert estate and gift taxes to taxes on inheritances. All told, these changes would make taxes more progressive and raise substantial revenue, reducing the debt-to-GDP ratio by 32 percentage points by 2050 (Appendix Table 11.1).

Filing income taxes is an annual ritual for most people. The first step for the taxpayer is calculating his or her adjusted gross income (AGI). Taxpayers add up

Figure 11.1. How to calculate income tax liability. Author's illustration.

their wages and salaries, business income (other than corporations), retirement income, interest, dividends, realized capital gains (the difference in price between assets that are sold and their purchase price), farm income, rent, royalties, some Social Security benefits, and a few other items, and adjust this sum for certain alimony payments, IRA contributions, and a few other factors (Figure 11.1).

Taxpayers can take either a standard deduction or the sum of their itemized deductions, whichever is greater, and therefore more beneficial for them. In 2018, the standard deduction was $12,000 for individuals and $24,000 for married couples filing jointly. Taxpayers can take itemized deductions for mortgage interest (on the first $750,000 of loan principal for a primary residence), up to $10,000 in state and local income and property taxes, charitable contributions, excess medical expenses, and investment interest payments, among other items. About 11 percent of all tax filers itemized their deductions when filing their 2018 taxes, including more than three-quarters of those in the top 1 percent of filers.[3]

Subtracting deductions from AGI yields taxable income, which faces marginal tax rates ranging from 10 percent to 37 percent (rates for married couples filing jointly are shown in Figure 11.2). Dividends and capital gains face lower rates, with the top rate peaking at 20 percent. Complex rules allow a 20 percent deduction in some circumstances for income from pass-through business entities (sole proprietorships, partnerships, limited liability companies, and S corporations).[4]

A taxpayer may file as an individual, part of a married couple filing jointly, a married individual filing separately, or a head of household (an unmarried person with children). The tax brackets—the income thresholds at which each new rate kicks in—differ by filing status. Overall, about 72 percent of those who file taxes (and 77 percent of all households including non-filers) are in tax brackets of 12 percent or less. Only 2 percent of households were in tax brackets above 24 percent.

Applying the tax rates to taxable income yields gross tax liability. Taxpayers may also claim various credits, the largest of which are for earned income and children (see Chapter 9). Other credits subsidize everything from higher education to home energy efficiency. Tax liability is gross tax liability minus credits. The Earned Income Credit and part of the Child Tax Credit are refundable.[5]

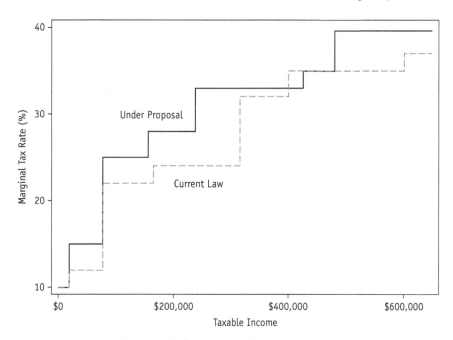

Figure 11.2. Marginal tax rate schedule, proposal vs. current law, married couples filing jointly. Gale et al. (2018).

High-income taxpayers—single taxpayers with modified adjusted gross incomes over $200,000 (married couples filing jointly with income above $250,000)—must pay a surtax of 3.8 percent on net investment income (the NIIT) and 0.9 percent on wages (which, combined with the 2.9 percent Medicare payroll tax, raises the tax on wages by 3.8 percent above the income tax).[6]

Capital gains—profits from the sale of assets—receive favored tax treatment in several ways. First, gains do not face any tax until or unless they are realized— that is, until the asset is sold. That gives taxpayers the advantages of deferring taxes and timing the sale to offset losses. Second, when they are realized, capital gains on assets held for at least a year are taxed at a maximum rate of 23.8 percent (combining an income tax rate of 20 percent and the NIIT of 3.8 percent on high-income households).[7] Third, the "angel of death" loophole means that assets held until the owner's death escape all income taxes.[8] The asset's basis (the purchase price for tax purposes) is "stepped up" to equal its value at the time of the owner's passing, so neither the owner nor inheritor ever pays income tax on the accrued gains.

The Tax Cuts and Jobs Act of 2017 implemented numerous changes to the personal income tax. In order to skirt budget rules that limited the overall revenue loss, Congress stipulated that many of the provisions would expire by 2025, including several of those described earlier.[9]

"Tax expenditures" are subsidies that policymakers put into the tax code in the form of deductions, credits, and other tax preferences.[10] In many ways, these preferences are the tax equivalent of government spending—which is where the term tax "expenditure" comes from.

In total, tax expenditures substantially reduce revenue. In 2018, they cost the government more than $1.3 trillion in lost revenue, which is about 6.3 percent of GDP, almost 80 percent of income tax revenues, and more than outlays for Social Security or the combination of Medicare and Medicaid.[11]

Generally, they are not "loopholes." The most expensive provisions subsidize items like retirement saving, healthcare, mortgage interest, charitable contributions, capital gains, entrepreneurship, low-income earners, working parents, and state and local taxes that benefit tens of millions of households. Many of these items have been in the income tax in some form for decades and they're considered core elements of social policy.

Tax expenditures are tilted toward high-income households. In 2015, benefits for these households totaled more than 13 percent of the pre-tax income of the top 1 percent, but only 6 percent of the income of households in the middle.[12] That's because high-income households are likelier to use these provisions and because exemptions and deductions create "upside-down" subsidies that benefit the well-off. Even if they reduce taxable *income* of different beneficiaries by the same amount, they reduce *taxes* more for higher-income households, who face higher marginal tax rates. In contrast, a dollar's worth of credit reduces everyone's taxes by the same amount (provided the credit is fully refundable).

A focus on tax expenditures is essential to tax reform. Broadening the tax base and taxing all forms of income at the same rate—that is, closing tax expenditures—is often the right direction for tax reform, and it has much to offer. It raises efficiency by encouraging people to make choices based on economic rather than tax reasons. It improves fairness by not playing favorites across different sources or uses of income. It simplifies taxes by reducing the number of artificial distinctions that taxpayers can make.

As noted, taxes will have to rise to meet the fiscal challenge the nation faces. Critics assert that higher taxes stymie economic growth and that tax cuts boost it. Indeed, the idea that tax cuts raise growth is taken as gospel in some quarters. This is one of the clearest cases, however, where ideology dominates the policy discussion. The real story is more complex.

By themselves, tax cuts can either increase or reduce growth. Lower tax rates boost the reward for firms to invest and hire and for people to work and save. In addition, lower tax rates shift resources from untaxed sectors, where there's presumably too much economic activity, toward taxed sectors, where there's presumably too little. For both reasons, tax cuts can boost the size of the economy. But there's more to the story.

First, tax cuts raise the after-tax income that people receive from their current activity, which *lessens* their need to work, save, and invest, and, thus, could reduce such activity. Over the last 200 years, for example, wages rose dramatically, but the length of the workweek declined substantially. Thus, tax cuts—which boost after-tax wages—may not work as intended.

Second, tax cuts must be paid for, and how they're financed matters. If they're financed with increased government debt, the borrowing will reduce long-term growth and thus offset some or all of the direct effects of the tax cut on growth (Chapter 4).[13]

The evidence shows that the *level* of taxes does not appear to have much impact on growth. US historical data show huge shifts in taxes with virtually no observable shift in growth rates (Figure 11.3).[14] From 1870 to 1912, the United States had no income tax, and tax revenues were less than 3 percent of GDP. From 1913 to 1950, taxes averaged almost 11 percent of GDP. By 1950, the economy had entered a new period with permanently higher taxes (and government

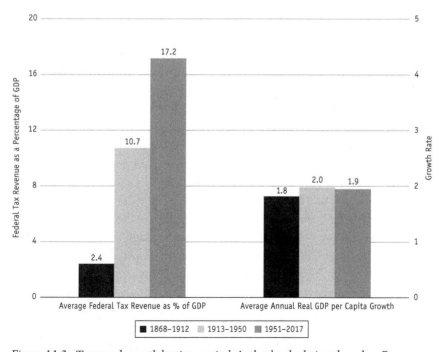

Figure 11.3. Taxes and growth by time period. Author's calculations based on Bureau of Economic Analysis (2018); Office of Management and Budget (2018); Slemrod and Bakija (2017).

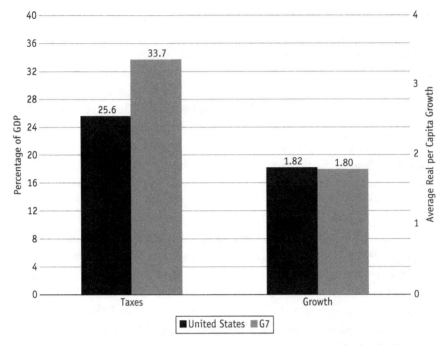

Figure 11.4. Taxes and growth, 1970–2015, United States vs. G7. Author's calculations based on OECD (2017a, 2017b).

spending). From 1950 to 2017, federal revenues averaged more than 17 percent of GDP. Despite the radical differences in taxes as a share of the economy, the annual growth rate of real GDP per person barely budged. It averaged about 2 percent in each period.[15]

Cross-country comparisons yield similar findings. Over the 1970–2015 period, taxes at all levels of government were *much* higher as a share of GDP on average in the other G7 countries (34 percent) than in the United States (26 percent). Yet, real per capita annual growth was virtually identical in those countries (1.82 percent) and the United States (1.80 percent) (Figure 11.4).[16] (One reason the other G7 countries can raise more revenue than the United States without hurting growth is that they employ value-added taxes, which burden consumption rather than saving and investment, as discussed in Chapter 13.)

Obviously, many things besides taxes affect economic growth. But it is noteworthy that differences in revenues of the magnitudes shown in US history and across countries do not have a noticeable impact on per capita growth rates.

Just as tax levels appear to have little impact on growth, so, too, do deficit-financed changes in *tax rates*. After Ronald Reagan's 1981 tax cut reduced top individual income tax rates by more than 20 percentage points, and reduced capital income taxes, the economy did, in fact, grow robustly. But almost all the growth, according to Reagan's chief economist, was due to monetary policy that slashed interest rates massively and helped the economy bounce back from a severe recession after 1982.[17]

The Bush tax cuts in 2001 and 2003 tell a similar story. Between 2001 and 2007 (before the financial crisis and Great Recession), the economy grew at a lackluster pace—real per capita income rose by 1.7 percent annually, compared to 2.2 percent from 1950 to 2001, despite the tax cuts and expansionary monetary policy. Gains were concentrated in housing and finance, two sectors that were not favored by the 2001 and 2003 tax cuts.[18]

If tax cuts boost growth, tax increases should stall the economy. Bill Clinton's tax increase in 1993, which raised the top rate from 31 to 39.6 percent, didn't cause the economic boom that followed. But, at the very least, the experience shows that higher taxes on high-income households need not interfere with faster economic growth.

More recently, several states experimented with tax cuts with little obvious success. The most notorious case is Kansas, where Governor Sam Brownback promised that a moderate tax cut for individuals and a big one for businesses would be "like a shot of adrenaline into the heart of the Kansas economy." Since the 2012 tax cut, however, Kansas's economy has lagged behind neighboring states. In the face of poor growth and persistent spending needs, the Republican state legislature in 2017 reversed much of Brownback's tax cut.[19]

International evidence generates the same conclusion. Research shows little correlation between how countries change their top income tax rate and how much their economies grow. From 1960–1964 to 2006–2010, the top income tax rate fell by more than 40 percentage points in the United States, but barely changed in Spain and Germany. Yet, average growth rates between the two periods in the three countries were almost identical (Figure 11.5).[20]

To be clear, deficit-financed tax cuts can boost the economy in the short run as they put money in people's pockets. But as discussed in Chapter 4, long-term growth requires boosting the supply side—the economy's capacity. Deficit-financed income tax cuts make the long-term budget situation worse, siphon off capital, and thus have small impacts on long-term growth.[21]

Tax *reform*—defined here as changes that broaden the base and reduce tax rates in a revenue- and distributionally neutral way—creates a theoretical presumption of raising the size of the economy by directing resources to their best economic use rather than their best tax-motivated use. But tax reform is a rare event in US history, and the Tax Reform Act of 1986 appears to have had little effect on long-term growth.[22]

Finally, even if they raise economic growth somewhat, deficit-financed tax cuts will make the *fiscal situation* worse. The Congressional Budget Office

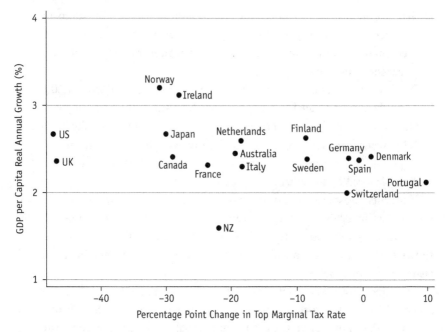

Figure 11.5. Changes in tax rates and growth, 1960–1964 to 2006–2010. Growth is adjusted for initial gross domestic product (GDP) in 1960. Piketty, Saez, and Stantcheva (2014).

estimates that the 2017 tax cut will raise deficits, even after allowing for the tax cut to raise economic growth.[23]

In short, the theory indicates that tax changes will have the most positive effects on growth when they avoid giving windfall gains; offer strong incentives to work, save, and invest more; and minimize debt financing. The data show that these effects appear to be minor, that even major differences in the level of taxes do not affect growth much, and that deficit-financed tax rate cuts do not help long-term growth much but hurt the fiscal situation. These findings imply that tax increases can be part of a fiscal solution without doing significant harm to the economy.

Fairness is crucial to any tax system. For personal taxes, fairness has three aspects. The first is how taxes affect people of different generations. When taxes don't fully finance current spending, the government borrows, shifting the burden of paying for spending to future generations. At times, that's appropriate—during a war, for example, government financing needs increase, and victory benefits future as well as current generations. But financing everyday expenses with debt clearly pushes the burden of paying for current programs to future generations.

The second aspect is how the tax system treats people at different income levels (vertical equity). Almost everyone believes the tax system should be progressive, meaning it should take a bigger share of the income of rich than poor people.[24] But people disagree about how progressive it should be. The federal tax system as a whole, and the income tax in particular, are progressive (Chapter 1).

The third aspect is how taxes treat people at about the same income levels (horizontal equity). There's widespread agreement in principle that a fair tax should provide equivalent treatment to households or individuals with equivalent economic status. In practice, however, it's hard to determine what's an equivalent situation. Do we place too much or too little burden on one-earner versus two-earner families? Parents versus childless adults? Homeowners versus renters? Married couples versus singles?

All three dimensions of fairness play a role in shaping the reforms discussed later in this chapter.

Paying taxes is a burden; tax complexity adds insult to injury. Taxes have always been complicated for well-off families with complex financial arrangements. Now, complexity can afflict lower- and middle-income households too, as they grapple with the definition of dependents, the earned income and child credits, and related issues.

The costs of administering the tax system include the time and out-of-pocket costs of individuals and businesses to comply with taxes and the administrative costs of government. Despite the vastly increased use of software packages to file taxes, estimates suggest that these "narrow" costs have been rising steadily.[25] Complexity also has broader costs. It gives people and businesses opportunities and incentives to organize their economic activities in certain ways. It makes the tax system so confusing that seemingly all taxpayers think they are getting a worse deal than everyone else.

A key question, though, is not how complicated the system is, but whether we get good value for the complexity. Here, the distinction between individual perspectives and the economy-wide perspective is important. Someone who gets a $1,000 tax cut for completing ten extra lines on the tax form might think that's a good deal. But suppose everyone gets a $1,000 tax cut for filling out 10 extra lines. On average, it would have been simpler to give everyone a $1,000 tax cut without completing any extra lines at all. So, everyone's added complexity has no redeeming social gain.

In a way, it's remarkable that the tax system is so complicated. After all, people disagree vehemently on how high taxes should be and who should pay them, but doesn't everyone want a simpler tax system? In fact, while people prefer simplicity, holding other factors constant, there is almost no such thing as "just" simplifying the tax system. Almost any tax change involves trade-offs between incentives and the distribution of taxes as well, and simplicity seems always to get the short end of the stick.

For example, taxpayers don't mind complex provisions that reduce their taxes. That is, they put lower taxes ahead of simpler taxes. Likewise, taxpayers and political leaders put the idea of taxing people based on their individual characteristics (like income, family size, or charitable contributions) ahead of simplicity. This requires tracing income from the business sector (where it is generated) to the household sector. It requires reporting and documenting individual characteristics. And it requires that tax rates vary with individual characteristics, creating incentives to shift income to people with lower income and to periods when income would otherwise be low.

In addition, political leaders almost always put tax incentives ahead of simplicity, despite politicians' promises to make taxes so simple that taxpayers will be able to put their tax return on a postcard. Lower tax rates on capital gains compared to other income give people incentive to convert income into the tax-preferred form. An enormous part of the tax code is devoted to the single issue of defining whether a source of income is a capital gain or not. Lower taxes on business income compared to wages similarly gives individuals incentives to relabel income. Giving preferential treatment to a particular good is a significant source of complexity. A recent court case focused on whether Snuggies were blankets or robes. Why? Because they are taxed differently.[26]

Finally, people put social policy ahead of simplicity. Let's say you want to subsidize childcare but you don't want to subsidize children's ski lessons in Aspen. We need a line between what's covered and what isn't. That line must cover all situations, and so the task of drawing that line can grow complicated, especially as taxpayers and their advisers look for ways to get around the rules.

While it's fashionable to harp on how complicated the income tax is, there is an important way in which the tax helps to *simplify* people's lives: The form 1040 is "one-stop shopping." Given all of our tax expenditures, it's simpler and more efficient to have them all on the same form than to require people to fill out other forms to get them. That the income tax form serves as the application for literally dozens of government programs reduces citizens' overall cost of dealing with government.

Consider the Free Application for Federal Student Aid (FAFSA). It used to require that students collect tax records and enter data by hand into the form. The complexity made it less likely that students, especially from low-income families, received financial aid.[27] In 2009, Congress and the Education Department simplified the application by automatically transferring tax information onto the FAFSA, saving families time, reducing data-entry mistakes, and making the program more effective.

Tax avoidance—finding legal ways to reduce tax liability, such as taking a deduction for one's mortgage interest payments—is perfectly legal. Tax evasion—the act of not paying taxes that are owed—is illegal and a significant problem. Evasion can be deliberate, as when people choose not to report income or pay taxes. It can also be inadvertent, as when people make unintentional mistakes in tax filing. In either case, when a person evades taxes, it reduces revenues, which raises the deficit, subsequently requiring higher taxes on the rest of us or requiring cuts in government spending.

The amount of unpaid taxes that are legally due—the "tax gap"—is larger than most people realize. Detailed IRS studies, updated to 2017, imply that that year's tax gap was about $535 billion. At 2.8 percent of GDP, the gap was about 80 percent as large as the deficit that year and 16 percent as large as federal revenues.[28] In short, if we collected every dollar of taxes that were owed, our fiscal problems would be largely gone. That may be impossible, however, unless we're willing to give the IRS more authority and resources to investigate tax fraud.

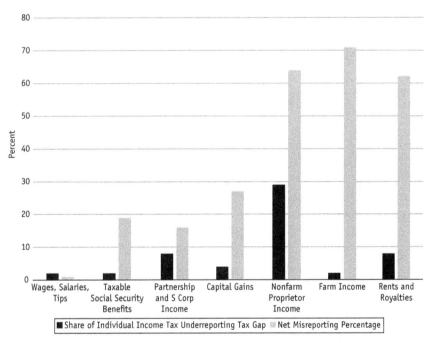

Figure 11.6. Income tax gap and misreporting by major income type. Columns do not add up to 100 percent. Omitted income categories include interest income, dividend income, state income tax refunds, pensions and annuities, unemployment compensation, alimony income, Form 4797 income, and other income. Other sources of the gap include unallocated marginal effects, errors with income offsets or filing status, and errors with tax credits. Together, these factors contribute to less than half of the individual income tax underreporting tax gap. Internal Revenue Service (2016).

Evasion rates depend on the tax system's administrative features. Compliance is highest when third parties report income information to the government and withhold taxes. Only 1 percent of income from wages and salaries is misreported on tax forms (Figure 11.6).[29] Compliance is lower when a third party reports the income but doesn't withhold taxes. Some 16 percent of partnership income and 27 percent of capital gains are unreported to the government by the recipient and thus escape the tax system. The lowest compliance rates occur when there is no cross-party reporting of income and no taxes withheld. Thus, *more than 60 percent* of farm income and sole proprietorship income is not reported to the government.[30] In fact, almost 30 percent of the entire individual income tax underreporting tax gap is associated with sole proprietorship income (Figure 11.6).[31]

Over the years, many people have considered replacing the income tax with a consumption tax.[32] Given our fiscal challenges, we don't have the luxury of substituting one tax for another. We need to implement a national consumption tax (Chapter 13), but not at the expense of the income tax. We can, however, reform the income tax to raise more revenue in a fairer and simpler way by following several principles (Appendix Table 11.1 shows the revenue gains).

Raise Taxes on High-Income Households

Raising taxes on the rich is the right idea at the right time for several reasons. For starters, high-income households have experienced skyrocketing income over the past 40 years, but their average tax rate has remained relatively constant (Chapter 5). In a progressive system, average tax rates should rise as income rises, so they're due for an increase. Moreover, most of the benefits of growth in recent decades have gone to high-income households (Chapter 5). To the extent that addressing our fiscal challenge translates to more growth in the future, much of the gain will accrue to high-income households, so they should pay for the benefit. In addition, raising taxes on high-income households is the *only* significant way to have them share in the burden of resolving our long-term fiscal problem.

Closing loopholes related to capital gains would raise significant revenue in a very progressive manner. More than 90 percent of the tax benefits from long-term capital gains tax rates went to households in the top 20 percent of income in 2017, including 73 percent to the top 1 percent.[33] I propose that we should tax dividends and capital gains at a top rate of 24.2 percent rather than 20 percent; including the 3.8 percent net investment income tax, the combined tax would equal the 28 percent rate under the 1986 Tax Reform Act.[34] I also propose that we tax unrealized capital gains at death; raise the lower rate on capital gains income from its current 15 percent rate to 20 percent; and treat "like-kind exchanges" as sales subject to immediate capital gains tax. Currently, in like-kind exchanges, investors and corporations can indefinitely postpone capital gains taxes on sales of tangible assets—such as real estate—by trading them for a similar asset (say, a different piece of real estate). The law exempts both parties from capital gain on the sale.

Carried interest is a type of commission paid to an investment fund manager for investing other people's money well. Under current law, it's taxed as a capital gain. It should be taxed as ordinary income.

Target Tax Expenditures

A central goal of tax reform should be to define the tax base consistently, broadly, and simply. Eliminating special provisions makes taxes simpler, fairer, and more efficient, and the expanded base raises revenues. Reforming tax expenditures raises revenues in a progressive and efficient way that cuts de facto government spending. As such, it could appeal to both conservatives and liberals.

Not all tax expenditures are bad or inappropriate, though many policy discussions tend to lump them together. In fact, many of the major tax expenditures make sense. The deduction for medical expenses helps families that face extremely expensive health situations. The deduction for charitable contributions encourages people to contribute directly to charity and is based on the reasonable premise that givers shouldn't pay tax on the funds they give away.[35]

But we should eliminate numerous tax expenditures. Many small tax expenditures qualify as targeted loopholes, including, but not limited to, preferential capital gains treatment of coal royalties, income from certain timber sales, deductions for bonds used to finance sports stadiums, and special rules for certain film and television production expenses. Eliminating them would save $10 billion per year.

In terms of major tax expenditures, we have already discussed capital gains and carried interest. In Chapter 7, I noted the need to curtail the exclusion of employer-provided health insurance. In Chapter 12, I propose eliminating many tax expenditures for business income.

The other major tax expenditure ripe for repeal is the mortgage interest deduction. It doesn't raise home ownership rates much, if at all. Many new US homeowners do not itemize or are in the 12 percent bracket or lower, so the MID gives them little or no current benefit.[36] A large MID change in Denmark had virtually no impact on homeownership.[37] Canada, the United Kingdom, and Australia have no subsidies for mortgage debt, yet their home ownership rates are slightly higher than ours.[38]

Instead, the deduction encourages the construction of larger, more expensive houses, which leads to higher energy costs, urban sprawl, and fewer investment funds available for business.[39] By encouraging people to finance homes with too much debt, the deduction increased the likelihood that people would default when housing prices fell in the financial crisis, thus making the Great Recession worse.[40] The deduction is also regressive, providing most benefits to high-income households. While it's often regarded as a middle-class birthright, only 5 percent of the benefits go the middle 20 percent, compared to roughly three-quarters that go to the top 20 percent.[41] Only 6 percent of those in the middle even take the deduction, compared to about 37 percent in the top 20 percent. And it's expensive, reducing revenues by about $32 billion in 2018.[42]

We should phase out the deduction by reducing the maximum deductible interest by 10 percent per year for the next 10 years. The phase-out should be gradual to avoid abrupt changes in housing markets that could put more households underwater. We should replace it with a refundable tax credit of $10,000 for each of the approximately 2 million first-time homeowners each year.[43] That would encourage homeownership, not home indebtedness. At a cost of about $20 billion per year, it would be less expensive, more progressive, and far more effective than the MID in boosting homeownership rates.

Be Fiscally Responsible

The 2017 Tax Cut and Jobs Act (TCJA) introduced numerous changes to income tax rates, the income thresholds at which the rates kick in, and structural features of the tax. Many of the individual income tax provisions will expire over the next few years, but the budget baseline in Chapter 3 assumes that policymakers will extend them, as they have other previous tax cuts. Given our fiscal situation, this is a tax cut we cannot afford. But it's not easy to untangle some of the rules for various reasons. So, we focus here just on changes to the income tax rates and the brackets for taxable income.

I propose that as of 2021, the rates and brackets for ordinary income return to their pre-TCJA levels, adjusted for inflation. This would raise the rate structure from its current 10 to 37 percent range to 10 to 39.6 percent (Figure 11.2) and would raise substantial amounts of revenue.

Enforce the Law

When people don't pay their taxes, they are not just cheating the government, they are ripping off their neighbors. Adequately funding the IRS to pursue tax enforcement would raise revenues on net and assure the public that the system isn't rigged in favor of the wealthy. We should give the Internal Revenue Service the resources it needs to enforce and administer the system. As noted, unpaid federal taxes exceed half a trillion dollars per year. Many taxpayers simply do not pay the taxes they owe, while the IRS lacks the resources to enforce payment.[44]

The IRS is falling further and further behind state-of-the-art computing. Many of its computer systems and programs belong in museums; they are running applications from the 1960s.[45] Meanwhile, Congress has asked the IRS to assume new administrative and enforcement responsibilities, related to interpreting and implementing the TCJA, the Affordable Care Act, the American Opportunity Tax Credit, expansions of the earned income tax credit, and the Foreign Account Tax Compliance Act.[46] Lower funding combined with increased responsibility generates predictable results: worse taxpayer service, fewer audits, and worse enforcement of the tax system.[47] We will never capture 100 percent of taxes owed, but the IRS could do far more if it had the resources. Cutting IRS spending, as policymakers have done in recent years, is penny-wise and pound-foolish.

We should enact a proposal from the Obama administration for added IRS spending on tax enforcement and compliance.[48] It would also allow the IRS to hire more employees so that the agency can do its work more efficiently. The program would cost $17 billion in its first decade and raise $64 billion directly, and more indirectly by encouraging greater compliance with tax law. The net $47 billion directly raised would be a start, but it would only be about 1 percent of the overall tax gap over the next decade, and we should look for other ways to close the gap.

Simplify Taxes

Massive simplification is the Holy Grail of tax reform—desirable and unattainable. For all sorts of reasons—politics, trade-offs with fairness, and so on—we will never get a simple, clean tax system. Still, we can make taxes simpler by, for instance, consolidating family, work, and dependent provisions; streamlining education incentives and saving incentives; and providing a percentage exclusion for capital gains and dividends rather than a separate rate schedule.

In addition, policymakers should let the IRS pre-populate people's tax returns with information it receives from third parties. This could greatly simplify filing for as many as 50 million taxpayers with relatively minor changes to the tax code.[49] Such systems exist in dozens of countries and would relieve the hassles of filing and compliance for the households least able to address them. Taxpayers could elect to have the tax agency prepare their return, and tax filing would occur in four steps: interested taxpayers provide basic information to the tax authority (name, address, Social Security number, dependents, etc.); the tax authority calculates tax liabilities, given the information returns it receives from employers, financial institutions, and other payers and the information it gets from the taxpayer; the taxpayer reviews and adjusts these calculations; and refunds or tax payments are processed. California piloted a similar program that became quite popular.[50]

Reform Asset Transfer Taxes

Taxes on estates and gifts have shrunk dramatically over the past 40 years. Less than 0.1 percent of all estates are subject to the estate tax, down from a peak of 7.65 percent in 1977.[51] But by taxing wealth transfers from one generation to the next, they play an important role in making taxes more progressive and slightly offsetting disparities in opportunity across economic classes.

Critics argue that the taxes adversely affect entrepreneurship and family farms, with the children of business owners and farmers who die forced to sell their inherited businesses and farms to pay the tax. There's little to no evidence to support these claims, however, nor was there even in earlier years when the exemption was much lower than today. Several analyses, including by the American Farm Bureau Federation and *New York Times*, did not reveal a *single* farm that went out of business due to estate tax liability.[52] In fact, only 80 small businesses and farms faced the estate tax in 2017, paying a total of $30 million, equal to 0.15 of 1 percent of total estate tax revenue.[53]

As baby boomers die, they could potentially transfer massive amounts of resources to the next generation. If left untaxed, those transfers will exacerbate the inequality that has widened over the past 40 years and fuel additional revenue shortfalls.

To help level the intergenerational playing field, I propose that we convert the estate tax to an inheritance tax on recipients. It would apply to all gifts and inheritances above a $2.1 million threshold, and the tax rate would equal the heir's income tax rate plus 15 percentage points.[54] That would integrate income and estate taxes. It would also change the moral direction of the debate—rather than focus on those who accumulated wealth, it would justify the levy as a windfall tax on those who, merely by their luck to be born into a rich family, inherited significant wealth. The distributional impact would be largely similar to that of the estate tax, targeting those who receive the largest inheritances.

The income tax plays a central role in federal taxes. Taxes on asset transfers play a key role in moderating inequality. Reforms of both taxes could help raise revenues and reduce inequality.

Notes

1. As discussed in Chapter 6, this is not a universally held position. Some conservatives favor a tax system that does not raise adequate revenue to finance current government spending because they think that the higher deficits will force spending cuts and bring about a smaller government.
2. Williamson (2017).
3. Tax Policy Center (2018a).
4. Gale and Krupkin (2018).
5. To see how this works, note that a married couple filing jointly with two children and wages of $100,000 in 2018 would have taxable income of $76,000 if they take the standard deduction, so they would be in the 12 percent tax bracket—that is the rate they would face on the next dollar of income. They would face gross income tax liability of $8,739 (the sum of 10 percent on the first $19,050 of taxable income and 12 percent on the next $56,950). They would be eligible for $4,000 in child credits, which would reduce their net tax liability to $4,739, so their tax payments would be about 4.7 percent of their AGI.
6. About 0.1 percent of all taxpayers—all of them upper-middle-class or upper-income—also have to pay alternative minimum tax (AMT). People have to pay their regular income liability or their AMT liability, whichever is larger. The AMT exempts almost all lower-income and middle-class households by providing a large exemption—in 2018, $70,300 for single taxpayers and $109,400 for married couples filing jointly. It taxes a broader base at flatter rates (26 percent and 28 percent) than the regular income tax.
7. In 2018, the tax rate on most long-term capital gains (and qualified dividends) was zero for joint taxpayers with total taxable income of $77,200 or less, 15 percent for those with taxable income between $77,201 and $479,000, and 20 percent for those with taxable income above $479,000.
8. Journalist and commentator Michael Kinsley first coined the term "angel of death" (Kinsley 1987). To illustrate the loophole, consider someone who buys stock for $100. After 20 years, the stock is worth $1,000. If the owner sells it at that point, the capital gains tax would apply to $900. If the owner instead dies at that point, no tax is paid on the capital gain—by the owner or the inheritor.
9. The Tax Cut and Jobs Act of 2017 made major changes to the income tax (Gale et al. 2018). It set statutory tax rates between 10 and 37 percent, down from a prior range of 10 to 39.6 percent. The law also changed the income thresholds for each tax bracket. The top bracket now begins at a higher income threshold ($600,000 compared to $480,000 for married couples filing jointly). It repealed personal exemptions but raised the standard deduction and the child credit and created a new dependent credit. It slightly restricted the MID, cut the maximum state and local income and property tax deduction from an unlimited amount to $10,000, and limited medical deductions. It eliminated the penalty for not having health insurance (see Chapter 7). The law changed some rules regarding capital gains, changed the way the tax brackets are indexed (see Chapter 8), provided a

new deduction and other changes for pass-through businesses (see Chapter 12), and made major changes to the corporate income tax (see Chapter 12).

10. Formally, tax expenditures are rules that deviate from a "normal" tax system. They can take the form of exclusions, exemptions, or deductions from income; credits; a preferential tax rate; or a deferral of taxes owed. Prominent examples include the mortgage interest deduction, the exclusion of employer health insurance premiums, and the earned income credit. To develop tax expenditure estimates, the government implicitly defines a normal system as a broad-based, progressive income tax with personal exemptions, standard deductions, and tax rates that are at current levels, where all forms of income are taxed at the same rate, except unrealized capital gains, which are untaxed. This definition of a normal system is controversial. Some people think the normal base should be consumption, others argue that the normal system should be more or less progressive than it is, or that unrealized capital gains should be included. Note that the size of tax expenditures depends on the level of tax rates, and that the use of tax expenditures distorts conventional measures of the size of government by understating both spending and revenues.

11. Congressional Budget Office (2018); Joint Committee on Taxation (2018). The revenue impact is larger when tax expenditures are measured simultaneously, so that interaction effects are taken into account. Burman, Toder, and Geissler (2008), for example, found that interactions raised the total cost of a large subset of tax expenditures in the individual income tax estimated simultaneously by between 5 and 8 percent in 2007, compared with the sum of the costs of the separate estimates. Even if the normal tax base were consumption rather than income, about two-thirds of the items would still be considered tax expenditures. Under a consumption tax, the deferrals applicable to capital gains, mortgage interest, and retirement saving would not be considered tax expenditures, since the current tax treatment would represent the normal treatment of saving under a consumption tax (Marron and Toder 2013).

12. Toder, Berger, and Zhang (2016).

13. Federal tax cuts can also generate responses from other governmental entities—including the Federal Reserve Board, state governments, and foreign governments—that reduce growth. Cuts in US taxes that induce capital inflows from abroad, for example, may encourage other countries to reduce their taxes to retain capital or attract US funds. To the extent that other countries respond, the net effect of income tax cuts on growth will be smaller than otherwise.

14. The data are courtesy of Slemrod and Bakija (2017), updated with data from the Bureau of Economic Analysis (2018) and the Office of Management and Budget (2018).

15. Hungerford (2012) plotted the annual real per capita GDP growth rate against the top marginal income tax rate and the top capital gains tax rate from 1945 to 2010, a period that spanned wide variation in the top rate. The fitted values suggest that higher tax rates are not associated with higher or lower real per capita GDP growth rates to any significant degree. In multivariate regression analysis, neither the top income tax rate nor the top capital gains tax rate has a statistically significant association with the real GDP growth rate.

16. OECD (2017a, 2017b).

17. Feldstein (1986). Of the change in real GNP during that period, Feldstein finds that only about 2 percentage-points of the 15-percentage point rise cannot be explained by monetary policy. A defense buildup boosted spending, and an influx of baby boomers (who were between 17 and 35 years old in 1981) and women expanded the labor force, leaving very little room for tax policy to have affected growth. In a separate study, Feldstein and former Congressional Budget Office director Doug Elmendorf found no evidence that the 1981 tax cuts got people to work more (Feldstein and Elmendorf 1989). They found that the strength of the recovery over the 1980s could be ascribed to monetary policy.

18. By 2006, prime-age males were working the same amount they were in 2000—before the tax cuts—and women were working less, inconsistent with the view that lower tax rates raise labor supply (Eissa 2008). Gale and Potter (2002) estimated that the 2001 tax cut

would have little or no net effect on GDP over the next 10 years and could have even reduced it; that is, they found that the negative effect of higher deficits and the decline in national saving would outweigh the positive effect of reduced marginal tax rates. Desai and Goolsbee (2004) argued that the effects of the 2003 tax cuts were likely to be small, and Yagan (2015) presented empirical evidence that the 2003 tax cuts had little impact on investment or employment.

19. Gale, Krupkin, and Rueben (2017). Evidence from other states is equally unsupportive of the supply-side notion that tax cuts boost growth.

20. Piketty, Saez, and Stantcheva (2014). See also Slemrod (1995).

21. Gale and Samwick (2017) reviewed this literature. Detailed simulations suggest that a radical reform—one that eliminates the standard deductions, all itemized deductions, and preferential treatment of fringe benefits and had a flat rate on all income (including wage and capital income)—could boost the size of the economy by 3 to 5 percentage points in the long run (Altig et al. 2001). These changes would be extremely regressive and are well beyond the scope of what is seriously proposed in policy circles, but they show the upper bound potential of even radical reform and thus help to convey why more modest reforms have small effects on growth.

22. Auerbach and Slemrod (1997) addressed numerous features of the Tax Reform Act of 1986 on economic growth and its components. They suggest that, although there may have been substantial impacts on the timing and composition of economic activity—for example, a reduction in tax sheltering activity—there was little effect on the overall level of economic activity. They concluded that there were small impacts on saving, labor supply, entrepreneurship, and other productive activities.

23. Congressional Budget Office (2018). These issues are discussed in detail in Gale and Samwick (2017). For surveys of the effects of taxes on saving, labor supply, and small business activity, see Bernheim (2002) and Gale and Brown (2013).

24. There are exceptions. Critics of progressive tax systems sometimes cite the Bible as providing the case for either an equal-per-head tax (Fugate 2012) or a fixed share of income (such as the biblical tithe).

25. Slemrod and Bakija (2017). This estimate includes enforcement and compliance activities for federal individual and corporate income taxes. Compliance costs include but are not limited to the costs of tax preparers or tax software, expenses incurred by third parties to collect taxes (i.e., tax withholding for employees), and the opportunity costs of time for completing tax forms and recordkeeping. Enforcement costs include IRS activities to collect the taxes that are owed. Earlier estimates by the authors (Slemrod and Bakija 2004, 2008) found that compliance costs were in the 10 to 13.5 percent range).

26. Flood (2017). The Court ruled that Snuggies should be classified as blankets rather than robes, thus allowing them to face a lower import tariff rate.

27. Dynarski and Scott-Clayton (2006).

28. Internal Revenue Service (2016). This refers to the net tax gap, which is equal to the gross tax gap less enforced and other late payments.

29. This is formally defined in Internal Revenue Service (2016) as the net misreported amount divided by the sum of the absolute values of the amounts that should have been reported, expressed as a percentage.

30. Internal Revenue Service (2016).

31. The IRS estimates an EITC improper payment rate of about 22 percent to 26 percent for fiscal year 2017. But, as noted by taxpayer advocate Nina Olsen, this rate may be overestimated because it reflects unintentional errors due to the complexity of filing requirements rather than intentional fraud (Greenstein, Wancheck, and Marr 2018).

32. For example, see Aaron and Gale (1996); Altig et al. (2001); Hall and Rabushka (2007).

33. Tax Policy Center (2017b).

34. In President Obama's 2017 budget, the administration proposed increasing the top capital gains tax rate to 28 percent, including the value of the net investment income tax

(24.2 percent plus the 3.8 percent NIIT), which is almost identical to this proposal. The administration also proposed elimination of the stepped-up basis for capital gains (Office of Management and Budget 2016).

35. One approach to reform, proposed by Mitt Romney in 2012, is to cap an individual's overall tax expenditures at either a dollar amount or a percentage of income. Romney proposed capping itemized deductions at $17,000, $25,000, or $50,000 (Romney 2012; Gale, Brown, and Looney 2012). This has the political advantage of not explicitly limiting any particular subsidy, but it does not distinguish between effective and ineffective tax expenditures, and questions inevitably arise over which tax expenditures should be included in the cap. Feldstein, Feenberg, and MacGuineas (2011) proposed a 2-percent-of-AGI cap on all tax expenditures.

36. Kolomatsky (2017). Indeed, there is an argument that the deduction actually reduces home ownership rates in some markets by subsidizing home purchases for high-income earners who increase their housing consumption, rather than reducing barriers to home ownership for lower-income earners (Hilber and Turner 2014).

37. Gruber, Jensen, and Kleven (2017).

38. Bartlett (2013). Nor was the deduction created to boost home ownership. It was present in the original 1913 income tax, which applied only to households in the top 2 percent of the income distribution and was imposed on redistributional grounds. It is hard to believe that home ownership rates among that group of households was an important public policy concern.

39. Gruber, Jensen, and Kleven (2017).

40. McDonald and Johnson (2010).

41. Tax Policy Center (2018b).

42. Joint Committee on Taxation (2018). Drukker, Gayer, and Rosen (2017) estimate that the rebalancing-adjusted revenue loss is about 90 percent of the conventionally estimated revenue loss to account for the fact that investors would change their portfolios if the deduction were eliminated.

43. Gale, Gruber, and Stephens-Davidowitz (2007); Genworth Mortgage Insurance (2017).

44. Government Accountability Office (2016); Mnuchin (2017).

45. Koskinen (2015).

46. Marr and Murray (2016).

47. In 2015, the IRS audited only 0.8 percent of individual and 1.3 percent of corporate returns, compared to 1.0 and 2.1 percent, respectively, in 1998. The audit rate for households with income over $1 million has fallen by 40 percent since 2010 (Government Accountability Office 2016; Internal Revenue Service 2010, 2015).

48. Office of Management and Budget (2016).

49. Department of the Treasury (2003); Gale and Holtzblatt (1997); Government Accountability Office (1997).

50. Goolsbee (2006).

51. Joint Committee on Taxation (2015); Tax Policy Center (2017c).

52. Johnston (2001).

53. Tax Policy Center (2017a). Two other provisions give special preferences to farms and closely held businesses, generally defined as a business with a small number of shareholders. The first, called special use valuation, allows farmers to value their farms based on their current use rather than their most profitable use. This provision allows owners to reduce the value of their assets by 40 to 70 percent. Under the second, if a farm or business comprises at least 35 percent of the gross estate, owners can pay the tax they owe in installments over 14 years. Over the first five years, only interest payments would be due. In the following years, interest plus principal would be due. Interest rates would be lower than normal.

54. Batchelder (2009, 2016, 2017).

Appendix Table 11.1 **Personal Tax Reform Policies**

Policy	2021 Revenue Change	2050 Revenue Change	2050 Debt Effect
Tax capital gains at death and raise top capital gains rate to 24.2%	0.10	0.12	−3.1
Raise lower capital gains rate to 20%	0.02	0.02	−0.6
Tax like-kind exchanges	0.03	0.03	−0.8
Treat carried interest as ordinary income	0.01	0.01	−0.2
Eliminate $10B of various loopholes	0.04	0.04	−1.2
Phase out mortgage interest deduction	0.02	0.18	−4.1
Create a first-time homeowner credit	−0.10	−0.10	2.8
Restore pre-TCJA tax rates and brackets	0.64	0.76	−20.0
Increase IRS enforcement	0.03	0.04	−0.8
Convert estate tax to an inheritance tax	0.12	0.13	−3.7
Total	**0.91**	**1.22**	**−31.7**

Notes: All numbers are referenced as a percentage of GDP. Total may not equal sum due to rounding. Capital gains, like-kind exchanges, carried interest, mortgage interest deduction, marginal tax rate, and expiring provision estimates grow with baseline income tax revenues. Loophole, homeowner credit, IRS enforcement, and inheritance tax estimates grow with GDP. IRS enforcement revenue change is the gross effect. The net effect in 2050 is 0.03 percent of GDP due to the associated spending increases.

Sources: Batchelder (2016); Congressional Budget Office (2016, 2018); Drukker, Gayer, and Rosen (2017); Joint Committee on Taxation (2017, 2018); McClelland (2017); Office of Management and Budget (2016); Tax Policy Center (2018b).

12

Taxing Business

The Boston Tea Party was a central event in early American history. In common lore, the colonists rose up against British taxation, but the protest was actually about a corporate tax exemption—on imported tea—through which Britain protected the East India Company.[1]

More than two centuries later, Americans remain concerned about business loopholes. Headlines scream that major corporations pay lower effective tax rates than many middle-class families.[2] Almost two-thirds of respondents in recent polls express concern that corporations don't pay their fair share of taxes.[3]

People are right to care about business taxes. How a country taxes its businesses can be central to its economic performance. Businesses employ workers, make investments, develop innovative production techniques, and provide goods and services to each other and consumers.

But the conversation is more complicated than it may appear. First, the nation's business landscape is remarkably diverse, and corporations are taxed differently from other types of businesses. Second, although businesses write tax checks to the government, they *don't* bear the ultimate burden of taxes—people do. Businesses pass along the cost of their taxes to consumers via higher prices, to workers via lower wages, to their owners and shareholders via lower returns, or to someone else. Third, the impact of taxing businesses depends not only on the headline tax rate but also on the various provisions that are either "incentives," if you like them, or "loopholes," if you don't.

Ideally, a business tax would be neutral; it would not affect firms' choices about investing, hiring, financing, and so on. On that basis, our current system fails in numerous ways.

We can make the system more neutral by eliminating special preferences for non-corporate businesses and changing the corporate tax so that it focuses on cash flows rather than profits. Once we have a cash-flow tax, we can raise the rate—from its current 21 percent to 25 percent—to raise revenues without reducing incentives for most types of investment. These and other changes described here would reduce tax avoidance and help rationalize the tax system. Taken together, they would reduce the debt-to-GDP ratio in 2050 by 22 percentage points.

Although we often equate "business" with "corporation," about 95 percent of American businesses are not standard (or "C") corporations. Sole proprietorships are owned and often operated by a single person. Two or more people or entities can form partnerships. The owners of a limited liability corporation can choose to be taxed as a partnership or a traditional corporation. S-corporations are closely held organizations, and unlike partnerships, they must distribute net income proportionally to each owner's share. Although these entities—collectively called "pass-throughs" for tax purposes—operate under a variety of rules, they have one thing in common. They don't face business-level taxes. Rather, the owners pay tax on their business earnings through the individual income tax.

Until recently, income from pass-through businesses was taxed just like other forms of income. The 2017 tax act created a complex deduction for pass-through income. Joint filers with taxable income below $315,000 ($157,500 for singles) are eligible for a 20 percent deduction of their qualified business income (QBI). At higher income levels, the deduction depends—in a complicated and capricious way—on what the business does, the wages it paid, and how much investment property it owns.[4]

Besides the new deduction, small businesses receive other subsidies.[5] Most prominently, they can write off their entire investments on the first million dollars per year of investment in equipment and software. Combined with the deduction for interest payments, they can generate a negative effective tax rate on new investments. In addition, capital gains on a business owner's "sweat equity" are treated very generously.

Most sole proprietorships are small businesses. They are typically owned by moderate- and middle-income households and represent less than half of the owner's income.[6] But not all pass-throughs are small. Businesses with annual receipts above $50 million represent about 0.3 percent of S-corporations and partnerships, but they earn more than 30 percent of all receipts among those types of organizations.[7]

The other 5 percent of businesses are corporations (technically called C corporations) and face a separate corporate income tax. Having a corporate income tax lets the nation tax monopolist profits and foreigners, tax-exempt entities, and retirement saving plans that hold corporate stock. It also provides a backstop to the income tax to help prevent tax avoidance.

The corporate income tax rate of 21 percent applies to the domestic income of US corporations and the US income of foreign corporations with permanent establishments here. For several decades, the US corporate income tax rate was higher than the OECD average—which, critics argued, put US corporations at a competitive disadvantage with those of other countries—but the 2017 tax act reduced the rate to about the OECD average (Figure 12.1).

The tax collects almost all of its revenue from big businesses.[8] It applies to corporate profits, calculated as gross business income (from the sale of goods and services, rents, royalties, interest, dividends, etc.) minus business costs that include employee compensation, supplies, advertising, a limited amount of interest payments, non-federal taxes, repairs, bad debts, and depreciation of assets (the decline in the value of an asset over time). The tax lets firms immediately deduct 100 percent of their investments in equipment, though that feature is scheduled to phase out under current law beginning in 2023. Firms may deduct net operating losses for up to 80 percent of taxable income and carry forward unused losses indefinitely.

Although corporations pay the tax to the government, they do not bear its economic burden. Rather, they pass it along to individuals, via higher prices, lower wages, smaller dividends, or other adjustments. Capital owners bear about 75 percent of the burden, according to several analyses, with workers bearing the remaining 25 percent.[9] Because owners of capital bear so much of the burden, the corporate tax overall is very progressive (when the burden is assigned to

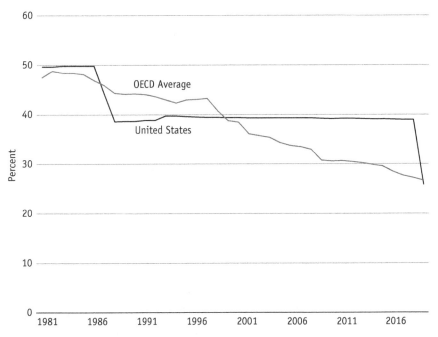

Figure 12.1. OECD vs. US combined (all levels of government) corporate tax rates, 1981–2018. OECD (2018).

households by income level). Households in the top 1 percent of the income distribution (including wages and capital income) bear almost half of the burden.[10]

The composition of business activity is sensitive to taxes. Over the past 40 years, business activity has shifted away from corporations and toward pass-throughs. In 1980, pass-throughs represented 83 percent of all businesses and 25 percent of net business income; by 2012, those figures had risen to 95 and 64 percent, respectively (Figure 12.2).[11] Much of this shift is due to a more favorable tax treatment of pass-throughs compared to corporations and more liberalized rules for owning S corporations.

The shift has had important consequences. It has helped drive the widening income gap, since the vast majority of partnership and S corporation income goes to households in the top 1 percent.[12] It has cost the government increasing amounts of revenue, rising to more than $100 billion per year as of 2011.[13] With the shift in business composition and other factors, corporate tax revenue has fallen over time. In 1980, the tax raised 2.3 percent of GDP. By 2017, it raised only two-thirds as much, just 1.5 percent of GDP. After the 2017 overhaul cut corporate taxes, the tax raised only about 1.2 percent of GDP in revenue in 2018.[14] Corporate taxes have fallen, even though corporate profits have risen

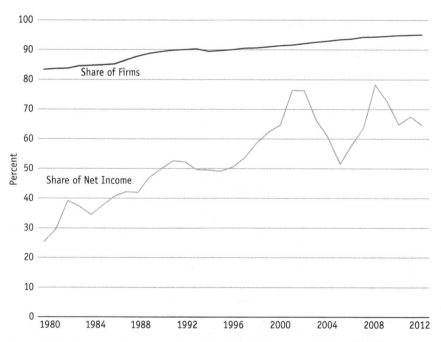

Figure 12.2. The rise of pass-through entities. Internal Revenue Service (2015).

dramatically as a share of GDP over the past 40 years, because of increased avoidance and more generous tax subsidies.[15]

The taxation of business raises numerous issues. The first of them involves one of the best-known economic "factoids"—the claim that small businesses create most new jobs.[16] In fact, however, it is young firms, most of which happen to be small, that create new jobs and innovate significantly. Employment growth is not common for small businesses. As they age, most small firms do not hire many, if any, new workers.[17]

Tax policies that create more generous incentives can boost investment and hiring modestly among existing businesses.[18] But people can also use businesses to shelter or hide income. *Higher* personal tax rates cause people to start businesses, presumably because owning a business offers the opportunity to shelter income or evade taxes.[19] Indeed, as noted in Chapter 11, almost two-thirds of income earned by sole proprietors is not reported to the government even though it should be—and thus is not taxed. Moreover, according to a recent Treasury Department study, partnership income is "opaque" and "murky," and more than one-third of it goes either to partners that could not be traced in tax return data or to circular partnerships—a group of partnerships that collectively own each other.[20] These findings suggest high levels of tax avoidance and possibly evasion.

The 2017 tax act changed the corporate system in major ways. In prior years, critics often complained that corporate profits were taxed twice. Corporations paid taxes on their profits, and then individuals paid taxes when they received the profits as dividends or sold their stocks and realized capital gains. Double taxation raised the effective tax rate on corporate investments that were financed with equity, thus raising the cost of making such investments and, in turn, reducing the level of investment and, with it, the rate of economic growth. It also gave pass-throughs more favorable tax treatment than corporations and encouraged firms to retain earnings rather than pay dividends. Because interest payments to debt holders were deductible for businesses but dividend payments to shareholders were not, double taxation created a bias toward debt financing.

These concerns were often overblown, however. In recent years, only about 25 percent of corporate equity faced taxation at both the business and the individual level, and even then, it usually faced reduced rates at each stage.[21] Many corporations paid much less than the official rate because they took advantage of a wide array of exemptions, deductions, and tax subsidies. Some of the largest corporations have paid almost no federal corporate income tax in recent years, in part by moving profits overseas.[22] Individuals paid reduced rates on realized capital gains and dividends, and lots of stock was held by tax-exempt entities, like foundations, or in retirement saving plans.[23] Non-taxation of corporate income was as big an issue as double taxation, and the uneven taxation created economic inefficiencies.

To a certain extent, the 2017 tax cut turned double taxation concerns on their head. Corporate income is still taxed at both the business and individual levels, but the sharp reduction in the corporate tax rate to 21 percent gives strong incentives for wealthy individuals without an immediate need for cash to shelter their income in corporations.[24] Virtually nothing prevents business taxpayers from switching from pass-through to corporation status—they need only to check a box on their tax form.

The biggest changes in the 2017 tax law applied to the taxation of foreign income. International economic issues have grown dramatically more important in recent decades as communications and other technologies have made the world smaller and firms larger. The sum of exports and imports were 27 percent of GDP in 2017, compared to just 11 percent in 1970.[25]

Before the 2017 act, firms paid taxes on their actively earned foreign income only when they "repatriated" the funds—that is, brought them back to their domestic parent.[26] This system was complex, raised little revenue, and gave firms ways to reduce taxes on their domestic earnings by shifting income overseas. To avoid the tax, US companies held more than $2.6 trillion in untaxed profits in their foreign affiliates by 2015.[27]

Under the 2017 tax law, multinational firms can now bring back new foreign profits without facing US tax. But don't expect that to have a big effect on the economy. Many people mistakenly believe that, previously, these funds were "trapped" overseas and couldn't help the economy.[28] In practice, they were mostly held in banks, which could lend the funds to others, or used to buy government bonds. Firms now must pay a "deemed repatriation" tax on their previously accumulated, untaxed foreign earnings. The tax rate is 15.5 percent for cash holdings and 8 percent for illiquid assets, and they must pay it over eight years.

But if the tax system only taxed firms' domestic income, companies would have strong incentives to shift real investment and reported income overseas and to shift deductions into the United States. Several provisions aim to reduce the extent to which companies take those actions. A minimum tax on global intangible low-taxed income (called GILTI) imposes a 10.5 percent minimum tax on profits that US corporations earn abroad in excess of a firm's "normal" return (defined as 10 percent on tangible property held abroad).[29] The GILTI tax rate rises to 13.125 percent starting in 2026. GILTI acts as a "stick" to prevent companies from moving their intangible assets overseas.

The base erosion and anti-abuse tax (BEAT) is another "stick." It imposes a minimum tax of 10.5 percent on otherwise deductible payments between a

US corporation and its foreign subsidiary. Specifically, BEAT taxes at a 10.5 per-cent rate the sum of a corporation's taxable income and all deductible payments (other than costs of goods sold) to foreign affiliates. The firms pay the larger of their BEAT or regular corporate tax.[30] The goal is to stop what is called "earnings stripping," a process by which firms can move earnings out of the United States into lower-taxed countries.

The law also provides a "carrot" to encourage firms to locate intangible assets in the United States. Foreign-derived intangible income (FDII) is income that companies earn from exporting products whose intangible assets are held in the United States. FDII is taxed at 13.125 percent rather than the 21 percent corpo-rate rate under the 2017 tax law, rising to 16.406 percent after 2025.

Many areas of business taxation need reform. (Revenue estimates are shown in Appendix Table 12.1.)

The 2017 tax law made major changes to business taxation that, in many cases, were not well thought out. The rules regarding the new deduction for pass-through businesses will cause numerous problems. They're ineq-uitable—about 44 percent of the benefits go to taxpayers with incomes greater than $1 million per year.[31] They provide windfall gains to owners who made investments in the past, which won't increase current invest-ment. They will create enormous opportunities to game the tax system. As one example, doctors or lawyers might split their operations into two companies: one that provides medical or legal services, and another that contracts with the service provider and acts as a leasing firm that owns all the property and equipment.[32] The rules will also create incentives for people to relabel wage income as business income. The rules do not make sense because they don't reflect any underlying principle. At worst, the new rules will prove unadministrable and generate massive tax avoidance. They should be repealed, so that wages and business income are taxed at the same rate.

There are a few "good housekeeping" reforms that we should pursue. We should subject corporations' like-kind exchanges to capital gains taxes, just as I propose for the individual income tax (Chapter 11). Also, we should close the "John Edwards/Newt Gingrich loophole."[33] Owners of S corporations pay pay-roll taxes on "reasonable compensation," but not on the rest of their income from the business. That incentivizes them to under-report reasonable compensation. The law should stipulate instead that owners of all pass-through businesses pay self-employment tax on their share of the business's income.[34]

More fundamentally, I propose that we move to a 25 percent corporate cash-flow tax. Specifically, I would (1) raise the corporate tax rate to 25 percent, (2) allow expensing—full first-year write-offs of investment in equipment, structures, and inventories—and (3) eliminate the deduction for corporate interest payments.

My rationale is straightforward. Raising the rate to 25 percent will reduce the extent to which the tax system provides windfall gains, which are expensive and unproductive, to previous investment. Eliminating the interest deduction sets debt and equity financing on equal footing and removes the tax system's distortion in favor of debt. With that, expensing sets the *effective* tax rate on new investments to *zero*. This may seem counterintuitive because the tax rate is 25 percent, but expensing effectively makes the government a silent partner in the investment. A firm that invests a dollar in a project this year gets a 25-cent deduction (the government's "contribution"). If, say, the project pays off to the tune of $2 next year, the government gets 50 cents in taxes. Both the firm and the government get the same return—in this case, 100 percent—on their investments. The government's "investment" takes the form of granting a deduction in the first year and receiving tax revenues in subsequent years.

Setting the effective tax rate on new investment to zero has three important implications. First, it lowers the effective tax rate on (most) investments. Second, it eliminates all distortions in effective tax rates across investments, which generate major economic costs.[35] Third, it would make the United States very competitive internationally. Leading conservative economist Robert Barro and prominent liberal economist Jason Furman, who served as chair of President Obama's Council of Economic Advisers, estimate that such a change would bring a dramatic boost in investment and economic growth compared to the current system.[36]

My proposal would tax exports and allow deductions for imports. If those provisions were switched so that the tax was "border adjusted"—exports were exempt from tax and imports were not deductible—the result would be what's called a destination-based cash-flow tax (DBCFT). The DBCFT has bipartisan roots. President George W. Bush's Advisory Panel on Federal Tax Reform proposed one in 2005.[37] More recently, Berkeley economist Alan Auerbach proposed one in a 2010 paper sponsored by the Center for American Progress, an avowedly liberal organization, and the Brookings Institution. House Republicans proposed a variation in 2016.[38]

Whether to border-adjust is an interesting question. It would make the United States an even more attractive place to invest because it would not tax profits earned in the United States, just sales in the nation. It would eliminate a host of complexities in international tax policy and eliminate all US tax incentives for American firms to move profits, productions, or headquarters overseas.

Nevertheless, for several reasons, I believe we should hold off on border adjustment. First, it would raise the specter of the government giving large refunds every year to major corporations that exported significant amounts. Second, despite some popular claims, border adjustments will not raise long-term revenue. Currently, the United States imports more than it exports, so a border adjustment—which taxes imports and exempts exports—would raise money in the short run. But in the long run, exports and imports must roughly balance, so we would lose money in future years on a border adjustment.

In addition, if it raised exchange rates significantly, border adjustment would give an enormous tax cut—several trillion dollars—to foreign investors in the United States, at the expense of American taxpayers, and it would wreak havoc on the finances of countries that borrow in US dollars. If it did not raise exchange rates significantly, the price of imports to America would rise substantially, which would hurt low-income people in the United States. Also, the two new taxes proposed in subsequent chapters—a value-added tax (Chapter 13) and a carbon tax (Chapter 14)—*should* be border-adjusted to work properly. For all these reasons, I believe that border-adjusting the corporate tax would be too large a policy leap at this point.

There's no perfect way to treat foreign income under the tax code. The new international tax rules are clearly designed to combat corporate efforts to avoid taxes by moving assets and income overseas and dumping their costs into the United States. But GILTI, BEAT, and FDII create new categories of income and expenses that will take years for corporations and the government to sort out. Firms' efforts to find ways around these provisions will add compliance costs, reduce revenues, and require more IRS enforcement resources.[39]

GILTI gives firms unintended incentives to invest in tangible assets— factories—overseas. And because it's based on worldwide average tax rates rather than per country taxes, it gives firms incentives to shelter income in tax havens. If BEAT works as intended, it will hurt the significant number of big businesses that use global supply chains, even if they're not engaging in egregious behavior. In the future, GILTI provisions will probably need to be tightened and BEAT provisions loosened, but it's too soon to tell exactly how they should be changed. The FDII provisions should be repealed, however. They will not prove particularly helpful in stimulating investment, given the generous treatment of research and experimentation expenses already proposed in Chapter 10. They will also likely face challenges from other countries in the World Trade Organization for violating a rule against selective export subsidies.

More generally, we don't yet know how other countries will respond to the recent tax legislation. They could plausibly challenge BEAT as well, for what might seem a selective import tariff. And whether other nations will merely stand by and let the United States become a "low corporate tax" country compared to many of its competitors is an open question. They could reduce their own corporate tax rates, continuing a "race to the bottom." They could otherwise strengthen tax incentives to attract reported profits and production.

How we tax businesses is central to our economic welfare. The 2017 tax act made many changes to business taxation. We now have the opportunity to enhance the best features and remedy the mistakes.

Notes

1. Thorndike (2005, 2010).
2. Leonhardt (2016).
3. Gallup (2017); Pew Research Center (2015).
4. Here's how the rules work. For income from a "specified service trade or business," if taxable income is between $315,000 and $415,000 (for taxpayers who are married and filing jointly), the unlimited deduction for qualified business income phases out as income rises, and the deduction cannot exceed the applicable share of the greater of (a) 50 percent of W-2 wages paid by the business or (b) 25 percent of wages plus 2.5 percent of qualified property for the business. If taxable income is above $415,000, income from specified service trades or businesses is not eligible for the deduction. A specified service trade or business is defined as "any trade or business involving the performance of services in the fields of health, law, consulting, athletics, financial services, brokerage services, or any trade or business where the principal asset of such trade or business is the reputation or skill of one or more of its employees or owners, or which involves the performance of services that consist of investing and investment management trading, or dealing in securities, partnership interests, or commodities." For all other pass-through businesses, qualified business income does not phase out, and the 20 percent deduction is partially limited over the $315,000 to $415,000 taxable income range by the greater of either (a) 50 percent of W-2 wages for the business or (b) 25 percent of wages plus 2.5 percent of qualified property for the business. However, the limit is gradually applied over the income range. For a more detailed explanation of the pass-through provisions, see Gale and Krupkin (2018).
5. Gale and Brown (2013).
6. Gleckman (2016). In 2016, almost 40 percent of all business tax returns were sole proprietors whose income was less than $82,000 (in the third quintile or lower). For almost all of these, business income was a small fraction (much less than half) of their total income.
7. Keightley (2012); Tax Policy Center (2016). Owners of limited liability corporations and S corporations enjoy the benefits of limited liability even though the businesses do not face corporate income tax.
8. In 2013, for example, firms with assets of more than $2.5 billion accounted for just one out of every 1,800 corporations but paid 70 percent of all corporate income taxes (Internal Revenue Service 2016).
9. The Congressional Budget Office (2018b) and Joint Committee on Taxation (2013) allocate 25 percent of the burden to workers and 75 percent to capital. The Urban-Brookings Tax Policy Center allocates 20 percent of the burden to workers and 80 percent to owners of capital, the latter figure including 60 percent to shareholders and 20 percent to all holders of capital (Nunns 2012). The US Treasury allocates about 18 percent to workers, and 82 percent to capital, of which 63 percent is assigned to shareholders and the rest to all capital (Cronin et al. 2012).

10. Congressional Budget Office (2018b). This is based on the assumption that 75 percent of the burden is borne by owners of capital (including shareholders), while 25 percent is borne by labor.
11. Internal Revenue Service (2015). Net business income is measured as net income less deficit.
12. Cooper et al. (2016).
13. Cooper et al. (2016).
14. Congressional Budget Office (2018a).
15. Bureau of Economic Analysis (2018a).
16. Harrison (2013).
17. Gale and Brown (2013); Haltiwanger, Jarmin, and Miranda (2010); Pugsley and Hurst (2011).
18. Carroll et al. (1998a, 1998b); Gentry and Hubbard (2004).
19. Bruce (2002); Gurley-Calvez and Bruce (2008).
20. Cooper et al. (2016).
21. Rosenthal and Austin (2016).
22. Gardner, McIntyre, and Phillips (2017); McIntyre, Phillips, and Baxandall (2015).
23. It is natural to note that balances in tax-deferred saving accounts are eventually taxed, when they are withdrawn, but the costs of those taxes are offset by the fact that the original contribution to the account is tax deductible. So corporate earnings that accrue to owners of tax-deferred saving accounts do not face double taxation on net.
24. Looney (2017a). Certain rules related to personal holding companies and accumulated earnings limit the ability of wage earners simply to incorporate themselves to get the lower rate (Desai 2018).
25. Bureau of Economic Analysis (2018b).
26. Passively earned income, for example on financial assets, was taxed separately as it was earned, but was subject to complex rules that allowed for avoidance of tax on much of this income.
27. Joint Committee on Taxation (2016).
28. Looney 2017(b) reports that more than 90 percent of Microsoft's $124 billion in deferred cash before the 2017 tax overhaul was invested in US government and agency securities or other US debt. Among the 15 companies with the largest cash balances—companies that held almost $1 trillion in cash "offshore"—about 95 percent of the total cash was invested in the United States.
29. Companies can use 80 percent of their foreign tax credits, calculated on a worldwide basis, to offset this minimum tax. The combination of the 10.5 percent minimum tax and the credit for 80 percent of foreign taxes means that the US minimum tax would not apply to foreign profits (in excess of a "normal return") that pay a foreign income tax rate of 13.125 percent or higher. If the foreign income tax rate is 13.125 percent, the US foreign tax credit would be 10.5 percent of applicable profits (0.80 x 13.125), exactly offsetting the US 10.5 percent tax.
30. The tax is levied only on corporations with average annual gross receipts of at least $500 million and those that have made related party deductible payments exceeding 3 percent of the corporation's total deductions for that year.
31. Joint Committee on Taxation (2018b).
32. There are many more ways enterprising taxpayers can use this provision to reduce their taxes. For details and examples, see Kamin et al. (2018).
33. Koba (2014).
34. In addition, the law should be changed so that the definition of self-employment income for all owners/partners who participated in more than 500 hours would pay self-employment tax on all of their business income. Congressional Budget Office (2016, Revenue Option 23).
35. Office of Tax Policy (2017).

36. Barro and Furman (2018).
37. President's Advisory Panel on Federal Tax Reform (2005).
38. Auerbach (2010); Ryan (2016). The tax was also proposed by the Meade Commission in the United Kingdom in 1978. The business tax that was part of the Flat Tax (Hall and Rabushka 2007) and X-tax (Bradford 1986) was a cash-flow tax, but was not destination-based.
39. For example, FDII allows a special deduction to provide an incentive for US multinational companies to keep in the United States the intangible assets they use for exports. Firms may try to game the export condition on the deduction by selling products to foreign distributors who then resell products back into the United States. BEAT imposes a new minimum tax that disallows the deduction for certain payments firms make to their foreign affiliates in order to limit their ability to shift US-source income to low-tax foreign countries. But firms may avoid this limitation by routing what would have been intra-firm transactions through third parties or by bundling other components into cost-of-goods-sold, which is not subject to BEAT. Firms may engage in significant tax planning to avoid the impact of GILTI, in part by offsetting excess foreign tax credits accrued on intangible profits in high-tax countries to offset the minimum tax on income in lower-tax countries. There are also complicated interactions between GILTI and BEAT. See Sullivan (2018a, 2018b).

Appendix Table 12.1 **Business Tax Reform Policies**

Policy	2021 Revenue Change	2050 Revenue Change	2050 Debt Effect
Eliminate pass-through deduction	0.23	0.23	−6.3
Eliminate FDII provisions	−0.03	0.06	−1.5
Tax like-kind exchanges	0.01	0.01	−0.3
Close Gingrich/Edwards loophole	0.06	0.07	−1.9
Increase rate to 25 percent, expense all investment, and eliminate interest deductions	−0.13	0.64	−12.0
Total	**0.14**	**1.00**	**−22.0**

Notes: All numbers are referenced as a percentage of GDP. Total may not equal sum due to rounding. The pass-through estimate grows with baseline income tax revenues. The like-kind exchange and FDII estimates grow with baseline corporate tax revenues. The Gingrich/Edwards estimate grows with Social Security revenues as outlined in Chapter 8.

Sources: Congressional Budget Office (2016, 2018a); Joint Committee on Taxation (2017, 2018a); Nunns et al. (2016).

13

Taxing Consumption

To solve the nation's fiscal problem, we'll need more revenue than we can get by reforming existing taxes. The two most effective alternatives to raise revenue are new consumption taxes, discussed in this chapter, and carbon taxes, as we'll discuss in Chapter 14.

America has never had a national broad-based consumption tax. In 2015, consumption taxes—mainly at the state and local level—raised just 2 percent of GDP in the United States, compared to almost 6 percent in other OECD countries.[1]

Although consumption taxes come in many forms, we will focus on a value-added tax (VAT)—the world's most common consumption tax, which is in place in more than 160 countries, including every economically advanced nation except the United States.[2] Think of a VAT as a retail sales tax for consumers but collected in parts at each stage of production rather than all at once at the retail level.

VATs have much to offer. Most important, they raise money. Asked why he robbed banks, Willie Sutton supposedly said, "Because that's where the money is."[3] In tax reform, VATs are "where the money is." In OECD countries other than the United States, VATs are the third largest revenue source, behind income and payroll taxes. VATs are more conducive to economic growth than income taxes and easier to enforce than retail sales taxes. Critics argue that a federal VAT could hurt low-income households, small businesses, the elderly, and state and local governments. But these concerns are either overblown or easily addressed.

This chapter proposes a broad-based national VAT that provides relief from its burden for low-income households and exempts small businesses. The tax would start in 2021 at 5 percent and phase in one additional percentage point per year until it reaches 10 percent.[4] By 2050, the tax would reduce the debt-to-GDP ratio by about 70 percentage points and thus would be the largest single component of fiscal reform.

A business's "value added" is the difference between its gross sales and its purchase of goods and services from other businesses. That's equal to its payments to workers (including fringe benefits) plus business profits (net sales minus labor compensation).

Suppose a farmer grows wheat and sells it to a baker for $40. The baker turns the wheat into bread and sells it to consumers for $100. The baker's value added is $60—the difference between sales and purchases. Let's further assume (to keep it simple) that the farmer has no input costs so that his value added is $40. The total value added at each stage of production is equal to the retail sale price of the good, in this case $100.

Governments can tax value added in different ways (Table 13.1). In the credit-invoice method that almost all developed countries use, each business pays the government the VAT collected on its sales minus a credit for the VAT it pays on its input purchases. If the VAT were 10 percent in the earlier example, the farmer would charge the baker $44 overall, pay $4 in VAT to the government, and keep $40, which is equal to her value added. The baker would charge consumers $110, pay $6 in VAT (the difference between the $10 he owes on sales and the $4 credit for the VAT he paid the farmer) and keep $60 ($110 minus $44 minus $6), which is equal to his value added. Consumers pay $110 for the bread and the government receives $10 in taxes.

Consumer payments, tax revenues, and after-tax allocations to each producer are the same under a 10 percent VAT as under a well-functioning, 10 percent retail sales tax (Table 13.1). Thus, like the sales tax, the VAT is a consumption tax.

Table 13.1. **Taxes, Sales, and Value Added under Alternative Taxes**

		(1) Value Added	(2) Tax Collected on Sales	(3) Total Sales (Including Tax)	(4) Tax Credits	(5) Net Tax Payments (2)–(4)	(6) Net Receipts
No Taxes	Farmer[1]	40	0	40	0	0	40
	Baker	60	0	100	0	0	60 (= 100 – 40)
Retail	Farmer	40	0	40	0	0	40
Sales Tax	Baker	60	10	110	0	10	60 (= 110 – 40 – 10)
Credit	Farmer	40	4	44	0	4	40 (= 44 – 4)
Invoice	Baker	60	10	110	4	6	60 (= 110 – 44 – 10 + 4)
VAT							

Note:
[1] The occupations in Table 13.1 follow the example in the text.

The VAT is a relatively new tax. It was designed by two people, independently, in the early 20th century. Wilhelm von Siemens, a German businessman, designed the VAT to resolve problems that arose in implementing sales taxes. Thomas S. Adams, an American, thought the VAT was a better version of the corporate income tax.

European governments implemented VATs in the 1960s and 1970s to replace sales and turnover taxes. Developing countries implemented VATs starting in the 1980s. Almost all countries maintain separate corporate income taxes. The spread of the VAT was "the most important event in the evolution of tax structure in the last half of the 20th century," says Sijbren Cnossen, a leading tax expert from Maastricht University in the Netherlands.[5]

A VAT that's levied uniformly over time on all goods and services has several key attributes. It doesn't distort relative prices or consumer choices among goods. Nor does it affect household saving choices or businesses' investment or financing choices. Like income or payroll taxes, however, the VAT distorts household labor supply choices because it creates a wedge between what one earns and how much in the way of taxed goods one can consume.

A VAT operates seamlessly in an increasingly globalized world, in which more and more goods and services cross national borders. The VAT is border adjustable; it would zero-rate exports and tax imports. That's consistent with world trade agreements and other countries' practices and would not disrupt the global supply chains that modern corporations use so effectively.[6]

A VAT has administrative advantages over retail sales taxes. In the VAT, the chain of crediting creates a natural audit trail. In a transaction between two businesses, the seller knows that the buyer is reporting the transaction to claim a credit, so the seller has more incentive to report the transaction and pay tax. In contrast, a retail sales tax contains no similar incentive.[7] The retailer responsible for sending the check to the government for the tax it collects knows the government may not have a record of the transaction. Also, the retailer can't always tell whether the buyer is a consumer who should pay the tax or a business that should not—and has little incentive to find out. If the retailer doesn't impose a sales tax on consumer purchases, that's tax evasion. If the retailer does impose a tax on business purchases, the tax "cascades," building up over successive stages of production, raising and distorting prices depending on the number of stages of production. By providing a credit for taxes paid, the VAT avoids cascading. Last, when evasion occurs at the retail level, all tax revenues on the sale are lost under a retail sales tax, whereas only the tax on value added at the retail level is lost under a VAT.[8]

As a result, most countries, states, and localities have found that, as a practical matter, retail sales tax rates of 10 percent or higher aren't enforceable. All of this helps explain why so many countries have replaced their sales and turnover taxes with VATs.[9]

In practice, VATs differ in their tax rates and tax base. Typically, VATs have a "standard" rate for most goods and services. In 2016, it averaged 17 percent in the OECD's 34 other countries but varied widely—from 27 percent in Hungary to 5 percent in Canada.[10] VAT bases also vary widely, covering an average of 52 percent of potential VAT revenues.[11]

Almost all countries apply preferential rates to some goods and services, making them either "zero-rated" or "exempt." For a "zero-rated good," the government doesn't tax the retail sale but still allows full credits for the VAT that businesses pay on inputs. That ultimately reduces the price of a good. Governments zero-rate some goods—often food or utilities—just as US state sales taxes often exempt similar items. Since these items represent a greater share of the budget for low-income families than high-income families, zero-rating makes the tax more progressive. The effect on progressivity is less than people tend to think, however, because high-income families spend more in absolute terms on these items than low-income families do. A per-person or per-family allowance, described later, more effectively targets the funds toward low-income households.

In contrast, if a good or business is "exempt," the government doesn't tax the sale of the good, but producers can't claim a credit for the VAT they pay on inputs. Because exempt goods or businesses break the VAT's chain of credits on input purchases, they can actually raise prices and revenues. Hence, governments generally only use exemptions when value added is hard to define, such as with financial and insurance services.

Most countries also exempt some small businesses from VAT—partly be-cause they form a powerful political constituency and partly because the ad-ministrative costs of taxing them are high relative to the revenue raised. The definition of "small business" varies but usually relates to gross revenues below a certain level, which ranged from close to zero to almost $120,000 among OECD countries in 2016. As noted, a VAT exemption is a mixed blessing. It reduces compliance costs for businesses, but those businesses can't claim credits for the VAT they pay on their input purchases. In addition, an exemption may reduce the demand for a business's product, since other companies prefer to buy their inputs from firms that are in the VAT system so that they can claim credits for the taxes they pay. As a result, countries allow small businesses to register for the VAT even if they don't have to.[12]

A US VAT should have several key features.[13] First, it should rest on a broad base. That makes the tax more efficient in economic terms and avoids wasteful "line drawing" about whether products are taxable—for example, whether a Halloween costume is "clothing" (which might be exempt) or a "toy" (which might not). Applying the VAT to food is particularly important. Food accounts for a large share of spending. And if the tax applies to a necessity like food, policymakers will be hard-pressed to make a case for giving other goods preferential treatment.

Despite the importance of a broad base, a few exemptions are appropriate. A VAT, for instance, should exempt spending on education, which is an investment. It should exclude spending by charitable organizations and state and local governments, which have enjoyed tax-preferred status in the United States. It should exempt small businesses (with gross revenue under $200,000) but allow them to register if they wish.[14] It should exempt financial services because value added in their transactions is hard to calculate. Since the government cannot make money by taxing itself, it should exempt federal spending.[15] A VAT structured along these lines—and allowing for plausible levels of tax evasion— would apply to 55 percent of potential VAT revenues, which would be a somewhat broader base than in most European countries.[16]

The VAT rate should start at 5 percent in 2021 and rise by 1 percentage point each year until it reaches 10 percent. By phasing in a VAT, policymakers would give individuals and businesses some time to adjust to it. But they should not impose the VAT during a recession, since it would reduce consumer spending that could help return a weak economy to full capacity.

The VAT should provide relief to low- and moderate-income households, but it should not subsidize particular goods or services. Instead, it should give a refundable tax credit to low-income working families equal to the VAT rate times their earnings up to the poverty line, and it should boost benefits to recipients of government transfer payments to offset any impact of the VAT on their inflation-adjusted benefits.[17]

When fully phased in, a VAT with these features would reduce deficits by 2.6 percent of GDP per year, not counting its effect on net interest payments.[18] How that 2.6 percent is divided between taxes and spending depends on what happens to the consumer price level.

Assuming—for the moment—that it did not raise the price level, the VAT would raise gross revenue by 3.7 percent of GDP (Table 13.2). It would reduce other tax revenues, though. For example, the more the VAT collected, the lower corporate profits would be. Taking this into account and counting the assistance for lower-income households, the VAT would generate about 1.0 percent of GDP in net annual revenue. It would also reduce government spending on transfers, state and local grants, and other items by 1.5 percent of GDP. If the VAT caused prices to rise, the effects on the deficit would be the same, but

Table 13.2. **Primary Deficit Effects of a 10 Percent VAT**

	Percent of GDP
Gross VAT Revenue	3.66
Less Offsets for Other Taxes	−1.34
Less Rebate	−1.29
Net VAT Revenue	1.03
Reductions in Federal Spending	−1.55
Net Effect on Primary Deficit	**−2.57**

Source: Toder, Nunns, and Rosenberg (2012); author's calculations.

revenues would increase by more and spending would fall by less than if consumer prices stayed constant.

One common criticism is that VATs are regressive. Combined with low-income assistance, however, the proposed VAT would be progressive. When the tax is fully phased in, households in the bottom fifth of income would see a drop in after-tax income of just 0.8 percent—about $100 per year in 2018 dollars. The middle fifth would see a drop of 3.7 percent, or about $2,200 per year. The top fifth would see a drop of 4.7 percent, or about $12,600 per year.[19] Because it would tax any eventual consumption out of households' existing wealth, the VAT would impose a burden on those holdings, notably even among extremely wealthy households who are often able to avoid income and estate taxes through careful avoidance techniques.

Low- or moderate-income elderly households would not be hurt. In principle, the transition to a consumption tax can be tough on the elderly. Imagine that you've spent your working life (when your income exceeds your consumption) paying an income tax, and then, during your retirement (when your consumption will probably exceed your income), the government adds a consumption tax. You might justifiably feel that you're paying two taxes on your lifetime earnings. In practice, though, to the extent that a VAT raised prices, low-income elderly households would not be affected. Social Security, Medicare, and Medicaid—the main sources of income for low- and moderate-income elderly households—are effectively indexed for inflation. Social Security provides cost-of-living adjustments. The health programs provide specific covered services. The per-person allowances described in this chapter would provide further assistance. Thus, we can inoculate the low-income elderly from the burden of a consumption tax while increasing the burden on the high-income elderly, who can more easily afford it.

Conservatives and libertarians fear that a VAT will fuel the growth of government. Anti-tax activist Grover Norquist says, "VAT is a French word for 'big government.'" Referring to policymakers, the Cato Institute's Daniel Mitchell warns that a VAT would be like "giving keys to a liquor store to a bunch of alcoholics."[20] Critics offer three reasons a VAT would enlarge government. These arguments, however, do not withstand closer scrutiny.

First, critics complain that because a VAT is a "hidden tax," buried in the price of a good, policymakers can raise it without people noticing the impact. There is, in fact, some evidence that hidden taxes are easier for policymakers to raise, and VATs have been "hidden" in many countries.[21] But they need not be hidden. Policymakers can require that VAT payments be reported on receipts, as in Canada, France, and other countries. In the United States, state sales taxes are reported that way.

Second, critics claim that any increase in government revenues will fuel more spending. If we want policymakers to control government spending, they say, we should cut revenues and, in this way, "starve the beast" of government. That view may seem logical—the more money the government has, the easier it is to spend it—and some evidence supports it. But as discussed in Chapter 6, US history suggests that the opposite is more often the case. Policymakers tend to cut taxes and increase spending simultaneously, and also to raise taxes and cut spending simultaneously.[22] Thus, when policymakers are ready to address the fiscal challenge and create a VAT, they'll likely couple it with spending cuts.

Third, some conservative critics fear that the VAT is *too efficient*—it raises revenue with such minimal economic distortion and administrative costs that it prompts the public to demand higher spending.[23] The record, however, largely belies concerns that VATs are fueling bigger government. For starters, VAT revenues and rates have not risen inexorably in countries with them. From 1980 to 1988, after VATs were phased in, the tax raised an average of 5.6 percent of GDP in revenues in industrialized countries that had a VAT. Between 2010 and 2015, they raised the same share of GDP.[24]

Furthermore, although overall revenues have risen significantly in European countries with VATs, VATs don't seem to be the reason. A study of 16 Western European countries from 1965 to 2015 found that VAT revenue rose by 5.6 percent of GDP, but excise and other sales taxes offset almost all of that change, falling by 5.2 percent. Indeed, in many instances, policymakers in those countries enacted a VAT with the explicit goal of replacing less efficient sales and other taxes. Total revenue in those countries rose substantially—by about

10 percent of GDP—so the VAT increase in excess of the sales tax reductions was only a tiny fraction of the total tax increase.[25]

In addition, some evidence suggests the causation actually runs the other way. In other words, it is the public's demand for higher spending that fuels demands for a VAT in order to fund the higher spending in an efficient manner.[26]

Thus, predictions that a VAT will drive out-of-control government spending do not reflect the record. And while the VAT may have prompted somewhat higher spending in some countries, the dynamic would likely be very different in the United States. Given the need for both spending cuts and revenue increases to address the fiscal challenge, any new revenue stream would likely be accompanied by spending cuts, not increases.

A national VAT would have significant implications for the sales taxes on which most states and many localities rely. Sales taxes are the second largest state and local revenue source. Some policymakers and experts view consumption taxes as the states' prerogative and express concern that a national VAT would impinge on states' ability to administer their own sales taxes. Their concerns are understandable, but in fact, a national VAT could significantly help states rather than hurt them.

Currently, state sales taxes are poorly designed. They exempt many goods and most services, which makes them unfair and inefficient. They collect a significant amount of revenue from taxing business purchases, which should be exempt; this causes cascading (described earlier).[27] With a national VAT, states could convert their sales taxes to VATs with the same base as the federal tax. That would let states raise revenue with minimal economic distortion and ease their revenue collection from transactions such as interstate mail order and internet sales, which they now find hard to tax for political and compliance reasons.[28] State administrative costs would fall.

In fact, if the United States followed the example of Canada, discussed later, the federal government could collect revenue on behalf of states, remit the funds to the states, and relieve states of most administrative costs altogether. At the very least, states could "piggyback" on federal VAT administration—easing taxpayer compliance costs and government administrative costs—just as they do now with the income tax.[29] If states and localities adopted the federal VAT structure, they could replace existing sales tax revenues with an average VAT rate of 5 percent.[30] The combined federal, state, and local average VAT rate, which would be 15 percent, would still be lower than the OECD average.

We can further assuage concerns about regressivity, government's growth, transparency, and state impacts by focusing attention on Canada's VAT.[31] In

1991, Canada implemented a 7 percent national VAT to replace a tax on sales by manufacturers. It was introduced by the Conservative Party, which sought to address concerns about competitiveness and the government's fiscal situation. To address distributional concerns, Canada applied a zero rate to certain necessities—for example, groceries, medicines, and rent—and added a refundable credit to the income tax for lower-income people. Transfer payments were already indexed for inflation and were highly progressive, which further offset the VAT's regressivity. As noted, Canada's VAT is completely transparent: it's listed separately on receipts and invoices, just like US sales taxes.

At least in Canada, fears about a VAT have proved unfounded. It didn't decimate provincial consumption taxes; some provinces have converted their sales taxes to the VAT base, while others haven't. The tax hasn't risen inexorably; policymakers cut the standard VAT rate to 6 percent in 2006 and then 5 percent in 2008. It hasn't fueled government spending; Canada's general government tax revenue and spending have generally fallen as a share of its economy since 1991.[32]

But even if the worst fears about a VAT haven't borne fruit in other countries, the political obstacles to enacting one in the United States remain considerable. Policymakers mulled broad-based consumption taxes in the 1930s to plug the budget, in the 1940s to fund World War II, in the 1970s to share revenues with states and localities, and in the 1980s and 1990s as part of overall tax reform—all to no avail. That makes the VAT, as one expert noted, "the most studied tax system that has never been seriously considered by Congress."[33]

Politicians have notoriously long memories, and in that spirit, former Democratic House Ways and Means Committee chairman Al Ullman looms large. He proposed a VAT in 1979 and lost his reelection bid a year later. To be sure, many factors contributed to his loss—he was often away from his district, where his only residence was a hotel room, and 1980 was a big year for Republican candidates. His experience, though, has served as a warning to politicians who may be considering a VAT. So, too, does the experience of Canada's Conservative Party, which was decimated in the election after it enacted a VAT.[34]

Nevertheless, all is not bleak. Leading policymakers have proposed VATs numerous times in recent years. Conservatives may decry the VAT as an instrument of European socialism, but they have proposed VATs themselves, just under alternative pretenses. They treat the VAT like the wizards in J. K. Rowling's *Harry Potter* books treat Voldemort—careful never to say the name. The "destination-based cash flow" tax that House Speaker Paul Ryan and Ways and Means Committee chair Kevin Brady proposed in the 2016 Republican "Blueprint" is just a VAT with a wage deduction. VATs are embedded in Ryan's "business consumption tax," libertarian Kentucky senator Rand Paul's "Fair and Flat Tax," 2012 Republican presidential candidate Herman Cain's "9-9-9" proposal, and

Republican senator Ted Cruz's "Business Flat Tax." VATs have also been proposed (and renamed) in Senate Finance Committee Democrat Ben Cardin's "progressive consumption tax" and the Bipartisan Policy Center's 2010 Rivlin-Domenici commission report, which called it a "deficit reduction sales tax."[35] Although these leading policymakers proposed to use the resulting revenues differently, they all viewed the VAT favorably for three reasons: it raises lots of money; it creates few negative economic incentives; and it's administratively sound.

So why don't we have a VAT yet? Back in 1988, Harvard economist Larry Summers, who would later serve as Treasury secretary and National Economic Council chairman, summarized the VAT's political prospects this way: "Liberals think it's regressive and conservatives think it's a money machine," he said, predicting that policymakers will enact a VAT when liberals realize it's a money machine and conservatives realize it's regressive.[36]

You won't find a better description of the political problem. His statement, however, also holds the key to reaching a political accord. Although liberals fear it would be regressive, a VAT can be part of a progressive strategy. European countries impose regressive VATs, but they also spend more generously than the United States on low-income families and children and on social policy initiatives like universal healthcare and paid family leave. And though conservatives fear it's a money machine, the VAT is efficient and can be part of a compromise with liberals that limits spending and highlights the need to finance any new spending increases.

All told, the VAT has much to offer, if both sides can move past their ideological blinders.

Notes

1. All references to VAT data from OECD countries are from OECD (2016, 2017) and are weighted by GDP, unless otherwise noted.
2. The leading academic proponent of a VAT is Graetz (1997, 2008, and 2013). For excellent summaries of issues related to the VAT, see Tax Analysts (2011). Retail sales taxes and value-added taxes are consumption taxes that are placed on transactions. The "flat tax" (Hall and Rabushka 1985) is a value-added tax that is separated into two parts, with wages taxed at the individual level after an exemption amount is provided, and non-wage value added is taxed at the business level. The X-tax (Bradford 1986; Viard and Carroll 2012) is the same as the flat tax except it features graduated tax rates on wage income and sets the business tax rate equal to the top rate on wages. Alternatively, consumption can be taxed by subtracting saving from income, as proposed in the "USA" (Unlimited Saving Allowance) tax by Domenici, Kerrey, and Nunn (1995) and Seidman (1997). The destination-based cash flow tax proposed by Auerbach (2010) is also a variant on a VAT that includes a wage deduction.
3. Federal Bureau of Investigation (2015).

4. The proposed tax rates are equivalent to a mark-up at the cash register, in the same way that retail sales taxes are typically quoted. In technical terms, the proposed VAT rate is a tax-exclusive rate (Gale 2005).

5. Cnossen (2011).

6. While proponents sometimes argue that it would help domestic companies, a VAT is actually neutral in terms of international trade, treating these items as a retail sales tax would.

7. See Cnossen (2011) and Pomeranz (2015) for discussion of these incentives under a VAT. In the income tax, businesses withhold income and payroll taxes on behalf of workers and send the money to the government. As a result, evasion rates on wage income are quite low. The exception is tips, which serves to prove the point (Gale and Holtzblatt 2002).

8. There are other problems with a national retail sales tax (Gale 2005; President's Advisory Panel on Tax Reform 2005). Advocates have argued that a 23 percent national sales tax rate would be sufficient to replace virtually all federal taxes, but the calculation is flawed, and the actual rate would need to be much higher to maintain real government spending and revenues.

9. Tanzi (1995). VATs do have some administrative problems of their own. While tax evasion is typically lower under a VAT than under an income tax, it is not always low; one study estimated a 40 percent evasion rate in the Italian VAT (Tanzi 1995). Informal sectors of the economy, such as tip income or babysitting, will escape a VAT, as well as income or sales taxes. Taxing certain sectors, like financial services, has proven difficult under a VAT because it's hard to identify the value added. New types of fraud, involving businesses that collect the VAT on their sales and then disappear with the proceeds, have emerged in recent years in Europe.

10. This figure is weighted by GDP. The unweighted average is 19 percent.

11. The OECD (2016) uses the VAT revenue ratio (VRR) to estimate countries' effectiveness in collecting all possible VAT revenue. The VRR is the ratio of VAT revenue to the revenue that would be realized if the VAT were applied at the standard rate to the entire potential tax base with perfect compliance. A VRR close to 1 indicates a broad base with few exemptions and credits, as well as effective collection of the tax.

12. Gale, Gelfond, and Krupkin (2016).

13. The VAT proposed here is based on the VAT with a broad base and rebate, analyzed by Toder, Nunns, and Rosenberg (2012).

14. A recent study by several Treasury Department economists finds that if the United States were to institute a 10 percent VAT, the optimal exemption level based on sales would be about $200,000, and it would thus exempt about 43 million businesses. That exemption would be higher than in most other countries, but the 10 percent rate would be lower than in most other countries. At a 20 percent rate, which is close to the OECD average, the optimal exemption would be $90,000, which is within the range of exemptions in other countries (Brashares et al. 2014).

15. There is a case for taxing all the government items mentioned earlier under a VAT—namely, it would put the prices they pay on a more equal footing with those paid in the private sector. But taxing federal spending would not change the required rate or the net revenue—it would just add equally to federal revenue levels and federal spending requirements (Gale 2005).

16. Toder, Nunns, and Rosenberg (2012). Consistent with this estimate, Brashares et al. (2014) estimate that revenue would drop by 10 percent due to a small business threshold of $200,000 with optional registration. Toder, Nunns, and Rosenberg (2012) would substitute taxation of new housing purchases and home improvements for taxing of implicit and explicit rental payments.

17. Toder, Nunns, and Rosenberg (2012) explain that the rebate has two components: a refundable earnings credit on income taxes and an adjustment to cash transfer payments. The credit would phase in with income for a tax unit, up to a ceiling equal to the weighted average federal poverty threshold across tax units. In this case, income includes amounts

taxpayers report on income tax returns of wages, pensions, and other withdrawals from retirement accounts, plus 80 percent of self-employment income. The credit rate applied to this eligible income would be the effective rate of VAT as a percentage of income. The second component would consist of an adjustment made each year in the government's computation of benefits for each form of cash transfer payment to maintain the benefit at the level that would have been computed using the pre-VAT level of wages. Beneficiaries of cash transfer payments would not need to claim this portion of the rebate on their tax return; it would automatically be included in their benefits.

18. Toder, Nunns, and Rosenberg (2012) show that a 7.7 percent tax-exclusive VAT combined with the assistance for low-income earners would reduce the deficit by 2.0 percent of GDP. This is equivalent to a tax-inclusive rate of 7.15 percent. The 10 percent tax-exclusive rate proposed in this chapter is the equivalent of a 9.09 tax-inclusive rate. The figure in the text is derived by multiplying 2.0 percent of GDP by the ratio of 9.09/7.15. They also show that the 7.7 percent VAT would reduce other revenues by about 1.1 percent of GDP, that adding the rebate would cost about 1.0 percent of GDP, and that federal spending would reduce by 1.2 percent of GDP. Adjusting those figures to account for a 10 percent VAT generates the figures in the text (with rounding).

19. Percentage reductions in after-tax income are taken from Toder, Nunns, and Rosenberg (2012). Dollar amounts are based on the Tax Policy Center's post–Tax Cuts and Jobs Act baseline for 2018 (TPC Staff 2017). If households are classified by their consumption levels rather than their income levels, the VAT is proportional—the tax burden as a share of consumption remains unchanged as consumption rises.

20. Cassidy (2005); Mitchell (2010).

21. Finkelstein (2009).

22. Bartlett (2007); Becker and Mulligan (2003); Gale and Orszag (2004); Romer and Romer (2010).

23. Mitchell (2011).

24. OECD (2017). For a similar analysis, see Keen (2013).

25. These figures update calculations in Sullivan (2012), using data from OECD (2017). All 16 countries are included in the analysis, regardless of whether they had a VAT in 1965.

26. Lee, Kim, and Borcherding (2013). Keen and Lockwood (2006) find that about one-fifth of VAT revenues in OECD countries contributed to increases in overall spending. They show, however, that the estimate is fragile.

27. Gale (2005). See also McLure (2002), who refers to the "nutty" world of state sales taxes.

28. In light of the Supreme Court case *South Dakota v. Wayfair*, states have the authority to collect sales taxes on transactions in which the seller does not have a physical presence in that state (also known as "nexus"). If there were a national VAT, states that aligned their own VAT base with the national VAT base would be able to more easily collect tax on sales within their states by businesses that had no nexus.

29. Of course, a federal VAT would also have direct effects on states if it taxes purchases by state government. The Tax Policy Center's Jim Nunns and Eric Toder show, however, that if the federal VAT exempts state and local government spending, as proposed, the effects on state budgets would be either neutral or positive (Nunns and Toder 2015).

30. The 5 percent rate is calculated by dividing the 2 percent of GDP in state and local sales tax revenue from OECD (2017) by the effective tax base of 40 percent of GDP from Toder, Nunns, and Rosenberg (2012). Note that a state VAT that substituted for existing sales taxes would not have offsetting revenue or price level effects.

31. Sullivan (2011).

32. OECD (2017).

33. Schenk (2011).

34. In 2010, the US Senate went out of its way to disparage the VAT, voting 85-13 to support the statement: "The Value Added Tax is a massive tax increase that will cripple families on fixed income and only further push back America's economic recovery." The

Senate statement was a mere "Sense of the Senate" resolution—an expression of sentiment, not a piece of legislation—and lawmakers often forget or discard such resolutions when they get down to writing new law (Avi-Yonah 2011).

35. Ryan (2008); Paul (2015); Urban-Brookings Tax Policy Center (2011); Cardin (2015); Debt Reduction Task Force (2010); Cruz Campaign (2015).

36. Rosen (1988).

14

Improving the Environmental Outlook

Imagine a policy that reduces the debt, makes the economy fairer and more efficient, cuts pollution, lowers the chances of an environmental catastrophe, encourages innovation in clean energy technology, and leads to fewer government regulations. Throw in better health, less traffic, and less dependence on foreign oil. A fantasy? No, it's a carbon tax—that is, a tax on emissions of carbon dioxide and, ideally, other "greenhouse gases" like methane and nitrous oxide, with the tax imposed in proportion to their effects on global warming.[1]

The main source of greenhouse gas emissions is human activity—in particular, the combustion of fossil fuels, including coal, oil, and natural gas. When released into the atmosphere, the gases trap heat near the earth's surface, generating rising global temperatures that create adverse environmental effects, such as coastal flooding, extreme weather, and lower crop yields. Under current projections, these effects will intensify over time, with potentially dire economic and environmental effects for the United States and much of the world.

This problem exists for a simple but profound reason: businesses and people don't need to consider how their decisions on what to make and what to buy, respectively, will affect greenhouse gas emissions or climate change because they don't bear the full cost of their decisions. A properly designed tax would make producers and consumers face those costs, prompting them to change their behavior in ways that reduce emissions. For these reasons, the carbon tax is routinely considered an auspicious way to reduce emissions.[2]

Policymakers should enact a tax on all carbon dioxide (CO_2) emissions in the energy sector (which accounts for 97 percent of all CO_2 emissions). It would begin in 2021 at $30 per ton of emissions and rise by 5 percent per year above inflation through 2050. It would reduce US CO_2 emissions by 56 percent relative to what would occur otherwise by 2040, and reduce them by greater amounts over time. It would raise gasoline prices by around 8 percent in 2021, which should prove manageable for most households, especially if the carbon tax is coupled with additional income support for low-income households.[3]

The tax would help address the fiscal challenge, raising $110 billion in 2021, rising to $195 billion in 2030. By 2050, it would reduce the debt-to-GDP ratio by more than 18 percentage points.[4]

The United States imposes very low taxes on fossil fuels relative to our European counterparts. Several countries—and even some US localities—have established carbon taxes. More nations will likely do so to comply with recent global climate and emissions agreements. The United States should do so as well.

The case for reducing emissions stems from four facts. First, the planet is warming. The average global temperature has risen by 0.85 degrees Celsius since 1880 and is now rising faster than before. US temperatures are following a similar pattern. "Warming of the climate system is unequivocal," the Intergovernmental Panel on Climate Change (IPCC) concluded recently.[5]

Second, the main cause of global warming is human activity. Human activity—including the burning of fossil fuel and deforestation of vast tracts of land—"is *extremely likely* to have been the dominant cause of the observed warming since the mid-20th century" (emphasis in original), the IPCC concludes. The scientific consensus that human activity is driving global warming is as strong as the consensus that cigarette smoking can lead to lung cancer.[6] Even the major oil companies have accepted the idea.[7]

Third, rising global temperatures hurt the economy, the environment, and even our national security. By making extreme weather events more frequent and more severe, climate change disrupts economic activity and our infrastructure of roads and bridges. The public health hazards are well documented. Climate change–induced stressors such as weeds, precipitation extremes, and diseases could reduce the availability of farmable land, hurting the nation's food supply.[8] Increased air pollution raises asthma rates and can contribute to a greater risk of death from heart disease. Warmer weather allows for the spread of diseases such as the Zika virus (and other mosquito-borne illnesses) and Lyme disease.[9] Left unattended, global warming also could harm US interests around the world. Under President Obama, the Defense Department released a road map to mitigate the potential negative effects of climate change.[10] Under President Trump, Defense Secretary James Mattis noted, "Climate change can be a driver of instability, and the Department of Defense must pay attention to potential adverse impacts generated by this phenomenon."[11]

Fourth, these problems will grow unless we address them. US temperatures are projected to rise 3 to 5 degrees Celsius (roughly 5 to 9 degrees Farenheit) over the 21st century if the past rate of increase in global emissions continues. Scientists generally agree that a 2-degree Celsius rise relative to pre-industrial levels is the highest increase that we could endure while avoiding dangerous environmental changes; some scientists think the threshold increase is actually 1.5

degrees Celsius.[12] Since the average global temperature has already risen by 0.85 degrees since 1880 and is rising at an increasing rate, we have little room to spare.

The impact of greenhouse gases on global temperature depends on total emissions in the atmosphere. Most greenhouse gases remain in the atmosphere for long periods. Consequently, even if we substantially reduce annual emissions, the gases already in the atmosphere will change only slowly. Limiting the temperature increase to only 2 degrees since the Industrial Revolution would require a 70 percent reduction in human-related emissions relative to current levels by 2050 and further reductions after that.[13] As with fiscal policy more generally, the longer we take to address climate change, the more abrupt and disruptive the changes will have to be.[14]

The best way to reduce emissions is to create a carbon tax. An alternative approach—more regulations that prohibit businesses from producing all the greenhouse gases that they otherwise would—would impose costs on producers and raise prices for consumers but not generate any new tax revenues. Although a carbon tax would impose costs on businesses, it also raises revenue that can pay for policy changes. In addition, and perhaps most importantly, it would give businesses and consumers the flexibility to respond in the least costly way.

A carbon tax is also better than what's known as a cap-and-trade system. In such a system, the government auctions off a set number of permits to let businesses emit carbon, which firms buy and then trade among themselves. Under that system, carbon prices fluctuate with market demand, creating uncertainty that reduces investment and innovation. Another problem is that when cap-and-trade systems are introduced, influential businesses often pressure governments to give them enough permits to accommodate their current emissions.[15] That reduces revenue, rewards past polluting behavior, and penalizes new firms that don't have a history of generating emissions.

To help address global warming and the fiscal challenge, the United States should adopt the carbon tax designed in 2018 by experts Warwick McKibbin, Adele Morris, Peter Wilcoxen, and Weifeng Liu.[16] It would apply to (1) fossil fuels that are extracted domestically; (2) fossil fuels that are imported; and (3) non-fossil processes, like cement manufacturing, that produce CO_2 emissions. It would not tax exports of fossil fuels or carbon that's not emitted into the atmosphere. It would protect low-income households from the burden of the tax. It would begin in 2021 at $30 per ton of carbon dioxide emissions and rise by 5 percent per year above inflation.

Their proposal makes sense for numerous reasons. For starters, a carbon tax should cover as many greenhouse gas emissions as possible. That would level the playing field, ensuring that businesses and people bear the social costs when they make production and consumption choices. The more inclusive the tax, the larger the reductions in emissions and the greater the revenue. This tax's broad base would cover almost 80 percent of domestic greenhouse gas emissions— more than almost any other carbon tax in the world.[17]

The tax would vary with the carbon content of fossil fuels. Because a fuel's carbon content is directly related to the CO_2 emissions it creates when it's burned, taxing carbon content is equivalent to taxing CO_2 emissions. In addition, the tax would be imposed at "upstream" production points: petroleum at the refinery, coal at the mine, and natural gas at the wellhead. That would simplify tax administration and reduce compliance costs by limiting the number of firms that would pay the tax and tying tax collection to information that the government already collects from these firms.

The tax would not affect carbon that's not released into the atmosphere and, thus, doesn't increase global warming. For example, businesses would receive rebates for the CO_2 that they captured from combustion at power plants and stored in the ground.[18] To ensure that it doesn't hurt US producers in foreign markets, the tax would apply to imports of unprocessed fossil fuels and would exempt exports.[19]

To understand the tax rate, we need to focus on the "social cost of carbon" (SCC), a concept that measures the economic damage that a one-ton increase in carbon emissions generates. The Environmental Protection Agency defines the SCC as a "comprehensive estimate of climate change damage and includes changes in net agricultural productivity, human health, property damages from increased flood risk, and changes in energy system costs."

Estimating the SCC is complex and uncertain.[20] For one thing, it depends on complicated technical aspects of the environment and the economy—for example, how much sea levels will rise and how that will affect the economy. For another, because climate change addresses events that take place far into the future, even small differences in how much people value the future compared to the present can dramatically alter the estimated SCC. For still another, the SCC depends on how risk-averse society is—how much it values avoiding events that are highly improbable but extremely damaging (such as flooding in a major city). Finally, SCC estimates differ depending on whether global or national effects are considered. Global measures of the SCC are often 10 times as large as the US costs.[21]

In 2015, a federal interagency working group examined multiple scenarios and estimated that the global SCC would be about $52 per ton to society in 2019.[22] The underlying estimates varied widely, indicating significant uncertainty. Even so, almost all of the estimates were significantly above zero, which means that people and businesses do not bear the full societal costs of their actions with regard to carbon emissions.

In sharp contrast, in 2017, the Trump administration estimated that the SCC is between $1 and $6 per ton in 2020 (in 2011 dollars). These estimates are vastly different from earlier published figures because the current administration discounted future outcomes at a much higher rate than other studies, and it only included the direct domestic benefits from carbon mitigation rather than the global benefits. Because of these flaws, I continue to use the Obama administration's 2015 estimates.

In a simple world, the tax rate on carbon would equal the SCC. But while the SCC covers environmental costs of carbon emissions, it omits several factors that are relevant for setting the tax rate. These include interactions with other taxes, non-climate environmental effects (for example, reduction in emissions of other noxious gases and particulate matter), non-environmental benefits (e.g., reduced traffic congestion), innovation, and other countries' emissions, as well as whether to set the tax based on global or national measures.

Almost all countries with carbon taxes have set the rate below the federal government's estimated SCC. In 2017, rates ranged from $1 to $140 per ton in other countries.[23] Carbon taxes that have very high rates typically cover a very small share of emissions.[24] A variety of leading research teams have proposed plans for the United States to tax almost all CO_2 emissions and set an initial carbon tax rate between $11 and $50 per ton if it took effect in 2019, rising between 1 and 5 percentage points a year above inflation.[25]

The proposed plan—a $30-per-ton tax in 2021, rising 5 percent a year above inflation through 2050—is just more than half as big as the SCC, but toward the higher side of the range of proposals for the United States. Setting the tax rate lower than the estimated SCC seems appropriate because US policy may not want to include all global costs. Setting the tax at the higher end of the range of previous proposals also seems appropriate since we are aiming to address the long-term debt problem as well as the environmental issues raised by greenhouse gas emissions. The tax rate would rise over time because the cost of emissions rises as more greenhouse gases accumulate in the atmosphere. A rising rate will also encourage producers to innovate toward less carbon-intensive technologies, and it would give businesses and people time to adjust.

Finally, policymakers should include assistance for those most vulnerable to the carbon tax's effects. The tax will manifest itself through higher prices of goods that use carbon in production. As a result, the tax will be regressive, meaning that those at the bottom will pay a larger share of their incomes to cover the burden.[26]

Using 15 percent of carbon tax revenues to help low-income households would fully offset the costs of the tax on households below 150 percent of the poverty level.[27] That relief could come in the form of payroll tax rebates, income tax credits, or an electronic debit card that households could use to make purchases. Importantly, the relief should boost income, not subsidize the price of energy, because the latter would partially undo the environmental effects of the tax.

A carbon tax that applies to a broad base of emissions at a significant rate allows changes in other federal policies. For example, since the tax would raise the price of energy from fossil fuels compared to non-carbon alternatives (solar, wind, water, nuclear), policymakers would no longer need to subsidize consumer or business purchases of clean energy technologies such as solar panels or hybrid vehicles. But they should still subsidize basic research and development on clean energy and energy-efficient technologies. Even with the incentives for clean energy that the carbon tax would create, the private sector will likely not do enough of this research because some of the gains will go to society rather than to the researcher involved.

A carbon tax would also allow reductions in other federal regulations that aim to limit greenhouse gas emissions—for example, Clean Air Act regulations and fuel economy standards. But major rule changes should wait until the carbon tax is running effectively.

What would a carbon tax do? Most obviously, it would cut greenhouse gas emissions.[28] Fossil fuels will rise in price relative to other goods—coal by the greatest percentage, followed by oil, and then natural gas. That will encourage businesses to switch to less emissions-intensive production processes and invest in clean energy technologies. Consumers would cut back on carbon-intensive products. They may switch from conventional gas-powered automobiles to hybrid or alternative-fueled vehicles. Carbon taxes in British Columbia, Australia, and the European Union significantly reduced emissions.[29]

In the United States, emissions grew continually until 2005 and have generally been trending down since then due to the Great Recession, rising energy efficiency, and lower natural gas prices that prompted consumers to switch from coal to natural gas (Figure 14.1). The proposed carbon tax would reduce CO_2 emissions by about 35 percent relative to what they would have been in 2025 and by about 56 percent by 2040.[30] The resulting reduction in pollution will improve human health, and the resulting higher gasoline prices will encourage behaviors that reduce traffic congestion and driving accidents.[31] The tax would reduce our dependence on foreign oil and create market incentives for using renewable energy sources.

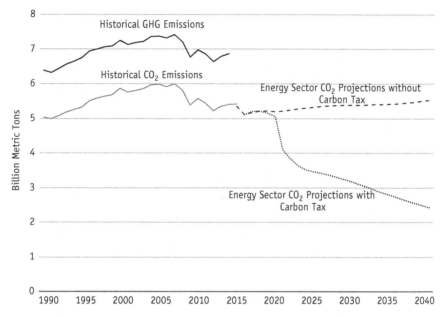

Figure 14.1. United States greenhouse gas and carbon dioxide emissions, 1990–2040. Environmental Protection Agency (2016a); McKibbin et al. (2018).

The faster emissions shrink, the less money the tax will raise. But annual revenues will not fall until "many decades" from now.[32] And that would be a good problem to have because it would reflect less climate change.[33]

A carbon tax will affect the economy broadly because fossil fuels are used widely. Electricity, transportation, and industrial production are the three largest sources of greenhouse gas emissions (30 percent, 26 percent, and 21 percent, respectively). The coal mining industry, already in decline, would lose the greatest share of its jobs, followed by oil and gas extraction and natural gas utilities, construction, transportation, and chemical production.[34]

Any type of carbon pricing policy would likely reinforce the coal industry's declining employment over time; the number of workers fell by two-thirds between 1987 and 2017. Those job losses have damaged many communities, but the jobs are not coming back, as options including natural gas have made coal less attractive. Policymakers should provide transitional financial assistance for affected workers, communities, and industries to help them and to garner political support in Congress to enact a carbon tax. Fortunately, that assistance would require only a tiny share of the revenue from the tax.[35] In 2016, there were only 51,000 workers employed in the US coal mining industry.[36] Even giving each of them a one-time (generous) severance payment of $250,000 would only cost

$13 billion, less than 1 percent of the 10-year revenue gain from implementing a carbon tax.

Across the economy, a new tax will reduce workers' after-tax earnings, which may reduce the number of hours they're willing to work. The tax will raise the price of fossil fuel and, in turn, raise the cost of new physical capital (buildings, machines, computers, and so on), which will reduce investment. How all of this will affect economic growth will depend on how policymakers use the new revenue that a carbon tax will generate.[37]

Even if it reduces economic growth slightly, the tax will prove worthwhile because it will improve the well-being of Americans. By reducing emissions, a carbon tax can improve health, reduce traffic congestion and road accidents, and reduce the destructive effects of global warming. Thus, focusing just on the growth effects of a carbon tax provides an overly narrow perspective on its beneficial effects to society.[38]

The politics of enacting a carbon tax are difficult. There are enormous differences across the political parties. In a 2016 poll by the Pew Research Center, 79 percent of liberal Democrats said that global warming is "mostly due" to human activity but only 15 percent of conservative Republicans share that view. Even more striking, while 70 percent of liberal Democrats trusted climate scientists to provide accurate information on climate change, only 15 percent of conservative Republicans did.[39] The 2016 Democratic Party platform said that "carbon dioxide, methane, and other greenhouse gases should be priced to reflect their negative externalities, and to accelerate the transition to a clean energy economy."[40] In sharp contrast, President Trump has said that "global warming was created by and for the Chinese in order to make U.S. manufacturing non-competitive."[41] The 2016 Republican platform praised coal as "an abundant, clean, affordable, reliable domestic energy source" and rejected "any" carbon tax.[42] In 2015, 91 percent of Senate Republicans voted to reject the idea that human activity significantly contribute to climate change (though they agreed that climate change is real).[43] In 2016, House Republicans voted unanimously against a carbon tax.[44]

But, dig deeper, and the politics get muddled. Not all liberals support the tax. Liberal voters in Washington State opposed a carbon tax in a November 2016 vote (due to controversy about how the revenue would be used). And despite Republican opposition, there is a good conservative case for a carbon tax.[45] The tax would eliminate a market inefficiency, reduce inefficient regulations, and end wasteful federal subsidies. It would let businesses plan ahead more easily than with a cap-and-trade system, under which future carbon prices would be uncertain. It would reduce the chance of catastrophic climate outcomes. And it would reduce the pressure for more regulation, a policy that conservatives would oppose even more strongly than a carbon tax.

For all of these reasons, Republican senator John McCain promised to fight climate change during his 2008 presidential campaign, after sponsoring a bill to reduce carbon emissions by 65 percent by 2050 relative to 1990 levels.[46] More recently, the conservative-leaning Climate Leadership Council published its own proposal for a carbon dividends program in 2017.[47] The tax would begin in 2019 at $40 per ton and increase at an annual rate of 2 percent above inflation. All proceeds would go to households through a quarterly dividend payment that the Social Security Administration would administer. The tax would come with a significant rollback of environmental regulations, a full repeal of the Clean Power Plan, and border tax adjustments.

Public opinion is conflicted as well. The public agrees that global warming is human-induced and problematic, but it does not support a carbon tax strongly.[48] Public support for a carbon tax grows if the revenues would be returned to the public via rebates or used for renewable energy research rather than to reduce the deficit.[49] As of 2016, over 160 Senate and House Republicans and eight governors have signed a "No Climate Tax Pledge," opposing any climate change legislation that raises revenues but leaving the door open for revenue-neutral changes, such as those discussed above.[50] Even Exxon recently announced that it prefers a revenue-neutral carbon tax to regulation.[51] Shell, while not yet fully endorsing a carbon tax, acknowledges climate change is a real problem and notes that one step to limit its negative impacts would be to require a carbon pricing scheme.[52]

Since a carbon tax can contribute greatly to an overall fiscal solution, a revenue-neutral change represents a missed opportunity on the fiscal front.

Climate change is a global issue.[53] The United States and Europe have generated about half of all greenhouse gas emissions since the Industrial Revolution, but the balance has shifted over time. In 2016, China produced 29 percent of all new emissions, followed by the United States at 14 percent, all of Europe at 10 percent, and India at 7 percent.[54] The US share is slated to fall further as our emissions decline and China's and India's rise. Clearly, even large changes in US emissions will not significantly affect global outcomes anywhere near as much as they could if they were matched with changes from other countries. Should the United States take unilateral action? The question raises three issues, none of which should deter America from acting on its own if that's the only realistic option.

The first is what's known as the "free-rider problem," in which those who benefit from a public good don't pay for it. In this case, the extent of global warming depends on total atmospheric emissions. Every country has an incentive to do nothing and let other countries impose the costs of reducing emissions on their own citizens (in the form of, for instance, a carbon tax). But if every country did nothing, nobody would address the problem.

Second, unilateral US action could make some US-based industries less competitive in global markets. But industries that are both energy-intensive and compete heavily with foreign companies comprise only about 2.4 percent of US output and less than 1 percent of employment, and a carbon tax's impact even on these industries would be small.[55] And, as noted above, border tax adjustments would address these issues, as could diplomatic engagement.

Third, if a carbon tax works as planned and reduces the US demand for fossil fuels, world fuel prices would fall and other countries' fuel consumption would rise. That would offset some of the benefits from a US carbon tax, but research suggests the impact would be small.[56]

Not only are all three of these issues manageable, but US concerns about them are less valid than they used to be. After all, the United States is coming late to this party. As of 2017, 42 countries that account for 15 percent of global emissions imposed a price on carbon through some mechanism, and 21 countries had a carbon tax, including the United Kingdom, Japan, and South Africa.[57] The European Union functions as the world's largest cap-and-trade system, and many EU member states also have a carbon tax.[58] China also recently implemented a cap-and-trade system.

Several US states and jurisdictions now have carbon pricing schemes. Through the Regional Greenhouse Gas Initiative, nine northeastern states created the nation's first mandatory, market-based emissions reduction program, requiring that each of the nine states participate in a cap-and-trade program to limit emissions from electric power plants. California also maintains a cap-and-trade program, while Boulder, Colorado, created the nation's first tax on carbon emissions in 2007. Washington and Oregon are establishing a carbon pricing regime.

Two recent treaties ensure that the process of pricing carbon will continue. In 2015, 197 countries representing 96 percent of global emissions met in Paris and set national emissions targets that would collectively limit future global warming to less than 2 degrees Celsius, and the agreement has since taken effect. At the summit, the United States committed to reduce its overall greenhouse gas emissions in 2025 to 26–28 percent below 2005 levels. The proposed carbon tax would let us meet that goal.[59]

However, as part of a broader effort to overturn or weaken climate and energy regulations, President Trump pulled the United States out of the Paris agreement in 2017, leaving America as the only nation that's not a signer.[60] But the Paris accords still command widespread support. Later that year, 14 states plus Puerto Rico (covering over a third of the US population) formed the US Climate Alliance, committing themselves to meeting their share of the Paris emissions reduction target. In addition, 383 US mayors (half of whose cities aren't in states in the US Climate Alliance) pledged to maintain their commitment to the Paris agreement and intensify their city's efforts to meet their climate goals.[61] Even before Trump's decision to pull out of the Paris agreement, over 350 companies signed a letter to the president expressing their support for the agreement.[62]

In Kigali, Rwanda, in 2016, 197 nations agreed to reduce global hydro-fluorocarbon (HFC) emissions by 80 percent by 2047. HFCs are used in air conditioning, building insulation, and aerosols, and they are extremely potent (trapping up to 10,000 times as much heat as carbon dioxide). If fully implemented, this agreement alone could reduce global temperatures by up to 0.44 degrees Celsius.[63] While the Paris treaty is not legally binding and must rely on voluntary compliance and periodic reporting to facilitate change, the Kigali agreement is legally binding on its signatories, which include the United States.[64]

As these two agreements make clear, the global community is acting. It's time for the United States to act as well.

Notes

1. This chapter uses evidence and analysis from several recent articles on the carbon tax, including Calder (2015); Dinan (2013); IPCC (2014); Marron, Toder, and Austin (2015); Morris (2013, 2016a); Morris and Mathur (2014); NOAA (2016); Walsh et al. (2014); and World Bank (2017). Generally available facts and analyses that are not specifically cited in the text may be found in these articles.
2. Economists strongly support carbon taxes and gasoline taxes, which are closely related to carbon levies. See Fuchs, Krueger, and Poterba (1998); Levitt (2007); Mankiw (2009, 2013); IGM Forum (2011, 2012). Nevertheless, there is disagreement among economists about how to use the revenues raised from a carbon tax.
3. Barron et al. (2018).
4. Carbon tax payments would be a deductible business expense and so would reduce revenues from the individual and corporate income tax. The Congressional Budget Office (2009) estimates the size of the offset to be about 25 percent of gross tax revenue. The figures in the text take this offset and an additional 15 percent offset for low-income earners into account and report net revenue.
5. Created by the United Nations and the World Meteorological Organization in 1988, the IPCC is the authoritative source for climate research, drawing on research of thousands of the world's leading scientists.
6. American Association for the Advancement of Science (2014).
7. Irfan (2018); Roberts (2018).
8. Melillo et al. (2014).
9. Belluz (2017).
10. Department of Defense (2014).
11. Revkin (2017).
12. Sanderson, O'Neill, and Tebaldi (2016). While scientists debate the merits of using a single average temperature threshold to represent the dangers of global warming, the 2-degree limit has become a benchmark (Victor and Kennel 2014; Knopf et al. 2012; Smith et al. 2009; Rogelj et al. 2011; Meinshausen et al. 2009). Some believe that a 1.5-degree threshold is necessary and feasible (Tschakert 2015; Rogelj 2015). One study asserts that the 0.5 degrees mark "the difference between events at the upper limit of present-day natural variability and a new climate regime" (Schleussner et al. 2016, p. 327). The difference

would translate into significantly more variable climate effects—including longer heat waves, more rainfall, a higher risk of coral bleaching, and lower crop yields.

13. Walsh et al. (2014).

14. Nordhaus (2008).

15. Viard (2009).

16. McKibbin et al. (2018).

17. The proposal applies only to CO_2 emissions in the energy sector. As such, it would cover the vast majority of US greenhouse gas emissions in a relatively simple manner. Ideally, however, a carbon tax would cover as many greenhouse gases and sources as possible. Other greenhouse gases—methane, nitrous oxide, and hydrofluorocarbons—are significantly more potent in terms of global warming than carbon dioxide per ton of emission. Methane, for example, traps 25 times more heat than carbon dioxide, although it does not have the ocean acidification effects that carbon dioxide does. Recent trends suggest that methane levels are increasing at a rapid pace, mostly due to food production methods (Saunois et al. 2016). Some greenhouse gas sources—such as nitrous oxide emitted from fertilizers in certain weather and soil conditions—are not suitable for taxation because they are produced through diffuse processes, making it hard to identify a responsible party or measure the emissions. Nevertheless, methane from landfills and coal beds is relatively straightforward to measure and would be feasible to tax.

18. Fossil fuels are also used to make products like asphalt, chemical feedstock, waxes, and lubricants. To the extent that the CO_2 is stored within the products themselves rather than emitted into the atmosphere, the products should not face a carbon tax.

19. Emissions that are embedded in imports or exports could be taxed or exempted, respectively, through a potentially complex procedure. See Morris (2013) and McKibbin et al. (2018). The tax should be able to be designed to be consistent with World Trade Organization rules (Calder 2015; Hillman 2013; Samans 2016).

20. National Academies of Sciences, Engineering, and Medicine (2017).

21. Marron, Toder, and Austin (2015).

22. Environmental Protection Agency (2016b). The estimates omit several items that are hard to value, for example, the costs of possible animal extinction, ocean acidification, or the complete collapse of the Greenland Ice Sheet and the resulting flooding of major cities (Interagency Working Group on the Social Cost of Carbon 2010). The Interagency Working Group on the Social Cost of Carbon (2010, 2015) produced estimates of the global SCC for use in regulatory analyses by integrating numerous scenarios run through three advanced climate models. These models estimate the magnitude of changes in the climate, changes in the economy, and how they affect each other. Each is based on slightly different assumptions, but they all convert changes in emissions to changes in greenhouse gas concentrations in the atmosphere. They convert those changes into temperature changes, and those temperature changes into economic impacts. They include five different sets of GDP, population, and emissions growth scenarios, as well as three different discount rates. Putting all of this together, the group developed 45 different SCC distributions for each year, which are then separated by discount rate and combined into probability distributions to generate a plausible range of the SCC for each rate. Using their best estimates for the economic impact, an intermediate value for weighting the future (a discount rate of 3 percent), and considering global costs, the group found that the average estimated cost of a metric ton of CO_2 emission across the various scenarios would be $42 in 2020 using 2007 dollars. I extrapolate what the SCC would be in 2019 based on a linear change from 2015 and 2020 and then update that value to 2019 dollars. The results were sensitive to the discount rate employed. Using different discount rates for the future (discount rates of 2.5 percent and 5 percent) produced average effects ranging from $15 to $77 per metric ton. The results also showed a high degree of variance. Using the 95th percentile of estimated costs, as a measure of a plausible "worst-case" scenario, and an intermediate interest rate, the costs equaled $153 per ton (in 2019 dollars).

23. World Bank (2017).
24. Marron, Toder, and Austin (2015).
25. Rates are adjusted to 2019 dollars and rounded to the nearest dollar. For a representative sample, see Fawcett et al. (2018); Jorgenson et al. (2015); Morris (2013); McKibbin et al. (2015); Paltsev at al. (2007); NERA Economic Consulting (2013); Rausch and Reilly (2012); Congressional Budget Office (2013b); Shapiro, Pham, and Malik (2008); Rausch et al. (2010); Horowitz et al. (2017); Goulder and Hafstead (2013); Williams III and Wichman (2015). Additionally, recent legislation in Congress proposed a $49/ton tax on carbon in 2018, increasing 2 percentage points a year above inflation. The US Treasury estimated the fiscal and distributional impacts of a $49 carbon tax beginning in 2019, increasing 2 percentage points per year above inflation. The authors find that the tax would raise $194 billion in 2019 and $2.2 trillion through 2028 (Horowitz et al. 2017).
26. The regressivity is dampened if households are classified based on consumption or lifetime income rather than current, annual income (Poterba 1991).
27. Morris (2013). An 11 percent rebate would be sufficient to protect the bottom quintile while an 18 percent rebate would protect the bottom three deciles (Mathur and Morris 2012).
28. The Congressional Budget Office (2013b) estimates that a $25 per ton tax on emissions from electricity, manufacturing, and transportation with an increase of 2 percent above inflation each year would reduce emissions by 10 percent in the first decade. Jorgenson et al. (2015) find that a $20 tax growing at 5 percent above inflation would reduce emissions by 20 percent in its 15th year and 30 percent in its 35th year. McKibbin et al. (2015) estimate that a $15 tax growing at 4 percent above inflation could reduce emissions by 20 percent in its 25th year. Shapiro, Pham, and Malik (2008) find that an initial $14 tax rising to $50 in 2030 would reduce emissions by 30 percent after 20 years. Metcalf (2009) finds that a $15 per ton tax that increases over time would reduce greenhouse gas emissions by 14 percent. All dollars are indexed for the year of original publication.
29. Elgie (2014); Sumner, Bird, and Smith (2009). The tax in British Columbia initially reduced emissions but became less effective after the tax rate was frozen over time. One study suggests that in the initial years, the tax reduced emissions by 5 to 15 percent below the counterfactual (Murray and Rivers 2015). The British Columbia government announced that beginning in April 2018, it would begin to increase the rate again until it reaches $50 per ton in 2021 (Porter 2016).
30. McKibbin et al. (2018). Baseline emissions align with those published by the Energy Information Administration's Annual Energy Outlook for 2016 and do not include any effects of the Clean Power Plan, which is in legal limbo.
31. Parry, Walls, and Harrington (2007); Currie et al. (2014).
32. Morris (2013); Congressional Budget Office (2013a).
33. Climate change has small effects on the spending side of the budget. Although relief efforts like those following Hurricane Sandy in 2012 are well publicized, the costs of disaster relief, flood and crop insurance, fire management, and other programs subject to climate change are quite small—about 1 percent of spending.
34. Congressional Budget Office (2010).
35. As an illustrative calculation, there are about 50,000 coal miners, and their average earnings are about $60,000 per year. If transitional support provided a one-time payment equal to three full years of salary for every coal miner, the cost would be $9 billion (National Mining Association 2016; US Department of Labor 2016).
36. Bureau of Labor Statistics (2018); Morris (2016b).
37. Studies suggest a general ordering of growth effects: highest (and potentially positive) if corporate income tax rates were cut; intermediate (and usually negative) if individual income tax or payroll tax rates were reduced; and smallest if the funds are rebated to individuals (McKibbin et al. 2012; Goulder and Hafstead 2013; NERA Economic Consulting 2013;

Carbone et al. 2013). The carbon tax proposed here is part of a broader set of proposals, so it is unclear how to assign a particular use of the revenues.

38. Economists often refer to the potential for a "double dividend," namely, that the carbon tax will both (1) create a cleaner environment and generate other benefits by correcting a market failure and (2) improve economic efficiency by using carbon tax revenues to reduce other tax rates. While the first component would almost certainly occur, the second benefit will occur only if the efficiency costs of a carbon tax—namely, its interactions with other taxes—is smaller than the efficiency gains from reductions in other taxes. Research suggests that the second dividend often does not occur (Marron, Toder, and Austin 2015; Goulder 2013).

39. Funk and Kennedy (2016).

40. Democratic Platform Committee (2016).

41. Trump (2012).

42. Committee on Arrangements for the 2016 Republican National Convention (2016).

43. Plumer (2015).

44. Library of Congress (2016).

45. Shultz and Becker (2013); Spillman (2016); Taylor (2015).

46. Norris and Horsley (2008).

47. Bailey and Bookbinder (2017); Baker et al. (2017). Several major companies, including Shell, BP, ExxonMobil, and General Motors, have come out in support of the Climate Leadership Council's carbon tax plan as "founding members."

48. In a 2016 Gallup poll, 82 percent of Americans thought global warming was a critical or important threat to US interests over the next decade. Two-thirds said global warming is caused by human activity. More than half thought that policymakers should make environmental protection a priority, even at the risk of limiting economic growth; the same share thought the government was doing too little to protect the environment (Gallup 2016). Politics seems to play a large role—almost all Democrats with high levels of scientific knowledge agree that climate change is mostly due to human activity and half of those with low scientific knowledge believe this. Among Republicans, there is no significant difference between the two groups (Funk 2017). But support for a carbon tax is weak. When asked about a carbon tax, 34 percent of Americans state that they support the tax. That percentage increases to 56 percent, however, when surveyers also state that the revenue from the tax would be returned to the public as a tax rebate (Amdur, Rabe, and Borick 2014). In another survey, researchers asked Americans how much they would be willing to pay to combat climate change if the cost appeared as a monthly fee on their energy bill. Twenty-nine percent of Americans responded that they were willing to pay $20 per month and 17 percent were willing to pay $40 per month (Energy Policy Institute at the University of Chicago 2016). Despite the relatively low public support, economists broadly agree that a carbon tax is an efficient policy to reduce emissions. A University of Chicago survey of leading economists found that 90 percent of economists agree or strongly agree with the statement that a carbon tax is a less expensive way to reduce CO_2 emissions than a collection of regulations (IGM Forum 2011). Eighty-seven percent agreed with the statement that a federal carbon tax would produce fewer negative externalities than an equivalent increase in marginal tax rates (IGM Forum 2012).

49. Amdur, Rabe, and Borick (2014).

50. No Climate Tax (2016).

51. Exxon may have a financial incentive to support a carbon tax because it is the country's largest natural gas producer.

52. Roberts (2018).

53. Antholis and Talbott (2010).

54. Janssens-Maenhout et al. (2017).

55. Marron, Toder, and Austin (2015); Fischer, Morgenstern, and Richardson (2013); US Department of Labor (2015, 2016); Aldy and Pizer (2009).

56. Morris and Mathur (2014).
57. Australia implemented a $23 per ton carbon tax in 2012, but repealed it in 2014 for political reasons. Since then, carbon pricing has been a controversial issue, and the uncertainty has led to an increasingly unstable and expensive energy market (Aly 2017).
58. World Bank (2017).
59. Barron et al. (2018).
60. The broader effort includes rules to expand oil and gas drilling in protected areas and an executive order that would begin to unravel the Clean Power Plan. Federal agencies have begun to remove the words "climate change" from their websites (Davenport 2018; Popovich, Albeck-Ripka, and Pierre-Louis 2018).
61. America's Pledge (2017); Goulder and Hafstead (2017).
62. Kennedy (2016).
63. Velders (2016).
64. Under the Paris treaty, countries are required to reconvene in staggered five-year intervals to present updated plans that increase emissions reductions beyond their initial goals and to make a public statement on their progress toward achieving their emissions reductions plans (Davenport 2015). The Kigali agreement is an amendment to the 1987 Montreal Protocol, which banned ozone-depleting coolants called chlorofluorocarbons, and hence is legally binding. The HFCs that are being phased out under the Kigali agreement were created to evade the Montreal Protocol's ban on chlorofluorocarbons.

Epilogue

It is difficult to make predictions, as the saying goes, especially about the future. I don't know what's going to happen, but here's the story I hope historians can tell come 2050.

While the economy was strong and interest rates were low, it was easy for Americans to ignore the problems simmering under the surface. The nation's deficits—including the growing long-term fiscal imbalance and the systematic underinvestment in its own people and infrastructure—were not unknown but were not compelling. (To paraphrase Mark Twain, they were like the weather: everybody talked about them, but nobody did anything about them.)

Then a crack appeared in the mirror. The economy faltered, bringing a rise in deficits. Interest rates rose, boosting government interest payments, and helping politicians relearn that railing against interest payments as a waste was a vote-getter. A trade war escalated, emphasizing our dependence on foreign capital.

A charismatic new leader arose who actually spoke the hard truth and got people to listen.

The public and political leaders began to take seriously the notion that rising debt and underinvestment were threatening the American Dream. The problems that had been hiding in plain sight for years became clear as day. The trust fund exhaustion dates for Social Security and Medicare suddenly seemed a lot closer than people had realized before.

Members of the public got agitated. After years of denial, it was as if they moved rapidly through the remaining stages of grief—from anger to bargaining, depression, and eventually acceptance of the situation. This was not their grandfathers' debt problem.

Policymakers—newly wise, cynically following public opinion, or maybe a little of both—began to take action.

Of course, they started with a commission. But this commission was different. First of all, each party got to pick some of the members representing the other party. Conservatives chose liberals who realized that spending cuts had to be part of the solution and that they couldn't simultaneously argue, first, that debt was not of a concern but, second, that conservatives' relentless drive to cut taxes was bad policy. Liberals chose conservatives who understood that revenues had to rise and that cutting taxes and raising spending every time they were in power was a flawed long-term strategy. Second, Congress had to vote up or down on the commission's proposals.

After a few false starts, beginning 2021 or thereabouts, a newly elected president and a motivated Congress enacted a series of laws similar to the proposals described in earlier chapters.

They saw the danger of rising healthcare costs but also recognized the incredible value of healthcare spending. They controlled costs by raising competition among providers, eliminating wasteful spending, and taxing health insurance plans. And they made sure that all people, especially children, had adequate care.

They took seriously the notion that Social Security needed reforms but also recognized the program as a linchpin of security for each generation in its retirement. They put the program back on a solvent path but preserved its considerable powers to protect people against poverty and other risks.

Liberals accepted the need to trim Social Security but insisted on investing more in the American people. In response, policymakers took a long position on America and invested in children, nutrition, childcare, maternity leave, and job training.

Both sides acknowledged that more and better infrastructure and research and development were in the country's interest, and they put their money where their mouth was.

Conservatives recognized the need to raise revenue but wanted to do so in the most efficient way possible—and they largely succeeded.

Policymakers ended their head-in-the-sand insanity and imposed a carbon tax. After the United States imposed a carbon tax, it negotiated with China to impose one as well. The two countries became world leaders who got other countries to follow suit. In the process, they corrected an enormous market failure to price carbon appropriately and helped save the planet.

The United States joined the rest of the world in creating a value-added tax, which does not burden saving or investment. As Larry Summers predicted, liberals came to love the revenue potential and conservatives didn't mind the regressivity. Because the VAT and carbon taxes are regressive, policymakers added relief for low-income households at a small fraction of the overall revenue gain.

Policymakers made sensible improvements to the corporate tax—reducing the effective tax rate on most new investments to zero, eliminating distortions across investments, and collecting revenue by reducing windfall gains on past investments.

The public revolted against the tax loopholes benefiting the rich. Once policymakers accepted that there was a fiscal problem, they realized that the money had to come from somewhere. Eliminating loopholes raised taxes on a group that had done extraordinarily well in the past several decades yet had not seen an increase in tax rates. It created not just a sense, but the actuality, of shared sacrifice. But don't worry about the 1 percent—they are doing fine.

The IRS got the money it needed to enforce the tax system better and as a result cut evasion dramatically, raising revenues and making the tax system fairer in the process.

The results of all of this have been pretty satisfying. We may not have a balanced budget (or a balanced budget amendment), but deficits are low. The public debt is not zero, but it's manageable and stable at around 60 percent of GDP, and it is lower than it was in 2018. The debt is growing at or below the overall economic growth rate. Interest costs are reasonable.

Healthcare spending is still substantial, as befitting an aging and wealthy economy, but spending growth is under control, the quality of care is up, and virtually everyone has health insurance coverage.

Social Security is solvent and protecting tens of millions of households from economic insecurity.

Rather than turning the country into a nation of moochers, higher social spending invigorated the low-income population, powering a new round of American ingenuity and hard work, and bringing them better health, more education, higher wages, lower poverty, safer neighborhoods, and more opportunity.

The economy is doing quite well. Higher taxes did not stymie growth—as they hadn't historically in the United States or Europe—because well-designed tax increases are efficient ways to raise revenue. Instead, lower debt freed up capital, a renewed corporate tax boosted investment, increased infrastructure made the private sector more effective, and more research increased the rate of innovation. Higher social spending and better child care and maternity leave policies boosted the quality and quantity of labor effort. Inequality is down; economic mobility is up. America has become, once again, the land of opportunity. Lower greenhouse gas emissions have kept the planet cleaner and cooler.

All in all, experts agree that the whole experience confirms the observation, allegedly made by Winston Churchill, that "you can always count on Americans to do the right thing . . . after they have exhausted all of the other options."

References

Introduction

Ballhaus, Rebecca. 2017. "President Trump Promises 'Giant Tax Cut for Christmas.'" *Wall Street Journal*, December 13.

CBS News. 2017. "CBS News Poll: Americans Say Tax Plan Helps Wealthy, Not Middle Class." CBS News, December 7.

Committee for a Responsible Federal Budget. 2017. "Debt Fixer." Committee for a Responsible Federal Budget, Washington, DC. http://www.crfb.org/debtfixer/.

Debt Reduction Task Force. 2010. "Restoring America's Future: Reviving the Economy, Cutting Spending and Debt, and Creating a Simple, Pro-Growth Tax System." Senator Pete Domenici and Dr. Alice Rivlin, Bipartisan Policy Center, Washington, DC.

Hacker, Jacob, and Paul Pierson. 2005. "Abandoning the Middle: The Bush Tax Cuts and the Limits of Democratic Control." *Perspectives on Politics* 3 (1): 33–53.

Hutchins Center on Fiscal and Monetary Policy. 2018. "The Fiscal Ship." Brookings Institution, Washington, DC. http://fiscalship.org/.

Kennedy, John F. 1962. "Annual Message to Congress on the State of the Union." Delivered on January 11.

Moynihan, Daniel Patrick. 2010. *Daniel Patrick Moynihan: A Portrait in Letters of an American Visionary.* Ed. Steven Weisman. New York: Public Affairs.

National Commission on Fiscal Responsibility and Reform. 2010. "The Moment of Truth: Report of the National Commission on Fiscal Responsibility and Reform." Washington, DC.

Peter G. Peterson Foundation. 2011. "The 2011 Fiscal Summit: The Solutions Initiative." Peter G. Peterson Foundation, Washington, DC.

Peter G. Peterson Foundation. 2015. 2015 Fiscal Summit: Opportunity for America. "The Solutions Initiative III." Peter G. Peterson Foundation, Washington, DC.

Reinhart, Carmen, and Kenneth Rogoff. 2009. *This Time Is Different: Eight Centuries of Financial Folly.* Princeton, NJ: Princeton University Press.

Chapter 1

American Petroleum Institute. 2015. "Gasoline Taxes: Combined Local, State, and Federal (Cents Per Gallon) Rates Effective 10/01/2015." http://www.api.org/~/media/Files/Statistics/Gasoline-Tax-Map.pdf.

Austin, D. Andrew. 2015. "The Debt Limit: History and Recent Increases." Congressional Research Service, Washington, DC.

Boards of Trustees, Federal Hospital Insurance and Federal Supplementary Medical Insurance Trust Funds. 2018. "2018 Annual Report of the Boards of Trustees of the Federal Hospital

Insurance and Federal Supplementary Medical Insurance Trust Funds." Medicare, Department of Health and Human Services, Washington, DC.

Center on Budget and Policy Priorities. 2018a. *Policy Basics Archive.* Washington, DC: Center on Budget and Policy Priorities.

Center on Budget and Policy Priorities. 2018b. "Policy Basics: The Earned Income Tax Credit." Center on Budget and Policy Priorities, Washington, DC.

Centers for Medicare and Medicaid Services. 2018. "National Health Expenditure Accounts." Department of Health and Human Services, Washington, DC.

Congressional Budget Office. 2018a. "The Budget and Economic Outlook: 2018 to 2028." Congressional Budget Office, Washington, DC.

Congressional Budget Office. 2018b. "The Distribution of Household Income and Federal Taxes, 2014." Congressional Budget Office, Washington, DC.

Cronin, Julie Anne, Emily Y. Yin, Laura Power, and Michael Cooper. 2012. "Distributing the Corporate Income Tax: Revised U.S. Treasury Methodology." US Department of the Treasury, Washington, DC.

Desilver, Drew. 2018. "Congress Has Long Struggled to Pass Spending Bills on Time." Pew Research Center, Washington, DC.

Food and Nutrition Service. 2018. "FY15 through FY18 *National View Summary.*" Supplemental Nutrition Assistance Program (SNAP), United States Department of Agriculture, Washington, DC.

Fox, Liana. 2017. "The Supplemental Poverty Measure: 2016." Current Population Reports, US Census Bureau, Washington, DC.

Fullerton, Don, and Gilbert E. Metcalf. 2002. "Tax Incidence." In *Handbook of Public Economics*, vol 4. Edited by Alan J. Auerbach and Martin Feldstein, 1787–872. Amsterdam: Elsevier.

Gruber, Jonathan, and Alan B. Krueger. 1990. "The Incidence of Mandated Employer-Provided Insurance: Lessons from Workers' Compensation Insurance." NBER Working Paper No. 3557. National Bureau of Economic Research, Cambridge, MA.

Heniff, Bill, Jr. 2015. "Debt Limit Legislation: The House "Gephardt Rule." Congressional Research Service, Washington, DC.

Johnston, David Cay. 2001. "Talk of Lost Farms Reflects Muddle of Estate Tax Debate." *New York Times*, April 8.

Joint Committee on Taxation, US Congress. 2013. "Modeling the Distribution of Taxes on Business Income." JCX-14-13. Joint Committee on Taxation, US Congress, Washington, DC.

Joint Committee on Taxation. 2018. "Estimates of Federal Tax Expenditures for Fiscal Years 2017–2021." JCX-34-18. Joint Committee on Taxation, US Congress, Washington, DC.

Kadet, Anne. 2017. "National Debt Clock Returns from the Shop, Finds It's Off by $687 Billion." *Wall Street Journal*, November 29.

Kaiser Family Foundation. 2013. "2013 Survey of Americans on the U.S. Role in Global Health." Henry J. Kaiser Family Foundation, Menlo Park, CA.

Marron, Donald, and Eric Toder. 2013. "Tax Policy and the Size of Government." National Tax Association Proceedings, 104th Annual Conference on Taxation, New Orleans, LA.

McIntyre, Robert S., Matthew Gardner, and Richard Phillips. 2014. "The Sorry State of Corporate Taxes: What Fortune 500 Firms Pay (or Don't Pay) in the USA and What They Pay Abroad—2008 to 2012." Citizens for Tax Justice and Institute on Taxation and Economic Policy, Washington, DC.

McIntyre, Robert S., Richard Philips, and Phineas Baxandall. 2015. "Offshore Shell Games 2015: The Use of Offshore Tax Havens by Fortune 500 Companies." U.S. Public Interest Research Group Education Fund and Citizens for Tax Justice, Washington, DC.

Nunns, James R. 2012. "How TPC Distributes the Corporate Income Tax." Tax Policy Center, Washington, DC.

Organisation for Economic Co-operation and Development (OECD). 2016. "Social Spending," *Society at a Glance 2016.* OECD Data. OECD, Paris.

OECD. 2017a. "General Government." *National Accounts at a Glance.* OECD Statistics. OECD, Paris.

OECD. 2017b. "Health Spending." *Health at a Glance.* OECD Data. OECD, Paris.

OECD. 2017c. "Infrastructure Investment." *ITF Transport Outlook 2017.* OECD Data. OECD, Paris.

OECD. 2017d. "Revenue Statistics—Comparative Tables." OECD Stat. OECD, Paris.

OECD. 2018. "Taxing Energy Use 2018: Companion to the Taxing Energy Use Database." OECD, Paris.

Pew Research Center. 2014. "The News IQ Quiz." Online Quiz: October. Pew Research Center, Washington, DC.

Quote Investigator. 2015. "It Is Better to Know Nothing than to Know What Ain't So." http://quoteinvestigator.com/2015/05/30/better-know/.

Sherman, Arloc. 2017. "Census Says Four Programs—Which House Eyes for Cuts—Keep Millions from Poverty." Center on Budget and Policy Priorities, Washington, DC.

Social Security Administration. 2016. "Income of the Population 55 or Older, 2014." Social Security Administration, Office of Retirement and Disability Policy, Washington, DC.

Social Security Administration. 2017. "SSI Monthly Statistics: Table 1. Recipients (by type of payment), Total Payments, and Average Monthly Payment, February 2016–February 2017." Social Security Administration, Washington, DC.

Tax Policy Center. 2016. "Who Pays the Estate Tax?" *Tax Policy Center Briefing Book.* Washington, DC: Urban Institute and Brookings Institution.

Tax Policy Center. 2017a. "T17-0308—Estate Tax Returns and Liability under Current Law and the House and Senate Versions of the Tax Cuts and Jobs Act, 2018–2027." Tax Policy Center, Washington, DC.

Tax Policy Center. 2017b. "T17-0312—Conference Agreement: The Tax Cuts and Jobs Act; Baseline: Current Law; Distribution of Federal Tax Change by Expanded Cash Income Percentile, 2018." Tax Policy Center, Washington, DC.

Tax Policy Center. 2017c. "T17-0335—Tax Units with Zero or Negative Federal Individual Income Tax under Current Law and the Tax Cuts and Jobs Act, 2018–2027." Tax Policy Center, Washington, DC.

Tax Policy Center. 2018. "Distribution of Federal Payroll and Income Taxes by Expanded Cash Income Percentile, 2018." Tax Policy Center, Washington, DC.

US Department of the Treasury. 2013. "The Potential Macroeconomic Effect of Debt Ceiling Brinkmanship." October 2013 Report. US Department of the Treasury, Washington, DC.

US Department of the Treasury. 2018. "Debt Limit." Initiatives. https://www.treasury.gov/initiatives/Pages/debtlimit.aspx.

Williams, Roberton. 2015. "New Estimates of How Many Households Pay No Federal Income Tax." *Tax Vox,* October 6. Tax Policy Center, Washington, DC.

Williamson, Vanessa S. 2018. "Public Ignorance or Elitist Jargon? Reconsidering Americans' Overestimates of Government Waste and Foreign Aid." Brookings Institution, Washington, DC.

Chapter 2

Auerbach, Alan J., Jason Furman, and William G. Gale. 2007. "Still Crazy after All These Years: Understanding the Budget Outlook." *Tax Notes,* May 21.

Auerbach, Alan J., and William G. Gale. 2001. "Tax Cuts and the Budget." *Tax Notes,* March 26.

Auerbach, Alan J., and William G. Gale. 2009a. "The Economic Crisis and the Fiscal Crisis: 2009 and Beyond." Brookings Institution, Washington, DC.

Auerbach, Alan J., and William G. Gale. 2009b. "The Economic Crisis and the Fiscal Crisis: 2009 and Beyond. An Update." Brookings Institution, Washington, DC.

Auerbach, Alan J., and William G. Gale. 2011. "Tempting Fate: The Federal Budget Outlook." Tax Policy Center, Washington, DC.

Auerbach, Alan J., and William G. Gale. 2016. "Once More unto the Breach: The Deteriorating Fiscal Outlook." Brookings Institution, Washington, DC.

Auerbach, Alan J., William G. Gale, and Aaron Krupkin. 2018. "The Federal Budget Outlook: We Are Not Winning." *Tax Notes*, July 30: 643.

Balkin, Jack M. 2012. "The Not-So-Happy Anniversary of the Debt-Ceiling Crisis." *Atlantic*, July 31.

Bank, Steven A., Kirk J. Stark, and Joseph J. Thorndike. 2008. *War and Taxes*. Washington, DC: Urban Institute Press.

Bartlett, Bruce. 2014. "The 50th Anniversary of the Kennedy Tax Cut." *Tax Notes* 142: 749.

Birnbaum, Jeffrey H., and Alan S. Murray. 1987. *Showdown at Gucci Gulch: Lawmakers, Lobbyists, and the Unlikely Triumph of Tax Reform*. New York: Random House.

Brown, E. Cary. 1956. "Fiscal Policy in the Thirties: A Reappraisal." *American Economic Review* 46 (5): 857–79.

Brown, E. Cary. 1989. "Episodes in the Public Debt History of the United States." Presented at the Conference on Capital Markets and Debt Management, Castelgondolfo, Italy.

Brownlee, W. Elliot. 2004. *Federal Taxation in America: A Short History*. Cambridge: Cambridge University Press.

Bureau of Economic Analysis. 2013. "Gross Domestic Product (GDP)." *National Economic Accounts*. Washington, DC: US Department of Commerce.

Churchill, Winston. 1905. *Why I Am a Free Trader*. London: Review of Reviews.

Clinton, William. 1996. State of the Union Address, January 23.

Congressional Budget Office. 2001. "The Budget and Economic Outlook: Fiscal Years 2002–2011." White House, Washington, DC

Congressional Budget Office. 2010. "Historical Data on the Federal Debt." Congressional Budget Office, Washington, DC.

Congressional Budget Office. 2012. "What Accounts for the Slow Growth of the Economy after the Recession?" Congressional Budget Office, Washington, DC.

Congressional Budget Office. 2016. "The Budget and Economic Outlook: 2016 to 2026." Congressional Budget Office, Washington, DC.

Council of Economic Advisers. 2013. "Economic Activity during the Government Shutdown and Debt Limit Brinksmanship." White House, Washington, DC.

Elmendorf, Douglas W. 2013. "How Eliminating the Automatic Spending Reductions Specified by the Budget Control Act Would Affect the U.S. Economy in 2014." Congressional Budget Office, Washington, DC.

Gale, William G., and Peter R. Orszag. 2004. "Economic Effects of Making the 2001 and 2003 Tax Cuts Permanent." Brookings Institution, Washington, DC.

Gordon, John Steele. 2010. *Hamilton's Blessing: The Extraordinary Life and Times of Our National Debt*. New York: Walker.

Government Accountability Office. 2015. "DEBT LIMIT: Market Response to Recent Impasses Underscores Need to Consider Alternative Approaches." Government Accountability Office, Washington, DC.

Hausman, Joshua K. 2016. "Fiscal Policy and Economic Recovery: The Case of the 1936 Veterans' Bonus." *American Economic Review* 106 (4): 1100–1143.

Hormats, Robert D. 2007. *The Price of Liberty: Paying for America's Wars from the Revolution to the War on Terror*. New York: Times Books.

Johnson, Simon, and James Kwak. 2012. *White House Burning: The Founding Fathers, Our National Debt, and Why It Matters to You*. New York: Pantheon Books.

Krugman, Paul. 2017. "Zombies of Voodoo Economics." *New York Times*, April 24.

Madison, James. 1970. Letter to Henry Lee, April 13. https://founders.archives.gov/documents/Madison/01-13-02-0106.

Makin, John H., and Norman J. Ornstein. 1994. *Debt and Taxes*. New York: Times Books.

National Commission on Fiscal Responsibility and Reform. 2010. "The Moment of Truth: Report of the National Commission on Fiscal Responsibility and Reform." Washington, DC.

Office of Management and Budget. 2003. "The Real Fiscal Danger." In *Budget of the United States Government Fiscal Year 2004*. White House, Washington, DC.

Office of Management and Budget. 2018. "Historical Tables." White House, Washington, DC.

"Pollock v. Farmers' Loan & Trust Co." 1895. The Oyez Project at IIT Chicago–Kent College of Law, accessed September 19, 2015, http://www.oyez.org/cases/1851-1900/1894/1894_893.

Posen, Adam S. 2014. "Introduction: The Costs of Behaving Badly." In *Flirting with Default: Issues Raised by Debt Confrontations in the United States*, PIIE Briefing No. 14-1, pp. 1–2. Peterson Institute for International Economics, Washington, DC.

Poterba, James M. 1994. "Budget Policy." In *American Economic Policy in the 1980s*. Chicago: University of Chicago Press.

Raju, Manu, and Jake Sherman. 2013. "GOP Shuns Shutdown, but Not Default." *Politico*, September 26.

Reagan, Ronald. 1980. "Ronald Reagan/John Anderson Presidential Debate." Transcript. Baltimore, MD, September 21.

Romer, Christina D. 2009. "Lessons from the Great Depression for Economic Recovery in 2009." Prepared remarks for presentation at the Brookings Institution, Washington, DC, March 9.

Romer, Christina D., and David H. Romer. 2009. "Do Tax Cuts Starve the Beast? The Effect of Tax Changes on Government Spending." *Brookings Papers on Economic Activity*, Spring 2009: 139–214.

Social Security Administration. 2015. "Congress Passes H.R. 1314, the Bipartisan Budget Act of 2015." *Social Security Legislative Bulletin*, November 3, 114–18.

Swann, Nikola, John Chambers, and David Beers. 2011. "Research Update: United States of America Long-Term Rating Lowered to 'AA+' on Political Risks and Rising Debt Burden." Standard & Poor's, New York.

Taylor, Timothy. 2014. "How Milton Friedman Helped Invent Income Tax Withholding." *Conversable Economist*, April 12.

Thorndike, Joseph J. 2008. "Four Things That Everyone Should Know about New Deal Taxation." *Tax Notes*, November 24.

Toynbee, Arnold J. 1957. *A Study of History*. New York: Oxford University Press.

Wallis, John Joseph. 2000. "American Government Finance in the Long Run: 1790 to 1990." *Journal of Economic Perspectives* 14 (1): 61–82.

Weisman, Steven R. 1983. "Budget Tie-Up: Reagan at the Crossroads." *New York Times*, News Analysis section, April 20.

White, Bill. 2014. *America's Fiscal Constitution: Its Triumph and Collapse*. New York: Public Affairs.

Chapter 3

Aaron, Henry J. 2014. "The Economics and Politics of Long-Term Budget Projections." Working Paper 8, Hutchins Center on Fiscal and Monetary Policy, Brookings Institution, Washington, DC.

Aaron, Henry J. 2015. "The Myth Behind America's Deficit." *Fortune*, September 10.

Auerbach, Alan J. 1994. "The U.S. Fiscal Problem: Where We Are, How We Got Here, and Where We're Going." *NBER Macroeconomics Annual* 9: 141–86.

Auerbach, Alan J. 2014. "Fiscal Uncertainty and How to Deal with It." Working Paper 6, Hutchins Center on Fiscal and Monetary Policy, Brookings Institution, Washington, DC.

Auerbach, Alan, William G. Gale, and Benjamin Harris. 2014. "Federal Health Spending and the Budget Outlook: Some Alternative Scenarios." Brookings Institution, Washington, DC.

Auerbach, Alan, William G. Gale, and Aaron Krupkin. 2016. "Interest Rates and the Federal Budget Outlook." Brookings Institution, Washington, DC.

Auerbach, Alan J., William G. Gale, and Aaron Krupkin. 2018. "The Federal Budget Outlook: We Are Not Winning." *Tax Notes*, July 30: 643.

Ball, Laurence M., Douglas W. Elmendorf, and N. Gregory Mankiw. 1998. "The Deficit Gamble." *Journal of Money, Credit, and Banking* 30 (4): 699–720.

Board of Trustees, Federal Old-Age and Survivors Insurance and Federal Disability Insurance Trust Funds. 2018. "The 2018 Annual Report of the Board of Trustees of the Federal Old-Age and Survivors Insurance and Federal Disability Insurance Trust Funds." Social Security Administration, Washington, DC.

The Boards of Trustees, Federal Hospital Insurance and Federal Supplementary Medical Insurance Trust Funds. 2018. "2018 Annual Report of the Boards of Trustees of the Federal Hospital Insurance and Federal Supplementary Medical Insurance Trust Funds." Department of Health and Human Services, Washington, DC.

Burman, Leonard E., Jeffrey Rohaly, Joseph Rosenberg, and Katherine C. Lim. 2010. "Catastrophic Budget Failure." *National Tax Journal* 63 (3): 561–83.

Committee for a Responsible Federal Budget. 2018. "Debt Could Be Twice the Size of the Economy by Mid-Century." Committee for a Responsible Federal Budget, Washington, DC.

Congressional Budget Office. 2015. "The 2015 Long-Term Budget Outlook." Congressional Budget Office, Washington, DC.

Congressional Budget Office. 2017. "Estimates of Automatic Stabilizers." Congressional Budget Office, Washington, DC.

Congressional Budget Office. 2018a. "The Budget and Economic Outlook: 2018 to 2028." Congressional Budget Office, Washington, DC.

Congressional Budget Office. 2018b. "The 2018 Long-Term Budget Outlook." Congressional Budget Office, Washington, DC.

Debt Reduction Task Force. 2010. "Restoring America's Future." Bipartisan Policy Center, Washington, DC.

Engen, Eric M., and R. Glenn Hubbard. 2005. "Federal Government Debt and Interest Rates." In *NBER Macroeconomics Annual 2004*, vol. 19. Edited by Mark Gertler and Kenneth Rogoff, 83–160. Cambridge, MA: MIT Press.

Gale, William G., and Peter R. Orszag. 2004. "Budget Deficits, National Saving, and Interest Rates." *Brookings Papers on Economic Activity* 2: 101–210.

Gordon, Robert J. 2016. *The Rise and Fall of American Growth: The U.S. Standard of Living since the Civil War.* Princeton, NJ: Princeton University Press.

Goss, Stephen C. 2016. "Understanding Social Security's Long-Term Fiscal Outlook: Putting Financial Challenges in Perspective." *Actuary* (April/May): 16–24.

Government Accountability Office. 2015a. "Debt Limit: Market Responses to Recent Impasses Underscores Need to Consider Alternative Approaches." GAO-15-476. Government Accountability Office, Washington, DC.

Government Accountability Office. 2015b. "State and Local Governments' Fiscal Outlook: 2015 Update." GAO-16-260SP. Government Accountability Office, Washington, DC.

Hamilton, James D., Ethan S. Harris, Jan Hatzius, and Kenneth D. West. 2015. "The Equilibrium Real Funds Rate: Past, Present, and Future." NBER Working Paper No. 21476. National Bureau of Economic Research, Cambridge, MA.

Irwin, Neil. 2015. "Why Very Low Interest Rates May Stick Around." *New York Times*, December 14, 2015.

Johnson, Simon, and James Kwak. 2012. *White House Burning: The Founding Fathers, Our National Debt, and Why It Matters to You.* New York: Pantheon.

Joint Committee on Taxation. 2015. "Technical Explanation of the Protecting Americans from Tax Hikes Act of 2015, House Amendment #2 to the Senate Amendment to H.R. 2029 (Rules Committee Print 114-40)." Joint Committee on Taxation, Washington, DC.

Kamin, David. 2014. "In Good Times and Bad: Designing Legislation That Responds to Fiscal Uncertainty." Working Paper 7, Hutchins Center on Fiscal and Monetary Policy. Brookings Institution, Washington, DC.

Kogan, Richard, Chad Stone, Bryann DaSilva, and Jan Rejeski. 2015. "Difference between Economic Growth Rates and Treasury Interest Rates Significantly Affects Long-Term Budget Outlook." Center on Budget and Policy Priorities, Washington, DC.

Krugman, Paul. 2013a. "On the Non-Equivalence of Greenhouse Gases and Entitlement Spending." *New York Times*, January 17.

Krugman, Paul. 2013b. "Fight the Future." *New York Times*, June 16.

Laubach, Thomas. 2009. "New Evidence on the Interest Rate Effects of Budget Deficits and Debt." *Journal of the European Economic Association* 7 (4): 858–85.

Malakoff, David. 2014. "Renewal of R&D Tax Credit Seems Like Sure Bet after U.S. House Vote." *Science*, December 4.

National Commission on Fiscal Responsibility and Reform. 2010. "The Moment of Truth." White House, Washington, DC.

Office of Management and Budget. 2011. *Analytical Perspectives: Budget of the U.S. Government, Fiscal Year 2012*. White House, Washington, DC.

Office of Management and Budget. 2018. *Historical Tables*. White House, Washington, DC.

Peterson-Pew Commission on Budget Reform. 2010. "Getting Back in the Black." Peterson-Pew Commission on Budget Reform, Washington, DC.

Summers, Lawrence. 2013. "Larry Summers: America's Many Deficits." *Washington Post*, January 21.

US Census. 2014. "Table 3. Projections of the Population by Sex and Selected Age Groups for the United States: 2015 to 2060." *2014 National Population Projections Tables*. Washington, DC: US Government Printing Office.

US Department of the Treasury. 2017. "Analysis of Growth and Revenue Estimates Based on the U.S. Senate Committee on Finance Tax Reform Plan." December 11.

Weisman, Jonathan. 2013. "Many in G.O.P. Offer Theory: Default Wouldn't Be that Bad." *New York Times*, October 8.

Zivney, Terry L., and Richard D. Marcus. 1989. "The Day the United States Defaulted on Treasury Bills." *Financial Review* 24 (3): 475–89.

Chapter 4

Abbas, S. M., Nazim Belhocine, Asmaa A. El-Ganainy, and Mark A. Horton. 2010. A Historical Public Debt Database. International Monetary Fund, Washington, DC.

Alesina, Alberto F., and Silvia Ardagna. 2010. "Large Changes in Fiscal Policy: Taxes versus Spending." In *Tax Policy and the Economy*, vol. 24. Edited by Jeffrey R. Brown. Chicago: University of Chicago Press.

Auerbach, Alan, and Yuriy Gorodnichenko. 2017. "Fiscal Stimulus and Fiscal Sustainability." Presented at Fostering a Dynamic Global Economy, a symposium hosted by the Federal Reserve Bank of Kansas City, August 24–26, Jackson Hole, WY.

Ball, Laurence, and N. Gregory Mankiw. 1995. "What Do Budget Deficits Do?" In *Budget Deficits and Debt: Issues and Options*, 95–119. Kansas City: Federal Reserve Bank of Kansas City.

Barro, Robert J. 1974. "Are Government Bonds Net Wealth?" *Journal of Political Economy* 82 (6): 1095–117.

Barro, Robert J. 2012. "Stimulus Spending Keeps Failing." *Wall Street Journal*, May 9.

Barro, Robert J., and Jason Furman. 2018. "Macroeconomic Effects of the 2017 Tax Reform." *Brookings Papers on Economic Activity*, Spring 2018.

Bartlett, Bruce. 2013. "For Many Hard-Liners, Debt Default Is the Goal." Economix Blog, *New York Times*, October 14.

Baum, Anja, Cristina Checherita-Westphal, and Philipp Rother. 2013. "Debt and Growth: New Evidence for the Euro Area." *Journal of International Money and Finance* 32: 809–21.

Bernheim, B. Douglas. 1989. "A Neoclassical Perspective on Budget Deficits." *Journal of Economic Perspectives* 3 (2): 55–72.

Blinder, Alan S., and Mark Zandi. 2015. "The Financial Crisis: Lessons for the Next One." Center on Budget and Policy Priorities, Washington, DC, October 15.

Bureau of Economic Analysis. 2018. "Table 5.1. Saving and Investment by Sector." National Income and Product Accounts Tables. US Department of Commerce, Washington, DC.

Caner, Mehmet, Thomas Grennes, and Fritzi Koehler-Geib. 2010. "Finding the Tipping Point—When Sovereign Debt Turns Bad." World Bank Working Paper no. 5391. World Bank, Washington, DC.

Cecchetti, Stephen G., M. S. Mohanty, and Fabrizio Zampolli. 2011. "Achieving Growth amid Fiscal Imbalances: The Real Effects of Debt." Presented at Achieving Maximum Long-Run Growth, a symposium sponsored by the Federal Reserve Bank of Kansas City (MO), August 25–27, Jackson Hole WY.

Chinn, Menzie D., Barry Eichengreen, and Hiro Ito. 2011. "A Forensic Analysis of Global Imbalances." NBER Working Paper 17513. National Bureau of Economic Research, Cambridge, MA.

Chinn, Menzie D., and Hiro Ito. 2005. "Current Account Balances, Financial Development and Institutions: Assaying the World 'Savings Glut.'" NBER Working Paper 11761. National Bureau of Economic Research, Cambridge, MA.

Chinn, Menzie D., and Hiro Ito. 2008. "Global Current Account Imbalance: American Fiscal Policy versus East Asian Savings." *Review of International Economics* 16 (3): 479–98.

Chodorow-Reich, Gabriel, Laura Feiveson, Zachary Liscow, and William Gui Woolston. 2012. "Does State Fiscal Relief during Recessions Increase Employment? Evidence from the American Recovery and Reinvestment Act." *American Economic Journal: Economic Policy* 4 (3): 118–45.

Chudik, Alexander, Kamiar Mohaddes, M. Hashem Pesaran, and Mehdi Raissi. 2015. "Is There a Debt-Threshold Effect on Output Growth?" Working Paper No. 15/197. International Monetary Fund, Washington, DC.

Congressional Budget Office. 2015. "Estimated Impact of the American Recovery and Reinvestment Act on Employment and Economic Output in 2014." Congressional Budget Office, Washington, DC.

Congressional Budget Office. 2016. "The 2016 Long-Term Budget Outlook." Congressional Budget Office, Washington, DC.

Congressional Budget Office. 2018. "The Budget and Economic Outlook: 2018–2028." Congressional Budget Office, Washington, DC.

DeLong, J. Bradford, and Lawrence H. Summers. 2012. "Fiscal Policy in a Depressed Economy." *Brookings Papers on Economic Activity*, Spring: 233–97.

Dornbusch, Rudi. 1997. "Murder, Money, & Mexico." Interview with PBS *Frontline*, April.

Egert, Balazs. 2013. "The 90% Public Debt Threshold: The Rise and Fall of a Stylized Fact." OECD Economics Department Working Papers, No. 1055. OECD, Paris.

Elmendorf, Douglas W., and N. Gregory Mankiw. 1999. "Government Debt." In *Handbook of Macroeconomics*, vol 1. Edited by J. B. Taylor and M. Woodford. Philadelphia: Elsevier Science.

Engen, Eric M., and R. Glenn Hubbard. 2005. "Federal Government Debt and Interest Rates." In *NBER Macroeconomics Annual 2004*, vol. 19. Edited by Mark Gertler and Kenneth Rogoff, 83–160. Cambridge, MA: MIT Press.

Feinstein, C. H. 1981. "Capital Accumulation and the Industrial Revolution." In *The Economic History of Britain since 1700*. Edited by Roderick Floud and Donald McCloskey. Cambridge: Cambridge University Press.

Feldstein, Martin. 2009. "Fall in US Household Wealth Likely to Spur a Long Recession." *Taipei Times*, March 3.

Friedman, Benjamin. 1988. *Day of Reckoning: The Consequences of American Economic Policy under Reagan and After*. New York: Random House.

Gale, William G., and Peter R. Orszag. 2004. "Budget Deficits, National Saving, and Interest Rates." *Brookings Papers on Economic Activity* 2: 101–210.

Hemingway, Ernest. 1926. *The Sun Also Rises*. New York: Scribner's.

Herndon, Thomas, Michael Ash, and Robert Pollin. 2014. "Does High Public Debt Consistently Stifle Economic Growth? A Critique of Reinhart and Rogoff." *Cambridge Journal of Economics* 38 (2): 257–79.

Hills, Sally, Ryland Thomas, and Nicholas Dimsdale. 2010. "The UK Recession in Context—What Do Three Centuries of Data Tell Us?" *Bank of England Quarterly Bulletin* (Q4): 277–91.

Huntley, Jonathan. 2014. "The Long-Run Effects of Federal Budget Deficits on National Saving and Private Domestic Investment." Congressional Budget Office, Washington, DC.

IGM Forum. 2013. "Fiscal Policy and Savings." University of Chicago, Booth School of Business, July 8.

International Monetary Fund. 2010. "Will It Hurt? Macroeconomic Effects of Fiscal Consolidation." In *World Economic Outlook: Recovery, Risk, and Rebalancing*. Washington, DC: International Monetary Fund.

International Monetary Fund. 2018. "Brighter Prospects, Optimistic Markets, Challenges Ahead." World Economic Outlook Update. Washington, DC: International Monetary Fund.

Ito, Tatsuo. 2014. "BOJ Becomes Top Holder of Japan Government Bonds." *Wall Street Journal*, June 18.

Joint Committee on Taxation. 2017. "Macroeconomic Analysis of the Conference Agreement for H.R. 1, The 'Tax Cuts and Jobs Act.'" JCX-69-17. Joint Committee on Taxation, Washington, DC.

Krishnamurthy, Arvind, and Anette Vissing-Jorgensen. 2012. "The Aggregate Demand for Treasury Debt." *Journal of Political Economy* 120 (2): 233–67.

Krugman, Paul. 2003. "A Fiscal Train Wreck." *New York Times*, March 11.

Krugman, Paul. 2011. "On the Inadequacy of the Stimulus." *New York Times*, September 5.

Laubach, Thomas. 2009. "New Evidence on the Interest Rate Effects of Budget Deficits and Debt." *Journal of the European Economic Association* 7 (4): 858–85.

Macroeconomic Advisors, LLC. 2013. "The Cost of Crisis-Driven Fiscal Policy." Report for the Peter G. Peterson Foundation, Washington, DC.

Marshall, Tyrone C., Jr. 2011. "Debt Is Biggest Threat to National Security, Chairman Says." *DoD News*, September 22. United States Department of Defense, Washington, DC.

Page, Benjamin R., Joseph Rosenberg, James R. Nunns, Jeffrey Rohaly, and Daniel Berger. 2017. "Macroeconomic Analysis of the Tax Cuts and Jobs Act." Tax Policy Center, Washington, DC.

Page, Benjamin, and Marika Santoro. 2010. "Economic Impacts of Waiting to Resolve the Long-Term Budget Imbalance." Congressional Budget Office, Washington, DC.

Persson, Torsten, and Lars E. O. Svensson. 1989. "Why a Stubborn Conservative Would Run a Deficit: Policy with Time-Inconsistent Preferences." *Quarterly Journal of Economics* 104 (2): 325–45.

Posen, Adam S. 2014. "Introduction: The Costs of Behaving Badly." In *Flirting with Default: Issues Raised by Debt Confrontations in the United States*, PIIE Briefing No. 14-1, pp. 1–2. Peterson Institute for International Economics, Washington, DC.

Reinhart, Carmen, and Kenneth Rogoff. 2009. *This Time Is Different: Eight Centuries of Financial Folly*. Princeton, NJ: Princeton University Press.

Reinhart, Carmen M., and Kenneth S. Rogoff. 2010. "Growth in a Time of Debt." *American Economic Review* 100 (2): 573–78.

Reinhart, Carmen M., and Kenneth S. Rogoff. 2011. "The Forgotten History of Domestic Debt." *The Economic Journal* 121 (552): 319–50.

Romer, Christina, and David Romer. 2017. "Why Some Times Are Different: Macroeconomic Policy and the Aftermath of Financial Crises." NBER Working Paper 23931, National Bureau of Economic Research, Cambridge, MA.

Rubin, Robert E., Peter R. Orszag, and Allen Sinai. 2004. "Sustained Budget Deficits: Longer-Run U.S. Economic Performance and the Risk of Financial and Fiscal Disarray." Paper presented at the AEA-NAEFA Joint Session, Allied Social Science Associations Annual Meetings, Andrew Brimmer Policy Forum, National Economic and Financial Policies for Growth and Stability, San Diego, January 4.

Schultze, Charles. 1989. "Of Wolves, Termites and Pussycats." *Brookings Review* 7 (3): 26–33.

Tax Foundation Staff. 2017. "Preliminary Details and Analysis of the Tax Cuts and Jobs Act." Tax Foundation Special Report No. 241. Tax Foundation, Washington, DC.

University of Pennsylvania. 2017. "The Tax Cuts and Jobs Act, as Reported by the Conference Committee (12/15/17): Static and Dynamic Effects on the Budget and the Economy." Penn Wharton Budget Model. University of Pennsylvania, Philadelphia.

Ursua, Jose, and Dominic Wilson. 2012. "Risks to Growth from Build-ups in Public Debt." *Global Economics Weekly* 12/10. New York: Goldman Sachs.

US Department of the Treasury, Fiscal Service. 2018. "Federal Debt Held by Foreign and International Investors." https://fred.stlouisfed.org/series/FDHBFIN.

Weisman, Jonathan. 2013. "Many in G.O.P. Offer Theory: Default Wouldn't Be that Bad." *New York Times*, October 8.

Wilson, Daniel J. 2012. "Fiscal Spending Jobs Multipliers: Evidence from the 2009 American Recovery and Reinvestment Act." *American Economic Journal: Economic Policy* 4 (3): 251–82.

Woo, Jaejoon, and Manmohan S. Kumar. 2010. "Public Debt and Growth." IMF Working Paper 10-174. International Monetary Fund, Washington, DC.

Woo, Jaejoon, and Manmohan S. Kumar. 2015. "Public Debt and Growth." *Economica* 82: 705–39.

World Bank. 2018. "GDP (Current US$)." World Bank National Accounts Data. World Bank, Washington, DC.

Zandi, Mark. 2017. "US Macro Outlook: A Plan that Doesn't Get It Done." https://www.economy.com/dismal/analysis/299138.

Chapter 5

Aaronson, Daniel, and Bhashkar Mazumder. 2008. "Intergenerational Economic Mobility in the United States, 1940 to 2000." *Journal of Human Resources* 43 (1): 139–72.

Academy of Achievement. 1991. "Interview: Milton Friedman, Nobel Prize in Economics." Stanford, CA, January 31.

Agnello, Luca, and Ricardo M. Sousa. 2014. "How Does Fiscal Consolidation Impact on Income Inequality?" *Review of Income and Wealth* 60 (4): 702–26.

Aguiar, Mark, and Mark Bils. 2015. "Has Consumption Inequality Mirrored Income Inequality?" *American Economic Review* 105 (9): 2725–56.

Aizer, Anna, Shari Eli, Joseph Ferrie, and Adriana Lleras-Muney. 2014. "The Long-Term Impact of Cash Transfers to Poor Families." NBER Working Paper 20103. National Bureau of Economic Research, Cambridge, MA.

Alesina, Alberto, and Roberto Perotti. 1996. "Income Distribution, Political Instability, and Investment." *European Economic Review* 40 (6): 1203–28.

Alesina, Alberto, and Dani Rodrik. 1994. "Distributive Politics and Economic Growth." *Quarterly Journal of Economics* 109 (2): 465–90.

Auerbach, Alan J., Jagadeesh Gokhale, and Laurence J. Kotlikoff. 1991. "Generational Accounts: A Meaningful Alternative to Deficit Accounting." In *Tax Policy and the Economy*, vol. 5. Edited by David Bradford, 55–110. Cambridge, MA: MIT Press.

Auerbach, Alan J., Jagadeesh Gokhale, and Laurence J. Kotlikoff. 1994. "Generational Accounting: A Meaningful Way to Evaluate Fiscal Policy." *Journal of Economic Perspectives* 8 (1): 73–94.

Auerbach, Alan J., Laurence J. Kotlikoff, and Darryl R. Koehler. 2016. "U.S. Inequality, Fiscal Progressivity, and Work Disincentives: An Intragenerational Accounting." NBER Working Paper 22032. National Bureau of Economic Research, Cambridge, MA.

Autor, David H. 2014. "Skills, Education, and the Rise of Earnings Inequality among the 'Other 99 Percent.'" *Science* 344 (6186): 843–51.

Autor, David H., Alan Manning, and Christopher L. Smith. 2016. "The Contribution of the Minimum Wage to US Wage Inequality over Three Decades: A Reassessment." *American Economic Journal: Applied Economics* 8 (1): 58–99.

Barro, Robert J. 2000. "Inequality and Growth in a Panel of Countries." *Journal of Economic Growth* 5 (1): 5–32.

Batini, Nicoletta, Giovanni Callegari, and Julia Guerreiro. 2011. "An Analysis of U.S. Fiscal and Generational Imbalances: Who Will Pay and How?" IMF Working Paper 11/72. International Monetary Fund, Washington, DC.

Bloom, Nicholas. 2017. "Corporations in the Age of Inequality." *Harvard Business Review*, April 7.

Board of Governors of the Federal Reserve System. 2016. "Flow of Funds, Balance Sheets, and Integrated Macroeconomic Accounts, Fourth Quarter 2015." *Financial Accounts of the United States*. Washington, DC: Federal Reserve System.

Bricker, Jesse, Alice Henriques, Jacob Krimmel, and John Sabelhaus. 2016, Spring. "Measuring Income and Wealth at the Top Using Administrative and Survey Data." *Brookings Papers on Economic Activity*. Washington, DC: Brookings Institution Press.

Brown, David W., Amanda E. Kowalski, and Ithai Z. Lurie. 2015. "Medicaid as an Investment in Children: What Is the Long-Term Impact on Tax Receipts?" NBER Working Paper 20835. National Bureau of Economic Research, Cambridge, MA.

Bureau of Economic Analysis. 2016. "Section 2: Personal Income and Outlays." *National Income and Product Accounts Tables*. US Department of Commerce. Washington, DC: US Government Printing Office.

Bureau of Labor Statistics. 2016. "Labor Force Statistics from the Current Population Survey." US Bureau of Labor Statistics, United States Department of Labor, Washington, DC.

Bureau of Labor Statistics. 2017. "Union Affiliation Data from the Current Population Survey." US Bureau of Labor Statistics, United States Department of Labor, Washington, DC.

Burkhauser, Richard V., Jeff Larrimore, and Kosali I. Simon. 2012. "A 'Second Opinion' on the Economic Health of the American Middle Class." *National Tax Journal* 61 (1): 7–32.

Card, David. 2001. "The Effect of Unions on Wage Inequality in the U.S. Labor Market." *Industrial and Labor Relations Review* 54 (2): 296–315.

Card, David, and Alan B. Krueger. 1995. *Myth and Measurement: The New Economics of the Minimum Wage*. Princeton, NJ: Princeton University Press.

Case, Anne, and Angus Deaton. 2015. "Rising Morbidity and Mortality in Midlife among White Non-Hispanic Americans in the 21st Century." *Proceedings of the National Academy of Sciences* 112 (49): 15078–83.

Causa, Orsetta, and Asa Johansson. 2010. "Intergenerational Social Mobility in OECD Countries." *OECD Journal: Economic Studies* 2010 (1): 1-45.

Chetty, Raj, Nathaniel Hendren, Patrick Kline, Emmanuel Saez, and Nicholas Turner. 2014b. "Is the United States Still a Land of Opportunity? Recent Trends in Intergenerational Mobility." *American Economic Review Papers and Proceedings* 104 (5): 141–47.

Chetty, Raj, Nathaniel Hendren, Patrick Kline, and Emmanuel Saez. 2014a. "Where Is the Land of Opportunity? The Geography of Intergenerational Mobility in the United States." *Quarterly Journal of Economics* 129 (4): 1553–623.

Chetty, Raj, Nathaniel Hendren, and Lawrence F. Katz. 2016. "The Effects of Exposure to Better Neighborhoods on Children: New Evidence from the Moving to Opportunity Experiment." *American Economic Review* 106 (4): 855–902.

Chyn, Eric. 2016. "Moved to Opportunity: The Long-Run Effect of Public Housing Demolition on Labor Market Outcomes of Children." Job Market Paper, University of Michigan, Ann Arbor.

Cingano, Federico. 2014. "Trends in Income Inequality and Its Impact on Economic Growth." OECD Social, Employment, and Migration Working Papers, No. 163. OECD, Paris.

Clark, Gregory. 2014. *The Son Also Rises: Surnames and the History of Social Mobility*. Princeton, NJ: Princeton University Press.

Congressional Budget Office. 2014. "The Effects of a Minimum-Wage Increase on Employment and Family Income." Congressional Budget Office, Washington, DC.

Congressional Budget Office. 2016. "The Distribution of Household Income and Federal Taxes, 2013." Congressional Budget Office, Washington, DC.

Congressional Budget Office. 2018. "The Distribution of Household Income, 2014." Congressional Budget Office, Washington, DC.

Corak, Miles 2013a. "Income Inequality, Equality of Opportunity, and Intergenerational Mobility." *Journal of Economic Perspectives* 27 (3): 79–102.

Corak, Miles. 2013b. "Inequality from Generation to Generation: The United States in Comparison." In *The Economics of Inequality, Poverty, and Discrimination in the 21st Century*. Edited by Robert Rycroft. Santa Barbara, CA: ABC-CLIO.

Corak, Miles, and Andrew Heisz. 1999. "The Intergenerational Earnings and Income Mobility of Canadian Men: Evidence from Longitudinal Income Tax Data." *Journal of Human Resources* 34 (3): 504–33.

Corak, Miles, Matthew J. Lindquist, and Bhashkar Mazumder. 2014. "A Comparison of Upward and Downward Intergenerational Mobility in Canada, Sweden and the United States." *Labour Economics* 30: 185–200.

Council of Economic Advisers. 2015. "Worker Voice in a Time of Rising Inequality." White House Council of Economic Advisers Issue Brief, Washington, DC.

Deming, David. 2009. "Early Childhood Intervention and Life-Cycle Skill Development: Evidence from Head Start." *American Economic Journal: Applied Economics* 1(3): 111–34.

Fields, Gary S. 2001. *Distribution and Development: A New Look at the Developing World*. New York: Russell Sage Foundation/Cambridge, MA: MIT Press.

Forbes, Kristin J. 2000. "A Reassessment of the Relationship between Inequality and Growth." *American Economic Review* 90 (4): 869–87.

Frank, Robert H. 2016. *Luck and Success: Good Fortune and the Myth of Meritocracy*. Princeton, NJ: Princeton University Press.

Friedman, Milton. 1962. *Capitalism and Freedom*. Chicago: University of Chicago Press.

Furman, Jason, and Peter Orszag. 2015. "A Firm-Level Perspective on the Role of Rents in the Rise of Inequality." Presentation at "A Just Society," Centennial Event in Honor of Joseph Stiglitz. Columbia University, New York.

Gale, William, Hilary Gelfond, Aaron Krupkin, Mark J. Mazur, and Eric Toder. 2018. "The Effects of the Tax Cuts and Jobs Act: A Preliminary Analysis." Urban-Brookings Tax Policy Center, Washington, DC.

Gale, William G., and Andrew A. Samwick. 2017. "Effects of Income Tax Changes on Economic Growth." In *The Economics of Tax Policy*. Edited by Alan Auerbach, Len Burman, and Kent Smetters: New York: Oxford University Press.

Galea, Sandro, Melissa Tracy, Katherine J. Hoggatt, Charles DiMaggio, and Adam Karpati. 2011. "Estimated Deaths Attributable to Social Factors in the United States." *American Journal of Public Health* 101 (8): 1456–65.

Gokhale, Jagadeesh. 2012. "Fiscal and Generational Imbalances and Generational Accounts: A 2012 Update." CATO Working Paper. Cato Institute, Washington, DC.

Gold, Matea, and Anu Narayanswamy. 2016. "The New Gilded Age: Close to Half of All Super-PAC Money Comes from 50 Donors." *Washington Post*, April 15.

Goldin, Claudia, and Lawrence F. Katz. 2009. *The Race between Education and Technology*. Cambridge, MA: Belknap Press.

Guvenen, Fatih, Greg Kaplan, Jae Song, and Justin Widener. 2017. "Lifetime Income in the United States over Six Decades." NBER Working Paper No. 23371. National Bureau of Economic Research, Cambridge, MA.

Hauser, Robert M. 2010. "Intergenerational Economic Mobility in the United States: Measures, Differentials, and Trends." UW-Madison Center for Demography and Ecology working paper. University of Wisconsin, Madison.

Hertz, Thomas. 2007. "Trends in the Intergenerational Elasticity of Family Income in the United States." *Industrial Relations: A Journal of Economy and Society* 46 (1): 22–50.

Hoover, Herbert. 1936. "New Deal Agricultural Policies and Some Reforms." Speech in Lincoln, Nebraska, January 16.

Hoynes, Hilary, Diane Whitmore Schanzenbach, and Douglas Almond. 2016. "Long-Run Impacts of Childhood Access to the Safety Net." *American Economic Review* 106 (4): 903–34.

Kaplan, George A., Elise R. Pamuk, John W. Lynch, Richard D. Cohen, and Jennifer L. Balfour. 1996. "Inequality in Income and Mortality in the United States: Analysis of Mortality and Potential Pathways." *British Medical Journal* 312: 999–1003.

Kaplan, Steven N., and Joshua D. Rauh. 2013. "Family, Education, and Sources of Wealth among the Richest Americans, 1982–2012." *American Economic Review* 103 (3): 158–62.

Kass, David. 2013. "Warren Buffett's Meeting with University of Maryland MBA Students— November 15, 2013." Commentary on Warren Buffett and Berkshire Hathaway, December 8. University of Maryland, College Park, MD. http://blogs.rhsmith.umd.edu/davidkass/2013/12.

Kearney, Melissa S., and Benjamin H. Harris. 2014. "The 'Ripple Effect' of a Minimum Wage Increase on American Workers." Hamilton Project, Brookings Institution, Washington, DC.

Kearney, Melissa S., and Phillip Levine. 2014. "Income Inequality and Early, Non-Marital Childbearing." *Journal of Human Resources* 49: 1–31.

Kearney, Melissa S., and Phillip Levine. 2016. "Income Inequality, Social Mobility, and the Decision to Drop Out of High School." *Brookings Papers on Economic Activity*. Brookings Institution, Washington, DC, Spring.

Keeley, Brian. 2015. *Income Inequality: The Gap between Rich and Poor*. OECD Insights. OECD, Paris.

Kelly, Morgan. 2000. "Inequality and Crime." *Review of Economics and Statistics* 82 (4): 530–39.

Kennedy, Bruce P., Ichiro Kawachi, and Deborah Prothow-Stith. 1996. "Income Distribution and Mortality: Cross Sectional Ecological Study of the Robin Hood Index in the United States." *British Medical Journal* 312: 1004–7.

Kleinbard, Edward D. 2014. *We Are Better than This: How Government Should Spend Our Money*. New York: Oxford University Press.

Kneebone, Elizabeth, and Natalie Holmes. 2016. "U.S. Concentrated Poverty in the Wake of the Great Recession." Brookings Institution, Washington, DC.

Kopczuk, Wojciech. 2015. "What Do We Know about the Evolution of Top Wealth Shares in the United States?" *Journal of Economic Perspectives* 29 (1): 47–66.

Kotlikoff, Laurence J. 1986. "Deficit Delusion." *Public Interest* 84 (Summer 1986): 53–65.

Kroll, Luisa. 2015. "Inside the 2015 Forbes 400: Facts and Figures about America's Wealthiest." *Forbes*, September 29.

Krueger, Alan B. 2012. "The Rise and Consequences of Inequality in the United States." Speech at the Center for American Progress, Washington, DC, January 12.

Kuznets, Simon. 1955. "Economic Growth and Income Inequality." *American Economic Review* 45 (1): 1–28.

Lee, Chul-In, and Gary Solon. 2009. "Trends in Intergenerational Income Mobility." *Review of Economics and Statistics* 91 (4): 766–72.

Marmot, Michael. 2015. *The Health Gap*. London: Bloomsbury Press.

Meer, Jonathan, and Jeremy West. 2016. "Effects of the Minimum Wage on Employment Dynamics." *Journal of Human Resources* 51 (2): 500–22.

Miller, Claire Cain. 2015. "Class Differences in Child-Rearing Are on the Rise." *New York Times*, December 17.

Newport, Frank. 2011. "Americans Prioritize Economy over Reducing Wealth Gap." Gallup poll from November 28 to December 1.

Norden, Lawrence, Brent Ferguson, and Douglas Keith. 2016. "Five to Four." Brennan Center for Justice, New York.

OECD. 2016a. "Education Attainment." *Education Database*. OECD, Paris.

OECD. 2016b. "Income Distribution and Poverty." OECD Social and Welfare Statistics. OECD, Paris.

Okun, Arthur M. 1975. *Equality and Efficiency: The Big Tradeoff*. Washington, DC: Brookings Institution Press.

Olsen-Phillips, Peter, Russ Choma, Sarah Bryner, and Doug Weber. 2015. "The Political One Percent of the One Percent: Megadonors Fuel Rising Cost of Elections in 2014." Sunlight Foundation, Washington, DC.

Ostry, Jonathan D., Andrew Berg, and Charalambos G. Tsangarides. 2014. "Redistribution, Inequality, and Growth." IMF Staff Discussion Note 14/02. International Monetary Fund, Washington, DC.

Parker, Kim. 2014. "Families May Differ, but They Share Common Values on Parenting." American Trends Panel Survey April 29–May 27. Pew Research Center, Washington, DC.

Persson, Torsten, and Guido Tabellini. 1994. "Is Inequality Harmful for Growth?" *American Economic Review* 84 (3): 600–621.

Pew Research Center. 2014a. "Beyond Red vs. Blue: The Political Typology." Pew Research Center Political Typology, Washington, DC.

Pew Research Center. 2014b. "Most See Inequality Growing, but Partisans Differ over Solutions." Pew Research Center, Washington, DC.

Piketty, Thomas. 2013. *Capital in the Twenty-First Century*. Cambridge, MA: Harvard University Press.

Piketty, Thomas, and Emmanuel Saez. 2016. Updated data for "Income Inequality in the United States, 1913–1998." *Quarterly Journal of Economics* 118 (1): 1–39.

Piketty, Thomas, Emmanuel Saez, and Stefanie Stantcheva. 2014. "Optimal Taxation of Top Labor Incomes: A Tale of Three Elasticities." *American Economic Journal: Economic Policy* 6 (1): 230–71.

Piketty, Thomas, Emmanuel Saez, and Gabriel Zucman. 2017. "Distributional National Accounts: Methods and Estimates for the United States." National Bureau of Economic Research, Cambridge, MA.

Posner, Richard. 2012. "Luck, Wealth, and Implications for Policy." *Becker-Posner Blog*, October 14. http://www.becker-posner-blog.com/2012/10/luck-wealth-and-implications-for-policy-posner.html.

Powdthavee, Nattavudh, and Andrew J. Oswald. 2014. "Does Money Make People Right-Wing and Inegalitarian? A Longitudinal Study of Lottery Winners." Warwick Economics Research Paper Series (TWERPS) 1039. Economics Department, University of Warwick, Coventry, UK.

Prat, Andrea, Riccardo Puglisi, and James M. Snyder Jr. 2010. "Is Private Campaign Finance a Good Thing? Estimates of the Potential Informational Benefits." *Quarterly Journal of Political Science* 5 (3): 291–318.

Putnam, Robert D., Carl B. Frederick, and Kaisa Snellman. 2012. "Growing Class Gaps in Social Connectedness among American Youth." The Saguaro Seminar: Civic Engagement in America, Kennedy School of Government, Harvard University, Cambridge, MA.

Reardon, Sean F. 2011. "The Widening Academic Achievement Gap between the Rich and the Poor: New Evidence and Possible Explanations." In *Whither Opportunity? Rising Inequality, Schools, and Children's Life Chances*. Edited by Greg J. Duncan and Richard Murnan. New York: Russell Sage Foundation.

Reeves, Richard V. 2017. *Dream Hoarders*. Washington, DC: Brookings Institution Press.

Reeves, Richard V., and Isabel V. Sawhill. 2016. "Modeling Equal Opportunity." *RSF: The Russell Sage Foundation Journal of the Social Sciences* 2 (2): 60–97.

Rose, Stephen J. 2016. "The Growing Size and Incomes of the Upper Middle Class." Urban Institute, Washington, DC.

Sacerdote, Bruce. 2007. "How Large Are the Effects from Changes in Family Environment? A Study of Korean American Adoptees." *Quarterly Journal of Economics* 122 (1): 119–57.

Saez, Emmanuel, and Gabriel Zucman. 2016. "Wealth Inequality in the United States since 1913: Evidence from Capitalized Income Tax Data." *Quarterly Journal of Economics* 131 (2): 519–78.

Sawhill, Isabel. 2014. *Generation Unbound: Drifting into Sex and Parenthood without Marriage*. Washington, DC: Brookings Institution Press.

Scheve, Kenneth, and David Stasavage. 2016. *Taxing the Rich: A History of Fiscal Fairness in the United States and Europe*. Princeton, NJ: Princeton University Press.

Schwartz, Marvin. 1982. "Preliminary Estimates of Personal Wealth, 1982: Composition of Assets." Internal Revenue Service, Washington, DC.

Smith, Matthew, Danny Yagan, Owen Zidar, and Eric Zwick. 2017. "Capitalists in the Twenty-First Century." National Bureau of Economic Research, Cambridge, MA.

Solt, Frederick. 2008. "Economic Inequality and Democratic Political Engagement." *American Journal of Political Science* 52 (1): 48–60.

Sorensen, Ted. 2008. *Counselor: A Life at the Edge of History.* New York: HarperCollins.

Statistics of Income Division. 2015. "The 400 Individual Income Tax Returns Reporting the Largest Adjusted Gross Incomes Each Year, 1992–2013." Statistics of Income Division, Research, Analysis and Statistics, Internal Revenue Service, Washington, DC.

Tjepkema, Michael, Russel Wilkins, and Andrea Long. 2013. "Socio-Economic Inequalities in Cause-Specific Mortality: A 16-Year Follow-Up Study." *Canadian Journal of Public Health* 104 (7): 472–78.

United States Department of Labor. 2009. "History of Federal Minimum Wage Rates under the Fair Labor Standards Act, 1938–2009." US Department of Labor, Wage and Hour Division, Washington, DC.

Winship, Scott. 2014. "No, the Rich Are Not Taking All of the Economic Pie." *Economic Policies for the 21st Century.* New York: Manhattan Institute.

Chapter 6

Americans for Tax Reform. 2012. "Myths and Facts about the Taxpayer Protection Pledge." Americans for Tax Reform, Washington, DC, June 20.

Americans for Tax Reform. 2013. "About the Taxpayer Protection Pledge." Americans for Tax Reform, Washington, DC.

Associated Press. 2008. "McCain Backs Off His No-New-Tax Pledge." Associated Press, July 29.

Auerbach, Alan J. 2008. "U.S. Experience with Federal Budget Rules," Ifo Institute for Economic Research at the University of Munich, *CESifo DICE Report* 7 (1): 41–48.

Auerbach, Alan J., and William G. Gale. 2000. "Perspectives on the Budget Surplus." *National Tax Journal* 53 (3): 459–72.

Auerbach, Alan J., Jagadeesh Gokhale, and Laurence J. Kotlikoff. 1991. "Generational Accounts—A Meaningful Alternative to Deficit Accounting." In *Tax Policy and the Economy.* Edited by D. Bradford, vol. 5, 55–110, Cambridge, MA: MIT Press.

Auerbach, Alan J., Jagadeesh Gokhale, and Laurence J. Kotlikoff. 1994. "Generational Accounting: A Meaningful Way to Evaluate Fiscal Responsibility." *Journal of Economic Perspectives* 8 (1): 73–94.

Bartlett, Bruce. 2007. "'Starve the Beast': Origins and Development of a Budgetary Metaphor." *Independent Review* 12 (Summer): 5–26.

Bartlett, Bruce. 2011. "Reagan's Forgotten Tax Record." February 22. http://capitalgainsandgames .com/blog/bruce-bartlett/2154/reagans-forgotten-tax-record.

Boards of Trustees, Federal Hospital Insurance and Federal Supplementary Medical Insurance Trust Funds. 2004. "2004 Annual Report of the Boards of Trustees of the Federal Hospital Insurance and Federal Supplementary Medical Insurance Trust Funds." Department of Health and Human Services, Washington, DC.

Bowman, Karlyn, Andrew Rugg, and Jennifer Marsico. 2013. "Public Opinion on Taxes: 1937 to Today." AEI Public Opinion Studies. American Enterprise Institute, Washington, DC.

Carroll, Royce, Jeff Lewis, James Lo, Nolan McCarty, Keith Poole, and Howard Rosenthal. 2015. "DW-NOMINATE Scores with Bootstrapped Standard Errors." http://voteview.com/ dwnomin.html.

CBS News/*New York Times.* 2010. "The Tea Party Movement." CBS News/*New York Times* Poll conducted February 5–10.

CBS News/*New York Times.* 2011. "The Economy, the Budget Deficit, and Gun Control." CBS News/*New York Times* Poll conducted January 15–19.

Coburn, Tom. 2012. "Norquist's Phantom Army." *New York Times*, July 15.

Congress.gov. 2018. "H.R. 1892 — Bipartisan Budget Act of 2018." Library of Congress, 115th Congress, Washington, DC. https://www.congress.gov/bill/115th-congress/house-bill/1892.

Congressional Budget Office. 1995. "Who Pays and When? An Assessment of Generational Accounting." Congressional Budget Office: Washington, DC, November.

Congressional Budget Office. 2008. "Capital Budgeting." Congressional Budget Office, Washington, DC.

DeBonis, Mike. 2016. "Congress Acts to Avert Government Shutdown after Striking Deal on Flint Aid." *Washington Post*, September 28.

Dews, Fred. 2017. "A Primer on Gerrymandering and Political Polarization." Brookings Institution, Washington, DC.

Dickerson, John F. 2004. "Confessions of a White House Insider." *Time*, January 10.

Enten, Harry. 2017. "The GOP Tax Cuts Are Even More Unpopular than Past Tax Hikes." FiveThirtyEight, November 29. https://fivethirtyeight.com/contributors/harry-enten/page/5/.

Gallup. 2017. "Taxes." *In Depth: Topics A to Z*. http://www.gallup.com/poll/1714/taxes.aspx.

Garver, Rob. 2014. "These Top Economists All Agree on the Biggest Problem the U.S. Faces." *Fiscal Times*, February 24.

Government Accountability Office. 1983. "Pros and Cons of a Separate Capital Budget for the Federal Government." Report to the Committee on Environment and Public Works, United States Senate, by the Comptroller General of the United States. Government Accountability Office, Washington, DC.

Greenstein, Robert, and Richard Kogan. 2011. "A Constitutional Balanced Budget Amendment Threatens Great Economic Damage." Center on Budget and Policy Priorities, Washington, DC.

Hare, Christopher, and Keith Poole. 2014. "The Polarization of Contemporary American Politics." *Polity* 46 (3): 411–29.

Hart, Peter, and Bill McInturff. 2011. "Study #11091." NBC News/*Wall Street Journal* Survey conducted February 24–28.

Horsley, Scott. 2013. "A Churchill 'Quote' That U.S. Politicians Will Never Surrender." *Morning Edition*, October 28.

Hubbard, Glenn, and Tim Kane. 2013. *Balance: The Economics of Great Powers from Ancient Rome to Modern America*. New York: Simon & Schuster.

Jacobs, Davina F. 2008. "A Review of Capital Budgeting Practices." IMF Working Paper 160. International Monetary Fund, Washington, DC.

Jones, Jeffrey M. 2011. "Americans Oppose Eliminating Income Tax Deductions." Based on a *USA Today*/Gallup poll conducted April 13. Gallup, Washington, DC.

Kaplan, Thomas. 2017. "With Tax Cuts on the Table, Once-Mighty Deficit Hawks Hardly Chirp." *New York Times*, September 28.

Keith, Robert. 2010. "The Statutory Pay-As-You-Go Act of 2010: Summary and Legislative History." Congressional Research Service, Washington, DC, April 2.

Kelly, Brennan, and William G. Gale. 2004. "The 'No New Taxes' Pledge." *Tax Notes*, July 12, 197–209.

Kelly, Walt. 1970. *We Have Met the Enemy*. Poster for first annual observance of Earth Day, April 22.

Kohut, Andrew. 2012. "Debt and Deficit: A Public Opinion Dilemma." Pew Research Center, Washington, DC.

Krugman, Paul. 2016. "Debt, Diversion, Distraction." *New York Times*, October 22.

Krugman, Paul. 2017. "Deficits Matter Again." *New York Times*, January 9.

Mann, Thomas. 2014. "Admit It, Political Scientists: Politics Really Is More Broken than Ever." *Atlantic*, May 26.

Mann, Thomas E., and Norman J. Ornstein. 2012. *It's Even Worse than It Looks: How the American Constitutional System Collided with the New Politics of Extremism*. New York: Basic Books.

Marcos, Cristina. 2017. "GOP Lawmaker: Donors Are Pushing Me to Get Tax Reform Done." *The Hill*, November 7.

Mayhew, David. 2011. *Partisan Balance*. Princeton, NJ: Princeton University Press.

Mettler, Suzanne, and Julianna Koch. 2012. "Who Says They Have Ever Used a Government Social Program? The Role of Policy Visibility." Cornell University, Ithaca, NY.

National Commission on Fiscal Responsibility and Reform. 2010. "The Moment of Truth." White House, Washington, DC.

Newport, Frank. 2013. "Dysfunctional Government Surpasses Economy as Top US Problem." Gallup, October 29, http://www.gallup.com/poll/165302/dysfunctional-gov-surpasses-economy-top-problem.aspx.

Norquist, Grover. 2003. "Transcript: Bill Moyers Interviews Grover Norquist." PBS, January 10.

Nussle, Jim. 2011. "Perspectives on Budget Process Reform." *Testimony before a Hearing of the House Budget Committee, United States House of Representatives*, 112th Congress.

O'Keefe, Ed. 2012. "Mitch McConnell, John Boehner Double Down on Deficit Concerns." *Washington Post*, May 20.

Olson, Mancur. 1965. *The Logic of Collective Action: Public Goods and the Theory of Groups*. Cambridge, MA: Harvard University Press.

Opinion Research Corporation. 2011. "CNN-Opinion Research Poll." Conducted March 11–13.

Ornstein, Norman. 2014. "What's Wrong with Washington? Tribalism." *Governance* 27 (2): 179–83.

Orszag, Peter. 2011. "Won't You Be My (Hyper-Partisan) Neighbor?" *Bloomberg View*, June 8.

Perlberg, Steven. 2013. "S&P: The Shutdown Took $24 Billion Out of the US Economy." *Business Insider*, October 16.

Pew Research Center. 2012a. "Deep Divisions over Debt Reduction Proposals." Pew Research Center, Washington, DC, October 12.

Pew Research Center. 2012b. "Only a Handful of Proposals for Reducing the Deficit Get Majority Support." Pew Research Center, Washington, DC, December 20.

Pew Research Center. 2013. "In Deficit Debate, Public Resists Cuts in Entitlements and Aid to Poor." Pew Research Center, Washington, DC, December 19.

Pew Research Center. 2014a. "Deficit Reduction Declines as Policy Priority." Pew Research Center, Washington, DC, January 27.

Pew Research Center. 2014b. "Political Polarization in the American Public." Pew Research Center, Washington, DC, June 12.

Pew Research Center. 2017a. "Top Frustrations with Tax System: Sense that Corporations, Wealthy Don't Pay Fair Share." Pew Research Center, Washington, DC, April 14.

Pew Research Center. 2017b. "With Budget Debate Looming, Growing Share of Public Prefers Bigger Government." Pew Research Center, Washington, DC, April 24.

Plumer, Brad. 2013. "Want to Get Rid of the Debt Ceiling Forever? Join the Club." *Washington Post*, January 23.

Poole, Keith, and Howard Rosenthal. 2015. "The Polarization of the Congressional Parties." *Polarized America*. http://voteview.com/political_polarization_2014.htm.

Portman, Robert. 2015. S.334 "End Government Shutdowns Act." 114th Congress. Introduced February 2.

Posner, Paul L. 2015. "Federal Budget Process Reform." Testimony to the House Budget Committee, July 28.

President's Commission on Budget Concepts. 1967. *Report of the President's Commission on Budget Concepts*. Washington, DC: President's Commission on Budget Concepts.

President's Commission to Study Capital Budgeting. 1999. *Report of the President's Commission to Study Capital Budgeting*. Washington, DC: President's Commission to Study Capital Budgeting.

Quote Investigator. 2012. "Americans Will Always Do the Right Thing—After Exhausting All the Alternatives." http://quoteinvestigator.com/2012/11/11/exhaust-alternatives/.

Rauch, Jonathan. 1994. *Demosclerosis, the Silent Killer of American Government*. New York: Times Books.

Rauch, Jonathan. 2013. "Rescuing Compromise." *National Affairs* 17 (Fall): 1–13.

Reagan, Ronald. 1982. "Televised Speech on Tax Policy," as reported by the *New York Times*, August 17.

Rivlin, Alice, and Pete Domenici. 2015. "Proposal for Improving the Congressional Budget Process." Bipartisan Policy Center, Washington, DC.

Romer, Christina D., and David H. Romer. 2009. "Do Tax Cuts Starve the Beast? The Effect of Tax Changes on Government Spending." *Brookings Papers on Economic Activity*, Spring 2009: 139–214.

Rucker, Philip. 2009. "Sen. DeMint Is Voice of Opposition to Health-Care Reform." *Washington Post*, July 28.

Ryan, Paul. 2012. Speech to the Republican National Convention. August 29.

Savransky, Rebecca. 2017. "Graham: 'Financial Contributions Will Stop' If GOP Doesn't Pass Tax Reform." *The Hill*, November 9.

Schultze, Charles. 2010. *The Public Use of Private Interest*. Washington, DC: Brookings Institution Press.

Sullivan, Sean. 2012. "Lindsey Graham, Peter King Break with Grover Norquist." *Washington Post*, November 25.

Tankersley, Jim. 2015. "Clinton and Sanders Are Divided over a Big Obama Promise: Not Raising Taxes on the Middle Class." *Washington Post*, November 13.

Thorndike, Joseph J. 2018. "Tax History: Everyone Knows Deficits Don't Matter—and Everyone Is Wrong." *Tax Notes*, February 20.

Washington Post/ABC News. 2015. "Washington Post-ABC News Poll March 26–29, 2015."

Wyden, Ron. 2010. "Tax Reform: Why Do We Need It? What Should We Do?" Remarks at conference hosted by Tax Analysts, Washington, DC, October 6.

Chapter 7

Agency for Healthcare Research and Quality. 2016. "National Scorecard on Rates of Hospital Acquired Conditions 2010 to 2015: Interim Data from National Efforts to Make Health Care Safer." Department of Health and Human Services, Washington, DC.

Archer, Diane. 2011. "Medicare Is More Efficient than Private Insurance." *Health Affairs*, September 20.

Baicker, Katherine, Amy Finkelstein, Jae Song, and Sarah Taubman. 2014. "The Impact of Medicaid on Labor Market Activity and Program Participation: Evidence from the Oregon Health Insurance Experiment." *American Economic Review: Papers and Proceedings* 104 (5): 322–28.

Baicker, Katherine, Sarah Taubman, Heidi Allen, Mira Bernstein, Jonathan Gruber, Joseph Newhouse, Eric Schneider, Bill Wright, Alan Zaslavsky, and Amy Finkelstein. 2013. "The Oregon Experiment—Effects of Medicaid on Clinical Outcomes." *New England Journal of Medicine* 368: 1713–22.

Baumol, William. 2013. *The Cost Disease: Why Computers Get Cheaper and Health Care Doesn't*. New Haven, CT: Yale University Press.

Berk, Marc L., and Zhengyi Fang. 2017. "Most Americans Have Good Health, Little Unmet Need, and Few Health Care Expenses." *Health Affairs* 36 (4): 742–46.

Blumenthal, David, and David Squires. 2016. "Drug Price Control: How Some Government Programs Do It." Commonwealth Fund, Washington, DC.

The Boards of Trustees, Federal Hospital Insurance and Federal Supplementary Medical Insurance Trust Funds. 2018. "2018 Annual Report of the Boards of Trustees of the Federal Hospital Insurance and Federal Supplementary Medical Insurance Trust Funds." Department of Health and Human Services, Washington, DC.

Bodenheimer, Tomas, Ellen Chen, and Heather Bennett. 2009. "Confronting the Growing Burden of Chronic Disease: Can the US Healthcare Workforce Do the Job?" *Health Affairs* 28 (1): 64–74.

Brooks, Tricia. 2014. "The Family Glitch." Health Policy Briefs. *Health Affairs*, November 10.

Brown, David, Amanda Kowalski, and Ithai Lurie. 2015. "Medicaid as an Investment in Children: What Is the Long-Term Impact on Tax Receipts?" NBER Working Paper No. 20835. National Bureau of Economic Research, Cambridge, MA.

Buettgens, Matthew, Lisa Dubay, and Genevieve Kenney. 2016. "Marketplace Subsidies: Changing the Family Glitch Reduces Family Health Spending but Increases Government Costs." *Health Affairs* 35 (7): 1167–75.

Butler, Stuart. 1989. "A Framework for Reform." In *Critical Issues: A National Health System for America*. Edited by Stuart M. Butler and Edmund F. Haislmaier. Washington, DC: Heritage Foundation.

Buttorff, Christine, Teague Ruder, and Melissa Bauman. 2017. *Multiple Chronic Conditions in the United States*. Santa Monica, CA: Rand Corporation.

Cassidy, Amanda. 2014. "Geographic Variation in Medicare Spending." Health Policy Briefs. *Health Affairs*, March.

Cawley, John, and Chad Meyerhoefer. 2012. "The Medical Care Costs of Obesity: An Instrumental Variables Approach." *Journal of Health Economics* 31 (1): 219–30.

Center on Budget and Policy Priorities. 2016. "Policy Basics: Introduction to Medicaid." Center on Budget and Policy Priorities, Washington, DC.

Centers for Medicare and Medicaid Services. 2008. "Chapter 6: Part D Drugs and Formulary Requirements." *Prescription Drug Benefit Manual*. Washington, DC: Department of Health and Human Services.

Centers for Medicare and Medicaid Services. 2018a. "National Health Expenditure Accounts." Department of Health and Human Services, Washington, DC.

Centers for Medicare and Medicaid Services. 2018b. "NHE Projections 2017–2026." National Health Expenditure Data. Department of Health and Human Services, Washington, DC.

Chaloupka, Frank J., Henry Saffer, and Michael Grossman. 1993. "Alcohol-Control Policies and Motor-Vehicle Fatalities." *Journal of Legal Studies* 22 (1): 161–86.

Chaloupka, Frank J., Henry Saffer, and Michael Grossman. 2002. "The Effects of Price on Alcohol Consumption and Alcohol-Related Problems." *Alcohol Research & Health* 26 (1): 22–35.

Chaloupka, Frank J., and Kenneth E. Warner. 2000. "The Economics of Smoking." *Handbook of Health Economics* 1B: 1539–627.

Chandra, Amitabh, Jonathan Holmes, and Jonathan Skinner. 2013. "Is This Time Different? The Slowdown in Health Care Spending." *Brookings Papers on Economic Activity*, Fall 2013, 261–302.

Chandra, Amitabh, and Jonathan Skinner. 2012. "Technology Growth and Expenditure Growth in Health Care." *Journal of Economic Literature* 50 (3): 645–80.

Chua, Kao-Ping, and Benjamin Sommers. 2014. "Changes in Health and Medical Spending among Young Adults under Health Reform." *Journal of the American Medical Association* 311 (23): 2437–39.

Clemens, Jeffrey, and Joshua D. Gottlieb. 2013. "In the Shadow of a Giant: Medicare's Influence on Private Physician Payments." NBER Working Paper 19503. National Bureau of Economic Research, Cambridge, MA.

Cohodes, Sarah, Daniel Grossman, Samuel Kleiner, and Michael Lovenheim. 2016. "The Effect of Child Health Insurance Access on Schooling: Evidence from Public Insurance Expansions." *Journal of Human Resources* 51 (3): 727–59.

Collins, Sara, Munira Gunja, and Michelle Doty. 2017. "How Well Does Insurance Coverage Protect Consumers from Health Care Costs?" Findings from the Commonwealth Fund Biennial Health Insurance Survey, 2016. Commonwealth Fund, Washington, DC.

Committee on a National Strategy for the Elimination of Hepatitis B and C, National Academies of Sciences, Engineering, and Medicine. 2017. *A National Strategy for the Elimination of Hepatitis B and C: Phase Two Report*. Edited by Gillian J. Buckley and Brian L. Strom. Washington, DC: National Academies Press.

Congressional Budget Office. 2012. "Raising the Excise Tax on Cigarettes: Effects on Health and the Federal Budget." Congressional Budget Office, Washington, DC.

Congressional Budget Office. 2013. "Options for Reducing the Deficit: 2014 to 2023." Congressional Budget Office, Washington, DC.

Congressional Budget Office. 2014a. "Comparing the Costs of the Veterans' Health Care System with Private-Sector Costs." Congressional Budget Office, Washington, DC.

Congressional Budget Office. 2014b. "Payments of Penalties for Being Uninsured under the Affordable Care Act: 2014 Update." Congressional Budget Office, Washington, DC.

Congressional Budget Office. 2015. "Budgetary and Economic Effects of Repealing the Affordable Care Act." Congressional Budget Office, Washington, DC.

Congressional Budget Office 2016. "Options for Reducing the Deficit: 2017 to 2026." Congressional Budget Office, Washington, DC.

Congressional Budget Office. 2017a. "A Premium Support System for Medicare: Updated Analysis of Illustrative Options." Congressional Budget Office, Washington, DC.

Congressional Budget Office. 2017b. "Repealing the Individual Health Insurance Mandate: An Updated Estimate." Congressional Budget Office, Washington, DC.

Congressional Budget Office. 2018a. "The Budget and Economic Outlook: 2018–2028." Congressional Budget Office, Washington, DC.

Congressional Budget Office. 2018b. "Federal Subsidies for Health Insurance Coverage for People under Age 65: 2018 to 2028." Congressional Budget Office, Washington, DC.

Congressional Budget Office. 2018c. "The 2018 Long-Term Budget Outlook." Congressional Budget Office, Washington, DC.

Cook, Philip J., and Christine Durrance. 2011. "The Virtuous Tax: Lifesaving and Crime-Prevention Effects of the 1991 Federal Alcohol-Tax Increase." NBER Working Paper 17709. National Bureau of Economic Research, Cambridge, MA.

Cromwell, Jerry, Debra Dayhoff, Nancy McCall, Sujha Subramanian, Rachel Freitas, and Robert Hart. 1998. "Medicare Participating Heart Bypass Center Demonstration." Centers for Medicare and Medicaid Services, Department of Health and Human Services, Washington, DC.

Curto, Vilsa, Liran Einav, Amy Finkelstein, Jonathan D. Levin, and Jay Bhattacharya. 2017. "Healthcare Spending and Utilization in Public and Private Medicare." NBER Working Paper 23090. National Bureau of Economic Research, Cambridge, MA.

Cutler, David. 1995. "Technology, Health Costs and the NIH." National Institutes of Health Roundtable on the Economics of Biomedical Research, Bethesda, MD.

Cutler, David. 2018. "What Is the US Health Spending Problem?" *Health Affairs* 37 (3): 493–97.

Davis, Karen, Kristof Stremikis, David Squires, and Cathy Schoen. 2014. "Mirror, Mirror on the Wall: How the Performance of the US Health Care System Compares Internationally." The Commonwealth Fund, Washington, DC.

Defense Health Agency. 2016. "Number of Beneficiaries." US Department of Defense. http://www.tricare.mil/About/Facts/BeneNumbers.aspx.

Dorn, Stan, and Matthew Buettgens. 2017. "The Cost of Not Expanding Medicaid: An Updated Analysis." Urban Institute and the Robert Wood Johnson Foundation, Washington, DC.

Finegold, Kenneth, Kelsey Avery, Bula Ghose, and Caryn Marks. 2015. "Health Insurance Marketplace: Uninsured Populations Eligible to Enroll for 2016." Office of the Assistant Secretary for Planning and Evaluation, US Department of Health and Human Services, Washington, DC.

Finkelstein, Amy. 2007. "The Aggregate Effects of Health Insurance: Evidence from the Introduction of Medicare." *Quarterly Journal of Economics* 122 (1): 1–37.

Finkelstein, Amy, Matthew Gentzkow, and Heidi Williams. 2016. "Sources of Geographic Variation in Health Care: Evidence from Patient Migration." *Quarterly Journal of Economics* 131 (4): 1681–726.

Finkelstein, Amy, Sarah Taubman, Bill Wright, Mira Bernstein, Jonathan Gruber, Joseph Newhouse, Heidi Allen, Katherine Baicker, and Oregon Health Study Group. 2012. "The Oregon Health Insurance Experiment: Evidence from the First Year." *Quarterly Journal of Economics* 127 (3): 1057–106.

Fisher, Elliott, Julie Bynum, and Jonathan Skinner. 2009. "The Policy Implications of Variations in Medicare Spending Growth." Dartmouth Atlas Project Brief Report. www.dartmouthatlas .org/downloads/reports/Policy_Implications_Brief_022709.pdf.

Fisher, Elliott, David Goodman, Jonathan Skinner, and Kristen Bronner. 2009. "Health and Health Care Spending, Quality and Outcomes." Dartmouth Atlas Project Topic Brief Report. www .dartmouthatlas.org/downloads/reports/Spending_Brief_022709.pdf.

Food and Drug Administration. 2015. "Generic Competition and Drug Prices." US Department of Health and Human Services, Silver Spring, Maryland.

Frakt, Austin. 2015. "To Reduce the Cost of Drugs, Look to Europe." *New York Times*, October 19.

Frakt, Austin. 2018a. "Medical Mystery: Something Happened to U.S. Health Spending After 1980." *New York Times*, May 14.

Frakt, Austin. 2018b. "Reagan, Deregulation and America's Exceptional Rise in Health Care Costs." *New York Times*, June 4.

Frakt, Austin, Steven Pizer, and Roger Feldman. 2012. "Should Medicare Adopt the Veterans Health Administration Formulary?" *Health Economics*, 21 (5): 485–95.

Fronstin, Paul, and M. Christopher Roebuck. 2016. "The Impact of an HSA-Eligible Health Plan on Health Care Services Use and Spending by Worker Income." *EBRI Issue Brief*, No. 425. Employee Benefit Research Institute, Washington, DC.

Furman, Jason. 2016. "Six Lessons from the U.S. Experience with Tobacco Taxes." Speech at Winning the Tax Wars: Global Solutions for Developing Countries, World Bank, Washington, DC, May 24.

Furman, Jason. 2017. "The Affordable Care Act: Seven Years Later." Presentation at the Century Foundation, Washington, DC.

Gagnon, Marc-Andre, and Sidney Wolfe. 2015. "Mirror, Mirror on the Wall: Medicare Part D Pays Needlessly High Brand-Name Drug Prices Compared with Other OECD Countries and with U.S. Government Programs." Carleton University, Ottawa, Ontario, Canada, and Public Citizen, Washington, DC.

Gallet, Craig A., and John A. List. 2003. "Cigarette Demand: A Meta-Analysis of Elasticities." *Health Economics* 12 (10): 821–35.

Garfield, Rachel, Melissa Majerol, Anthony Damico, and Julia Foutz. 2016. "The Uninsured: A Primer." Kaiser Family Foundation, Washington, DC.

Gawande, Atul. 2009. "The Cost Conundrum." *New Yorker*, June 1.

Hall, Keith. 2018. "Letter to the Honorable Lamar Alexander, Re: Appropriation of Cost-Sharing Reduction Subsidies." Congressional Budget Office, Washington, DC.

Hall, Robert, and Charles Jones. 2007. "The Value of Life and the Rise in Health Spending." *Quarterly Journal of Economics* (February): 39–72.

Hamel, Liz, Jamie Firth, Larry Levitt, Gary Claxton, and Mollyann Brodie. 2016. "Survey of Non-Group Health Insurance Enrollees, Wave 3." Kaiser Family Foundation, Washington, DC.

Hammond, Ross, and Ruth Levine. 2010. "The Economic Impact of Obesity in the United States." *Diabetes, Metabolic Syndrome and Obesity: Targets and Therapies* 3: 285–95.

Hartman, Micah, Anne Martin, Olivia Nuccio, Aaron Catlin, and the National Health Expenditure Accounts Team. 2010. "Health Spending Growth at a Historic Low in 2008." *Health Affairs* 29 (1): 147–55.

Healthcare.gov. 2017. "If You Don't Have Health Insurance: How Much You'll Pay." Department of Health and Human Services. https://www.healthcare.gov/fees/fee-for-not-being-covered/.

Hussey, Peter, Susan Ridgely, and Meredith Rosenthal. 2011. "The PROMETHEUS Bundled Payment Experiment: Slow Start Shows Problems in Implementing New Payment Models." *Health Affairs* 30 (11): 2116–24.

Ingold, John. 2016. "ColoradoCare Measure Amendment 69 Defeated Soundly." *Denver Post*, November 8.

Internal Revenue Service. 2017. "Revenue Procedure 2017–37." https://www.irs.gov/pub/irs-drop/rp-17-37.pdf.

International Agency for Research on Cancer. 2011. "Effectiveness of Tax and Price Policies for Tobacco Control." *IARC Handbooks of Cancer Prevention: Tobacco Control*, vol. 14. International Agency for Research on Cancer, Lyon, France.

Jiwani, Aliya, David Himmelstein, Steffie Woolhandler, and James G. Kahn. 2014. "Billing and Insurance-Related Administrative Costs in United States Health Care: Synthesis of Micro-Costing Evidence." *BMC Health Services Research* 14: 556.

Jost, Timothy. 2017. "CMS Releases 2016 ACA Marketplace Reinsurance and Risk Adjustment Data." *Health Affairs*, Blog, July 1.

Kaiser Family Foundation. 2012. "Massachusetts Health Care Reform: Six Years Later." *Focus on Health Reform*, May.

Kaiser Family Foundation. 2016. "Average Annual Workplace Family Health Premiums Rise Modest 3% to $18,142 in 2016: More Workers Enroll in High-Deductible Plans with Savings Options over Past Two Years." Kaiser Family Foundation, San Francisco, September 14.

Kanavos, Panos, Alessandra Ferrario, Sotiris Vandoros, and Gerard Anderson. 2013. "Higher US Branded Drug Prices and Spending Compared to Other Countries May Stem Partly from Quick Uptake of New Drugs." *Health Affairs* 32 (4): 753–61.

Kapczynski, Amy, and Aaron S. Kesselheim. 2016. "'Government Patent Use': A Legal Approach to Reducing Drug Spending." *Health Affairs* 35 (5): 791–97.

Kenney, Geneveive, and Christine Coyer. 2012. "National Findings on Access to Health Care and Service Use for Children Enrolled in Medicaid or CHIP." MACPAC Contractor Report No. 1. https://www.macpac.gov/wp-content/uploads/2015/01/Contractor-Report-No_1.pdf.

Kesselheim, Aaron, Jerry Avorn, and Ameet Sarpatwari. 2016. "The High Cost of Prescription Drugs in the United States: Origins and Prospects for Reform." *Journal of the American Medical Association* 316 (8): 858–71.

Kiley, Jocelyn. 2017. "Public Support for 'Single Payer' Health Coverage Grows, Driven by Democrats." Pew Research Center, Washington, DC.

Kipp, Richard, and Carol Ko. 2008. "Potential Cost Impacts Resulting from CMS Guidance on 'Special Protections for Six Protected Drug Classifications' and Section 176 of the Medicare Improvements for Patients and Providers Act of 2008 (MIPPA) (P.L. 110-275)." Milliman Consulting, Seattle, WA.

Kirzinger, Ashley, Bryan Wu, and Mollyann Brodie. 2016. "Kaiser Health Tracking Poll: September 2016." Kaiser Family Foundation. San Francisco, September.

Kliff, Sarah. 2018. "California's Ambitious Plan to Regulate Health Prices, Explained." *Vox*, April 11.

Koechlin, Francette, Luca Lorenzoni, and Paul Schreyer. 2010. "Comparing Price Levels of Hospital Services across Countries." Organization for Economic Cooperation and Development, Paris.

Lallemand, Nicole. 2012. "Reducing Waste in Health Care." *Health Affairs*, December 13.

Lochner, Kimberly, Christine Cox, Stephanie Bartee, Gloria Wheatcroft, and James Krometis. 2012. "Chronic Conditions among Medicare Beneficiaries, Chartbook: 2012 Edition." Centers for Medicare and Medicaid Services, Washington, DC.

Looney, Adam. 2017. "Measuring the Loss of Life from the Senate's Tax Cuts for Alcohol Producers." Brookings Institution, Washington, DC, November 22.

Lowry, Sean. 2014. "Alcohol Excise Taxes: Current Law and Economic Analysis." Congressional Research Service, No. 7-5700, Washington, DC.

Martin, Anne B., David Lassman, Benjamin Washington, Aaron Catlin, and the National Health Expenditure Accounts Team. 2012. "Growth in US Health Spending Remained Slow in 2010; Health Share of Gross Domestic Product Was Unchanged from 2009." *Health Affairs* 31 (1): 208–19.

Martin, Anne, David Lassman, Lekha Whittle, Aaron Catlin, and the National Health Expenditure Accounts Team. 2011. "Recession Contributes to Slowest Annual Rate of Increase in Health Spending in Five Decades." *Health Affairs* 30 (1): 11–22.

Mason, Melanie. 2017. "Single-Payer Healthcare Could Cost $400 Billion to Implement in California." *Los Angeles Times*, May 22.

Mazumder, Bhashkar, and Sarah Miller. 2016. "The Effects of the Massachusetts Health Reform on Household Financial Distress." *American Economic Journal: Economic Policy* 8 (3): 284–313.

Miller, Thomas, and James Capretta. 2014. "An Emerging Consensus: Medicare Advantage Is Working and Can Deliver Meaningful Reform." *Health Affairs*, November 6.

Mitchell, Alison, Evelyne Baumrucker, and Elicia Herz. 2014. "Medicaid: An Overview." Congressional Research Service, Washington, DC.

Muhelstein, David, Robert Saunders, and Mark McClellan. 2017. "Growth of ACOs and Alternative Payment Models in 2017." *Health Affairs*, Blog, June 28.

National Conference of State Legislatures. 2017. "Equalizing Health Provider Rates: All-Payer Rate Setting." National Conference of State Legislatures, Washington, DC.

National Institute for Health Care Management. 2012. "The Concentration of Health Care Spending." NIHCM Foundation Data Brief, July 2012, Washington, DC.

Newhouse, Joseph. 1992. "Medical Care Costs: How Much Welfare Loss?" *Journal of Economic Perspectives* 6 (3): 3–21.

Newhouse, Joseph, and Thomas McGuire. 2014. "How Successful Is Medicare Advantage?" *Milbank Quarterly* 92 (2): 351–94.

Ogden, Cynthia, and Margaret Carroll. 2010. "Prevalence of Overweight, Obesity and Extreme Obesity among Adults: United States, Trends 1960–1962 through 2007–2008." Centers for Disease Control and Prevention, Atlanta, GA.

Ogden, Cynthia, Margaret Carroll, Cheryl Fryar, and Katherine Flegal. 2015. "Prevalence of Obesity among Adults and Youth: United States, 2011–2014." NCHS Data Brief, Centers for Disease Control and Prevention, Atlanta, GA.

Organization for Economic Cooperation and Development. 2017. "OECD Health Statistics 2017." Organization for Economic Cooperation and Development, Paris.

Orszag, Peter. 2008. "Growth in Health Care Costs." Testimony before the US Senate Budget Committee. Congressional Budget Office, Washington, DC.

Orszag, Peter. 2013. "To Fix U.S. Budget, Reform Medical Malpractice Law." *Bloomberg*, February 27.

Papanicolas, Irene, Liana Woskie, and Ashish Jha. 2018. "Health Care Spending in the United States and Other High-Income Countries." *Journal of the American Medical Association* 319 (10): 1024–39.

Porter, Michael, and Robert Kaplan. 2016. "How to Pay for Health Care." *Harvard Business Review*, July–August.

Rampell, Catherine. 2018. "This Is What a Death Spiral Looks Like." *Washington Post*, May 14.

Romley, John A., and Paul B. Ginsburg. 2018. "Improving Bundled Payments in the Medicare Program." USC-Brookings Schaeffer Initiative for Health Policy, Washington, DC.

Roodman, David. 2015. "The Impacts of Alcohol Taxes: A Replication Review." Open Philanthropy Project. https://davidroodman.com/david/The%20impacts%20of%20alcohol%20taxes%206.pdf.

Rovner, Julie. 2014. "VA and Military Health Care Are Separate, Yet Often Confused." National Public Radio, Washington, DC.

Rudowitz, Robin, Samantha Artiga, and Rachel Arguello. 2014. "Children's Health Coverage: Medicaid, CHIP and the ACA." Kaiser Family Foundation, San Francisco.

Sheiner, Louise. 2014. "Why the Geographic Variation in Health Care Spending Cannot Tell Us Much about the Efficiency or Quality of Our Health Care System." Brookings Papers on Economic Activity. Brookings Institution, Washington, DC, Fall 2014.

Sheiner, Louise. 2015. "Health Spending Growth: The Effects of the Great Recession." Brookings Institution, Washington, DC.

Shih, Terry, Lena Chen, and Brahmajee Nallamothu. 2015. "Will Bundled Payments Change Health Care? Examining the Evidence Thus Far in Cardiovascular Care." *Circulation* 131 (24): 2151–58.

Smith, Sheila, Stephen Heffler, and Mark Freeland. 2000. "The Impact of Technological Change on Health Care Cost Spending: An Evaluation of the Literature." Health Care Financing Administration, Centers for Medicare and Medicaid Services, Baltimore, MD.

Soffen, Kim, and Kevin Uhrmacher. 2017. "Every County's Obamacare Marketplace Will Have an Insurer in 2018." *Washington Post*, September 5.

Sommers, Benjamin, Atul Gawande, and Katherine Baicker. 2017. "Health Insurance Coverage and Health—What the Recent Evidence Tells Us." *New England Journal of Medicine* 337 (6): 586–93.

Sommers, Benjamin D., Bethany Maylone, Robert J. Blendon, E. John Orav, and Arnold M. Epstein. 2017. "Three-Year Impacts of the Affordable Care Act: Improved Medical Care and Health among Low-Income Adults." *Health Affairs* 36 (6): 1–9.

Thorpe, Kenneth, Curtis Florence, David Howard, and Peter Joski. 2004. "Trends: The Impact of Obesity on Rising Medical Spending." *Health Affairs* W4: 480–86.

Trish, Erin. 2017. "Why Risk Adjustment Is a Crucial Component of Individual Market Reform." Brookings Institution, Washington, DC.

US Department of the Treasury. 2018. "Tax Expenditures." https://www.treasury.gov/resource-center/tax-policy/Pages/Tax-Expenditures.aspx.

Viscusi, W. Kip. 1995. "Cigarette Taxation and the Social Consequences of Smoking." In *Tax Policy and the Economy*, vol. 9. Edited by James M. Poterba. Cambridge, MA: MIT Press.

Wheaton, Sarah. 2014. "Why Single Payer Died in Vermont." *Politico*, December 20.

Zuckerman, Rachael, Steven Sheingold, John Orav, Joel Ruhter, and Arnold Epstein. 2016. "Readmissions, Observation, and the Hospital Readmissions Reduction Program." *New England Journal of Medicine* 374 (16): 1543–51.

Chapter 8

Aaron, Henry J. 2013. "Nudged, Pushed, or Mugged: Policies to Encourage Older Workers to Retire Later." In *Closing the Deficit: How Much Can Later Retirement Help?* Edited by Gary Burtless and Henry J. Aaron. Washington, DC: Brookings Institution Press.

Arias, Elizabeth, Melonie Heron, and Jiaquan Xu. 2017. "United States Life Tables, 2014." *National Vital Statistics Reports* 66 (4). Centers for Disease Control and Prevention, Atlanta, GA.

Autor, David H., and Mark G. Duggan. 2006. "The Growth in the Social Security Disability Rolls: A Fiscal Crisis Unfolding." *Journal of Economic Perspectives* 20 (3): 71–96.

Autor, David H., and Mark Duggan. 2010. "Supporting Work: A Proposal for Modernizing the U.S. Disability Insurance System." Center for American Progress and the Hamilton Project, Washington, DC.

Bipartisan Policy Center. 2015. "Improve the SSDI Program and Address the Impending Trust Fund Depletion: Consensus Recommendations of BPC's Disability Insurance Working Group." Bipartisan Policy Center, Washington, DC.

The Board of Trustees, Federal Old-Age and Survivors Insurance and Federal Disability Insurance Trust Funds. 2016. "The 2016 Annual Report of the Board of Trustees of the Federal Old-Age and Survivors Insurance and Federal Disability Insurance Trust Funds." Social Security Administration, Washington, DC.

The Board of Trustees, Federal Old-Age and Survivors Insurance and Federal Disability Insurance Trust Funds. 2018. "The 2018 Annual Report of the Board of Trustees of the Federal Old-Age and Survivors Insurance and Federal Disability Insurance Trust Funds." Social Security Administration, Washington, DC.

Center on Budget and Policy Priorities. 2016. "Policy Basics: Top Ten Facts about Social Security." http://www.cbpp.org/research/social-security/policy-basics-top-ten-facts-about-social-security.

Commission on Retirement Security and Personal Savings. 2016. "Securing Our Financial Future: Report of the Commission on Retirement Security and Personal Savings." Bipartisan Policy Center, Washington, DC.

Committee for a Responsible Federal Budget. 2014. "General Revenue & the Social Security Trust Funds." August 19. Committee for a Responsible Federal Budget, Washington, DC.

Congressional Budget Office. 2018. "The 2018 Long-Term Budget Outlook." Congressional Budget Office, Washington, DC.

Debt Reduction Task Force. 2010. *Restoring America's Future: Reviving the Economy, Cutting Spending and Debt, and Creating a Simple, Pro-Growth Tax System*. Washington, DC: Bipartisan Policy Center.

DeWitt, Larry. 2005. "Research Note #23." Research Notes & Special Studies by the Historian's Office, Social Security Administration, Washington, DC.

Diamond, Peter A., and Peter R. Orszag. 2005. *Saving Social Security: A Balanced Approach*. Washington, DC: Brookings Institution Press.

Fichtner, Jason J., and Jason S. Seligman. 2016. "Beyond All or Nothing: Reforming Social Security Disability Insurance to Encourage Work and Wealth." In *SSDI Solutions: Ideas to Strengthen the Social Security Disability Insurance Program*. Edited by Jim McCrery and Earl Pomeroy. Washington, DC: Committee for a Responsible Federal Budget.

Fox, Liana. 2017. "The Supplemental Poverty Measure: 2016." Current Population Reports, US Census Bureau, Washington, DC.

Gale, William G., Jonathan Gruber, and Peter R. Orszag. 2006. "Improving Opportunities and Incentives for Saving by Middle- and Low-Income Households." The Hamilton Project Discussion Paper 2006-02. Brookings Institution, Washington, DC.

Gale, William G., Sarah E. Holmes, and David C. John. 2015. "Social Security Coverage for State and Local Government Workers: A Reconsideration." *Journal of Retirement* 3 (2): 123–35.

Gale, William G., J. Mark Iwry, and Peter R. Orszag. 2005. "The Automatic 401(k): A Simple Way to Strengthen Retirement Savings." Brookings Institution, Retirement Security Project, Washington, DC.

Goss, Stephen C. 2016. Memorandum to Kent Conrad and James B. Lockhart III. Social Security Administration, October 11. https://www.ssa.gov/oact/solvency/BPCCRSPS_20161011 .pdf.

Iwry, J. Mark, and David C. John. 2009. "Pursuing Universal Retirement Security through Automatic IRAs." Retirement Security Project, Washington, DC.

Koenig, Gary, Jason J. Fichtner, and William G. Gale. 2018. "Supplemental Transition Accounts for Retirement: A Proposal to Increase Retirement Income Security and Reform Social Security." AARP, Washington, DC.

Liebman, Jeffrey B. 2015. "Understanding the Increase in Disability Insurance Benefit Receipt in the United States." *Journal of Economic Perspectives* 29 (2): 123–50.

Liebman, Jeffrey B., and Jack A. Smalligan. 2013. "An Evidence-Based Path to Disability Insurance Reform." In *15 Ways to Rethink the Federal Budget*. Washington, DC: Hamilton Project, Brookings Institution.

Manchester, Joyce, and Jae G. Song. 2011. "What Can We Learn from Analyzing Historical Data on Social Security Entitlements?" *Social Security Bulletin* 71 (4): 1–14.

Munnell, Alicia H. 2017. "Social Security's Financial Outlook: The 2017 Update in Perspective." Center for Retirement Research at Boston College, Boston, MA.

National Academies of Sciences, Engineering, and Medicine. 2015. *The Growing Gap in Life Expectancy by Income: Implications for Federal Programs and Policy Responses*. Washington, DC: National Academies Press.

National Center for Health Statistics. 2016. "12-Month-Ending General Fertility Rate: United States, 2014–Quarter 1, 2016." *Vital Statistics Rapid Release*. Atlanta, GA: Centers for Disease Control and Prevention.

National Commission on Fiscal Responsibility and Reform. 2010. *The Moment of Truth*. Washington, DC: White House.

OECD. 2017. *Pensions at a Glance 2017: OECD and G20 Indicators*. Paris: OECD Publishing.

Ortman, Jennifer M., and Victoria A. Velkoff. 2014. "An Aging Nation: The Older Population in the United States." *Current Population Reports*. Washington, DC: US Census Bureau.

Pang, Gaobo, and Sylvester Schieber. 2014. "Understanding Social Security's Income Replacement Measurements." SSRN Electronic Journal, January. DOI 10.2139/ssrn.2433181.

Ruffing, Kathy. 2013. "Social Security Benefits Are Modest by International Standards." *Off the Charts Blog*: Center on Budget and Policy Priorities, Washington, DC.

Social Security Administration. 2015. "Understanding the Benefits." SSA Publication No. 05-10024. Social Security Administration, Washington, DC.

Social Security Administration. 2016. "Income of the Population 55 or Older, 2014." Social Security Administration, Office of Retirement and Disability Policy, Washington, DC.

Social Security Administration. 2017a. "Disability Benefits." Publication No. 05-10029. Social Security Administration, Office of Retirement and Disability Policy, Washington, DC.

Social Security Administration. 2017b. "Individual Changes Modifying Social Security." Social Security Administration, Office of Retirement and Disability Policy, Washington, DC.

Chapter 9

American Enterprise Institute/Brookings Institution Working Group on Poverty and Opportunity. 2015. "Opportunity, Responsibility and Security: A Consensus Plan for Reducing Poverty and Restoring the American Dream." American Enterprise Institute and the Brookings Institution, Washington, DC.

Autor, David H. 2014. "Skills, Education, and the Rise of Earnings Inequality among the 'Other 99 Percent.'" *Science* 34 (6186): 843–51.

Baum, Sandy, and Judith Scott-Clayton. 2013. "Redesigning the Pell Grant Program for the Twenty-First Century." Discussion Paper, Hamilton Project, Brookings Institution, Washington, DC.

Barr, Andrew, and Chloe Gibbs. 2017. "Breaking the Cycle? Intergenerational Effects of an Anti-Poverty Program in Early Childhood." Texas A&M University, College Station.

Barr, Andrew, and Alex Smith. 2017. "Fighting Crime in the Cradle: The Effects of Early Childhood Food Stamp Access." Texas A&M University, College Station.

Bauer, Lauren, and Diane Schanzenbach. 2016. "The Long-Term Impact of the Head Start Program." Hamilton Project, Brookings Institution, Washington, DC.

Bettinger, Eric. 2004. "How Financial Aid Affects Persistence." NBER Working Paper No. 10242. National Bureau of Economic Research, Cambridge, MA.

Bettinger, Eric, Bridget Long, Philip Oreopoulos, and Lisa Sanbonmatsu. 2012. "The Role of Application Assistance and Information in College Decisions: Results from the H&R Block FAFSA Experiment." *Quarterly Journal of Economics* 127 (3): 1205–42.

Bitler, Marianne, and Janet Currie. 2005. "Does WIC Work? The Effects of WIC on Pregnancy and Birth Outcomes." *Journal of Policy Analysis and Management.* 24 (1): 73–91.

Bitler, Marianne, and Hilary Hoynes. 2016. "The More Things Change, the More They Stay the Same: The Safety Net and Poverty in the Great Recession." *Journal of Labor Economics* 34 (1): 403–44.

Bowden, John. 2018. "Carson Proposes Rent Increases for Americans on Housing Assistance." *Hill*, April 25.

Bulman, George, and Caroline Hoxby. 2015. "The Returns to the Federal Tax Credits for Higher Education." *Tax Policy and the Economy* 29: 13–88.

Card, David, Jochen Kluve, and Andrea Weber. 2010. "Active Labor Market Policy Evaluations: A Meta-Analysis." *Royal Economic Society Economic Journal* 120 (548): F452–77.

Card, David, and Alan B. Krueger. 1995. *Myth and Measurement: The New Economics of the Minimum Wage*. Princeton, NJ: Princeton University Press.

Carlson, Steven, and Zoe Neuberger. 2015. "WIC Works: Addressing the Nutrition and Health Needs of Low-Income Families for 40 Years." Center on Budget and Policy Priorities, Washington, DC.

Carniero, Pedro, and Rita Ginja. 2014. "Long-Term Impacts of Compensatory Preschool on Health and Behavior: Evidence from Head Start." *American Economic Journal* 6 (4): 135–73.

Cascio, Elizabeth, and Diane Schanzenbach. 2013. "The Impacts of Expanding Access to High-Quality Preschool Education." *Brookings Papers on Economic Activity*, Fall, 127–92. Brookings Institution, Washington, DC.

Cascio, Elizabeth, and Diane Schanzenbach. 2014. "Expanding Preschool Access for Disadvantaged Children." Hamilton Project, Brookings Institution, Washington, DC.

Cengiz, Doruk, Arindrajit Dube, Attila Lindner, and Ben Zipperer. 2017. "The Effect of Minimum Wages on the Total Number of Jobs: Evidence from the United States Using a Bunching Estimator." Presented at Allied Social Sciences Association Annual Meeting, Philadelphia, 2018.

Center on Budget and Policy Priorities. 2018a. "Chart Book: Economic Security and Health Insurance Programs Reduce Poverty and Provide Access to Needed Care." Center on Budget and Policy Priorities, Washington, DC.

Center on Budget and Policy Priorities. 2018b. "Policy Basics: The Earned Income Tax Credit." Center on Budget and Policy Priorities, Washington, DC.

Chetty, Raj, Nathaniel Hendren, and Lawrence Katz. 2015. "The Effects of Exposure to Better Neighborhoods on Children: New Evidence from the Moving to Opportunity Experiment." NBER Working Paper No. 21156. National Bureau of Economic Research, Cambridge, MA.

Congressional Budget Office. 2014. "The Effects of a Minimum Wage Increase on Employment and Family Income." Congressional Budget Office, Washington, DC.

Congressional Budget Office. 2015. "Federal Housing Assistance for Low-Income Households." Congressional Budget Office, Washington, DC.

Congressional Budget Office. 2017. "CBO's June 2017 Baseline Projections for the Student Loan Program." Congressional Budget Office, Washington, DC.

Congressional Budget Office. 2018. "The Budget and Economic Outlook: 2018–28." Congressional Budget Office, Washington, DC.

Cooper, David. 2016. "Balancing Paychecks and Public Assistance." Economic Policy Institute, Washington, DC.

Council of Economic Advisers. 2016. "Chapter 4: Inequality in Early Childhood and Effective Public Policy Interventions." In *Economic Report of the President*. Washington, DC: White House.

Currie, Janet, and Nancy Cole. 1993. "Welfare and Child Health: The Link between AFDC Participation and Birthweight." *American Economic Review* 83 (4): 971–85.

Currie, Janet, and Duncan Thomas. 1995. "Does Head Start Make a Difference?" *American Economic Review* 85 (3): 341–64.

Deming, David. 2009. "Early Childhood Intervention and Life-Cycle Skill Development: Evidence from Head Start." *American Economic Journal: Applied Economics* 1 (3): 111–34.

Department of Agriculture. 2018a. "National School Lunch Program Participation and Costs." USDA Food and Nutrition Service, Washington, DC.

Department of Agriculture. 2018b. "School Breakfast Program Participation and Costs." USDA Food and Nutrition Service, Washington, DC.

Department of Education. 2018. "Federal Student Loan Portfolio." Office of Federal Student Aid, Washington, DC.

Department of Health and Human Services. 2016. "LIHEAP Home Energy Notebook for Fiscal Year 2014." Administration for Children and Families Office of Community Services, Washington, DC.

Department of Health and Human Services. 2018a. "Head Start Program Facts Fiscal Year 2017." Administration for Children and Families, Washington, DC.

Department of Health and Human Services. 2018b. "TANF & SSP: Average Monthly Number of Recipients." Administration for Children and Families, Washington, DC.

Department of Labor. 2016. "Family and Medical Leave Act." Wage and Hour Division, Department of Labor, Washington, DC.

Department of Labor. 2018a. "Congressional Budget Justification Employment and Training Administration." Department of Labor, Washington, DC.

Department of Labor. 2018b. "FY 2019 Department of Labor Budget in Brief." Employment and Training Administration, Department of Labor, Washington, DC.

Dolan, Ed. 2014. "Could We Afford a Universal Basic Income?" *Economonitor*, January 13.

Dynarski, Susan. 2003. "Does Aid Matter? Measuring the Effect of Student Aid on College Attendance and Completion." *American Economic Review* 93 (1): 279–88.

Dynarski, Susan, and Daniel Kreisman. 2013. "Loans for Educational Opportunity: Making Borrowing Work for Today's Students." Hamilton Project, Brookings Institution, Washington, DC.

Dynarski, Susan, and Judith Scott-Clayton. 2006a. "The Cost of Complexity in Federal Student Aid: Lessons from Optimal Tax Theory and Behavioral Economics." *National Tax Journal* 59 (2): 319–56.

Dynarski, Susan, and Judith Scott Clayton. 2006b. "Simplify and Focus the Education Tax Incentives." NBER Tax Notes. National Bureau of Economic Research, Cambridge, MA.

Dynarski, Susan, and Judith Scott-Clayton. 2007. "College Grants on a Postcard: A Proposal for Simple and Predictable Federal Student Aid." Hamilton Project Discussion Paper 2007-01. Brookings Institution, Washington, DC.

Dynarski, Susan, and Judith Scott-Clayton. 2018. "The Tax Benefits for Education Do Not Increase Education." Brookings Institution, Washington, DC.

Engle, Patrice, and Maureen Black. 2008. "The Effect of Poverty on Child Development and Educational Outcomes." *Annals of the New York Academy of Sciences* 1136 (1): 243–56.

Executive Order 13828. 2018. "Reducing Poverty in America by Promoting Opportunity and Economic Mobility." *Federal Register* 83 (72): 15941–44.

Falk, Gene. 2017. "The Temporary Assistance for Needy Families Block Grant: A Primer on TANF Financing and Federal Requirements." Congressional Research Service, Washington, DC.

Fischer, Will, and Barbara Sard. 2017. "Chart Book: Federal Housing Spending Is Poorly Matched to Need." Center on Budget and Policy Priorities, Washington, DC.

Floyd, Ife. 2017. "TANF Cash Benefits Have Fallen by More than 20 Percent in Most States and Continue to Erode." Center on Budget and Policy Priorities, Washington, DC.

Fox, Liana. 2017. "The Supplemental Poverty Measure: 2017." US Census Bureau, Washington, DC.

Frongillo, Edward, Diana Jyoti, and Sonya Jones. 2006. "Food Stamp Program Participation Is Associated with Better Academic Learning among School Children." *Journal of Nutrition* 136 (4): 1077–80.

Furman, Jason. 2017. "Reducing Poverty: The Progress We Have Made and the Path Forward." Prepared Remarks for the Center on Budget and Policy Priorities, Washington, DC.

García, Jorge Luis, James Heckman, Duncan Ermini Leaf, and María José Prados. 2016. "The Life-Cycle Benefits of an Influential Early Childhood Program." HCEO Working Paper No. 2016-035. Human Capital and Economic Opportunity Global Working Group, Chicago.

Gault, Barbara, Heidi Hartmann, Ariane Hartmann, Jessica Milli, and Lindsey Reichlin. 2014. "Paid Parental Leave in the United States: What the Data Tell Us about Access, Usage and Economic and Health Benefits." Institute for Women's Policy Research, Washington, DC.

Golshan, Tara. 2018. "House Republicans' Push to Slash Food Stamps in the Farm Bill, Explained." *Vox*, April 25.

Government Accountability Office. 2012. "Improved Tax Information Could Help Families Pay for College." Government Accountability Office, Washington, DC.

Government Accountability Office. 2015. "Federal Low-Income Programs: Multiple Programs Target Diverse Populations and Needs." Government Accountability Office, Washington, DC.

Grogger, Jeffrey. 2003. "The Effects of Time Limits, the EITC, and Other Policy Changes on Welfare Use, Work, and Income among Female-Headed Families." *Review of Economics and Statistics* 85 (2): 394–408.

Hair, Nicole, Jamie Hanson, Barbara Wolfe, and Seth Pollak. 2015. "Association of Child Poverty, Brain Development, and Academic Achievement." *Journal of the American Medical Association Pediatrics* 169 (9): 822–29.

Hansen, Lee. 1983. "The Impact of Student Financial Aid on Access." In *The Crisis in Higher Education.* Edited by Joseph Froomkin. New York: Academy of Political Science.

Heckman, James, Rodrigo Pinto, and Peter Savelev. 2013. "Understanding the Mechanisms through Which an Influental Early Childhood Program Boosted Adult Outcomes." *American Economic Review* 103 (6): 2052–86.

Heinrich, Carolyn, Peter Mueser, Kenneth Troske, Kyung-Seong Jeon, and Daver Kahvecioglu. 2013. "Do Public Employment and Training Programs Work?" *IZA Journal of Labor Economics* 2 (6): 1–23.

Hollenbeck, Kevin. 2009. "Workforce Investment Act (WIA) Net Impacts and Rate of Return." W. E. Upjohn Institute for Employment Research, Kalamazoo, MI.

Holzer, Harry. 2018. "Jobs for the Working Class: Raising Earnings among Non-College Graduates." Brookings Institution, Washington, DC.

Hoxby, Caroline, and George Bulman. 2015. "How Tax Credits for Higher Education Affect College-Going." Internal Revenue Service, Washington, DC.

Hoynes, Hilary, Doug Miller, and David Simon. 2015. "Income, the Earned Income Tax Credit and Infant Health." *American Economic Journal: Economic Policy* 7 (1): 172–211.

Hoynes, Hilary W., Marianne E. Page, and Ann Huff Stevens. 2009. "Is a WIC Start a Better Start? Evaluating WIC's Impact on Infant Health Using Program Introduction." NBER Working Paper No. 15589. National Bureau of Economic Research, Cambridge, MA.

Hoynes, Hilary, and Ankur Patel. 2015. "Effective Policy for Reducing Inequality? The Earned Income Tax Credit and the Distribution of Income." NBER Working Paper No. 21340. National Bureau of Economic Research, Cambridge, MA.

Hoynes, Hilary, Diane Schanzenbach, and Douglas Almond. 2016. "Long-Run Impacts of Childhood Access to the Safety Net." *American Economic Review* 106 (4): 903–34.

Internal Revenue Service. 2017. "Individual Income Tax Returns Line Item Estimates, 2015." Internal Revenue Service Statistics of Income, Washington, DC.

Investment Company Institute. 2017. "529 Plan Data: December 2016." Investment Company Institute, Washington, DC.

Jackson, Margot. 2015. "Early Childhood WIC Participation, Cognitive Development and Academic Achievement." *Social Science and Medicine* 126: 145–53.

Joint Committee on Taxation. 2017. "Estimates of Federal Tax Expenditures for Fiscal Years 2016–2020." Joint Committee on Taxation, Washington, DC.

Kane, Thomas. 1995. "Rising Public College Tuition and College Entry: How Well Do Public Subsidies Promote Access to College?" NBER Working Paper 5164. National Bureau of Economic Research, Cambridge, MA.

Kearney, Melissa S., and Lesley J. Turner. 2013. "Giving Secondary Earners a Tax Break: A Proposal to Help Low- and Middle-Income Families." Hamilton Project Discussion Paper 2013-07. Brookings Institution, Washington, DC.

Khanani, Intisar, Jon Elam, Rick Hearn, Camille Jones, and Noble Maseru. 2010. "The Impact of Prenatal WIC Participation on Infant Mortality and Racial Disparities." *American Journal of Public Health* 100 (Supplement 1): S204–9.

Kids Count Data Center. 2017. "Child Population by Single Age." Annie E. Casey Foundation, Baltimore, MD.

Lafortune, Julien, Jesse Rothstein, and Diane Schanzenbach. 2016. "School Finance Reform and the Distribution of Student Achievement." IRLE Working Paper No. 100-16. Institute for Research on Labor and Employment, University of California–Berkeley.

LaLumia, Sara. 2012. "Tax Preferences for Higher Education and Adult College Enrollment." *National Tax Journal* 65 (1): 59–90.

Leachman, Michael, Nick Albares, Kathleen Masterson, and Marlana Wallace. 2016. "Most States Have Cut School Funding and Some Continue Cutting." Center on Budget and Policy Priorities, Washington, DC.

Lipsey, Mark, Kerry Hofer, Niano Dong, Dale Farran, and Carol Bilbrey. 2013. "Evaluation of the Tennessee Voluntary Prekindergarten Program: Kindergarten and First Grade Follow-Up Results from the Randomized Control Design." Peabody Research Institute, Vanderbilt University.

Long, Bridget Terry. 2003. "The Impact of Federal Tax Credits for Higher Education Expenses." NBER Working Paper No. 9553. National Bureau for Economic Research, Cambridge, MA.

Maag, Elaine. 2017. "Refundable Credits: The Earned Income Tax Credit and the Child Tax Credit." Tax Policy Center, Washington, DC.

Maag, Elaine. 2018. "Who Benefits from the Child Tax Credit Now?" Tax Policy Center, Washington, DC.

Marr, Chuck, Chye-Ching Huang, Cecile Murray, and Arloc Sherman. 2016. "Strengthening the EITC for Childless Workers Would Promote Work and Reduce Poverty." Center on Budget and Policy Priorities, Washington, DC.

Matthews, Dylan. 2016. "Basic Income: The World's Simplest Plan to End Poverty, Explained." *Vox*, April 25.

McConnell, Sheena, Erma Perez-Johnson, and Jillian Berk. 2014. "Proposal 9: Providing Disadvantaged Workers with Skills to Succeed in the Labor Market." In *Policies to Address Poverty in America*. Washington, DC: Hamilton Project, Brookings Institution.

Meer, Jonathan, and Jeremy West. 2016. "Effects of the Minimum Wage on Employment Dynamics." *Journal of Human Resources* 51 (2).

Meyer, Bruce, and Dan Rosenbaum. 2001. "Welfare, the Earned Income Tax Credit and the Labor Supply of Single Mothers." *Quarterly Journal of Economics* 116 (3): 1063–114.

Moffitt, Robert A., and John Karl Scholz. 2010. "Trends in the Level and Distribution of Income Support." In *Tax Policy and the Economy*. Edited by Jeffrey Brown, 111–52. Chicago: University of Chicago Press.

Moore, Kristen Anderson, Zakia Redd, Mary Burkhauser, Kassim Mbwana, and Ashleigh Collins. 2009. "Children in Poverty: Trends, Consequences, and Policy Options." Child Trends Research Brief, Washington, DC.

National Conference of State Legislatures. 2017. "State Minimum Wages." National Conference of State Legislatures, Washington, DC.

Office of Management and Budget. 2018. "Historical Tables." White House, Washington, DC.

Oreopoulos, Philip, and Uros Petronijevic. 2013. "Making College Worth It: A Review of Research on the Returns to Higher Education." NBER Working Paper No. 19053. National Bureau of Economic Research, Cambridge, MA.

Organization for Economic Cooperation and Development. 2017. "OECD Family Database." Directorate for Employment, Labour and Social Affairs, OECD, Paris.

Orr, Larry, Judith Feins, Robin Jacob, Erik Beecroft, Lisa Sanbonmatsu, Lawrence Katz, Jeffrey Liebman, and Jeffrey Kling. 2003. "Moving to Opportunity Interim Impacts Evaluation." Report prepared by Abt Associates and NBER for the US Department of Housing and Urban Development, Washington, DC.

Perez-Johnson, Irma, Quinn Moore, and Robert Santillo. 2011. "Improving the Effectiveness of Individual Training Accounts: Long-Term Findings from an Experimental Evaluation of Three Service Delivery Models." Mathematica Policy Research, Princeton, NJ.

Rank, Mark. 2013. "Poverty in America Is Mainstream." *New York Times*, November 2.

Rank, Mark, and Thomas Hirschl. 2015. "The Likelihood of Experiencing Relative Poverty over the Life Course." *PLoS ONE* 10 (7).

Rossin-Slater, Maya. 2013. "WIC in Your Neighborhood: New Evidence on the Impacts of Geographic Access to Clinics." *Journal of Public Economics* 102: 51–69.

Rossin-Slater, Maya. 2017. "Maternity and Family Leave Policy." NBER Working Paper No. 23069. National Bureau of Economic Research, Cambridge, MA.

Rossin-Slater, Maya, Christopher Ruhm, and Jane Waldfogel. 2011. "The Effects of California's Paid Family Leave Program on Mothers' Leave-Taking and Subsequent Labor Market

Outcomes." NBER Working Paper No. 02138. National Bureau of Economic Research, Cambridge, MA.

Sanbonmatsu, Lisa, Jens Ludwig, Lawrence Katz, Lisa Gennetian, Greg Duncan, Ronald Kessler, Emma Adam, Thomas McDade, and Stacy Lindau. 2011. "Moving to Opportunity for Fair Housing Demonstration Program: Final Impacts Evaluation." US Department of Housing and Urban Development, Washington, DC.

Sawhill, Isabel, and Adam Thomas. 2001. "A Hand Up for the Bottom Third: Toward a New Agenda for Low-Income Working Families." Brookings Institution, Washington, DC.

Schochet, Peter, John Burghardt, and Sheena McConnell. 2008. "Does Job Corps Work? Impact Findings from the National Job Corps Study." *American Economic Review* 98 (5): 1864–86.

Schochet, Peter Z., Ronald D'Amico, Jillian Berk, Sarah Dolfin, and Nathan Wozny. 2012. "Estimated Impacts for Participants in the Trade Adjustment Assistance (TAA) Program under the 2002 Amendments" and "Methodological Notes on the Impact Analysis." Final reports submitted to the US Department of Labor, Employment and Training Administration by Mathematica Policy Research, Princeton, NJ.

Seftor, Neil, and Sarah Turner. 2002. "Back to School: Federal Student Aid Policy and Adult College Enrollment." *Journal of Human Resources* 37 (2): 336–52.

Shambaugh, Jay, Lauren Bauer, and Audrey Breitweiser. 2018. "Returning to Education: The Hamilton Project on Human Capital and Wages." In *Revitalizing Wage Growth: Policies to Get American Workers a Raise*. Edited by Jay Shambaugh and Ryan Nunn, 25–50. Washington, DC: Brookings Institution Press.

Social Security Administration. 2017. "SSI Monthly Statistics: Table 1. Recipients (by Type of Payment), Total Payments, and Average Monthly Payment, February 2016–February 2017." Social Security Administration, Washington, DC.

Tax Policy Center. 2016. "What Is the Child Tax Credit?" Briefing Book. Tax Policy Center, Washington, DC.

Tax Policy Center. 2017. "T17-0178—Current Law Distribution of Tax Unites Receiving Pell Grants, AOTC and LLC, All Students, by Adjusted Gross Income, 2017." Tax Policy Center, Washington, DC.

Thomas, Tracy, Maureen Kolasa, Fan Zhang, and Abigail Shefer. 2014. "Assessing Immunization Interventions in the Women, Infants, and Children (WIC) Program." *American Journal of Preventative Medicine* 47 (5): 624–28.

Turner, Nicholas. 2011. "The Effect of Tax-Based Federal Student Aid on College Enrollment." *National Tax Journal* 63 (3): 839–62.

Waldfogel, Jane, Yoshio Higuchi, and Masahiro Abe. 1999. "Family Leave Policies and Women's Retention after Childbirth: Evidence from the United States, Britain and Japan." *Journal of Population Economics* 12 (4): 523–45.

Whitehurst, Grover J. 2017. "Why the Federal Government Should Subsidize Childcare and How to Pay for it." *Evidence Speaks Reports* 2 (11). Brookings Institution, Washington, DC.

Wimer, Christopher, Liana Fox, Irv Garfinkel, Neeraj Kaushal, and Jane Waldfogel. 2016. "Progress on Poverty? New Estimates of Historical Trends Using an Anchored Supplemental Poverty Measure." *Demography* 53 (4): 1207–8.

Wood, Michelle, Jennifer Turnham, and Gregory Mills. 2008. "Housing Affordability and Family Wellbeing: Results from Housing Voucher Evaluation." *Housing Policy Debate* 19 (2): 367–412.

Ziliak, James P. 2008. "Filling the Poverty Gap, Then and Now." In *Frontiers of Family Economics*, vol. 1. Edited by Peter Rupert, 39–114. Bingley, West Yorkshsire, UK: Emerald Publishing.

Chapter 10

American Society of Civil Engineers. 2016. "Failure to Act: Closing the Infrastructure Investment Gap for America's Economic Future." American Society of Civil Engineers, Reston, VA.

American Society of Civil Engineers. 2017. "2017 Infrastructure Report Card." American Society of Civil Engineers, Reston, VA.

Aschauer, David. 1989. "Is Public Expenditure Productive?" *Journal of Monetary Economics* 23 (2): 177–200.

Bom, Pedro R. D., and Jenny E. Ligthart. 2014. "What Have We Learned from Three Decades of Research on the Productivity of Public Capital?" *Journal of Economic Surveys* 28 (5): 899–916.

Boroush, Mark. 2017. "U.S. R&D Increased by $20 Billion in 2015, to $495 Billion; Estimates for 2016 Indicate a Rise to $510 Billion." NSF 18-306. National Science Foundation, Alexandria, VA.

Bureau of Economic Analysis. 2017. "National Income and Product Accounts: National Data." Bureau of Economic Analysis, Washington, DC.

Burtless, Gary. 2016. "Infrastructure Investment Lags Even as Borrowing Costs Remain Near Historic Low." *Inside Sources*, June 18.

Congressional Budget Office. 2010. "Potential Costs of Veterans' Health Care." Congressional Budget Office, Washington, DC.

Congressional Budget Office. 2011. "Alternative Approaches to Funding Highways." Congressional Budget Office, Washington, DC.

Congressional Budget Office. 2014a. "Federal Policies and Innovation." Congressional Budget Office, Washington, DC.

Congressional Budget Office. 2014b. "Growth in DoD's Budget from 2000 to 2014." Congressional Budget Office, Washington, DC.

Congressional Budget Office. 2015a. "Estimated Impact of the American Recovery and Reinvestment Act on Employment and Economic Output in 2014." Congressional Budget Office, Washington, DC.

Congressional Budget Office. 2015b. "Public Spending on Transportation and Water Infrastructure, 1956 to 2014." Congressional Budget Office, Washington, DC.

Congressional Budget Office. 2016a. "The Macroeconomic and Budgetary Effects of Federal Investment." Congressional Budget Office, Washington, DC.

Congressional Budget Office. 2016b. "Options for Reducing the Deficit: 2017 to 2026." Congressional Budget Office, Washington, DC.

Congressional Budget Office. 2017a. "Analysis of the Long-Term Costs of the Administration's Goals for the Military." Congressional Budget Office, Washington, DC.

Congressional Budget Office. 2017b. "An Analysis of the Obama Administration's Final Future Years Defense Program." Congressional Budget Office, Washington, DC.

Congressional Budget Office. 2017c. "Approaches to Changing Military Health Care." Congressional Budget Office, Washington, DC.

Congressional Budget Office. 2018. "The Budget and Economic Outlook: 2018 to 2028." Congressional Budget Office, Washington, DC.

Council of Economic Advisers. 2016. "Chapter 5: Technology and Innovation." *White House Council of Economic Advisers Economic Report of the President.* White House, Washington, DC.

Crawford, Neta C. 2017. "US Budgetary Costs of Post-9/11 Wars through FY2018: A Summary of the $5.6 Trillion in Costs for the US Wars in Iraq, Syria, Afghanistan and Pakistan, and Post-9/11 Veterans Care and Homeland Security." In *Costs of War.* Watson Institute of International and Public Affairs, Brown University.

Daniels, Seamus P., and Todd Harrison. 2018. "Making Sense of the Bipartisan Budget Act of 2018 and What It Means for Defense." Center for Strategic and International Studies, Washington, DC.

Deshpande, Manasi, and Douglas Elmendorf. 2008. "An Economic Strategy for Investing in America's Infrastructure." Hamilton Project, Brookings Institution, Washington, DC.

Dinan, Stephen. 2015. "Alaska Kills Infamous Bridge to Nowhere that Helped Put End to Earmarks." *Washington Times*, November 8.

Driessen, Grant A., and Marc Labonte. 2018. "Discretionary Spending Levels under the Bipartisan Budget Act of 2018." Congressional Research Service, Washington, DC.

Eisenhower, Dwight D. 1953. "The Chance for Peace." Address Delivered before the American Society of Newspaper Editors, April 16, Washington, DC.

Elmendorf, Doug. 2014. "Effects on Economic Growth of Federal Investment and Reductions in Federal Deficits and Debt." Congressional Budget Office, Washington, DC.

Engel, Eduardo, Ronald Fischer, and Alexandria Galetovic. 2011. "Public-Private Partnerships to Revamp U.S. Infrastructure." Hamilton Project, Brookings Institution, Washington, DC.

Federal News Service. 2012. "Transcript of Panel One: National Security Implications of America's Debt." Speech by Robert Gates and Admiral Michael Mullen. Center for Strategic and International Studies, Washington, DC, September 17.

Fernald, John. 1999. "Roads to Prosperity? Assessing the Link between Public Capital and Productivity." *American Economic Review* 89 (3): 619–38.

Gates, Robert M. 2010. "Department of Defense (DoD) Efficiency Initiatives." Memorandum for Secretaries of the Military Departments, August 16.

Government Accountability Office. 2012. "Highway Trust Fund: Pilot Program Could Help Determine the Viability of Mileage Fees for Certain Vehicles." Government Accountability Office, Washington, DC.

Gramlich, Edward M. 1994. "Infrastructure Investment: A Review Essay." *Journal of Economic Literature* 32 (3): 1176–96.

Harrison, Todd. 2016. "Analysis of the FY2017 Defense Budget." A Report of the CSIS International Security Program's Defense Outlook Series, Washington, DC.

Holtz-Eakin, Douglas. 1995. "Spatial Productivity Spillovers from Public Infrastructure: Evidence from State Highways." *International Tax and Public Finance* 2 (3): 459–68.

Industrial Research Institute. 2016. "2016 Global R&D Funding Forecast." *Industrial Research Institute and R&D Magazine*, Winter.

International Monetary Fund. 2014. "Chapter 3: Is It Time for an Infrastructure Push? The Macroeconomics Effects of Public Investment." In *World Economic Outlook: Legacies, Clouds, Uncertainties*. Washington, DC: International Monetary Fund.

Istrate, Emilia, and Robert Puentes. 2009. "Investing for Success: Examining a Federal Capital Budget and a National Infrastructure Bank." Brookings Institution, Washington, DC.

Joint Committee on Taxation. 2017. "Estimated Budget Effects of the Conference Agreement for H.R. 1, The 'Tax Cuts and Jobs Act.'" JCX-67-17. Joint Committee on Taxation, US Congress, Washington, DC.

Jones, Charles, and John Williams. 1998. "Measuring the Social Return to R&D." *Quarterly Journal of Economics* 113 (4): 1119–35.

Klein, Aaron. 2018. "Four Ways to Make Wiser Infrastructure Investments." Brookings Institution, Washington, DC.

Korn, David, Robert Rich, Howard Garrison, Sidney Golub, Mary Hendrix, Stephen Heinig, Bettie Sue Masters, and Richard Turman. 2002. "The NIH Budget in the 'Postdoubling' Era." *Science* 296: 1401–2.

Kremer, Michael. 2000a. "Creating Markets for New Vaccines: Part I: Rationale." NBER Working Paper No. 7716. National Bureau of Economic Research, Cambridge, MA.

Kremer, Michael. 2000b. "Creating Markets for New Vaccines: Part II: Design Issues." NBER Working Paper No. 7717. National Bureau of Economic Research, Cambridge, MA.

Kroft, Steve. 2014. "Falling Apart: America's Neglected Infrastructure." CBS News, November 23.

McCartney, Scott. 2016. "The Air Traffic System US Airlines Wish They Had." *Wall Street Journal*, April 27.

Munnell, Alicia H. 1992. "Policy Watch: Infrastructure Investment and Economic Growth." *Journal of Economic Perspectives* 6 (4): 189–98.

National Academy of Sciences. 2013. "Chapter 2: Impact of Photonics on the National Economy." In *Optics and Photonics: Essential Technologies for Our Nation*. Washington, DC: National Academy of Sciences.

National Economic Council and the President's Council of Economic Advisers. 2014. "An Economic Analysis of Transportation Infrastructure Investment." White House, Washington, DC.

National Transportation Safety Board. 2008. "Highway Accident Report: Collapse of I-35W Highway Bridge." National Transportation Safety Board, Washington, DC.

OECD. 2017. "ITF Transport Outlook 2017." OECD and International Transport Forum, Paris.

Office of Management and Budget. 2017. "Fact Sheet: The President's Fiscal Year 2018 Budget: Infrastructure Initiative." White House, Washington, DC.

Office of Management and Budget. 2018. "Historical Tables." White House, Washington, DC.

O'Hanlon, Michael. 2013. *Healing the Wounded Giant.* Washington, DC: Brookings Institution Press.

O'Hanlon, Michael. 2015. *The Future of Land Warfare.* Washington, DC: Brookings Institution Press.

O'Hanlon, Michael. 2016. *The $650 Billion Bargain: The Case for Modest Growth in America's Defense Budget.* Washington, DC: Brookings Institution Press.

Pool, Sean, and Jennifer Erickson. 2012. "The High Return on Investment for Publicly Funded Research." Center for American Progress. Washington, DC, December 10.

Rogers, J. David, G. Paul Kemp, H. J. Bosworth, and Raymond B. Seed. 2015. "Interaction between the US Army Corps of Engineers and the Orleans Levee Board Preceding the Drainage Canal Wall Failures and Catastrophic Flooding of New Orleans in 2005." *Water Policy* 17 (4): 707–23.

Romp, Ward, and Jakob de Haan. 2007. "Public Capital and Economic Growth: A Critical Survey." *Perspektiven der Wirtschaftspolitik* 8 (S1): 6–52.

Schanzenbach, Diane Whitmore, Ryan Nunn, and Greg Nantz. 2017. "If You Build It: A Guide to the Economics of Infrastructure Investment." Hamilton Project, Brookings Institution, Washington, DC.

Schaper, David. 2017. "10 Years after Bridge Collapse, America Is Still Crumbling." National Public Radio, Washington, DC, August 1.

Smith, Noah. 2018. "Domino's Pizza Fixing Potholes Is an Ominous Sign." *Bloomberg,* June 20.

Stockholm International Peace Research Institute. 2017. *SIPRI Military Expenditure Database.* Stockholm: SIPRI.

Summers, Lawrence H. 2016. "Larry Summers: When the Best Umps Blow a Call." *Washington Post,* July 14.

West, Darrell M., and John R. Allen. 2018. "How Artificial Intelligence Is Transforming the World." Brookings Institution, Washington, DC.

Whitlock, Craig, and Bob Woodward. 2016. "Pentagon Buries Evidence of $125 Billion in Bureaucratic Waste." *Washington Post,* December 5.

Winston, Clifford. 2013. "On the Performance of the US Transportation System: Caution Ahead." *Journal of Economic Literature* 51 (3): 773–824.

Winston, Clifford, and Ashley Langer. 2004. "The Effect of Government Highway Spending on Road Users' Congestion Costs." Report to the Federal Highway Administration, Washington, DC.

Chapter 11

Aaron, Henry, and William Gale. 1996. *Economic Effects of Fundamental Tax Reform.* Washington, DC: Brookings Institution Press.

Altig, David, Alan J. Auerbach, Laurence J. Kotlikoff, Kent A. Smetters, and Jan Walliser. 2001. "Simulating U.S. Tax Reform." *American Economic Review* 91 (3): 574–95.

Auerbach, Alan J., and Joel Slemrod. 1997. "The Economic Effects of the Tax Reform Act of 1986." *Journal of Economic Literature* 35 (2): 589–632.

Bartlett, Bruce. 2013. "The Sacrosanct Mortgage Interest Deduction." *New York Times,* August 6.

Batchelder, Lily. 2009. "What Should Society Expect from Heirs? The Case for a Comprehensive Inheritance Tax." *Tax Law Review* 63 (1): 1–111.

Batchelder, Lily. 2016. "The 'Silver Spoon' Tax: How to Strengthen Wealth Transfer Taxation." Washington Center for Equitable Growth, Washington, DC.

Batchelder, Lily. 2017. "Opportunities and Risks in Individual Tax Reform." Testimony before the Senate Committee on Finance, United States Senate, September 13.

Bernheim, Douglas. 2002. "Taxation and Saving." In *Handbook of Public Economics*, vol. 3. Edited by Alan Auerbach and Martin Feldstein, 1173–249. Amsterdam: Elsevier.

Bureau of Economic Analysis. 2018. "Real Gross Domestic Product Per Capita." *National Economic Accounts*. Washington, DC: US Bureau of Economic Analysis, Department of Commerce.

Burman, Leonard, Eric Toder, and Christopher Geissler. 2008. "How Big Are Total Individual Income Tax Expenditures, and Who Benefits from Them?" *American Economic Review* 98 (2): 79–83.

Congressional Budget Office. 2016. "Options to Reduce the Deficit, 2017 to 2026." Congressional Budget Office, Washington, DC.

Congressional Budget Office. 2018. "The Budget and Economic Outlook: 2018 to 2028." Congressional Budget Office, Washington, DC.

Desai, Mihir A., and Austan D. Goolsbee. 2004. "Investment, Overhang, and Tax Policy." *Brookings Papers on Economic Activity* 2: 285–355.

Drukker, Austin, Ted Gayer, and Harvey Rosen. 2017. "The Mortgage Interest Deduction: Revenue and Distributional Effects." Griswold Center for Economic Policy Studies Working Paper No. 251. Department of Economics, Princeton University.

Dynarski, Susan, and Judith Scott-Clayton. 2006. "The Cost of Complexity in Federal Student Aid: Lessons from Optimal Tax Theory and Behavioral Economics." *National Tax Journal* 59 (2): 319–56.

Eissa, Nada. 2008. "Evidence on Labor Supply and Taxes, and Implications for Tax Policy." In *Tax Policy Lessons from the 2000s*. Edited by Alan D. Viard, 45–91. Washington, DC: AEI Press.

Feldstein, Martin. 1986. "Supply Side Economics: Old Truths and New Claims." *American Economic Review* 76 (2): 26–30.

Feldstein, Martin, and Douglas W. Elmendorf. 1989. "Budget Deficits, Tax Incentives, and Inflation: A Surprising Lesson from the 1983–1984 Recovery." In *Tax Policy and the Economy*, vol. 3. Edited by Lawrence H. Summers, 1–23. Cambridge, MA: National Bureau of Economic Research.

Feldstein, Martin, Daniel Feenberg, and Maya MacGuineas. 2011. "Capping Individual Tax Expenditure Benefits." NBER Working Paper No. 16921. National Bureau of Economic Research, Cambridge, MA.

Flood, Brian. 2017. "Snuggies Are Blankets, Not Priestly Robes, Rules Trade Court." *Bloomberg BNA*, Arlington, VA, February.

Fugate, Robert. 2012. "The Head Tax: The Only God-Endorsed Civil Tax." *Faith for All of Life* July/August: 4–9.

Gale, William G., and Samuel Brown. 2013. "Small Business, Innovation and Tax Policy: A Review." *National Tax Journal* 66 (4): 871–92.

Gale, William G., Samuel Brown, and Adam Looney. 2012. "TPC's Analysis of Governor Romney's Tax Proposals: A Follow-Up Discussion." Urban-Brookings Tax Policy Center, Washington, DC.

Gale, William, Hilary Gelfond, Aaron Krupkin, Mark J. Mazur, and Eric Toder. 2018. "The Effects of the Tax Cuts and Jobs Act: A Preliminary Analysis." Urban-Brookings Tax Policy Center, Washington, DC.

Gale, William G., Jonathan Gruber, and Seth Stephens-Davidowitz. 2007. "Encouraging Homeownership through the Tax Code." *Tax Notes* 115 (12): 1171–89.

Gale, William, and Janet Holtzblatt. 1997. "On the Possibility of a No-Return Tax System." *National Tax Journal* (3): 475–85.

Gale, William G., and Aaron Krupkin. 2018. "Navigating the New Pass-Through Provisions: A Technical Explanation." Urban-Brookings Tax Policy Center, Washington, DC.

Gale, William G., Aaron Krupkin, and Kim Rueben. 2017. "Tax Policy Outside of the Emerald City." *Bloomberg BNA Daily Tax Report: State,* July 7.

Gale, William G., and Samara Potter. 2002. "An Economic Evaluation of the Economic Growth and Tax Relief Reconciliation Act." *National Tax Journal* 55 (1): 133–86.

Gale, William G., and Andrew A. Samwick. 2017. "Effects of Income Tax Changes on Economic Growth." In *The Economics of Tax Policy.* Edited by Alan J. Auerbach and Kent Smetters. New York: Oxford University Press.

Genworth Mortgage Insurance. 2017. "First Time Homebuyer Market Report." Genworth Mortgage Insurance Corporation, Richmond, VA, June.

Goolsbee, Austan. 2006. "The 'Simple Return': Reducing America's Tax Burden through Return-Free Filing." Discussion Paper 2006-04. Hamilton Project, Brookings Institution, Washington, DC.

Government Accountability Office. 1997. "Tax Administration: Alternative Filing Systems." Government Accountability Office, Washington, DC.

Government Accountability Office. 2016. "Internal Revenue Service: Preliminary Observations on the Fiscal Year 2017 Budget Request and 2016 Filing Season Performance. Government Accountability Office, Washington, DC.

Greenstein, Robert, John Wancheck, and Chuck Marr. 2018. "Reducing Overpayments in the Earned Income Tax Credit." Center on Budget and Policy Priorities, Washington, DC.

Gruber, Jonathan, Amalie Jensen, and Henrik Kleven. 2017. "Do People Respond to the Mortgage Interest Deduction? Quasi-Experimental Evidence from Denmark." NBER Working Paper No. 23600. National Bureau of Economic Research, Cambridge, MA.

Hall, Robert, and Alvin Rabushka. 2007. *The Flat Tax:* 2nd ed. Stanford, CA: Hoover Institution Press.

Hilber, Christian, and Tracy Turner. 2014. "The Mortgage Interest Deduction and Its Impact on Homeownership Decisions." *Review of Economics and Statistics* 96 (4): 618–37.

Hungerford, Thomas. 2012. "Taxes and the Economy: An Economic Analysis of the Top Tax Rate since 1945." Congressional Research Service, Washington, DC.

Internal Revenue Service. 2010. "Data Book, 2010." Publication 55B. US Department of the Treasury, Internal Revenue Service, Washington, DC.

Internal Revenue Service. 2015. "Data Book, 2015." Publication 55B. US Department of the Treasury, Internal Revenue Service, Washington, DC.

Internal Revenue Service. 2016. "Tax Gap Estimates for Tax Years 2008–2010." Internal Revenue Service, Washington, DC.

Johnston, David Cay. 2001. "Talk of Lost Farms Reflects Muddle of Estate Tax Debate." *New York Times,* April 8.

Joint Committee on Taxation. 2015. "History, Present Law, and Analysis of the Federal Wealth Transfer System." Joint Committee on Taxation, US Congress, Washington, DC.

Joint Committee on Taxation. 2017. "Estimated Budget Effects of the Conference Agreement for H.R.1. 'The Tax Cuts and Jobs Act." JCX-67-17. Joint Committee on Taxation, US Congress, Washington, DC.

Joint Committee on Taxation. 2018. "Estimates of Federal Tax Expenditures for Fiscal Years 2017–2021." JCX-34-18. Joint Committee on Taxation, US Congress, Washington, DC.

Kinsley, Michael. 1987. "The Angel of Death Loophole." *Washington Post,* June 25.

Kolomatsky, Michael. 2017. "Who's Buying a First Home?" *New York Times,* April 21.

Koskinen, John. 2015. "Prepared Remarks of John A. Koskinen, Commissioner of the Internal Revenue Service before the Tax Policy Center, Washington, DC." Tax Policy Center, Washington, DC, April 8.

Marr, Chuck, and Cecile Murray. 2016. "IRS Funding Cuts Compromise Taxpayer Service and Weaken Enforcement." Center on Budget and Policy Priorities, Washington, DC.

Marron, Donald, and Eric Toder. 2013. "Tax Policy and the Size of Government." *National Tax Association Proceedings,* 104th Annual Conference on Taxation: 30–40.

McClelland, Robert. 2017. "Raise the 15 Percent Tax Rate on Capital Gains to Boost Revenue in a Progressive Way." Urban-Brookings Tax Policy Center, Washington, DC.

McDonald, Jason, and Shane Johnson. 2010. "Tax Policies to Improve the Stability of Financial Markets." Bank of Italy Occasional Paper, Rome.

Mnuchin, Steven. 2017. "Treasury Secretary Confirmation Hearing." Before the Senate Finance Committee, January 19. CSPAN.

OECD. 2017a. "National Accounts at a Glance." *OECD.Stat.* OECD, Paris.

OECD. 2017b. "Revenue Statistics — OECD Countries: Comparative Tables." *OECD.Stat.* OECD, Paris.

Office of Management and Budget. 2016. "Budget of the United States Government, Fiscal Year 2017." White House, Washington, DC.

Office of Management and Budget. 2018. "Historical Tables." White House, Washington, DC.

Piketty, Thomas, Emmanuel Saez, and Stefanie Stantcheva. 2014. "Optimal Taxation of Top Labor Incomes: A Tale of Three Elasticities." *American Economic Journal of Economic Policy* 6 (1): 230–71.

Romney, Mitt. 2012. Discussion at the Second Presidential Debate, October 16.

Slemrod, Joel. 1995. "What Do Cross-Country Studies Teach about Involvement, Prosperity, and Economic Growth?" *Brookings Papers on Economic Activity* 2: 373–415. Brookings Institution, Washington, DC.

Slemrod, Joel, and Jon Bakija. 2004. *Taxing Ourselves: A Citizen's Guide to the Debate over Taxes.* 3rd ed. Cambridge, MA: MIT Press.

Slemrod, Joel, and Jon Bakija. 2008. *Taxing Ourselves: A Citizen's Guide to the Debate over Taxes.* 4th ed. Cambridge, MA: MIT Press.

Slemrod, Joel, and Jon Bakija. 2017. *Taxing Ourselves: A Citizen's Guide to the Debate over Taxes.* 5th ed. Cambridge, MA: MIT Press.

Tax Policy Center. 2017a. "Who Pays the Estate Tax?" Briefing Book. Urban-Brookings Tax Policy Center, Washington, DC.

Tax Policy Center. 2017b. "T17-0137—Tax Benefit of the Preferential Rates on Long-Term Capital Gains and Qualified Dividends." Tax Policy Center, Washington, DC.

Tax Policy Center. 2017c. "T17-0308—Estate Tax Returns and Liability under Current Law and the House and Senate Versions of the Tax Cuts and Jobs Act, 2018–2027." Tax Policy Center, Washington, DC.

Tax Policy Center. 2018a. "T18-0002—Impact on the Number of Itemizers of H.R.1, the Tax Cuts and Jobs Act (TCJA), by Expanded Cash Income Percentile." Tax Policy Center, Washington, DC.

Tax Policy Center. 2018b. "T18-0008—Impact on the Tax Benefit of the Itemized Deduction for Home Mortgage Interest Deduction (MID) of H.R.1, the Tax Cuts and Jobs Act (TCJA), by Expanded Cash Income Percentile, 2018." Tax Policy Center, Washington, DC.

Toder, Eric, Daniel Berger, and Yifan Zhang. 2016. "Distributional Effects of Individual Income Tax Expenditures: An Update." Tax Policy Center, Washington, DC.

US Bureau of Economic Analysis. 2018. "Real Gross Domestic Product per Capita." Retrieved from FRED, Federal Reserve Bank of St. Louis.

US Department of the Treasury. 2003. "Report to the Congress on Return-Free Tax Systems: Tax Simplification Is a Prerequisite." US Department of the Treasury, Washington, DC.

Williamson, Vanessa S. 2017. *Read My Lips: Why Americans Are Proud to Pay Taxes.* Princeton, NJ: Princeton University Press.

Yagan, Danny. 2015. "Capital Tax Reform and the Real Economy: The Effects of the 2003 Dividend Tax Cut." *American Economic Review* 105 (12): 3531–63.

Chapter 12

Auerbach, Alan J. 2010. "A Modern Corporate Tax." Center for American Progress, Washington, DC.

Barro, Robert, and Jason Furman. 2018. "The Macroeconomic Effects of the 2017 Tax Reform." *Brookings Papers on Economic Activity.* Brookings Institution, Washington, DC, Spring.

Bradford, David. 1986. *Untangling the Income Tax.* Cambridge, MA: Harvard University Press.

Bruce, Donald. 2002. "Taxes and Entrepreneurial Endurance: Evidence from the Self-Employed." *National Tax Journal* 55 (1): 5–24.

Bureau of Economic Analysis. 2018a. "Corporate Profits by Industry." *National Economic Accounts.* Washington, DC: US Department of Commerce.

Bureau of Economic Analysis. 2018b. "Gross Domestic Product (GDP)." *National Economic Accounts.* Washington, DC: US Department of Commerce.

Carroll, Robert, Douglas Holtz-Eakin, Mark Rider, and Harvey S. Rosen. 1998a. "Income Taxes and Entrepreneurs' Use of Labor." NBER Working Paper 6578. National Bureau of Economic Research, Cambridge, MA.

Carroll, Robert, Douglas Holtz-Eakin, Mark Rider, and Harvey S. Rosen. 1998b. "Entrepreneurs, Income Taxes, and Investment." NBER Working Paper 6374. National Bureau of Economic Research, Cambridge, MA.

Congressional Budget Office. 2016. "Options to Reduce the Deficit, 2017 to 2026." Congressional Budget Office, Washington, DC.

Congressional Budget Office. 2018a. "The Budget and Economic Outlook: 2018 to 2028." Congressional Budget Office, Washington, DC.

Congressional Budget Office. 2018b. "The Distribution of Household Income and Federal Taxes, 2014." Congressional Budget Office, Washington, DC.

Cooper, Michael, John McClelland, James Pearce, Richard Prisinzano, Joseph Sullivan, Danny Yagan, Owen Zidar, and Eric Zwick. 2016. "Business in the United States: Who Owns It and How Much Tax Do They Pay?" *Tax Policy and the Economy* 30 (1): 91–128.

Cronin, Julie-Anne, Emily Y. Lin, Laura Power, and Michael Cooper. 2012. "Distributing the Corporate Income Tax: Revised U.S. Treasury Methodology." Office of Tax Analysis Technical Paper 5, US Department of the Treasury, Washington, DC.

Desai, Mihir. 2018. "Tax Reform, Round 1." *Harvard Magazine* (May–June): 57–61.

Gale, William, and Samuel Brown. 2013. "Small Business, Innovation, and Tax Policy: A Review." *National Tax Journal* 66 (4): 871–92.

Gale, William, and Aaron Krupkin. 2018. "Navigating the New Pass-Through Provisions: A Technical Explanation." Brookings Institution, Washington, DC.

Gallup. 2017. "Taxes." *In Depth: Topics A to Z.* https://news.gallup.com/poll/1714/taxes.aspx.

Gardner, Matthew, Robert S. McIntyre, and Richard Phillips. 2017. "The 35 Percent Corporate Tax Myth: Corporate Tax Avoidance by Fortune 500 Companies, 2008 to 2015." Citizens for Tax Justice and the Institute on Taxation and Economic Policy, Washington, DC.

Gentry, William M., and R. Glenn Hubbard. 2004. "Tax Policy and Entry into Entrepreneurship." Mimeograph, Columbia University.

Gleckman, Howard. 2016. "Who Owns Pass-Through Businesses, and Who Would Benefit from Trump's Plan to Cut Their Taxes?" *TaxVox.* Urban-Brookings Tax Policy Center, Washington, DC.

Gurley-Calvez, Tami Bruce, and Donald Bruce. 2008. "Do Tax Cuts Promote Entrepreneurial Longevity?" *National Tax Journal* 61: 225–50.

Hall, Robert, and Alvin Rabushka. 2007. *The Flat Tax.* 2nd ed. Stanford, CA: Hoover Institution Press.

Haltiwanger, John, Ron Jarmin, and Javier Miranda. 2010. "Who Creates Jobs? Small vs. Large vs. Young." NBER Working Paper No. 16300. National Bureau of Economic Research, Cambridge, MA.

Harrison, J.D. 2013. "Who Actually Creates Jobs: Start-ups, Small Businesses or Big Corporations?" *Washington Post*, April 25.

Internal Revenue Service. 2015. "Table 1: Selected Financial Data on Businesses." SOI Tax Stats—Integrated Business Data." US Department of the Treasury, Washington, DC.

Internal Revenue Service. 2016. "Table 2—Returns of Active Corporations." SOI Tax Stats. US Department of the Treasury, Washington, DC.

Joint Committee on Taxation. 2013. "Modelling the Distribution of Taxes on Business Income." JCX-14-13. Joint Committee on Taxation, US Congress, Washington, DC.

Joint Committee on Taxation. 2016. "Letter to Kevin Brady and Richard Neal." Joint Committee on Taxation, US Congress, Washington, DC.

Joint Committee on Taxation. 2017. "Estimated Budget Effects of the Conference Agreement for H.R.1. 'The Tax Cuts and Jobs Act.'" JCX-67-17. Joint Committee on Taxation, US Congress, Washington, DC.

Joint Committee on Taxation. 2018a. "Estimates of Federal Tax Expenditures for Fiscal Years 2017–2021." JCX-34-18. Joint Committee on Taxation, US Congress, Washington, DC.

Joint Committee on Taxation. 2018b. "Tables Related to the Federal Tax System as in Effect 2017 through 2026." JCX-32R-18. Joint Committee on Taxation, US Congress, Washington, DC.

Kamin, David, David Gamage, Ari D. Glogower, Rebecca M. Kysar, Darien Shanske, Rueven S. Avi-Yonah, Lily L. Batchelder, J. Clifton Fleming, Daniel Jacob Hemel, Mitchell Kane, David S. Miller, Daniel Shaviro, and Manoj Viswanathan. 2018. "The Games They Will Play: Tax Games, Roadblocks, and Glitches Under the 2017 Tax Legislation." *Minnesota Law Review* 103. https://papers.ssrn.com/sol3/papers.cfm?abstract_id=3089423.

Keightley, Mark P. 2012. "Taxing Large Pass-Throughs as Corporations: How Many Firms Would Be Affected?" Congressional Research Service R42451. Congressional Research Service, Washington, DC.

Koba, Mark. 2014. "How the Gingrich-Edwards Tax Loophole Works." CNBC, March 5.

Leonhardt, David. 2016. "The Big Companies that Avoid Taxes." *New York Times*, October 18.

Looney, Adam. 2017a. "The Next Tax Shelter for Wealthy Americans: C-Corporations." Brookings Institution, Washington, DC.

Looney, Adam. 2017b. "Repatriated Earnings Won't Help American Workers—But Taxing Those Earnings Can." Brookings Institution, Washington, DC.

McIntyre, Robert, Richard Phillips, and Phineas Baxandall. 2015. "Offshore Shell Games 2015: The Use of Offshore Tax Havens by Fortune 500 Companies." Citizens for Tax Justice and US PIRG, Washington, DC.

Nunns, Jim. 2012. "How TPC Distributes the Corporate Income Tax." Urban-Brookings Tax Policy Center, Washington, DC.

Nunns, Jim, Len Burman, Ben Page, Jeff Rohaly, and Joe Rosenberg. 2016. "An Analysis of the House GOP Tax Plan." Tax Policy Center, Washington, DC.

OECD. 2018. "Table II.1—Corporate Income Tax Rates." *OECD Tax Database*. Paris: OECD Printing.

Office of Tax Policy. 2017. "The Case for Responsible Business Tax Reform." United States Department of Treasury, Washington, DC.

Pew Research Center. 2015. "Federal Tax System Seen in Need of Overhaul, Top Complaints: Wealthy, Corporations 'Don't Pay Fair Share.'" Pew Research Center, Washington, DC, March 19.

President's Advisory Panel on Tax Reform. 2005. "Simple, Fair and Pro-Growth: Proposals to Fix America's Tax System." President's Advisory Panel on Tax Reform, White House, Washington, DC.

Pugsley, Benjamin Wild, and Erik Hurst. 2011. "What Do Small Businesses Do?" *Brookings Papers on Economic Activity* 2011 (2): 73–118.

Rosenthal, Steven M., and Lydia S. Austin. 2016. "The Dwindling Taxable Share of U.S. Corporate Stock." *Tax Notes*, May 16.

Ryan, Paul. 2016. "A Better Way: Tax." A Better Way Blueprint, Washington, DC.

Sullivan, Martin. 2018a. "Economic Analysis: More GILTI Than You Thought." *Tax Notes* (February 12): 845–50.

Sullivan, Martin. 2018b. "Economic Analysis: Where Will Factories Go? A Preliminary Assessment." *Tax Notes* (January 29): 570–79.

Tax Policy Center. 2016. "Sources of Flow-Through Business Income by Expanded Cash Income Percentile; Current Law, 2016." Model Estimate T16-0184. Tax Policy Center, Washington, DC.

Thorndike, Joseph J. 2005. "A Tax Revolt or Revolting Taxes?" *Tax Analysts*, December 14.

Thorndike, Joseph J. 2010. "Four Things You Should Know about the Boston Tea Party." *Tax Analysts*, April 8.

Chapter 13

Auerbach, Alan. 2010. "A Modern Corporate Tax." Center for American Progress and the Hamilton Project, Washington, DC.

Avi-Yonah, Reuven S. 2011. "The Political Pathway: When Will the U.S. Adopt a VAT?" *VAT Reader*. Washington, DC: Tax Analysts.

Bartlett, Bruce. 2007. "'Starve the Beast': Origins and Development of a Budgetary Metaphor." *Independent Review* 12 (1): 5–27.

Becker, Gary S., and Casey B. Mulligan. 2003. "Deadweight Costs and the Size of Government." *Journal of Law and Economics* 46 (2): 293–340.

Bradford, David F. 1986. *Untangling the Income Tax*. Cambridge, MA: Harvard University Press.

Brashares, Edith, Matthew Knittel, Gerald Silverstein, and Alexander Yuskavage. 2014. "Calculating the Optimal Small Business Exemption Threshold for a US VAT." *National Tax Journal* 67 (2): 283–320.

Cardin, Ben. 2015. "Progressive Consumption Tax Act." http://www.cardin.senate.gov/pct.

Cassidy, John. 2005. "The Ringleader: How Grover Norquist Keeps the Conservative Movement Together." *New Yorker*, August 1.

Cnossen, Sijbren. 2011. "A VAT Primer for Lawyers, Economists, and Accountants." *VAT Reader*. Washington, DC: Tax Analysts.

Cruz Campaign. 2015. "The Simple Flat Tax Plan." Web page. https://www.tedcruz.org/tax_plan/index.html.

Debt Reduction Task Force. 2010. "Restoring America's Future: Reviving the Economy, Cutting Spending and Debt, and Creating a Simple, Pro-Growth Tax System." Bipartisan Policy Center, Washington, DC.

Domenici, Pete, Robert Kerrey, and Samuel Nunn. 1995. "USA Tax Act of 1995." 104th Congress, 1st Session.

Federal Bureau of Investigation. 2015. "Famous Cases & Criminals: Willie Sutton." https://www.fbi.gov/about-us/history/famous-cases/willie-sutton.

Finkelstein, Amy. 2009. "E-Z Tax: Tax Salience and Tax Rates." *Quarterly Journal of Economics* 124 (3): 969–1010.

Gale, William G. 2005. "The National Retail Sales Tax: What Would the Rate Have to Be?" *Tax Notes* 107 (7): 889–911.

Gale, William G., Hilary Gelfond, and Aaron Krupkin. 2016. "Entrepreneurship and Small Business under a Value-Added Tax." Brookings Institution, Washington, DC.

Gale, William G., and Janet Holtzblatt. 2002. "The Role of Administrative Factors in Tax Reform: Simplicity, Compliance, and Administration." In *United States Tax Reform in the Twenty-First Century*. Edited by George R. Zodrow and Peter Mieszkowski, 179–214. New York: Cambridge University Press.

Gale, William G., and Peter R. Orszag. 2004. "Bush Administration Tax Policy: Starving the Beast?" *Tax Notes* 105 (8): 999–1002.

Graetz, Michael. 1997. *The Decline (and Fall?) of the Income Tax*. New York: W.W. Norton.

Graetz, Michael. 2008. *100 Million Unnecessary Returns: A Simple, Fair, and Competitive Tax Plan for the United States*. New Haven, CT: Yale University Press.

Graetz, Michael. 2013. "The 'Competitive Tax Plan' Updated for 2015." Presentation at the National Tax Association, Tampa, FL.

Hall, Robert E., and Alvin Rabushka. 1985. *The Flat Tax*. Stanford, CA: Hoover Institution Press.

Keen, Michael. 2013. "The Anatomy of the VAT." *National Tax Journal* 66 (2): 423–46.

Keen, Michael, and Ben Lockwood. 2006. "Is the VAT a Money Machine?" *National Tax Journal* 59 (4): 905–28.

Lee, Dungeon, Dongil Kim, and Thomas E. Borcherding. 2013. "Tax Structure and Government Spending: Does the Value-Added Tax Increase the Size of Government?" *National Tax Journal* 66 (3): 541–70.

McLure, Charles E., Jr. 2002. "The Nuttiness of State and Local Taxes—and the Nuttiness of Responses Thereto." *State Tax Notes* 25 (12): 841–56.

Mitchell, Daniel J. 2010. "VAT Attack." *New York Post*, April 8.

Mitchell, Daniel J. 2011. "The Case against the Value-Added Tax." Cato Institute, Washington, DC.

Nunns, Jim, and Eric Toder. 2015. "Effects of a Federal Value-Added Tax on State and Local Governments." Urban-Brookings Tax Policy Center, Washington, DC. June 15.

OECD. 2016. *Consumption Tax Trends 2016*. Paris: OECD Publishing.

OECD. 2017. "Revenue Statistics—Comparison Tables." *OECD Stat*. Paris: OECD Publishing.

Paul, Rand. 2015. "Blow Up the Tax Code and Start Over." *Fair and Flat Tax Plan*. https://www.randpaul.com/news/rand-pauls-fair-and-flat-tax.

Pomeranz, Dina. 2015. "No Taxation without Information: Deterrence and Self-Enforcement in the Value Added Tax." *American Economic Review* 105 (8): 2539–69.

President's Advisory Panel on Tax Reform. 2005. "Simple, Fair and Pro-Growth: Proposals to Fix America's Tax System." President's Advisory Panel on Tax Reform, White House, Washington, DC.

Romer, Christina D., and David H. Romer. 2010. "The Macroeconomic Effects of Tax Changes: Estimates Based on a New Measure of Fiscal Shocks." *American Economic Review* 100 (3): 763–801.

Rosen, Jan M. 1988. "Tax Watch: The Likely New Forms of Taxes." *New York Times*, December 19.

Ryan, Paul. 2008. *Roadmap for America's Future Act of 2008*. 110th Congress, 2nd Session.

Schenk, Alan. 2011. "Prior Flirtations with VAT." *VAT Reader*. Washington, DC: Tax Analysts.

Seidman, Laurence S. 1997. *The USA Tax: A Progressive Consumption Tax*. Cambridge, MA: MIT Press.

Sullivan, Martin A. 2011. "VAT Lessons from Canada." *VAT Reader*. Washington, DC: Tax Analysts.

Sullivan, Martin A. 2012. "Was the VAT a Money Machine for Europe?" Washington, DC: Tax Analysts.

Tanzi, Vito. 1995. *Taxation in an Integrating World*. Washington, DC: Brookings Institution.

Tax Analysts. 2011. *The VAT Reader: What a Federal Consumption Tax Would Mean for America*. Falls Church, VA: Tax Analysts.

Toder, Eric, Jim Nunns, and Joseph Rosenberg. 2012. "Implications of Different Bases for a VAT." Urban-Brookings Tax Policy Center, Washington, DC.

TPC Staff. 2017. "Distributional Analysis of the Conference Agreement for the Tax Cuts and Jobs Act." Tax Policy Center, Washington, DC.

Urban-Brookings Tax Policy Center. 2011. "Herman Cain's 9-9-9 Tax Plan." Tax Policy Center, Washington, DC.

Viard, Alan D., and Robert Carroll. 2012. *Progressive Consumption Taxation: The X-Tax Revisited*. Washington, DC: AEI Press.

Chapter 14

Aldy, Joseph E., and William A. Pizer. 2009. "The Competitiveness Impacts of Climate Mitigation Policies." Resources for the Future, Washington, DC.

Aly, Waleed. 2017. "Australia Has a Climate Change Lesson for the World." *New York Times*, November 1.

Amdur, David, Barry G. Rabe, and Christopher P. Borick. 2014. "Public Views on a Carbon Tax Depend on the Proposed Use of Revenue." *Issues in Energy and Environmental Policy* 13. https://papers.ssrn.com/sol3/papers.cfm?abstract_id=2652403.

American Association for the Advancement of Science. 2014. "'What We Know: The Reality, Risks, and Responses to Climate Change." AAAS, Washington, DC.

America's Pledge. 2017. "America's Pledge Phase 1 Report: States, Cities and Businesses in the United States Are Stepping Up on Climate Action." November.

Antholis, William, and Strobe Talbott. 2010. *Fast Forward: Ethics and Politics in the Age of Global Warming*. Washington, DC: Brookings Institution Press.

Bailey, David, and David Bookbinder. 2017. "A Winning Trade: How Replacing the Obama-Era Climate Regulations with a Carbon Dividends Program Starting at $40/Ton Would Yield Far Greater Emissions Reductions." Climate Leadership Council, Washington, DC.

Baker, James, III, Martin Feldstein, Ted Halstead, N. Gregory Mankiw, Henry Paulson, George Schultz, Thomas Stepenson, and Rob Walton. 2017. "The Conservative Case for Carbon Dividends." Climate Leadership Council, Washington, DC.

Barron, Alexander, Allen Fawcett, Marc Hafstead, James McFarland, and Adele Morris. 2018. "Policy Insights from the IMF 32 Study on US Carbon Tax Scenarios." *Climate Change Economics* 9 (1): 1840003-1–1840003-47.

Belluz, Julia. 2017. "Climate Change Will Make People Sicker. Trump Is Pulling Out of Paris Anyway." *Vox*, June 1.

Bureau of Labor Statistics. 2018. "Employment, Hours and Earnings from the Current Employment Statistics Survey (National); Series ID: CES1021210001." US Department of Labor, Washington, DC.

Bush, George W. 2007. "State of the Union." Speech, January 23.

Calder, Jack. 2015. "Administration of a US Carbon Tax." In *Implementing a US Carbon Tax*. Edited by Ian Parry, Adele Morris, and Roberton Williams III, 38–61. New York: Routledge.

Carbone, Jared C., Richard D. Morgenstern, Roberton C. Williams III, and Dallas Burtraw. 2013. "Deficit Reduction and Carbon Taxes: Budgetary, Economic, and Distributional Impacts." Resources for the Future, Washington, DC.

Committee on Arrangements for the 2016 Republican National Convention. 2016. "Republican Platform 2016." RNC 2016, Cleveland, OH.

Congressional Budget Office. 2009. "The Role of the 25 Percent Revenue Offset in Estimating the Budgetary Effects of Legislation." Economic and Budget Issue Brief, Congressional Budget Office, Washington, DC.

Congressional Budget Office. 2010. "How Policies to Reduce Greenhouse Gas Emissions Could Affect Employment." Congressional Budget Office, Washington, DC.

Congressional Budget Office. 2013a. "Effects of a Carbon Tax on the Economy and the Environment." Congressional Budget Office, Washington, DC.

Congressional Budget Office. 2013b. "Options for Reducing the Deficit: 2014 to 2023." Congressional Budget Office, Washington, DC.

Currie, Janet, Joshua Graff Zivin, Jamie Mullins, and Matthew Neidell. 2014. "What Do We Know about Short and Long-Term Effects of Early-Life Exposure to Pollution?" *Annual Review of Resource Economics* 6 (1): 217–47.

Davenport, Coral. 2015. "Nations Approve Landmark Climate Accord in Paris." *New York Times*, December 12.

Davenport, Coral. 2018. "How Much Has 'Climate Change' Been Scrubbed from Federal Websites? A Lot." *New York Times*, January 10.

Democratic Platform Committee. 2016. "2016 Democratic Party Platform." Orlando, FL, July 21.

Department of Defense. 2014. "FY 2014 Climate Change Adaptation Roadmap." Department of Defense, Washington, DC.

Dinan, Terry. 2013. "Effects of a Carbon Tax on the Economy and the Environment." Congressional Budget Office, Washington, DC.

Elgie, Stewart. 2014. "British Columbia's Carbon Tax Shift: An Environmental and Economic Success." World Bank, Washington, DC, September 10.

Environmental Protection Agency. 2016a. "Inventory of US Greenhouse Gas Emissions and Sinks: 1990–2014." Environmental Protection Agency, Washington, DC.

Environmental Protection Agency. 2016b. "The Social Cost of Carbon." Environmental Protection Agency, Washington, DC.

Fawcett, Allen, James McFarland, Adele Morris, and John Weyant. 2018. "Introduction to the EMF 32 Study on US Carbon Tax Scenarios." *Climate Change Economics* 9 (1): 1840001-1–1840001-7.

Fischer, Carolyn, Richard Morgenstern, and Nathan Richardson. 2013. "Ensuring Competitiveness under a US Carbon Tax." Resources for the Future, Washington, DC.

Fuchs, Victor R., Alan B. Krueger, and James M. Poterba. 1998. "Economists' Views about Parameters, Values, and Policies: Survey Results in Labor and Public Economics." *Journal of Economic Literature* 36 (September): 1387–425.

Funk, Cary. 2017. "How Much Does Science Knowledge Influence People's Views on Climate Change and Energy Issues?" Pew Research Center, Washington, DC.

Funk, Cary, and Brian Kennedy. 2016. "The Politics of Climate." Pew Research Center, October 4.

Gallup. 2016. "Environment." 2016. Gallup Organization. http://www.gallup.com/poll/1615/environment.aspx.

Goulder, Lawrence. 2013. "Climate Change Policy's Interactions with the Tax System." *Energy Economics* 40: S3–S11.

Goulder, Lawrence H., and Marc A. Hafstead. 2013. "Tax Reform and Environmental Policy: Options for Recycling Revenue from a Tax on Carbon Dioxide." Discussion Paper, Resources for the Future, Washington, D.C.

Hafstead, Marc. 2017. "Projected CO2 Emissions Reductions under the American Opportunity Carbon Fee Act of 2017." Resources for the Future, Washington, DC.

Hillman, Jennifer. 2013. "Changing Climate for Carbon Taxes: Who's Afraid of the WTO?" German Marshall Fund of the United States, American Action Forum and Climate Advisers, Washington, DC.

Horowitz, John, Julie-Anne Cronin, Hannah Hawkins, Laura Konda, and Alex Yuskavage. 2017. "Methodology for Analyzing a Carbon Tax." US Department of the Treasury, Washington, DC.

IGM Forum. 2011. "Carbon Tax." Chicago Booth School, University of Chicago, December 20.

IGM Forum. 2012. "Carbon Taxes II." Chicago Booth School, University of Chicago, December 4.

Interagency Working Group on the Social Cost of Carbon. 2010. "Technical Support Document: Social Cost of Carbon for Regulatory Impact Analysis under Executive Order 12866." Interagency Working Group on the Social Cost of Carbon, Washington, DC.

Interagency Working Group on the Social Cost of Carbon. 2015. "Technical Support Document: Social Cost of Carbon for Regulatory Impact Analysis under Executive Order 12866." Interagency Working Group on the Social Cost of Carbon, Washington, DC.

IPCC. 2014. "Climate Change 2014: Synthesis Report." Contribution of Working Groups I, II and III to the Fifth Assessment Report of the Intergovernmental Panel on Climate Change. Core Writing Team, R. K. Pachauri and L. A. Meyer, eds. IPCC, Geneva, Switzerland.

Irfan, Umair. 2018. "Chevron Just Agreed in Court that Humans Cause Climate Change, Setting a New Legal Precedent." *Vox*, March 28.

Janssens-Maenhout, G., M. Crippa, D. Guizzardi, M. Muntean, E. Schaaf, J. G. J. Olivier, J. A. H. W. Peters, and K. M. Schure. 2017. "Fossil CO2 and GHG Emissions of All World Countries." European Commission JRC Science for Policy Report. Publications Office of the European Union, Luxembourg.

Jorgenson, Dale W., Richard J. Goettle, Mun S. Ho, and Peter J. Wilcoxen. 2015. "Carbon Taxes and Fiscal Reform in the United States." *National Tax Journal* (March): 121–37.

Kennedy, Merrit. 2016. "Hundreds of US Businesses Urge Trump to Uphold Paris Climate Deal." *National Public Radio*, November 17.

Knopf, Brigitte, Martin Kowarsch, Christian Flachsland, and Ottmar Edenhofer. 2012. "The 2°C Target Reconsidered." In *Climate Change, Justice and Sustainability*. Edited by Ottmar Edenhofer et al., 121–37. Dordrecht, Netherlands: Springer.

Levitt, Steven D. 2007. "Hurray for High Gas Prices!" *Freakonomics Blog*, June 18.

Library of Congress. 2016. "H.Con.Res.80—114th Congress (2015-2016)."

Mankiw, N. Gregory. 2009. "Smart Taxes: An Open Invitation to Join the Pigou Club." *Eastern Economic Journal* 35: 14–23.

Mankiw, N. Gregory. 2013. "A Carbon Tax That America Could Live With." *New York Times*, September 1.

Marron, Donald, Eric Toder, and Lydia Austin. 2015. "Taxing Carbon: What, Why and How." Tax Policy Center, Urban Institute and Brookings Institution, Washington, DC.

Mathur, Aparna, and Adele C. Morris. 2012. "Distributional Effects of a Carbon Tax in Broader US Fiscal Reform." Climate and Energy Economics Discussion Paper, Brookings Institution, Washington, DC.

McKibbin, Warwick, Adele Morris, and Peter Wilcoxen. 2012. "The Potential Role of a Carbon Tax in U.S. Fiscal Reform." Brookings Institution, Washington, DC.

McKibbin, Warwick J., Adele C. Morris, Peter J. Wilcoxen, and Yiyong Cai. 2015. "Carbon Taxes and US Fiscal Reform." *National Tax Journal* 68 (1): 139–55.

McKibbin, Warwick, Adele Morris, Peter Wilcoxen, and Weifing Liu. 2018. "The Role of Border Carbon Adjustments in a US Carbon Tax." *Climate Change Economics* 9(1): 1840011-1–1840011-41.

Meinshausen, M., N. Meinshausen, W. Hare, S. C. Raper, K. Frieler, R. Knutti, D. J. Frame, and M. R. Allen. 2009. "Greenhouse-Gas Emission Targets for Limiting Global Warming to 2°C." *Nature* 458 (7242): 1158–62.

Melillo, Jerry, Terese Richmond, Gary Yohe, eds. 2014. *Climate Change Impacts in the United States: The Third National Climate Assessment*. US Global Change Research Program. Washington, DC: US Government Printing Office.

Metcalf, Gilbert E. 2009. "Designing a Carbon Tax to Reduce US Greenhouse Gas Emissions." *Review of Environmental Economics and Policy* 3 (1): 63–83.

Morris, Adele C. 2013. "Proposal 11: The Many Benefits of a Carbon Tax." In *15 Ways to Rethink the Federal Budget*. Washington, DC: The Hamilton Project, Brookings Institution.

Morris, Adele. 2016a. "11 Essential Questions for Designing a Policy to Price Carbon." Brookings Institution, Washington, DC.

Morris, Adele. 2016b. "Build a Better Future for Coal Workers and Their Communities." Brookings Institution, Washington, DC.

Morris, Adele, and Aparna Mathur. 2014. "A Carbon Tax in Broader Fiscal Reform." Center for Climate and Energy Solutions, Arlington, VA.

Murray, Brian, and Nicholas Rivers. 2015. "British Columbia's Revenue-Neutral Carbon Tax: A Review of the Latest 'Grand Experiment' in Environmental Policy." Nicholas Institute Working Paper 15-04. Duke University, Durham, NC.

National Academies of Sciences, Engineering and Medicine. 2017. "Valuing Climate Damages: Updating Estimation of the Social Cost of Carbon Dioxide." Consensus Report, Committee on Assessing Approaches to Updating the Social Cost of Carbon, National Academies of Sciences, Engineering and Medicine, Washington, DC.

National Mining Association. 2016. "Profile of the US Coal Miner, 2015." National Mining Association, Washington, DC.

NERA Economic Consulting. 2013. "Economic Outcomes of a U.S. Carbon Tax." NERA Economic Consulting, Washington, DC.

NOAA. 2016. "State of the Climate: Global Analysis for Annual 2015." NOAA National Centers for Environmental Information, Washington, DC.

No Climate Tax. 2016. "Pledge Takers." Americans for Prosperity, Arlington, VA.

Nordhaus, William. 2008. *A Question of Balance*, 80–90. New Haven, CT: Yale University Press.

Norris, Michele, and Scott Horsley. 2008. "McCain Talks Climate Change in Oregon Speech." NPR, May 12.

Paltsev, Sergey, John M. Reilly, Henry D. Jacoby, Angelo C. Gurgel, Gilbert E. Metcalf, Andrei P. Sokolov, and Jennifer F. Holak. 2007. "Assessment of U.S. Cap-and-Trade Proposals." MIT Joint Program on the Science and Policy of Global Change Report No. 146. Massachusetts Institute of Technology, Cambridge, MA.

Parry, Ian, Margaret Walls, and Winston Harrington. 2007. "Automobile Externalities and Policies." *Journal of Economic Literature* 45 (June): 373–99.

Plumer, Brad. 2015. "The Senate Is Pretty Clearly a Hoax." *Vox*, January 21.

Popovich, Nadja, Livia Albeck-Ripka, and Kendra Pierre-Louis. 2018. "67 Environmental Rules on the Way Out under Trump." *New York Times*, January 31.

Porter, Eduardo. 2016. "Does a Carbon Tax Work? Ask British Columbia." *New York Times*, March 1.

Poterba, James. 1991. "Is the Gasoline Tax Regressive?" *Tax Policy and the Economy* 5: 145–64.

Rausch, Sebastian, Gilbert E. Metcalf, John M. Reilly, and Sergey Paltsev. 2010. "Distributional Implications of Alternative U.S. Greenhouse Gas Control Measures." NBER Working Paper 16053. National Bureau of Economic Research, Cambridge, MA.

Rausch, Sebastian, and John Reilly. 2012. "Carbon Tax Revenue and the Budget Deficit: A Win-Win-Win Solution?" MIT Joint Program on the Science and Policy of Global Change Report No. 228. Massachusetts Institute of Technology, Cambridge, MA.

Revkin, Andrew. 2017. "Trump's Defense Secretary Cites Climate Change as National Security Challenge." *ProPublica*, March 14.

Roberts, David. 2018. "Shell's Vision of a Zero Carbon World by 2070, Explained." *Vox*, March 30.

Rogelj, J., W. Hare, J. Lowe, D. P. van Vuuren, K. Riahi, B. Matthews, T. Hanaoka, K. Jiang, and M. Meinshausen. 2011. "Emission Pathways Consistent with a 2°C Global Temperature Limit." *Nature Climate Change* 1 (8): 413–18.

Rogelj, J., G. Luderer, R. C. Pietzcker, E. Kriegler, M. Schaeffer, V. Krey, and K. Riahi. 2015. "Energy System Transformations for Limiting End-of-Century Warming to Below 1.5°C." *Nature Climate Change* 5 (6): 519–27.

Samans, Richard. 2016. "Waking Up: America's Once-in-a-Generation Opportunity for Structural Economic Reform and Political Renewal." https://www.huffingtonpost.com/entry/waking-up_us_57ee7dc8e4b082aad9bad8db.

Sanderson, Benjamin M., Brian C. O'Neill, and Claudia Tebaldi. 2016. "What Would it Take to Achieve the Paris Temperature Targets?" *Geophysical Research Letters* 43 (13): 7133–42.

Saunois, Marielle, Rob Jackson, Phillippe Bousquet, Ben Poulter, and Pep Canadell. 2016. "The Growing Role of Methane in Anthropogenic Climate Change." *Environmental Research Letters* 11 (12): 120207.

Schleussner, Carl Friedrich, Tabea K. Lissner, Erich M. Fischer, Jan Wohland, Mahé Perrette, Antonius Golly, Joeri Rogelj, Katelin Childers, Jacob Schewe, Katja Frieler, Matthias Mengel, William Hare, and Michiel Schaeffer. 2016. "Differential Climate Impacts for Policy-Relevant Limits to Global Warming: The Case of 1.5C and 2C." *Earth System Dynamics* 7: 327–51.

Shapiro, Robert, Nam Pham, and Arun Malik. 2008. "The Economics and Environmental Science of Combining a Carbon Based Tax and Tax Relief." US Climate Task Force, Washington, DC.

Shultz, George P., and Gary S. Becker. 2013. "Why We Support a Revenue-Neutral Carbon Tax." *Wall Street Journal*, April 7.

Smith, J. B., et al. 2009. "Assessing Dangerous Climate Change through an Update of the Intergovernmental Panel on Climate Change (IPCC): Reasons for Concern." *Proceedings of the National Academy of Sciences* 106 (11): 4133–37.

Spillman, Benjamin. 2016. "Elon Musk Makes a Libertarian Argument for Carbon Tax." *Reno Gazette-Journal*, July 29.

Sumner, Jenny, Lori Bird, and Hillary Smith. 2009. "Carbon Taxes: A Review of Experience and Policy Design Considerations." Technical Report. National Renewable Energy Laboratory, Golden, CO.

Taylor, Jerry. 2015. "The Conservative Case for a Carbon Tax." Niskanen Center, Washington, DC.

Trump, Donald. 2012. Twitter Post. November 6, 11:15 AM.

Tschakert, P. 2015. "1.5°C or 2°C: A Conduit's View from the Science-Policy Interface at COP20 in Lima, Peru." *Climate Change Responses* 2 (1): 3.

United States Department of Labor. 2015. "Industry Employment and Output Projections to 2024." *Monthly Labor Review*. Bureau of Labor Statistics, Washington, DC.

United States Department of Labor. 2016. "Current Employment Statistics—CES (National)." Bureau of Labor Statistics, Washington, DC.

Velders, Guus. 2016. "Nations Agree to Kigali Amendment: Largest Near-Term Temperature Reduction from Single Agreement." Institute for Governance & Sustainable Development, Washington, DC.

Viard, Alan D. 2009. "Don't Give Away the Cap-and-Trade Permits!" *Tax Notes*, May 4.

Victor, D. G., and C. F. Kennel. 2014. "Climate Policy: Ditch the 2°C Warming Goal." *Nature* 514 (7520): 30–31.

Walsh, J., D. Wuebbles, K. Hayhoe, J. Kossin, K. Kunkel, G. Stephens, P. Thorne, R. Vose, M. Wehner, J. Willis, D. Anderson, S. Doney, R. Feely, P. Hennon, V. Kharin, T. Knutson, F. Landerer, T. Lenton, J. Kennedy, and R. Somerville. 2014. "Ch. 2: Our Changing Climate." In *Climate Change Impacts in the United States: The Third National Climate Assessment*. Edited by J. M. Melillo, Terese (T. C.) Richmond, and G. W. Yohe, 19–67. US Global Change Research Program. https://s3.amazonaws.com/nca2014/low/NCA3_Full_Report_02_Our_Changing_Climate_LowRes.pdf?download=1.

Williams, Roberton C., III, and Casey J. Wichman. 2015. "Macroeconomic Effects of Carbon Taxes." In *Implementing a US Carbon Tax*. Edited by Ian Parry, Adele Morris, and Roberton Williams III, 83–95. New York: Routledge.

World Bank. 2017. "State and Trends of Carbon Pricing (November)." World Bank, Washington, DC.

Index

Note: Figures and tables are indicated by an italic "*t*" or "*f*" following the page number. Note material is indicated by the page number followed by an italic "*n*" and the note number.